HOMSON

SE TECHNOLOGY

onal ■ Trade ■ Reference

REASON™ 2.5

POWER!

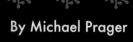

By Michael Prager

MUSKA LIPMAN
Publishing

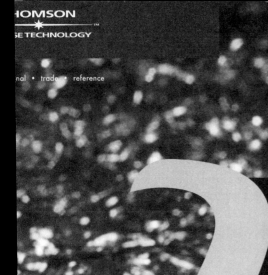

REASON™ 2.5
POWER!

By Michael Prager

Reason 2.5 Power!

Senior Vice President, Professional, Trade, Retail Group: Andy Shafran

Publisher: Stacy L. Hiquet

Credits: Senior Marketing Manager, Sarah O'Donnell; Marketing Manager, Heather Hurley; Manager of Editorial Services, Heather Talbot; Senior Acquisitions Editor, Kevin Harreld; Senior Editor, Mark Garvey; Associate Marketing Manager, Kristin Eisenzopf; Retail Market Coordinator, Sarah Dubois; Production Editor, Dan Foster, Scribe Tribe; Copy Editor, Kezia Endsley; Technical Editor, Orren Merton; Proofreader, Jenny Davidson; Cover Designer, Nancy Goulet; Interior Design and Layout, Marian Hartsough; Indexer, Kevin Broccoli.

Library of Congress Catalog Number: 2003108388

ISBN: 1-59200-138-6

5 4 3

MUSKA&LIPMAN
Publishing

Muska & Lipman Publishing
a Division of Course Technology
25 Thomson Place
Boston, MA 02210
www.courseptr.com

This book is dedicated to my parents
for their advice and support throughout the years.

And, of course, I dedicate this book to mi amore, Jeannie.
You are the air I breathe and make me believe I can do anything.

Above all, this book is dedicated to you, the reader.
I hope that this book helps you and guides you through
one of the best programs ever written, period. Make music!

Acknowledgments

Thanks to everyone at Course Technology for giving me the chance to write this book. It has been a real journey and pleasure to work with such fine individuals, and I look forward to doing it again soon. A special thanks goes to Mark Garvey for his insight and editing expertise. This book would not be as good as it is if it weren't for your help. Thanks to all of my friends and family who have encouraged and supported me with their kind thoughts and words of encouragement. My thanks to the library of the California State University of Northridge for providing a quiet place for me to write. Of course, this book wouldn't even exist if it weren't for the technology wizards of Propellerhead Software. Thank you so much for making a truly groundbreaking program that sparks genuine creativity. Thanks to all of my friends and contacts at Steinberg, Emagic, Cakewalk, Synapse Audio, Digidesign, MAudio, and Ableton. Your programs and products make music all the more fun to create.

About the Author

Michael Prager has been involved in music technology for more than ten years. As a graduate of many fine technology driven campuses, Michael has had the privilege of working with such companies as Steinberg, Spectrasonics, Sony Classical, Q Up Arts, *Keyboard Magazine*, audioMIDI.com, the Columbia College Hollywood, and Disney Interactive. Michael also co-founded VirtualStudioWorx.com and is a private consultant in the Los Angeles area. In 2002, Michael began work on a series of Artist Pro instructional DVDs, aimed at the professional and non-professional music market. With his wide knowledge of both PC and Macintosh-based software, Michael is currently completing production of these DVDs.

Contents

4   Creating Your First Reason Song   53

5   The Reason Sequencer—Close Up   81

10   The Malström—Close Up   217

11   NN-19—Close Up   235

12   NN-XT—Close Up   259

13   The Matrix—Close Up   289

14   Effects—Close Up   305

Introduction

Reason 2.5 Power! is dedicated to teaching you the ins and outs of one of today's most popular music production applications. Since its initial release in 2000, Reason has sold countless numbers of copies worldwide and has been used on several professional recordings while also gaining considerable popularity with the hobbyist musician community. This book is a perfect companion for any user of this fantastic program. Not only will you learn all there is to know about Reason, but you will also find several insightful and in-depth tutorials to teach you how to use this program to its fullest potential.

What You'll Find in This Book

Throughout this book, you'll find plenty of useful information, including:

- ▶ How to choose a computer as well as install and configure Reason
- ▶ A first look at the Reason interface
- ▶ In-depth tours of the individual devices of Reason
- ▶ Timesaving tutorials chock full of information and exercises
- ▶ How to use Reason with other popular Digital Audio Workstation (DAW) programs
- ▶ Information on mixing, burning, and publishing your Reason songs for your friends, family, and fans
- ▶ Additional Propellerhead technology and how to expand your knowledge of Reason

Whom This Book Is For

Reason 2.5 Power! is meant for any electronic music enthusiast who wants to write, record, mix, and remix music. If you are a beginner, this book will serve as an excellent tool to help you quickly learn and understand how Reason 2.5 works. If you are a musician experienced with computers and music, you'll also find plenty of good, useful information within these pages.

Because Reason 2.5 works on both Macintosh and Windows operating systems, this book is geared toward both operating systems, including figures and any relevant operating-system exclusive information.

How This Book Is Organized

Reason 2.5 Power! is divided into 18 chapters, plus several appendixes.

- ▶ **Chapter 1, "Introduction to Reason 2.5"**—A first look at and explanation of this synth station wonder.

▶ **Chapter 2, "Installing and Configuring Reason"**—This chapter focuses on selecting the right equipment for your Reason studio and how to install, configure, and optimize Reason to its full potential.

▶ **Chapter 3, "Getting Started with Reason 2.5"**—In this chapter, you are guided through the Reason interface for the first time by using the built-in default song for reference.

▶ **Chapter 4, "Creating Your First Reason Song"**—Why wait until the end of the book to start making music with Reason? In this chapter, you learn how to start using Reason right away by programming loops and synths.

▶ **Chapter 5, "The Reason Sequencer—Close Up"**—The Reason sequencer is the heart of the program. This chapter focuses on learning how the sequencer works and what it is capable of helping you accomplish in your music.

▶ **Chapter 6, "ReMix—Close Up"**—This chapter introduces and discusses reMix, which is used to mix, pan, and route all of the different signals in Reason.

▶ **Chapter 7, "Redrum—Close Up"**—Redrum is the drum machine that you have been dreaming of. This chapter shows you how to navigate and use Redrum quickly. You also learn how to program your own drum patterns using the built-in Pattern Sequencer.

▶ **Chapter 8, "Dr:rex—Close Up"**—Are you a loop-oholic? Dr:rex is the loop player that does tricks that no other synth can. Based on REX technology developed by Propellerhead, the loops loaded into Dr:rex can be used at virtually *any* tempo.

▶ **Chapter 9, "Subtractor—Close Up"**—This chapter introduces you to Reason's first virtual synth. Based on subtractive synthesis, the Subtractor is a versatile synth that delivers great sounds with ease and fun. In this chapter, you learn how the Subtractor works, and you also get a step-by-step tutorial to teach you how to program your own synth sounds.

▶ **Chapter 10, "The Malström—Close Up"**—Think you've seen every synth there is to see? The Malström is a truly original synth that combines the best of granular and wavetable synthesis. In this chapter, you learn every function of the Malström, and how to program your own synth sounds.

▶ **Chapter 11, "NN-19—Close Up"**—Sampling and electronic music go hand in hand these days. You can't have one without the other, and the NN-19 delivers the goods. This chapter serves as a great introduction to sampling and teaches you how to program a guitar sample patch from scratch.

▶ **Chapter 12, "NN-XT—Close Up"**—The NN-XT picks up where the NN-19 leaves off. If you are familiar with sampling, you'll quickly see how versatile this sampling powerhouse is. You learn how to program your own sample patch and also how to expand your sampling library with free utility programs provided by Propellerhead.

▶ **Chapter 13, "The Matrix—Close Up"**—The Matrix is old-school pattern sequencing at its best. This chapter focuses on teaching you how to use the Matrix to control Reason's devices and includes easy-to-understand tutorials.

▶ **Chapter 14, "Effects—Close Up"**—When you're finished programming your synths, it's time to top them off with reverb, delay, or distortion. Just about every kind of effect processor is included with Reason, as well as some you've never heard of. This chapter shows you each of these one by one and provides some real-world examples for how to use them.

▶ **Chapter 15, "Automation"**—This chapter focuses on using automation within Reason. You'll find that every parameter within the program can be programmed to work on its own.

▶ **Chapter 16, "Synchronization"**—Planning on using Reason with external hardware or sequencers? This chapter shows you how to synchronize Reason with other devices.

▶ **Chapter 17, "ReWire"**—Already using another sequencing software like Cubase, Logic, Pro Tools, or SONAR? This chapter shows you how to integrate Reason into any of these programs by using the Propellerhead technology called ReWire.

▶ **Chapter 18, "Mixing and Publishing Your Reason Songs"**—Once your song is mixed, effected, and automated, it's time to create a stereo mixdown of your creation. This chapter shows you how to accomplish this, plus how to burn your songs onto CDs and also how to publish and share your creations with other Reason users the world over.

Keeping the Book's Content Current

Everyone involved with this book has worked hard to make it complete and accurate. But as we all know, technology changes rapidly and a small number of errors might have crept in besides. If you find any errors or have suggestions for future editions, please contact Muska & Lipman at this website:

www.courseptr.com

You can also find updates, corrections, and other information related to the content of the book at this site.

1

Introduction to Reason 2.5

Welcome to the world of Propellerhead Reason 2.5! This program is every synthoholic's dream and desire when it comes to synthesizing and sequencing music. The easy-to-understand graphical user interface (or GUI) makes Reason an ideal music-creation tool for both amateur and professional musicians alike.

Since its release in 2000, Reason has been purchased and adored by thousands of users worldwide, and has been heavily used in many dance recordings and movie soundtracks. Its popularity is exceeded only by its creativity potential, thanks to the ingenious conception of Propellerhead Software.

In this chapter, I am going to outline the basics of the technology behind Reason 2.5 and we'll be sure to cover the following topics:

▶ An overview of Reason 2.5

▶ MIDI and how it relates to Reason

▶ Digital Audio basics and how they relate to Reason

What Is Reason 2.5?

Reason is music composition software that was conceived, developed, and released by Propellerhead Software in 2000. It supplies the best of both software synthesis and sequencing for creative music production aimed at the electronic music scene. Within Reason lies the capability to produce, sequence, and professionally mix electronic music that consists of every element from glossy synth leads, to acid-drenched bass lines, to bone-crunching "four on the floor" drum loops. As you can see in Figure 1.1, it's all here and virtually available at your fingertips.

Aside from synthesis, Reason also houses a powerful arsenal of real-time effects that rival just about any hardware-based effect module found in any professional studio. The list of effects ranges from reverbs, to delays, to chorus, and other popular effects such as vocoders and distortions. All of these tools are ready to go at the click of a mouse button and can be used in just about every creative way possible.

Figure 1.1
Reason's got everything
under the hood.

Here's a quick rundown of what Reason is and what it's capable of:

▶ **Virtual Synthesizers**—Reason's sounds are produced by virtual synthesizers and sound modules. These synths emulate the look and feel of hardware synths and sound modules found in a music production studio. Everything from drum machines, to analog synths, to samplers can be found within the Reason interface.

▶ **MIDI Sequencing**—Sequencing refers to the ability to record a performance using Reason synths, drum "machines," and so on. These performances are then stored on your computer and are available to edit and play back.

▶ **MIDI Editing**—Once the performance has been sequenced, editing those performances within Reason is where some of the real magic of computer music takes place. With editing, you can make both broad and intricate changes to the feel and sound of your song.

▶ **Routing and Mixing**—Just about any device in Reason can be virtually routed to another device by using the mouse and your creativity. Once you route the devices to other devices, Reason provides a virtual mixing board that resembles most popular hardware mixers found in studios. These virtual mixers can be used as master mixers for your entire song or as sub-mixers for other devices within Reason.

▶ **Real-Time Effects**—A good real-world music studio is nothing without the help of a healthy dose of hardware effects to produce cavernous reverbs and teeth grinding distortions. All of that potential can be found within Reason by supplying real-time effects that use your computer's processor to create ambiences that you never thought were possible.

▶ **Synchronization**—Aside from creativity, the name of the game in computer music is expandability. Propellerhead has created its own proprietary format called ReWire to allow Reason to be used with many popular pro-audio software titles like Cubase or Pro Tools.

In case this is your first time working with a program like this, it's best to first get your hands around some of the terminology and jargon by taking a quick tour through computer music history.

MIDI and Reason

MIDI is short for Musical Instrument Digital Interface. It is a communication protocol that was developed and implemented in 1983 by most of the major synthesizer manufacturers at the time, such as Roland, Korg, and Yamaha. The simplest way to explain what MIDI does is to describe a scenario in which a simple connection is made between two keyboards.

1. Assume that you have connected two keyboards via a MIDI cable, as shown in Figure 1.2. You are all set to transmit a MIDI signal from one keyboard, called the "master," to the other keyboard, called the "slave."

2. Press the "Middle C" key on your master keyboard. This sends a MIDI signal to the slave keyboard. This MIDI signal contains a series of messages telling the slave that a note was pressed, which note it was, and how hard you pressed the note. In MIDI terms, these events are called Note On, Note Number, and Note Velocity.

3. The slave keyboard responds to this data by playing the corresponding note on its own keyboard, using the parameters specified in the MIDI message from the master keyboard.

4. After playing the note on your master, you release the key, which sends another MIDI signal to the slave. This signal also contains a series of messages, including Note Off and Note Number.

5. The slave keyboard receives this message and releases the corresponding key on its own keyboard.

If you wanted to create a full music production using MIDI in the previous ten years or so, a boatload of hardware was required in order to compose, create, edit, and mix a piece of music. If you walked into any studio in the 90s, you would see racks and racks full of processors, synthesizers, and probably a few ADAT tape machines, not to mention a huge mixing console in the middle of everything. Just have a look at Figure 1.3.

Figure 1.2
Two keyboards can be connected together via MIDI.

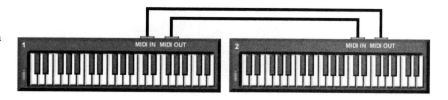

Figure 1.3
Back in the "good ol'
days" of recording.

Fast-forward to 2003, and you'll find that, for the purposes of recording audio, just about every studio has switched from tape machines to computers. It is also much more common to find studio musicians using software-based synthesizers rather than large costly hardware synths (see Figure 1.4).

Figure 1.4
Welcome to the Virtual
Studio.

Reason is a top-rated solution for the computer musician because it offers so many possibilities for composing and playing music, as follows:

▶ Reason is a fantastic MIDI sequencer, with every feature you could want for creating music using MIDI.

▶ Reason has a large selection of virtual synthesizers and sound modules suitable for nearly every style of music.

▶ Reason supplies a fantastic virtual mixer and real-time effects that rival just about any hardware rack effects.

MIDI IS NOT DIGITAL AUDIO

It's important to note that MIDI is not the same as digital audio. MIDI is essentially a language that transmits performance commands from one device to another.

On the other hand, digital audio is created by capturing analog signals and converting them into digital files.

Upon its initial release, MIDI allowed keyboard players to link up and access several different keyboards simultaneously. This allowed keyboardists to "layer" their sounds and create thick and heavy orchestrations in a live or studio setting. But that was just the beginning.

In the mid-80s, computer manufacturers began to develop a way of using a computer to communicate with keyboards and other peripherals via the MIDI standard. Although many computer companies integrated to MIDI by way of external hardware (remember the Commodore 64?), the now defunct Atari computer company released the 1040ST. It was one of the first computers to incorporate MIDI by including an interface on the side of the computer that sent and received MIDI signals (see Figure 1.5).

Software companies were also starting to see the potential impact of developing programs to help record MIDI events and play them back as a sequence of events, hence the term *sequencing*. One of the first programs to make it out of the starting gate was called Pro 24, released by a then small German software company called Steinberg. This program could record, edit, and play back MIDI events on multiple "virtual tracks." These virtual tracks are not like audio tracks on a tape machine, as they simply record and play MIDI data events, which is much different than audio events. Don't worry; I'll explain digital audio later in this chapter.

Figure 1.5
The Atari 1040ST.

WHAT'S THAT NAME AGAIN?

If the name Pro 24 doesn't ring a bell, that's probably because it doesn't exist anymore. Steinberg stopped development on Pro 24 to make way for its flagship program, Cubase, a very popular program that you'll take a look at toward the end of this book.

Let's have a look at a typical MIDI sequencing setup (see Figure 1.6).

1. The first component needed in a MIDI sequencing setup is a controller keyboard that sends and receives MIDI messages.

2. This master keyboard is connected to a MIDI interface, which receives and sends MIDI messages to the computer, the master keyboard, and any other MIDI peripherals (or slave devices) in your sequencing setup.

3. The MIDI interface is connected to a computer running a MIDI sequencing program. This program can receive, record, edit, and play back MIDI messages to the master and slave devices.

Figure 1.6
A typical MIDI studio setup.

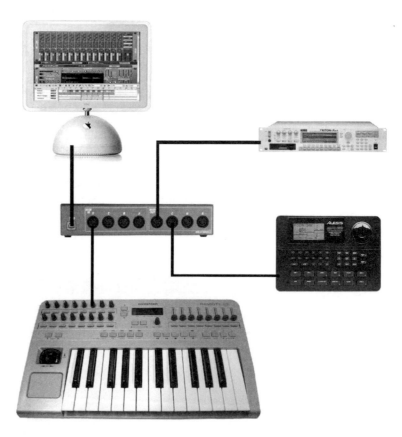

WHERE CAN YOU LEARN MORE ABOUT MIDI?
Although Reason is a very able MIDI sequencing program, the fact is that this book can't realistically cover every aspect of MIDI. For everything you might need to know about MIDI, check out *MIDI Power!*, by Robert Guerin (Muska & Lipman).

Digital Audio and Reason

When you get right down to it, Reason has virtually nothing to do with *recording* digital audio, as it is strictly a MIDI sequencing program. That said, Reason certainly does dip its big toe in the pool of digital audio, as all of its virtual synths and sound modules rely heavily on the existence and functionality of digital audio.

▶ The Redrum drum module synth uses digital samples in order to play back acoustic, electronic, or heavily processed drum sounds (see Figure 1.7). These digital samples are stored on your computer's hard drive and then loaded into RAM when used in Reason.

▶ The NN-XT and NN-19 sound modules are Reason's sample playback modules. They both play digital samples of real instruments, such as guitars, vocals, drums, and orchestral instruments (see Figure 1.8). As with Redrum, these sound modules store the samples on your computer's hard drive and are loaded into RAM when used.

▶ Dr:rex is a sound module that plays digitally sampled loops, which are stored and accessed just like the samples played by NN-XT, NN-19, and Redrum (see Figure 1.9).

▶ Reason's virtual synths, called the Subtractor and Malström (see Figures 1.10 and 1.11) are software emulations of hardware synths. Through a process called physical modeling, which you'll learn about later in this book, both synths produce sound by using different forms of synthesis, called Subtractive and Graintable.

▶ Once you have completed creating and mixing a song in Reason, you must then export your audio mix as a digital audio file. As you can see in Figure 1.12, Reason has many exporting options.

Figure 1.7
Redrum is the virtual drum machine that techno dreams are made of.

Figure 1.8
Whether you like your samplers easy or complex, the NN-19 and NN-XT will meet your needs.

Figure 1.9
Loops come alive in Dr:rex.

Figure 1.10
The Subtractor is a fantastic virtual analog synth for creating driving bass lines and dreamy pads.

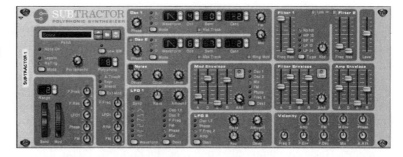

Figure 1.11
The Malström Graintable Synth is in a class by itself.

Figure 1.12
Reason offers many audio mixdown options.

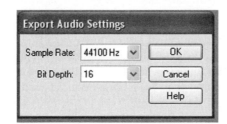

JUST THE TIP OF THE ICEBERG

This section contains just a brief overview of the sound modules in Reason. Each module has its own dedicated chapter in this book.

Much like an analog tape recorder, your computer has the capability to record sounds, such as a voice, guitar, drums, keyboards, kazoos, or whatever other instrument or sound you can think of. These sounds are then translated into digital data (called *samples*), which are then stored on your computer's hard drive. This data can then be played back and heard through your computer's speakers.

Thanks to enhanced and intuitive Graphical User Interfaces (or GUIs), using a computer to record and play back audio in a virtual studio is similar to the look and feel of an analog studio, but the actual process of accomplishing this task within your computer is much different. This section outlines the basics of how to record both analog and digital sound.

Analog Sound—Frequency and Amplitude

A sound can simply be defined as a vibration that is capable of being detected by a human ear. When our eardrums vibrate, we are "hearing a sound." The rate at which our eardrums (and the sound-producing object) vibrate is called the vibration's *frequency*.

Frequency is measured in units called Hertz (or Hz), named after the German scientist Heinrich R. Hertz. A Hertz is defined as the number of vibrational cycles that a sound produces in one second. A single Hertz is equal to one cycle per second, which is far too low a frequency for the human ear to detect. The Hertz unit is usually combined with metric system prefixes to produce various subdivisions. These are commonly known as the kilohertz (kHz), the megahertz (MHz), and the gigahertz (GHz).

A finely tuned human ear is capable of detecting a broad frequency range, from 20Hz to 22.05kHz (22,050Hz). The range narrows as we grow older, and as our hearing is dulled thanks to the effects of listening to loud noises over long periods of time. It's important to treat your hearing like gold!

So how does the frequency spectrum translate into musical terms? Consider a stringed instrument, such as a cello, which has a pretty wide frequency range, as an example. When a note is bowed on the lowest string, the string vibrations are very slow, as the diameter of the string is quite thick in comparison to the highest string. This produces a very low frequency vibration, which in turn means that the sounded note is very low in pitch. On the other end of that spectrum, if your cello player were to then play a note on the highest string, the vibrations would be much more rapid, creating a tone with higher frequency and pitch.

Frequency also has a counterpart element, called *amplitude*, which is simply the volume of the sound and is measured in units called *decibels*. Every sound has a frequency and amplitude. If you play one piano note softly, the frequency is constant and the amplitude is low. If you play the same note again, but press the key harder than before, the frequency will be the same, but the amplitude will be higher, producing a louder sound.

The graphical plotting of the frequency and amplitude of a sound is called a *waveform*. Frequency is represented on the horizontal axis, and amplitude is on the vertical. A very simple waveform with low amplitude looks something like Figure 1.13, and that same waveform with

Figure 1.13
A simple waveform with low amplitude.

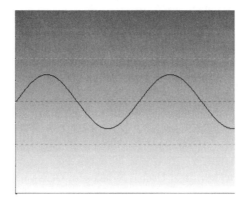

greater amplitude looks like Figure 1.14. If you were to draw a waveform with a low frequency, it would look something like Figure 1.15, whereas a higher frequency would look like Figure 1.16.

Figure 1.14
A little bit louder now.

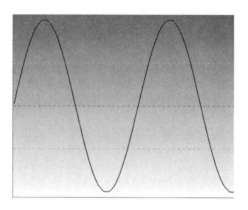

Figure 1.15
A waveform with a low frequency.

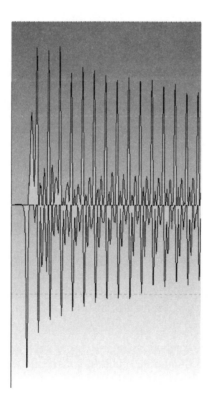

Figure 1.16
A waveform with a high
frequency.

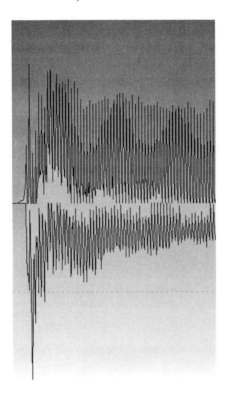

But sounds in the real world are most often not simple waveforms. They are typically much more complex, as there are numerous frequencies and amplitudes occurring simultaneously in just about any sound. With that in mind, look at Figure 1.17 to see a complex waveform. This figure is from a program for the PC called WaveLab.

Space—The Final Dimension

In addition to frequency and amplitude, the third and final dimension that defines sound is *space*. It can be thought of as a counterpart to amplitude, as it is space that defines the amplitude of a recorded sound through time. For example, let's say you are recording your hand clapping in a medium-sized room with the microphone placed in close proximity to your hands. The recorded sound will be very loud and present, as there is very little space between your hands and the microphone. Next, try recording your hand clapping again in the same room, but standing much farther from the microphone. The recorded sound will be much different from before, not only in amplitude, but also in character.

For certain instruments, a little space is needed in order to accurately capture its entire frequency range. A good example of this is a recording of an orchestral ensemble within a large auditorium, where the microphones are typically placed a good distance from the instruments.

For other instruments, such as drums or acoustic guitars, very little or no space is ideal for accurately capturing its frequency range. However, a commonly used technique for adding

Figure 1.17
Here's a much more complex waveform with a variety of frequencies and amplitudes.

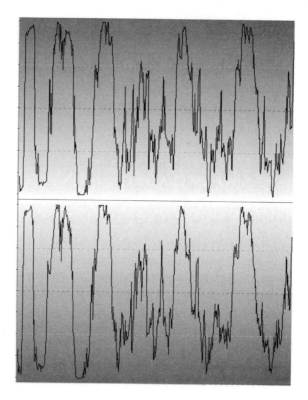

ambience or character to a recording of these instruments is to place an additional microphone far away from the instrument. This "ambient mic" is then mixed in with the close proximity microphones, resulting in an interesting recording.

Digital Audio and Sampling

Although both analog and digital audio generally have the same purpose and application, the technology behind how the two are recorded is very different. Frequency and amplitude are still both important in digital recording, they are just processed in another way, using a technology called *sampling*.

In 1928, an AT&T engineer named Harry Nyquist theorized that he could accurately record a waveform by sampling its frequency and amplitude electronically twice in one cycle, and then play these samples back perfectly replicated. Although this theory was to become the basis of digital audio as we know it, Nyquist unfortunately didn't have the available technology to prove his theory. Nevertheless, the Nyquist theory has been proven to some degree, and it is this theory that makes it possible to record audio digitally. Let me buy you a pint, Mr. Nyquist!

By using the Nyquist theory, one can simply describe the process of sampling.

1. Amplitude is measured as voltage values and then captured as numeric data called *bits*.

2. These bits are essentially binary data comprised of ones and zeros, each one representing "on," and each zero representing "off." Although bits can represent large numbered values, in computer terms these values translate into long strings of ones and zeros.

3. The more bits, the more possible measurements of amplitude. This essentially will mean more volume potential to musicians.

4. The rate at which these bits are captured is described as a frequency measured in kilohertz. This is called the *sampling rate*.

5. The higher the sampling rate, the better the overall clarity of the captured bits.

Earlier in the chapter, I stated that a human ear could detect sounds ranging from 20Hz to 20kHz. Wait a tick, isn't the frequency range of a CD much higher? Yes, this is true, as a CD has a sampling rate of 44.1kHz, which is more than twice the hearing potential of a human ear.

Recall, though, that the Nyquist theory that states that a waveform must be sampled twice during each cycle in order to reproduce the waveform accurately. This means that in order to reproduce the waveform clearly, the sampling rate has to be doubled in order to accurately reproduce a waveform, which would give you a potential of around 44.1kHz. Ta-da!

BIT DEPTH?

If you're just getting into digital audio, you should familiarize yourself with the jargon related to the field. At the top of your list should be *bit depth*.

Bit depth relates to the number of data bits that are needed in order to accurately capture analog signals at different amplitudes. As you read in the previous section, these bits are represented in the simple binary language of zeros and ones. For example, an 8-bit recording could have approximately 256 amplitude levels that would be represented as a rather long string of zeros and ones in binary (for example, 00001100, 10100010). A standard 16-bit recording would have nearly 65,535 amplitude levels that would be represented in a virtually endless string of zeros and ones.

Although a commercial audio compact disc has a standard bit depth of 16 bits, the professional recording studio typically records audio at a much higher bit depth, usually 24. This is to ensure that the recorded audio is being captured at its highest potential. The more bits available to digitally capture a sound, the more accurate that captured sound will be in terms of dynamic range.

You'll learn much more about this and other digital audio terms as you get deeper into Reason. Pretty soon, you'll be able to sling techno terms like a pro!

As you can see, Reason has a lot going on under the hood. Now that you have all of the "Mr. Wizard" stuff out of the way, it's time to install Reason, take a guided tour of the program, and start making some music!

2

Installing and Configuring Reason

Before diving into making music with Reason 2.5, you first need to consider installing, configuring, and optimizing the program. Although this might sound like a chore, it's really a simple task. I have installed Reason on a number of computers and operating systems, and I could pretty much do it blindfolded at this point. But worry not; I will lead you through this chapter with both eyes open, so you can breathe a sigh of relief.

This chapter covers the following topics:

▶ Equipping the ideal Reason studio

▶ Choosing a computer to use for Reason

▶ Installing Reason and configuring it for both PC and Mac

▶ Making small adjustments to let Reason rock your computer

The Ideal Reason Studio

With all that Reason is capable of, you might imagine it requires the latest in cutting-edge computing power. You will be surprised to learn that the actual requirements for a killer Reason studio are not so high. In this game, you are going to learn one important governing rule: keep it simple. Let's have a look at what goes into a Reason studio (see Figure 2.1).

▶ A computer that meets the system requirements listed on the Reason box

▶ A controller keyboard that can send MIDI signals

▶ A pair of speakers

▶ A mixing board

That wasn't such a long list, now was it? Let's examine each of these components.

Figure 2.1
Here's a typical Reason
studio that is ready to
rock and roll with the
best of them.

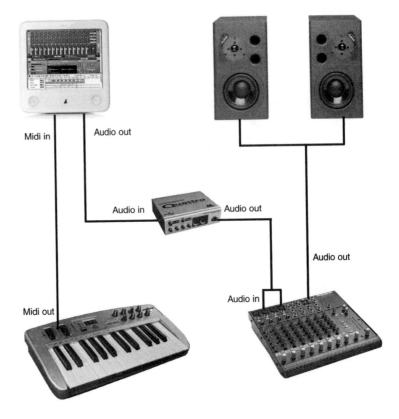

What's Under the Hood?

Whether you are buying a computer off the shelf at your local computer store, having a computer customized and built to your specifications, or making a brave attempt at buying the parts and building your own system, there are five factors (or commandments if you will) that will ultimately determine the performance you will get from Reason.

Here are the five commandments of computer building (you can say these out loud in your best Charlton Heston voice if you want):

▶ Thou shalt choose a Central Processing Unit, or CPU, that will be fast enough to get thy music grooving now and for a long time to come.

▶ Thou shalt purchase an abundance of Random Access Memory chips, or RAM, which will permit thy music to contain a sea of funky loops, drums, and samples.

▶ Thou shalt purchase a large enough hard drive to ensure that thy music can be saved in abundance.

▶ Thou shalt purchase a CD burner to back up thy precious music created within Reason.

▶ Thou shalt select a proper sound card to ensure that thy music sounds freakin' awesome.

Oh yes, there is one more commandment—one that's very important but not spoken nearly enough:

▶   Thou shalt have fun doing this!

CPU (Central Processing Unit)

The CPU is where all of the real-time processing for your computer is handled. Installed on the computer's motherboard, the CPU handles and regulates the flow of information throughout the entire computer, and, most importantly, gives you the juice you need to make Reason rock and roll inside your computer.

The only problem with selecting the right kind of CPU for your computer is that there are so many to choose from. Consider the following list of available CPUs for both PC and Mac.

▶   **Intel** has developed and released a long line of CPUs for the Windows platform called the *Pentium* series. At the time of this writing, the Pentium IV processor (see Figure 2.2) is the most current and can range in speeds from 1.6 to a blistering 3.06 Gigahertz (or GHz). You may also have heard of Intel's *Celeron* processor, but as this processor is not well equipped to handle the real-time audio processing of Reason, I recommend using the Pentium IV for best results.

▶   **AMD** is another company that has developed many CPUs for the Windows platform. The most currently available CPU at this time is the Athlon XP series (see Figure 2.3), which can run at speeds between 1.3GHz, and 2.1GHz, which is more than enough for Reason. AMD also produces other CPUs as well, including the Duron series, but just as with Celeron, the Duron isn't really up to the Reason challenge.

▶   **Apple** has simplified the whole CPU question by having three available processors, the G3, G4, and the new G5. These can be found in all of the current Apple systems, including the iBook, iMac (see Figure 2.4), and Power Mac computers. This processor ranges in speeds from 700 Megahertz (MHz) to 1.4GHz. The more elaborate high-end Power Macs are now available with dual processors, which can potentially double the overall performance of the computer, which can be useful when using Reason with other programs.

CHAPTER 2

Figure 2.2
The Pentium IV processor is an excellent choice for your Reason computer.

Figure 2.3
The AMD Athlon is a
cost-effective CPU for
Reason.

Figure 2.4
The Apple iMac is an
all-in-one powerhouse
solution for Reason.

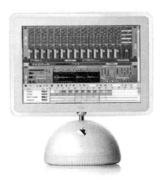

HOW MUCH IS ENOUGH?

How much processor power should you get? The simple answer is to purchase the fastest processor you can afford. In PC terms, the fastest Pentium IV or Athlon XP will do very nicely; with Apple computers, get the fastest G4 processor you can find and afford. Keep in mind that "bigger is always better" when it comes to buying or building a computer.

RAM (Random Access Memory)

Computers use two kinds of memory: permanent and temporary. Permanent memory can save and store data when the computer is powered down; temporary memory (called RAM, for Random Access Memory) stores data only when the computer is turned on. RAM stores and processes data while the computer is turned on, but loses that data when the computer is turned off. When it comes to Reason, the primary function of RAM is to store the temporary data that is loaded up within a Reason song file. Simply put, if you are using any samples, loops, or drum machines within a Reason song, that information is held in temporary memory, or RAM.

The best rule of thumb here is to make sure that you have a lot RAM installed in your computer. It will help Reason run more smoothly, and it will help prevent computer crashes that can sometimes happen due to a shortage of RAM. It's best to have at least 512 megabytes (MB) of RAM. This will give you plenty of headroom to work with. Just keep in mind that more is always better (and RAM is quite affordable these days), so feel free to splurge.

Hard Drive

Your computer's hard drive is your medium for permanent data storage. Among other things, it holds your operating system, your applications, and, above all, your Reason song files. The hard drive is also where you will eventually store the digital audio mixes of your Reason songs.

The first key to purchasing a good hard drive is to go with a well-known brand name. Western Digital, Seagate, Samsung, and Maxtor are all well-known and respected brands. Next, make sure that the drive meets the following list of requirements that will allow it to achieve good performance with Reason (and most other music-creation software):

> ▶ **Transfer rate**—How much digital data can the hard drive transfer per second? You'll want to make sure the hard drive has a transfer rate of at least 10 megabytes or higher per second.

> ▶ **Seek or access time**—How fast does the hard drive access information? The hard drive must have a seek time of 10 milliseconds (ms) or less in order to be used for digital audio.

> ▶ **Rotation speed**—How fast does the hard drive rotate? Many hard drives have a rotation speed of 5400 rotations per minute (RPM), but this generally won't cut it for digital audio. Look for a hard drive that has a rotation speed of 7200 RPM or better.

I remember buying my then butt-kicking Power Mac back in 1998 and being so impressed that it had a "large" hard drive of 4 gigabytes (GB). Today, programs such as Reason can use up that much storage space in no time. In order to give yourself plenty of room to work with, look for a hard drive with at least 40GB of storage space. You might even consider popping in an 80GB drive, because prices are so good these days.

THINKING AHEAD

Let's take a moment to consider an ugly fact of computing life: hard drive crashes. Like earthquakes, hard drive crashes are nearly impossible to predict. But they happen, and in all likelihood your hard drive will crash one day, no matter how well you care for your computer. But there's a cheap, easy remedy: Back your hard drive up to CD frequently. It's a good idea to burn your important files to CD-ROM weekly. If you don't own a CD burner, run right out and buy one as soon as possible. You'll be saving yourself from the future panic attacks and gray hairs that come with hard drive crashes.

ONE DRIVE, TWO DRIVE, RED DRIVE, BLUE DRIVE

Should you install two hard drives? The short answer is yes; a second hard drive is very helpful. You can perform quicker backups by copying data from one hard drive to another; and after all, as the saying goes, "two heads are better than one." But is this *necessary* for Reason? Not really, as the digital audio involved in a Reason song is stored in your computer's RAM, essentially making your second hard drive superfluous.

But, if your intention is to use Reason in conjunction with another Digital Audio Workstation (or DAW) program, such as Cubase or Pro Tools, a second hard drive will certainly be needed.

Because the prices of computer hardware are so reasonable these days, I would say if you have the cash, go for it; but remember that you can always upgrade your computer at a later date.

Sound Card—Your Digital Audio Connection

Your sound card is responsible for both playing back digital audio in Reason and providing the capability to create real-time performances within Reason while the program is running. To put it simply, the sound card is just about the most important part of your studio, with the possible exception of your creativity.

As there are so many cards available, you need to make sure yours supports one of the driver formats discussed next. The driver is software that comes with the sound card and that closely integrates the sound card with the operating system. This will ensure better accuracy and performance from Reason, as it will decrease the latency effect that can occur when using Reason as a real-time performance tool. If you are on the prowl for a new audio card, your timing couldn't be any better, because there are many affordable audio cards with mind-blowing features and reasonable price tags. For example, it's now possible to purchase a 24-bit/96kHz sound card for well under $200 at your local music shop.

THE LATENCY EFFECT

Latency, simply put, is the time lag between striking a note on your instrument and hearing that note played back through your studio speakers.

For example, on the Fourth of July, you see the fireworks explode in mid-air, but you have to wait almost a full second before you hear the explosion, depending on the distance between you and the fireworks. That is latency, plain and simple. But fireworks latency is a result of distance. In computer synthesis, the latency effect occurs because the instructions from your MIDI keyboard have to be processed inside your computer before your speakers can generate the sound.

ASIO Drivers

In 1996, the German company Steinberg developed and released a driver format called ASIO, or Audio Stream Input/Output. ASIO started a trend in digital audio technology by introducing an affordable way to use both the processing power of the computer's CPU and the DSP (Digital Signal Processing) of the sound card to produce a real-time audio performance in both PCs and Macs. To make things even better, Steinberg made the ASIO source code available to any company who wanted to write and design ASIO drivers for their audio cards and programs. The ASIO technology took off like a rocket to Mars, and is currently supported in more than 100 audio cards and numerous digital audio programs, such as Reason.

DirectX Drivers

If you are on the Windows platform and your sound card does not support ASIO drivers (it's pretty hard to find a card that doesn't these days), you will need to use the card's DirectX drivers instead. Developed by Microsoft using their DirectSound technology, DirectX is a common driver format. The driver is included with every consumer and professional digital sound card on the market today and is very easy to use and configure for pro audio and computer gaming. Later in this chapter, I show you how to set up your audio card for Reason and you will have another look at your audio card's DirectX driver.

WDM Drivers

In 2001, Microsoft released yet another driver format: WDM (Windows Driver Model). Built from the technology in the Windows NT operating system and supported in Windows 98/Me/XP, the WDM format is another in a long list of drivers supported by Reason 2.5.

CoreAudio Drivers

In 2002, Apple announced that they were releasing their own audio driver technology called CoreAudio, which essentially performs the same tasks as ASIO or WDM, except that it was designed and optimized for OSX. This driver format is quickly gaining popularity in the Macintosh community due to its ease of use and is sure to be a driver format you will hear more about in the months to come.

WHICH SOUND CARD SHOULD YOU PURCHASE?

It's almost impossible to say, because there are at least 100 audio cards to choose from that support the driver formats discussed here. The answer, for you, will depend largely on your needs and your budget. Appendix D, "Additional Propellerhead Information," contains a list of sound cards and more information, to help you make the best choice.

Would You Like a PC or Mac with That?

The PC/Mac debate reminds me of that old beer commercial where the drunks get into a shouting match of "Taste's Great! Less Filling!". I own and use both PCs and Macs on a daily basis in my studio. Each platform has its advantages and shortcomings. Here's my take on some of the differences:

► **Operating systems**—When I first started using Windows 98, I was instantly hooked on the intuitive graphical interface and felt that it had Mac's OS 8.5 beat by a mile. The distance between Macs and PCs only grew farther apart when I got my first look at Windows XP, as it has a very user-friendly interface and more new features than you can shake a stick at. This changed when I purchased my iBook and started digging into Mac OSX. Although OSX was still not quite ready for pro audio applications such as Reason and Cubase, it still had a slick new look to it that was addicting to use. Now with the current release of OS 10.2, and the planned OS 10.3, I certainly feel that the Mac OS is a worthy competitor to Windows.

► **Available software**—Let's face it, there is simply a lot more software available for the PC than for the Mac. But unless you are a computer gaming fanatic, most of these software titles are irrelevant, as they are not meant for music composition.

► **Price**—No matter what the pros and cons of PCs and Macs may be, the choice is usually going to come down to a matter of price. Until recently, PCs were known for being much less expensive than Macs. A complete PC that will do a decent job with Reason can be purchased for as low as $900, including a monitor. This doesn't include the price of Reason or a really great sound card, but it will certainly get you started and keep you going for a long time to come. Macintosh began to meet the PC price challenge a few years ago, with the introduction of the iMac and eMac computers. These fantastic little systems start at around $999 and come complete with a monitor and a somewhat decent sound card, and, like the budget PCs, the iMac and eMac will get you up and running and keep you going for a good long while.

**WINDOWS XP HOME OR PROFESSIONAL—
WHAT'S THE REAL DIFFERENCE?**

Windows XP currently comes in two flavors, Home Edition and Professional. You will spend an extra $100 purchasing XP Pro, so what real benefits can you expect? Here are the differences that matter to musicians:

► XP Pro can take advantage of computers built with two CPUs. Currently, I own a dual Pentium 3 (750MHz each) computer; so owning XP Pro is a real help as it allows me to use both CPUs at the same time, with supported programs (up to 1.5GHz). This might not be important to you and your computer, as single-CPU Pentium 4 computers are extremely fast and affordable.

► XP Pro can act as a server for networking computers together.

Unless you are a networking connoisseur and you have to have the best of the best, XP Home will certainly do the job.

If you're thinking about buying a new computer and are wondering if perhaps it's time to switch platforms, let me just suggest that you stick with what you already know. The whole point of buying Reason, and this book, is to enjoy being creative with Reason, not to do battle with a brand new operating system at the same time. Reason simply works great on both platforms and that's really all you need to know.

Choosing the Right MIDI Keyboard for Reason

For triggering all the synths and other instruments in Reason, it's important to have a MIDI keyboard of some kind. It could be a keyboard with its own built-in sounds, such as a Yamaha or Roland, or you could choose a MIDI controller keyboard, which is simply a MIDI keyboard without built-in sounds. If you have not purchased a keyboard yet but are intending to, I recommend purchasing one without built-in sounds. Why? Think of it this way; once you start using the synths in Reason, are you really going to need additional sounds from another keyboard? Probably not, as the synths in Reason will certainly give you the sounds sets that you will need to get the job done. Another disadvantage of getting a keyboard with built-in sounds is that Reason does *not* sequence external MIDI instruments and devices, making the purchase of this kind of keyboard a potential waste of money.

Controller keyboards (see Figures 2.5 and 2.6 for examples) are really the right choice for Reason, offering several key advantages:

▶ They cost far less than a keyboard with built-in sounds. A standard 25-key controller can be purchased for well under $200.

▶ They come in a wide variety of sizes and configurations. For example, if you are a classically trained piano student and you want to use a keyboard with weighted keys, there are several controller keyboards of this type that are available at your local Guitar Center. A traveling musician can buy a very small keyboard to hook up to her laptop computer.

▶ Most of the latest keyboard controllers support the USB (Universal Serial Bus) standard, which is great, because there is no need for any additional hardware, such as a MIDI interface.

▶ Many controller keyboards come with knobs and sliders that send out MIDI controller messages. These knobs and sliders can be assigned to specific editing functions within Reason (volume, cutoff, and resonance). For example, you might want to control the filters of the Subtractor, or possibly the parameters of the real-time effects. Many of the major manufacturers of these controllers have already set up specific templates for use with Reason.

READ THE MANUAL

If you are planning to purchase a USB keyboard or other USB peripheral, be sure to read the installation instructions for the keyboard prior to installing it. A good rule of thumb is to make sure that the USB keyboard is not connected to the computer unless otherwise noted in the instruction manual. Once the drivers have been installed, you will probably need to restart your computer to complete the installation. After the computer has restarted, you can then plug in and power up the USB keyboard and it should work just fine.

Figure 2.5
The Oxygen 8 by M-Audio gives you the best of both worlds by supplying assignable knobs for controlling specific Reason parameters, all in a compact keyboard.

Figure 2.6
The Evolution is another ideal controller keyboard.

Making a Sound Decision

All of the thrills and chills that the Reason synths produce will sound only as good as the speakers you select for your rig. Speakers come in a wide variety of brands, sizes, and quality, and you can bet it will take a bit of budgeting, researching, and auditioning before you're ready to make your final purchase decision.

First, you'll need to decide how much you are going to spend on a new pair of speakers. These days, you can price out a pair of speakers at anywhere between $200 and $500 for a decent pair. Just keep in mind the old saying "you get what you pay for" and plan to spend more than $200 for best results. If you want a second opinion, consult the Internet for some articles and reviews on possible speaker selections.

Generally, a day's trip to your local music store will get the job done. A lot of the better-known chain stores such as Guitar Center or Sam Ash have their speakers set up in an isolated room so you can properly fire them up and have a listen to each pair. You can also purchase most of these speakers online with online stores like audioMIDI.com or sweetwater.com.

Here are a few things to keep in mind while you are making a sound decision (pun intended).

▶ When you begin to audition speakers, try to find the *sweet spot* between the pair. This is the point in space at which the mix sounds properly balanced, not too heavy to either the left or the right sides. See Figure 2.7 to get a better idea.

Figure 2.7
The proper speaker
placement for the best
possible mixing solution.
Take a few extra minutes
to find the "sweet spot"
in your studio.

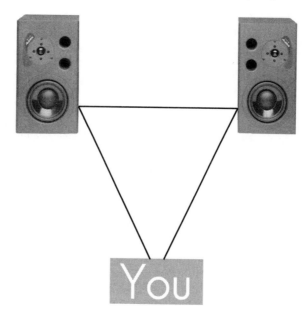

▶ Are you planning to buy a pair of speakers that require an amplifier, or a pair that contain their own power source? If you choose to purchase a separate amplifier, keep in mind that this will certainly affect the total price tag of your purchase.

▶ Bring along a CD of the kind of music you are planning to produce so that you can listen to that through the different pairs of speakers. Because this book is about Reason, a techno CD would probably be the right weapon of choice for this task. Make sure that you listen to the frequency response of the low end. You don't want it to sound too overwhelming or abusive to the rest of the mix.

As I mentioned, it might take a day or more of listening to various speakers before you reach a decision. The most important advice I can give is to let your ears be the judge. Don't be fooled by big brand names or the size of the woofers. They might be impressive to look at and tell your buddies about, but they could also end up being a bad investment.

TAKE COMMAND OF YOUR SUBS
One of the hottest add-ons to any speaker setup is the subwoofer. This speaker enhances the low end of the EQ curve enough to vibrate every part of your body and enrage any neighbor or older relative within earshot. Although these are killer additions to a studio, don't rely too heavily on them for mixing. They tend to color the sound and make your mixes especially bass heavy. Not everyone has a subwoofer in his or her speaker system, and if you mix using a subwoofer, your music will sound very different when played back on a system without one. Many subwoofers can be bypassed while mixing, which is recommended.

CHECK YOUR HEAD(SET)

Headphones are a great solution for bedroom musicians, as they allow you to work late at night without provoking a police intervention or a nasty look from your significant other. All kidding aside, even though headphones are useful, you should always plan to do your final mixes using speakers rather than headphones. There are a couple of key reasons for this.

First, you need to create a natural sounding stereo mix by adjusting the various signals and panning positions of the parts in your Reason song. This is easier to accomplish with speakers than with headphones.

Second, keep in mind that your potential audience is not likely to listen to your music on headphones. Nine times out of ten, they'll be listening to your music in their cars on the way to work or maybe at your latest rave party. Personally, when I am mixing a new song, I burn a test CD, run down to my car, and pop it in to listen. If it doesn't sound good there, it's back to the drawing board. So, although headphones are a good interim solution, don't forget how valuable a good set of speakers can be for your mix.

Selecting a Mixer

In your Reason studio, you might find yourself needing the ability to combine various audio sources at the same time. For example, you might have a few sound modules and drum machines that you would like to use in synchronization with Reason; or perhaps you would like to be able to plug in your guitar or mic and strum and sing along with your technophonic cacophony. Whatever the case may be, a little mixer of some kind would probably be a good investment. A couple of great budget mixers are those made by Mackie and Behringer. Both of these companies offer every kind of mixer you could want, from very simple to very complicated (see Figures 2.8 and 2.9).

Figure 2.8
The 1202 Mixer by Mackie is a good, solid unit for mixing.

Figure 2.9
The Behringer is a much more complex mixer, offering plenty of versatility.

Installing and Configuring Reason

Break out the champagne and start the party, because it's time to install Reason onto your computer. The Prop heads have gone to great lengths to create a relatively painless installation procedure that anyone can tackle. Before starting, though, take a minute to make sure you have everything you need.

▶ The Reason jewel case should contain three CDs, entitled Program Disc, Factory Sound Bank, and Orkester Sound Bank. All three are needed for installation and authorization of the program.

▶ In your Reason box, there should be a slip of paper with what looks like a credit card glued to it. This is your Reason Authorization Card, which contains your License number and your Registration code, and you will need both of these to install the program and register your program with Propellerhead. After installing Reason, pop the credit card into your wallet, so you will not lose it. You also might want to double up your efforts and write the codes down in a notebook or perhaps inside the Reason box.

LIVING IN THE PAST

Windows Me and XP include a very useful program called System Restore. This program takes a virtual "picture" of your computer setup, including your installed hardware and software, and then creates a Restore Point. This Restore Point can then be named and placed in a list that can be recalled later. Why is this useful? Well, let's suppose that after you install Reason, your computer starts acting a little funny—you start having unexplained crashes or lockups. It's pretty safe to assume that the installation of Reason caused some sort of conflict within the computer, resulting in the undesirable behavior. If you create a Restore Point before you install Reason (or any other program for that matter), you can recall that Restore Point at any time, restart your computer, and, upon rebooting, it will be as though you never installed Reason in the first place, thereby solving your crashing problems, as shown in Figure 2.10. At this point, you can then start to diagnose the problem by removing unnecessary hardware or additional software.

Figure 2.10
Create a Restore Point in Windows ME/XP by selecting Start > Programs > Accessories > System Tools > System Restore.

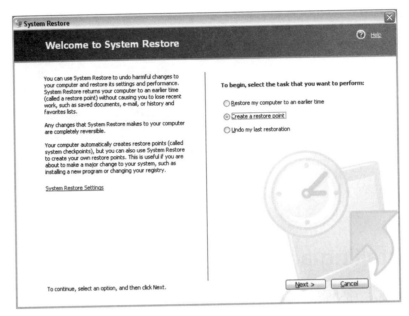

CRACK KILLS

Reason is one of the best-selling music software titles on the market today. Years of research and development went into conceiving and creating this program and others like it. As Reason is such as hot program, you can bet that there are a lot of illegal copies, called *cracks*, floating around the Internet, available for download.

Although cracked copies of software might seem tempting to download and install, it only makes things more difficult for software companies such as Propellerhead to stay afloat and keep producing fantastic software.

Propellerhead Software has a great reputation for addressing technical issues by updating their software titles regularly; it's important that you purchase and use an official version of Reason, as it will qualify you for technical support and product updates. Remember, software developers have to support their families too.

Installing the Program

If you've got the three CDs and your license, you're ready to begin.

1. Pop the Reason Program Disc into your computer and wait for your PC or Mac to recognize the disc. The installation program should start up on its own.

2. After scrolling through the License Agreement and selecting a place to install Reason, the Installation program will ask you if you want to install both of the ReFills CDs onto your hard drive along with the program (see Figure 2.11). They'll take up an additional gigabyte of space on your hard drive. If you select to not

Figure 2.11
If you have enough space on your hard drive, you should install both ReFill CDs.

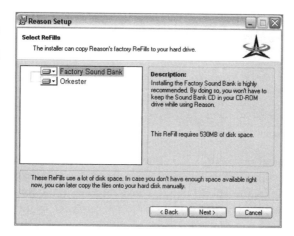

install them, you will be required to place these CDs in your CD-ROM drive every time you start Reason. Unless you are purposely trying to conserve space on your hard drive, I suggest just installing the whole enchilada now.

3. After setting your installation preferences, click the Next button to install the program. After about a minute, the Installation program will ask you to insert the Factory Sound Bank Disc (unless you specified otherwise). Just pop the Factory Sound Bank CD in and click the OK button to continue.

4. After about three minutes, the Installation program should prompt you to insert the Orkester Sound Bank Disc. As before, just pop in the CD and click on the OK button to continue.

5. A couple minutes later, the installation process should be finished. You can choose to restart your computer, which is always a good idea, or you can throw caution to the wind and start up Reason immediately.

6. Upon starting Reason for the first time, Reason will ask for you to insert the Orkester Sound Bank CD for verification (see Figure 2.12). Just pop the CD in and wait for Reason to automatically recognize the disc.

7. Reason will then prompt you to input your license number, which can be found on your authorization card (see Figure 2.13). After typing it, just click on the OK button to continue. Reason should now display the splash screen and start up.

Figure 2.12
Keep those CDs handy for the first time you launch Reason. You will need to pop them in to authorize the program.

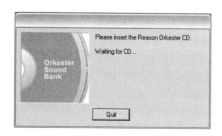

Figure 2.13
You will also need to enter the license number, which can be found in your Reason box.

Enter License Number

Please enter your user name, organization and license number, as included in your original package.

User Name: Michael

Organization:

License Number:

OK   Cancel   Help

8. When Reason first starts up, you will be prompted to register your copy and be given the options of doing so now or later. If you want to register it right then and there, your computer will need to be connected to the Internet. A web browser will launch and take you to the Registration page on the Propellerhead website, where you can enter your data and register your software. If you are not ready to do this right now, just click on the Register Later button and take care of it at another time.

SAVING SPACE

Because installing all of the Reason Sound Banks can eat up more than 1GB of hard drive space, you might be interested to know that you can install them on a second hard drive, or, as mentioned earlier, choose not to install them. If you want to install the Sound Banks onto another hard drive, you can either move them to the other hard drive after installing them on your main hard drive, or you can copy them from the Reason CDs.

If you choose not to install the Sound Banks, Reason will ask for both of the CDs when opening Reason and when you load a preset or sample. You should keep the CDs handy when using Reason. The program will also periodically ask you to insert the Program CD, as part of its copy protection scheme—another reason to keep those discs nearby.

Configuring Reason

After installing Reason and jumping through the authorization hoops, it's time to set your program preferences. You do so through the Preferences dialog box, which appears when you first start the program.

First, take a look at the General preferences page, in Figure 2.14.

▶ The Default Song portion of the General page allows you to select the song or template song you want to see when Reason boots up. By default, Reason starts up with the Built in song selected; it's a default song template that Propellerhead has put together as a tutorial to help get you started. As you will need this in the next chapter, make sure that you have the Built in option selected.

▶ On the Miscellaneous portion of the General page, you can optimize Reason to fit better with your computer (see Figure 2.15). The CPU Usage Limit assigns the desired amount of your computer's processor to Reason. Simply put, if you set

Figure 2.14
After Reason is authorized, you will need to set up the Audio, MIDI, and General preferences.

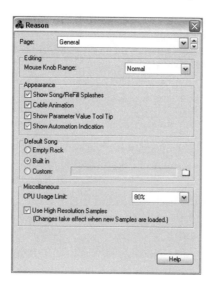

your CPU to 95 percent, you are allowing Reason to use up to 95 percent of your computer's processor before you get a message stating that you have exceeded the power of your CPU. If you are planning to use Reason along with other programs in your computer at the same time, it might be a good idea to set a limit on your CPU. If this is not the case, my money's on the "None" setting.

▶ The Use High Resolution Samples check box tells Reason to play any sample at its best possible resolution (see Figure 2.16). This means if you have loaded a 24-bit sample into the NN-XT sampler, this preference will allow you to listen to the sample at its best. However, this works only if you have a 24-bit audio card, or at least a card that has a playback resolution over 16 bits. Even if you have this option selected and you are using a 16-bit audio card (such as an old Sound Blaster card), the samples you are using may be 24 bits, but you'll hear them at 16 bits.

Figure 2.15
Try different CPU Usage settings to optimize Reason.

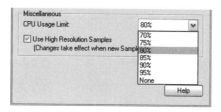

Figure 2.16
If you have a 24-bit audio card, select the Use High Resolution Samples check box.

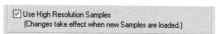

REASON TO THE RESCUE
If you click on the Help button in the lower-right corner of the Preferences page (see Figure 2.14), a Help menu will launch and give you a detailed explanation of every option in the Preferences page.

Next up, take a look at the Audio preferences page, which is accessed by navigating to the General pull-down menu and selecting Audio, as shown in Figure 2.17.

▶ First, you have to select the best audio card driver for Reason. Click on the Audio Card Driver pull-down menu and Reason will give you a list of available drivers that can be used with Reason.

▶ Below this is the sample rate. Reason can work with many sampling rates, varying from 22kHz to 96kHz. If this is your first time using Reason, stick with 44.1kHz.

▶ Below the sampling rate lies the buffer size, which plays an active role in determining the amount of latency. As you make adjustments to the slider control, notice that the output latency decreases or increases depending on which way you go. For your first time out, it's not important to use the lowest possible setting (see the following tip), but it should be set toward the left side.

▶ The Play in Background option tells Reason to keep on playing, even if you are using two applications at one time. Because I often use several applications at one time, I think this is a neat feature. You can select this option if you want.

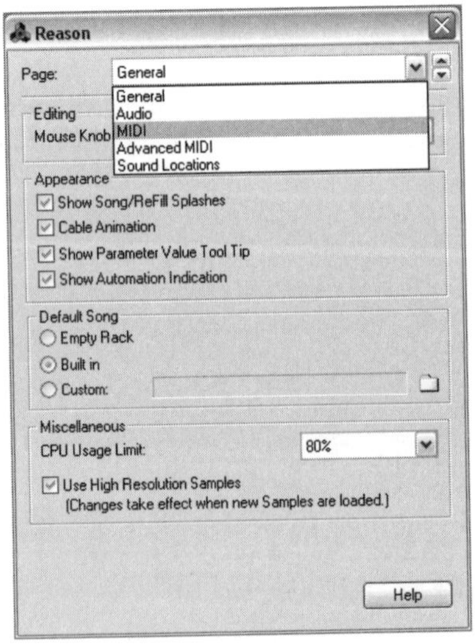

Figure 2.17
Use the pull-down menu in the Preferences window to switch between the different preference types.

HOW LOW CAN YOU GO?

The whole point of using a program like Reason is to be able to play and sequence its virtual synths and sound modules in real-time. This is where making adjustments to the output latency of your audio card comes into play. An audio card's *latency* is determined by the assigned buffer size, which is found in the Audio page of the Preferences window. A *buffer* is used to hold, or collect, data temporarily in a specific location. Simply put, the larger the buffer assigned to your audio card, the more data is stored before it is sent to the audio outputs. This is what causes latency. So, the name of the game here is to lower the buffer size to produce less latency.

Although it is tempting to try to use the lowest possible buffer setting in Reason, this sometimes produces bad audio results. While you are expecting to hear audio bliss through Reason, you might end up hearing a lot of nasty pops and clicks in the playback of your Reason songs. The simplest explanation for this is that the lower the buffer setting, the higher strain it puts on your CPU. If you have a faster computer, sometimes this is not a problem. But if you are using a slower computer, it's probably a better idea to increase the buffer.

The last page you'll look at in this window is the MIDI preferences page. Select the MIDI page from the pull-down menu; it should look something like Figure 2.18.

▶ The Port pull-down menu allows you to select the MIDI input device that will be used to send MIDI messages to the Reason sequencer. As you can see in Figure 2.19, I have quite a few options in my own rig here. Just select the port that is connected to your MIDI controller keyboard and you're set.

▶ The Channel pull-down menu allows you to select the MIDI channel that your controller uses to send and receive MIDI (you have 16 channels). Channel 1 is probably your best option at this point.

Figure 2.18
The MIDI preferences page.

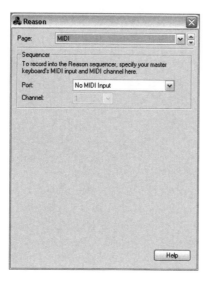

CHAPTER 2

Figure 2.19
Selecting the correct
MIDI port and channel
for your Reason setup.

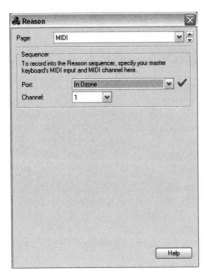

Click on the close window button, which is located at the top-right side of the preferences window on PCs or the top left for the Mac, and you are all set to go.

Throughout this chapter, you have looked at what goes into a typical Reason studio setup. You have also gone through the entire installation and configuration procedure. At this time, you should find yourself cocked, locked, and ready to rock into the next chapter, where you'll take a guided tour of the Reason interface and learn you how versatile this crazy little program really is.

3

Getting Started
with Reason 2.5

At first sight, Reason is a lot to take in—all those virtual mixers, synths, and sequencers can have you seeing double in no time. But the interface is logical, and if you've ever worked with a sequencer or recording gear of any kind, using Reason should feel familiar and intuitive almost from the start. The next couple of chapters cover the basics of navigating the Reason interface and creating music. Don't be surprised if you find yourself experimenting with Reason into the wee hours of the morning—or until your neighbors start pounding on the walls!

This chapter covers the following topics:

▶ Taking a first look at the devices in Reason

▶ Touring the Reason sequencer

▶ Basic routing in Reason

Reason by Default

Launch Reason, and the default song should pop up in a hot second (see Figure 3.1). As you can see, you have many virtual synths, effects, and a dandy mixer to start digging into.

First, have a listen to the groovy little tune that Propellerhead put together. You can use the spacebar on your computer keyboard to stop and start the song at any time. While the song is playing, use the navigation tools located at the right side of the program window (see Figure 3.2) to scroll up and down through the Reason Device Rack. As you scroll, take note of the basic graphic layout of Reason; it is divided into five main sections.

▶ *Inputs and Outputs*—These are found at the top of every song you will create in Reason. As you can see, this section handles the MIDI input and the audio output.

▶ *Mixer*—Although you can create as many mixers as you want in Reason, there is a single master mixer in every Reason song that controls the master levels of your song.

▶ *Effects*—Located just beneath the Reason Mixer are the real-time effects, which are routed to the auxiliary sends and returns in the Reason Mixer. In the Reason default song, there are two real-time effects loaded up and routed to the Mixer, but there are a total of four auxiliaries available per mixer.

Figure 3.1
The first time you boot
up Reason, the default
song loads up, which is a
perfect starting point to
begin honing your
remixing skills.

Figure 3.2
The navigation tools
allow you to scroll up
and down the Device
Rack.

▶ *Synths*—Right below the real-time effects are the virtual synths and sound modules. Additionally, there are a couple of Matrix sequencers in the default song, but let's take this one step at a time.

▶ *Reason Sequencer*—At the bottom of Reason is the main sequencer. This is where your synthesizer performances are recorded, stored, edited, and then played back.

Basic Studio Signal Flow

Before you begin to tour the Reason interface, it is important to have a basic understanding of how an audio signal is routed within a studio environment. This is commonly known as the *signal flow* (see Figure 3.3).

The *signal* refers to audio coming from any piece of studio equipment (hardware or software) that is capable of generating sound. For example, audio signals can come from:

▶ Synthesizers

▶ Guitars or basses

▶ Vocals

▶ Drums

Figure 3.3
A basic signal flow path. An instrument's signal is routed to the mixer, edited with effects, and then sent from the mixer to a recording device and/or speakers.

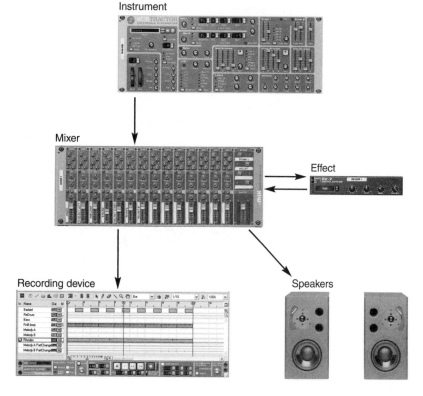

Instrument

Mixer

Effect

Recording device

Speakers

In the world of Reason, the synthesizers and samplers provide the signal. The virtual outputs of these Reason synths are then routed to the mixer.

The *mixer* is used to adjust the amplitude of every signal within a studio environment. Additionally, the mixer is used to manipulate the *timbre* or character of the signal by introducing equalization and effects, such as reverb, delay, and distortion. As you read on in this chapter, you will read about reMix, which is the virtual mixer in Reason.

Once the signals have been appropriately adjusted and manipulated, the mixed signal is then routed out of the mixer and into either a pair of speakers, or a recording device of some kind. In Reason, the mixed signal is routed to the outputs of your installed audio card.

Part of the mixing process is the addition of effects to many of the individual signals. An *effect processor* is a component in your studio that accepts a signal and introduces an audio effect, such as reverb, chorus, or delay. Effects are typically routed to and from the mixer through pathways known as *auxiliary sends*. Through the Aux Send, you can route a portion of any signal to any effect processor and then route the signal back to the mixer. The resultant signal is a combination of the original sound plus the added effect.

Reason's sends are located at the top of the reMix interface. The effect processors themselves are located right below reMix.

MIDI In Device/Audio Out

This device handles all of the routing for MIDI input devices and audio outputs. The MIDI input device allows you to assign any keyboard, drum machine, or other device that sends MIDI messages to a specific device in Reason, allowing for real-time performances of the Reason synths. The Audio Out portion of this device handles all of the audio output routing capabilities of Reason. There are up to 64 audio output possibilities available when you use Reason with a sound card that has multiple outputs or incorporate a Propellerhead technology called ReWire, discussed in Chapter 17, "ReWire." As shown in Figure 3.4, Reason automatically routes the audio outputs to the stereo left and right outputs of the active audio card.

Figure 3.4
The MIDI and audio modules provide a graphical view of how MIDI and audio are routed to and from Reason.

The Reason Mixer

No matter how many nifty sound modules or incredible effects you have, you won't get far without the services of a good mixing board. Reason's mixing board, called reMix, is a simple yet versatile mixing console that offers many creative possibilities when mixing your synthesized masterpieces. Many of the standard mixer controls are found here, such as level, pan, mute/solo, and auxiliary sends. Reason's mixer resembles a few well-known line mixers made by the likes of Behringer, Mackie, and Alesis (see Figure 3.5). This section dives deep into the Reason mixer and shows you some cool and creative techniques that hardware mixers can't match.

Figure 3.5
Most of the Reason modules resemble well-known hardware counterparts; reMix looks like many well-known hardware mixers.

SAVING SPACE
It's easy to be overwhelmed by the profusion of mixers, synths, and sound modules filling your screen. To conserve screen real estate, each Reason device is collapsible—simply click the little triangle at the upper-left of each device (see Figure 3.6) to toggle between the collapsed and expanded views. As you add more devices to your Reason projects, this method helps you save precious screen space.

Figure 3.6
Need to save some space in your Device Rack? Just click the triangle in the upper-left corner of any Reason module to expand and collapse it.

VIRTUALLY ENDLESS POSSIBILITIES

Reason gives you the capability to create as many devices as you want within one song. If you want to create a Reason song using multiple instances of the Subtractor, for instance, you can do it. If you fill up all of the channels in reMix, you can create a second remix and add more devices to it. This unique virtual studio environment gives free reign to your creativity.

The only limitation that you might encounter from time to time is your computer's CPU. As you begin to add more devices to your Reason song, the CPU will need to work harder to process the data. At some point, your CPU will reach its maximum potential and your song might occasionally drop out, which sounds kind of like a CD skip.

Real-Time Effects

If the virtual synths and sound modules in Reason are the main course, the real-time effects are certainly the desserts of pure decadence. Reason's real-time effects are the virtual equivalents of studio hardware, such as a reverb, flanger, or compressor. As you can see in Figure 3.7, the Reason default song contains two real-time effects: reverb and delay. These effects can be used as insert effects, in which the entire signal is routed to the effect and then into the Reason mixer, or they can be used as auxiliary effects, in which only a portion of the signal is sent to the effect and then back into the mixer. If that sounds confusing, don't worry; you'll be taking an in-depth look at the routing and use of each of Reason's real-time effects.

Figure 3.7
The Reason effects are the icing on the cake.

WHAT IS REAL TIME?

By now, you have read the phrase "real time" at least a couple of times, and I'm sure you have heard a lot of musicians and music magazines throw this term around. But what does *real time* actually mean in the world of Reason? It means that you can tweak and adjust the parameters of Reason's instruments and effects, and hear the results of your changes instantaneously, *while a song is playing*. To see for yourself, try this:

Open the Reason default song, press play, and make a few adjustments to the volume of different tracks as the song is playing. As you move the faders, you will hear the volume change. You can also change parameters of the reverb and delay, and you'll hear those changes instantly too. That's real time.

Synths, Sounds, Beats, and Treats

Continuing down the rack with Reason's default song loaded, below the effects come the virtual synths and sound modules that make up the orchestra of Reason. You'll take a quick look at these now, but each device is discussed in a chapter of its own later in the book. You'll learn how to program those dreamy pads, stabbing leads, and pulsating bass lines.

The Subtractor Polyphonic Synthesizer

The Subtractor is a polyphonic synthesizer modeled after a classic hardware analog synth. As seen in Figure 3.8, it contains two oscillators and a noise generator for producing tones, in addition to dual filters, LFOs, and envelopes for shaping and editing the tones. The Subtractor also features a wide range of polyphony, which limits and expands the number of possible simultaneous notes generated. This makes the Subtractor a very versatile synth for producing every kind of sound, from monophonic bass lines to percussion, to large-and-in-charge pad sounds that will make heads turn. And just in case you're not a synth tweaker by nature, the Subtractor comes with many presets that will satisfy your creativity for a long time to come. One of Subractor's lesser-known features is assignable velocity, or the amount of force used to play a note on your keyboard. Velocity information from a MIDI keyboard controller can be routed to a number of parameters, including phase, frequency modulation, and the filter envelope. This makes the Subtractor a virtual analog synth that is velocity sensitive for creating greater dynamic effects than any vintage hardware synth.

Scream 4—Sound Destruction Unit

Located just below the Subtractor is the Scream 4 real-time distortion effect (see Figure 3.9). Scream 4 is the distortion unit that will haunt your dreams and put any *Nine Inch Nails* CD to shame. Split up into three sections, Scream 4 allows you to shape your distortion. You simply select the type of distortion in the "Damage" section, use EQ with the "Cut" section, and finally top it off with resonance in the "Body" (where you can easily create a wicked wah-wah effect).

In the Reason default song, the Subtractor is routed directly to Scream 4, and then routed to reMix. As discussed in the previous section on real-time effects, Scream 4 is being used as an insert effect, where the entire signal is processed and then sent to reMix.

Figure 3.8
The Subtractor was the first available virtual synth in Reason 1.0 and is great for producing pads, leads, and bass lines.

Figure 3.9
No, it's not a sequel to a
Wes Craven movie. The
Scream 4 is the industrial
strength distortion effect
that every good techno
song needs.

Redrum Percussion Module

Redrum is a 10-channel drum machine that resembles a classic drum machine but that far
surpasses the sonic capabilities of older hardware drum machines. As shown in Figure 3.10, it
is split into two sections. The top part of the interface is where you work with the individual
percussion sounds. Each sound is assigned to its own virtual pad, and a number of its parameters
can then be edited, including its pitch, tone, and velocity. The lower portion of the Redrum
interface includes a step pattern-based sequencer that can run in perfect synchronization with the
tempo of your song. Within the sequencer portion of Redrum, a number of effects are available,
including shuffle, dynamics, and a flam for producing a drop stick roll effect. By the time you
finish reading the in-depth Chapter 7 "Redrum—Close Up" later in this book, you'll be the
percussion master.

Figure 3.10
Redrum is a step pattern
virtual drum machine.

WHAT ARE THOSE GREEN BOXES?

In the default song, you'll see a neon-green box drawn around the pattern box at
the bottom of the Redrum module (see Figure 3.11). Whenever you see a green box
around a knob or slider or other controller, it means that automation involving that
controller has been recorded. If you play the song through, you'll see the Redrum
pattern setting switch from pattern one to pattern two, and then back to pattern
one. There are several ways to program automation into your Reason songs, and
you'll learn all about automation later in Chapter 15.

Figure 3.11
Whenever you see a
green box around a knob
or slider in Reason, this
means that automation
has been written in.

The Matrix Analog Pattern Sequencer

The Matrix is an ultra-retro pattern-based sequencer that emulates a classic control voltage sequencer. In the days before MIDI, sequencing synthesizers was difficult, and the concept of controlled voltage sequencing was developed in order to make it easier. Imagine a rack-mounted switchboard that would simply have on and off switches to send controlled amounts of voltage to adjust note pitch, note length, and amplitude. This device would then be manually patched into the hardware synth that it was controlling, and there you have controlled voltage sequencing. The Matrix accomplishes this same task and so much more. The first Matrix sequencer you see (see Figure 3.12) while scrolling down the Device Rack is controlling a Subtractor synth by assigning note values and note velocities in a pattern-based form. If you look all the way down toward the bottom of the Device Rack, you'll see another Matrix that is controlling the Malström synth above it. Chapter 13, "The Matrix Sequencer—Close Up," explores some creative uses for controlling other Reason modules with the Matrix.

Dr:rex Loop Machine Extraordinaire

In most modern dance music, loops are a key element. In fact, you'll find loops being used in just about every kind of music today, even good old honky-tonk country. Dr:rex is Reason's loop player. It's based on a bit of older Propellerhead technology. Long before Reason was a spark in anyone's eye, Propellerhead introduced a program called ReCycle, an innovative loop-editing program that allowed musicians to use the same loop at different tempos. Although that might not sound very impressive today, with the endless number of loop editing programs on the market, you have to remember that in 1996 this was still new territory. In 1997, Propellerhead introduced an audio file format based on their ReCycle technology called the REX, or ReCycle Exclusive, file. Steinberg later added support for this file format into their program Cubase VST, making REX files an instant hit with virtual musicians everywhere. Dr:rex builds on that same technology, but has added a load of editing parameters that were unheard of then (see Figure 3.13).

Figure 3.12
What is the Matrix? It's a sequencer that simulates the old school control voltage sequencers of the 60s and 70s.

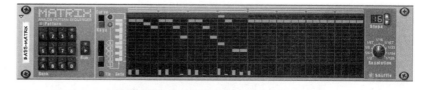

Figure 3.13
Dr:rex is the answer to your looping needs.

The NN-XT Advanced Sampler

The NN-XT sampler was introduced with Reason 2.0 in 2002 (see Figure 3.14). The NN-XT is a software-based sampler that is used to bring that acoustic or realistic element to your Reason songs. The NN-XT rivals most expensive hardware samples, such as those made by Akai and EMU. Propellerhead has also provided a boatload of samples, from acoustic pianos to orchestral instruments to guitar and voice, all of which sound great and are extremely useful in your music.

Figure 3.14
The NN-XT is a professional virtual sampler that includes an impressive sound library.

BUT WAIT, THERE'S MORE!

Prior to the release of version 2.0, Reason included a basic sampler called the NN-19. It resembles an old school Akai sampler, is less complicated than the NN-XT, is easy to navigate, and comes with many wonderful samples. The NN-19 is not part of the Reason default song, but you can read more about the NN-19 in Chapter 11, "NN-19 Close Up."

MORE IS BETTER

The NN-TX and Dr:rex are two very good reasons for increasing your computer's RAM sooner rather than later. Both the NN-XT and Dr:rex are RAM based, which means that the samples and loops that you load into your Reason song will use a significant amount of RAM. The last thing you want to do is limit your creative potential with Reason because you're short on memory.

The Malström Graintable Synthesizer

With the release of Reason 2.0, Propellerhead introduced an original synthesizer called Malström (see Figure 3.15). This virtual synth is unlike any other synthesizer, hardware or otherwise, because it is a completely original form of synthesis that creates blistering tones that will peel the paint off your studio walls. Based on a combination of two techniques known as granular and wavetable synthesis (to be discussed later), Malström has tonal possibilities that will knock your socks off. This synth is covered in Chapter 10, "Malström Close Up"—it's a page-turner!

Figure 3.15
The Malström sports a completely unique form of synthesis called "graintable."

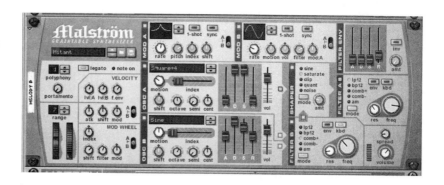

The Reason Sequencer—At First Glance

At the heart of any virtual studio lies the most important component, the sequencer. The sequencer is the tool used to record, edit, and play back notes and performances made with Reason's devices. In a way, it can be thought of as a virtual tape recorder, although it does not actually record audio. Rather, it records MIDI notes or impulses that are sent from a MIDI keyboard to the computer.

Sequencing has come a long way since my first encounter with MIDI—on the Atari 1040ST. As archaic as the Atari was, the MIDI sequencing programs available for it were even older looking, with very clunky interfaces and numerous crashing problems. Reason's sequencer (see Figure 3.16) is one of the most versatile yet easy-to-understand programs around. You'll take a quick look at the sequencer here, but for the details, check out Chapter 5, "The Reason Sequencer Close Up."

Figure 3.16
The Reason sequencer is perfectly laid out and easy to comprehend.

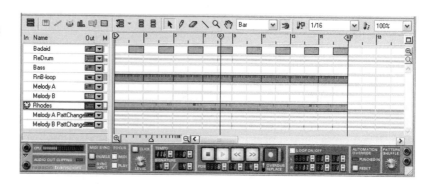

The Reason sequencer is divided into four functional areas:

▶ The Arrange view

▶ The Edit view

▶ The Editing and Quantization tools

▶ The Transport panel

The Arrange View

When a sequence has been created within the Reason sequencer, it becomes a "part." The Arrange view handles the "arrangement" of your these parts by providing a track list, a measure ruler, and a set of "locators." Take a look at each of these.

The Track List

The *track list* is used to organize and route MIDI data to each Reason device in a song (see Figure 3.17). Each device is given its own track, which displays its sequence within your song. Looking at the default song, you can see that there are nine separate tracks, each assigned to a different synth within the Reason Device Rack. In Chapter 5, you'll take an in-depth look at working with tracks.

Figure 3.17
Each Reason device can have its own corresponding track in the track list.

PEEK-A-BOO!
You can quickly navigate to any device in your Reason Rack simply by clicking on its corresponding track in the sequencer. Try it—Click on the "Redrum" track and the Redrum device instantly shows up in Device Rack. This is a very helpful tool to quickly scroll through the Reason devices without having to use the scroll bar on the right side of your Device Rack.

The Measure Ruler

The *measure ruler* is used to display the linear timeline within a Reason song. As you can see in Figure 3.18, a song's parts are governed by a measure-based timeline, which is read from left to right. If you press the spacebar to start up the default song, you'll notice a vertical line moving across the measures, which is topped by a flag with a "P" on it (see Figure 3.19). This is the Position Indicator; it indicates exactly where you are in the song at any given moment.

Figure 3.18
The measure ruler is used to display the linear timeline within a Reason song.

Figure 3.19
If you lose your place, just locate the Position Indicator (the P flag).

JUMP TO THE LEFT; JUMP TO THE RIGHT

Let the default song play, and try clicking on any point in the measure ruler; the Position Indicator will jump to that measure and keep playing.

Reason's Locator Points

Look at the measure ruler and you'll notice two vertical markers that are positioned at the beginning and end of the default song. These markers are known as "locators" (see Figure 3.20). They are sort of like virtual bookmarks, indicating the beginning and end of a song or loop. Press the spacebar to start the default song and watch as the Position Indicator reaches the right locator. As it does, you'll see the Position Indicator jump back to the beginning of the song, where the left locator is sitting. We'll take a closer look at the locator points in Chapter 5, "The Reason Sequencer—Close Up."

Figure 3.20
The locators can mark the beginning and end of a song, as well as serve as a very useful looping tool.

The Edit View

The Reason sequencer has a second way of viewing the MIDI data within your song, called the Edit view. This view is used to edit the performance, timing, and synth parameters within a song. In order to see the Edit view, you must switch from Arrange mode to Edit mode by clicking on the Switch to Edit Mode button in the upper-left corner of the Reason sequencer (see Figure 3.21).

Figure 3.21
Switching to Edit mode is a click of a button.

CHAPTER 3

In Edit mode, you can view and edit MIDI parameters and performance data using any of six separate data editors, called *lanes*. For example, on a track that contains a piano part, you can use the key lane to draw/edit/erase notes (see Figure 3.22). Or if you are using a Dr:rex loop player in a song, you can use the REX lane to edit its individual notes (see Figure 3.23).

To access any of these lanes, just click on their respective buttons, found in the upper-left corner of the Sequencer toolbar (see Figure 3.24).

Figure 3.22
The key lane.

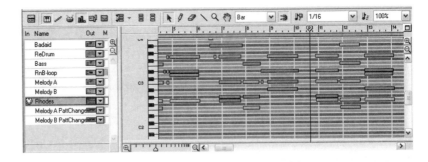

Figure 3.23
The REX lane.

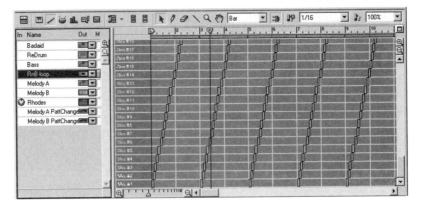

Figure 3.24
The Lane buttons are used to access any Lane Editor when in Edit mode.

The Editing and Quantization Tools

This next section takes a first look at the Editing and Quantization tools of the Sequencer toolbar (see Figure 3.25). By using these tools effectively, you can draw/erase/edit notes, automate your mix, and correct any timing problems with ease and precision.

Figure 3.25
The Editing and Quantization tools of the Sequencer toolbar.

The Editing Tools

Reason provides a set of tools that can be used in Arrangement or Edit mode. Many of these tools have obvious uses, such as the Pencil tool (see Figure 3.26) and the Erase tool (see Figure 3.27). A couple of the other tools have much more specialized functions, such as the Magnification tool for zoom, the Line tool for drawing straight and diagonal lines, and the Hand tool for scrolling through the arrangement in real time.

Figure 3.26
Use the Pencil tool to
draw in notes.

Quantization—Timing Is Everything

Aside from being the most important element in comedy, timing is also the most important element in music, unless you happen to be a fan of the music of John Cage. Some of us are not as rhythmically inclined as we would like to be, or possibly not the best synth players on the block (I fall into this category). That's where the Quantization tools come into play. They appear on the right side of the Sequencer toolbar. These tools help to correct timing problems when sequencing within Reason. For example, if you are playing a drum part and you just miss the last couple of drum hits by a beat or so, the Quantize tool can correct that mistake by shifting the misplayed notes to their correct places (see Figure 3.28). Sounds a little too good to be true, but believe me, it's a lifesaver.

Figure 3.27
Use the Eraser tool to
delete notes.

Figure 3.28
The Quantization tool is
the tool of all tools for
timing.

The Transport Panel

Below the Reason sequencer is the Transport panel. At first glance (see Figure 3.29), some of the controls look similar to those found on tape decks or CD players, but there is much more here than meets the eye. The Transport panel can be used to loop parts in songs, dictate the tempo and time signature, and help create a shuffle groove within a song, for all you Hip-Hop junkies.

Figure 3.29
The Reason Transport
controls.

CHAPTER 3

The Transport panel can also be used to control or monitor additional indicators and functions, such as:

▶ Display the amount of CPU used within a song.

▶ Indicate when an audio signal within Reason is distorting or "clipping."

▶ Produce an audible click or metronome track for keeping time.

▶ Activate synchronization functions.

You'll learn more about the Transport panel in Chapter 5.

Virtual Routing in Reason—Virtual Eye Candy

In addition to its power as a music composition tool, Reason 2.5 offers tremendous creative possibilities with virtual routing. Just like those expensive-looking patch bays found in hardware-based studios, Reason has its own virtual patch bay that is easy to use and a heck of a lot of fun to look at. Let's get patchin'!

The visual paradigm of the Reason interface is, of course, that of a rack of equipment—just like the gear racks used in real-world studios. And, as in real-world studios, the connections between pieces of gear in the rack are handled at the back of the rack. To see the "back" of Reason's virtual gear rack, press the computer keyboard's Tab key. You'll see the backs of the devices in your rack and the cable connections between them (see Figure 3.30).

Figure 3.30
Presto! Change-o!
Pressing the Tab key flips
the Reason interface
around.

As you scroll up and down the Device Rack, you'll notice that each of the virtual synth's audio outputs are routed to the mixer at the top of the rack.

1. Look at the back of the first Subtractor synth, below the real-time effects. As you can see in Figure 3.31, its audio output is routed to input 4 on the mixer.

2. Click and hold on the audio output of the Subtractor, and you will see a list of options, including the Disconnect option. Select disconnect, and watch as the virtual cable connecting the Subtractor to the mixer disappears. The synth has been virtually disconnected from reMix (see Figure 3.32).

3. Now click and hold on the Subtractor's audio output and start to drag the mouse up toward reMix. A gray virtual cable appears and follows your cursor as it moves (see Figure 3.33).

4. Drag the virtual cable up to channel 8's top input (the mono input) on the mixer and release the mouse. You should now see a red cable that connects the Subtractor to channel 8 (see Figure 3.34).

Figure 3.31
The Subtractor synth is routed to channel 4 in reMix.

Figure 3.32
Click and hold any connection within the Device Rack and you can virtually disconnect in a flash.

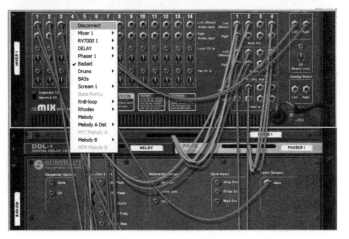

Figure 3.33
To route any device in Reason, just click and drag your virtual cable to any destination. This example is reconnecting the Subtractor to channel 8.

Figure 3.34
Subtractor has been routed to channel 8.

This example just scratches the surface of the endless routing possibilities with Reason. In later chapters, you'll learn some creative ways to use the virtual synths and other devices to create a routing frenzy within Reason.

HIDE THE CABLES

If all these cables are confusing, you can opt not to view them by unselecting the "Show Cables" preference, which is located in the Option pull-down menu.

This chapter took a brief tour of the Reason interface. As you can see, there was a lot of thought put into the creation of Reason. The more you use this application, the more you'll see how much the layout of the program makes sense, and pretty soon you'll find yourself virtually routing in your sleep.

4

Creating Your
First Reason Song

There are a few ways to create your first song in Reason. One way is to open the default song and erase all of the recorded tracks and use this as a starting place of sorts. Although this is a good way to begin, I believe the alternative is better. The second way is to start with a completely blank screen and create a new template and song from scratch. This method is easier than it might sound, and it's a quicker way to learn the software and free your creativity. In this chapter, you are going to create your first song in Reason by performing the following tasks:

▶ Create a reMix mixer and add some real-time effects

▶ Create a couple of virtual synths and sound modules

▶ Create a sequence of notes using a MIDI keyboard

▶ Mix your song with effects and create a digital audio file

Wiping the Slate Clean

Before you can begin, you should start by getting rid of the default song and resetting the Reason preferences to create a blank song template whenever the application is launched, or whenever a new song is created while Reason is running. Follow these steps to do so:

1. Select Edit > Preferences (see Figure 4.1).

2. This will bring up the Preferences window, with the General page active (see Figure 4.2).

Figure 4.1
Reason's Edit pull-down menu.

Figure 4.2
The Preferences window.

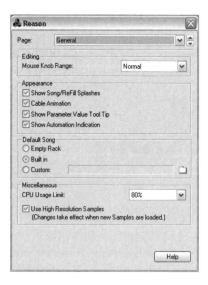

3. In the lower half of this dialog box is the Default Song section, where you select an empty rack, the standard default song, or a customized song. Select the empty rack option.

4. Close the Preferences window by clicking on the "X" in the upper-right corner (upper-left corner if you are using a Mac).

5. Select File > New (press Control+N in Windows; press Apple+N on the Mac). You should now see an empty song that looks like Figure 4.3.

Figure 4.3
Reason now opens with an empty rack. Notice that the right locator is placed at bar 9 by default.

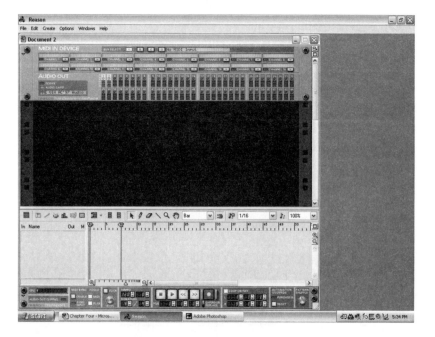

KEY COMMANDS—YOUR NEW BEST FRIEND

Key commands are keystroke combinations that allow you to perform the simplest and most complex tasks within your programs, including Reason. With the right combination of key commands, you can create new songs, save them, and cut and paste parts within Reason. They are real time savers. Most programs will also display their key commands within the pull-down menus of the program. Figure 4.4 shows Reason's File pull-down menu. To the left is the name of the function, whereas on the right side of the menu the corresponding keyboard command is listed.

Figure 4.4
Reason's key commands are listed in every pull-down menu.

Creating a reMix Mixer

You'll set up your first Reason song by creating a reMix device and routing some real-time effects and virtual synths to it.

There are two ways to create a device in Reason. First, you can select the Create pull-down menu and choose the device you want to create (see Figure 4.5). Second, you can right-click anywhere in the black empty space in the Device Rack. As shown in Figure 4.6, this will bring up the list of devices that can be created within the program. This can be done on the Mac by holding the Control key and then clicking anywhere in the empty rack space.

RIGHT MOUSE CLICKS FOR THE MAC

There are many two-button Mac-compatible mice available at your local computer store. If your local computer store does not have them in stock, then take a trip to the Apple Store website. Believe me, it's worth the investment.

Figure 4.5
The Create menu lets
you create any type of
Reason device.

Figure 4.6
Right-clicking in the
empty area of the Device
Rack will display the
Create menu.

Using one of these two methods, go ahead and create a reMix device by selecting the Mixer 14:2
option from the device list (see Figure 4.7)

SELF-ROUTING REASON

Press the Tab key to flip the Reason Device Rack around, and you'll see that Reason
has already routed the main outputs of reMix into the audio outputs of your sound
card (see Figure 4.8). Reason automatically routes any device you create to its
appropriate inputs, taking a lot of the guesswork out of creating and routing
devices. This becomes extremely handy, especially when you are new to the whole
idea of routing audio.

Figure 4.7
Creating a reMix device.

Figure 4.8
Reason can automatically route newly created devices.

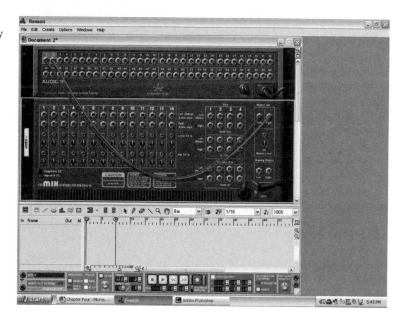

Routing the Effects

After creating the reMix device, it's now time to set it up with some sweet effects.

Using the Create pull-down menu or right-clicking in the empty space of the Device Rack, bring up the list of devices. Select RV-7 Digital Reverb and that effect will appear below reMix. Add a little delay, too. Create the DDL-1 Digital Delay Line. It will appear beside the reverb (see Figure 4.9).

Figure 4.9
Creating a few Reason effects is a snap.

SEND/INSERT EFFECTS

There are two ways to use real-time effects in Reason—as an *Insert* or as an *Auxiliary* (or Send).

An Insert effect is used to process the entire signal of a Reason device. For example, if you were to route the outputs of the Subtractor directly to the inputs of the COMP-01 Compressor, and then connect those outputs to the inputs of a reMix channel, this would be considered an insert effect.

An Auxiliary or Send effect is used to process an assigned *portion* of a Reason device's signal. That processed signal is then routed back into reMix and mixed together with the unprocessed or "dry" signal. For example, if you have a Subtractor routed to channel 1 on reMix and a RV-7 Reverb assigned to Aux 1 in reMix, you can use the Aux 1 knob found on channel one to "send" a portion of your dry signal to the RV-7. Once the signal is processed by the RV-7, it is then "returned" to reMix in order to be mixed in with the dry signal on channel 1.

You'll find a lot more information on this subject in Chapter 14, "Effects—Close Up."

Look at reMix; you will see that the reverb and delay have been automatically routed to the returns, which are found in the upper-right corner of reMix. Press Tab to verify that the outputs of the reverb and delay have been routed to the effect sends and returns of reMix (see Figure 4.10).

At this point, you can route a couple of additional effects to reMix, such as a chorus or distortion, because you have a total of four effect sends available to you. But for now, let's move on and create some synths. You can come back and add more effects later.

Figure 4.10
A quick look on the flip side, and you will see that the effects are already routed to reMix.

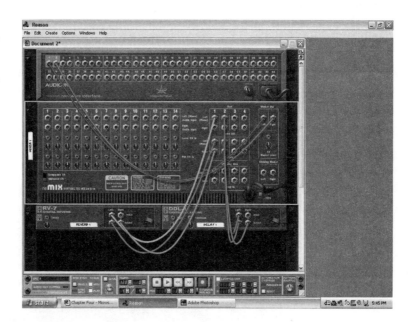

WHAT'S YOUR NAME?

Renaming devices in the rack is easy, and it will help prevent confusion as you add devices to your Reason songs. To rename a device, you can double-click on the name of any track in the track list of the Arrangement window and type the name you want, as shown in Figure 4.11.

You can also double-click on the name displayed on the device itself (see Figure 4.12) and type the new name.

Figure 4.11
Double-clicking on the track and typing a new name for your instrument.

Figure 4.12
Double-clicking on the device itself allows you to change its name as well.

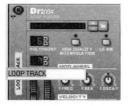

Is There a Dr:rex in the House?

The first virtual sound module that you are going to create is the Dr:rex loop player, so that you can have a steady beat to groove to. Next, you'll add a bass line along with some pads for ambience.

To create a Dr:rex device, select Create > Dr.REX Loop Player. The Dr:rex will pop up and be automatically routed to reMix (see Figure 4.13). You will see the label "Dr.REX 1" on channel 1 of the mixer, as shown in Figure 4.14.

Each time you create a new device, Reason automatically creates a sequencer track in the track list of the sequencer interface named after the device that was created, in this case Dr.REX 1. As an additional point of interest, look to the left of the track name. You can see an icon that resembles the end of a MIDI cable, as shown in Figure 4.15. This symbol tells you that this track has been armed and is ready to receive and record MIDI data. Clicking on the symbol will disarm the track and you will not be able to monitor live or record.

Figure 4.13
Creating a Dr:rex.

Figure 4.14
Once the Dr:rex has been created, you will see it displayed as such on channel 1 of reMix.

Figure 4.15
Once Dr:rex has been
created, Reason automati-
cally creates a sequencer
track and sets it up for
receiving MIDI data.

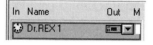

Now that you have created a Dr:rex module, it's time to load up a loop so you can start to groove
your way into your first tune. At the upper-left corner of the Dr:rex interface, there is a Patch
Browser, along with a couple of scroll buttons and a folder button. From here you can preview and
load REX loop files into Dr:rex.

1. Click on the folder button to launch the browser.

2. If this is your first time using the browser, you should click on the Find All ReFills
    button, located at the upper-right corner of the window (see Figure 4.16). Once
    you click on this button, you will see a file called Reason Factory Sound Bank, as
    shown in Figure 4.17. Double-click on this file to continue.

Figure 4.16
The Find All ReFills
button.

Figure 4.17
The Reason Factory
Sound Bank contains
sounds and patches for
Reason's virtual synths.

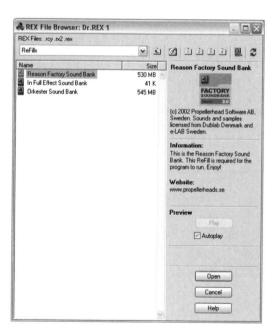

3. Double-click on the folder called Dr Rex Drum Loops (see Figure 4.18).

4. You will see a list of folders (see Figure 4.19) that contain drum loops of various styles of dance music. Depending on your mood, double-click on the folder of the style of loop you want to use.

Figure 4.18
The Dr Rex Drum Loops folder contains all the loops and fills that are formatted as REX files.

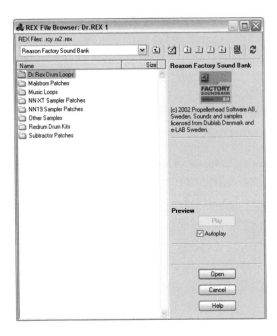

Figure 4.19
Propellerhead supplies a wide selection of styles to choose from. For this example, I have selected "Abstract Hip-Hop."

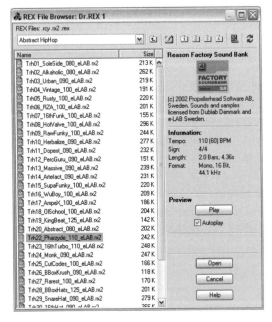

5. You will see a long list of loops to select from. You can select any loop you want by clicking on it once and clicking on the Play button in the lower-right corner. If you want to listen to the loop as soon as you highlight it, click the Autoplay check box (see Figure 4.20).

Figure 4.20
By selecting Autoplay, you will save yourself a lot of time when previewing loops.

6. Select the loop you want and click on the Open button at the lower-right corner of the browser window. This will load the loop into Dr:rex.

After selecting the loop that you want, Dr:rex will load it into the waveform display in the center of the Dr:rex interface, as shown in Figure 4.21. At this point, the loop has been loaded into the Dr: rex interface but not onto its sequencer track in the sequencer, so you won't hear it if you click on the Play button in the Transport panel. Toward the top center of the Dr:rex interface you will see a button called Preview. If you click on this button, Dr:rex will play the loop. To the right of the preview button is another button called To Track (see Figure 4.22). Click the To Track button to export the loop to the Dr:rex sequencer track.

Figure 4.21
The REX file has been loaded into the Dr:rex interface.

Figure 4.22
Click To Track and the sequencer track of the REX file is loaded. Notice that the loop is copied three additional times to fill up the empty space between bars 1 and 9.

DIFFERENT LOOP TEMPOS

When you are selecting a loop for Dr:rex, the Preview button plays the loop back at its original tempo. In this example, I selected a loop that had an original tempo of 100 BPM (beats per minute). But when I loaded the loop into Dr:rex, exported it to its sequencer track, and played it back, it sounded much faster than it had originally. The reason for this is the tempo of the song, which is found at the bottom portion of the transport control, is set to 120 BPM. This is the master tempo for the Reason song, and the REX loop will automatically speed up or slow down to fit that tempo.

Now that you have loaded a loop and copied it to the sequencer, you can add some reverb and delay to the loop to give it some character.

1. Press Play on the Transport control, or press the spacebar on your computer keyboard.

2. Scroll up the Device Rack to reMix. You are going to work on the first track, which is called DR REX 1.

3. At the top of channel 1 are the auxiliary sends. As you may recall, Aux 1 is a reverb and Aux 2 is a delay.

4. Click and hold on the first Aux knob and drag your mouse upward (see Figure 4.23). You should hear the loop playing back with a reverb effect.

Figure 4.23
Click and drag on the first Aux knob to assign a reverb effect to it.

5. You don't want to use too much reverb on a drum loop, as it sounds a little strange, so position the Aux send one knob to nine o'clock. This will produce a warm and mellow reverberation effect.

6. Now add a little delay by clicking on Aux 2's knob and setting it to nine o'clock as well.

7. You should now hear a slight reverb and delay effect on your drum loop. If you look at the reverb and delay meters below reMix, you will see they are working; the LED meters are hopping up and down.

Adding a Bass Line

The next virtual synth that you are going to create is the Subtractor. As you already got your groove thang started with Dr:rex, nothing could be better than a good ol' booty-shaking bass line.

You're going to draw in the bass line using the Pencil tool, so there will be no need for an external MIDI keyboard yet.

Click on Dr:rex to select it, and then select Create > Subtractor Analog Synthesizer. The synth is loaded below Dr:rex in the Device Rack, as shown in Figure 4.24. If you scroll back up to the mixer, you will see the name "Subtractor 1" listed vertically on channel 2. If you look at the sequencer in Figure 4.25, you'll also see a Subtractor MIDI track has been created and is armed to start recording.

Next, you will load a preset into the Subtractor by navigating to the upper-left corner of the Subtractor interface and clicking on the Browse Patch button. As in Dr:rex, the browser window opens and allows you to navigate and search for patches for the Subtractor. Double-click on the Reason Factory Sound Bank file and you will now see the Subtractor Patches folder. Double-click on this folder to see several subfolders containing Subtractor patches for just about every kind of dance music (see Figure 4.26).

Figure 4.24
Loading the Subtractor.

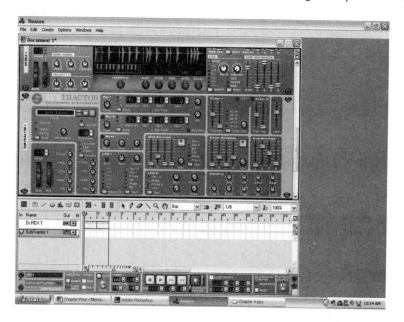

Figure 4.25
The Subtractor sequencer track has been created and is armed for MIDI input.

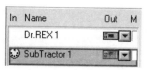

Figure 4.26
There are all sorts of different patches to choose from here, but you need a bass line for this example, so select the Bass folder.

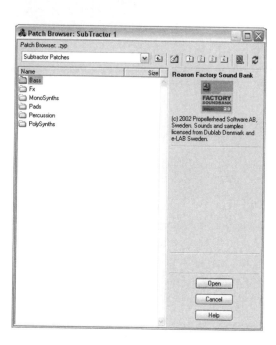

Because you are creating a bass line in this example, double-click on the Bass folder to display a long list of patches made especially for bass lines. Click on the bass patch called Ahab Bass and then click on the Open button toward the lower-right corner of the browser window. The Ahab Bass patch will appear in the upper-left window of the Subtractor interface (see Figure 4.27).

If it turns out the Ahab patch is not to your liking, you can easily scroll through the list of bass patches with just the click of a button. You can re-click the browse button and select another patch, or you can scroll through the patches in that folder by clicking the up and down arrow buttons beside the browse patch button. You can also click and hold on the patch name to choose another patch from the pop-up menu (see Figure 4.28). For the purposes here, try the Bass Guitar patch. You're now ready to sequence your first bass line.

Figure 4.27
The Ahab Bass patch has now been loaded into Subtractor.

Figure 4.28
So many bass patches, so little time.

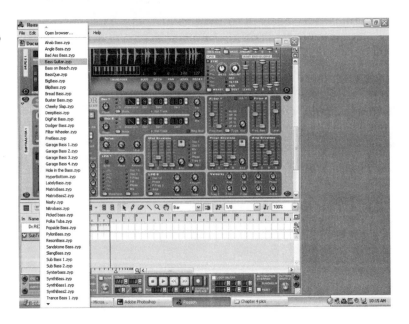

To sequence the bass line and lock in the mood and groove of your first Reason song, follow these steps:

1. First, create a two-bar loop in the sequencer in order to keep your first bass line to a manageable two bars. In the lower-right corner of the Transport panel, set the right locator to bar 3 and activate the Loop On/Off button (see Figure 4.29).

Figure 4.29
Set the right locator to bar 3 and activate the Loop On/Off button.

2. Next, you need to switch modes on the sequencer from Arrange to Edit. Navigate to the upper-left corner of the sequencer (see Figure 4.30) and click on the Switch to Edit Mode button. You should now see the key lane and the velocity lane.

Figure 4.30
Clicking the Edit Mode button is the easiest way to switch modes.

3. When I sequence MIDI events, I like to see as much of the virtual keyboard as possible. Reason has a handy tool that maximizes the sequencer window; it's located in the upper-right corner of the sequencer window (see Figure 4.31). Click once on the Maximize button to enlarge the sequencer window to its fullest potential.

Figure 4.31
You can maximize the Edit view in one click.

4. Now you're ready to draw in a few notes. Select the Pencil tool to start drawing in your sequence in the key lane (see Figure 4.32). Because this is your first time out, keep it simple; this is a bass line, and you want it to groove, not crowd the music. When you're finished drawing notes, you should see a sequence that looks something like Figure 4.33.

5. Click on the Maximize button to restore the sequencer window to its normal state, and click on the Switch to Arrange Mode button to see your bass line displayed in the sequencer along with the Dr:rex pattern, as in Figure 4.34.

Figure 4.32
Drawing in notes in Reason is simple.

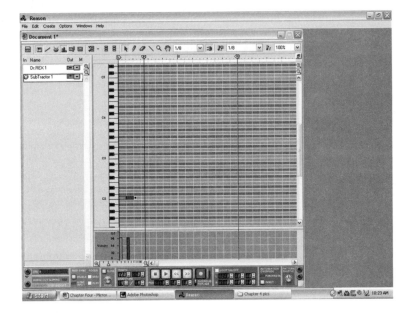

Figure 4.33
Now your two-bar bass loop is ready.

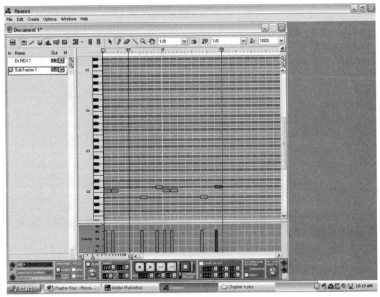

Figure 4.34
Our REX loop and bass line are ready to groove together.

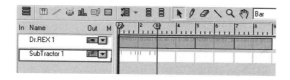

6. Next, you want to turn this sequence into a part that can be moved around freely, because this will also allow you to copy and paste this sequence anywhere in the Reason song. To do this, select the Pencil tool again and draw a box around the sequence by click dragging to the right, until you reach bar 3, as shown in Figure 4.35. Release the mouse and you will now have a drawn-in part.

Figure 4.35
Before you can move or copy your bass line, you need to change it into a part.

7. Now that a part has been created, you'll want to make duplicates of it so that it will run the same length as the REX groove. Select the Pointer tool and click on the part once, and then copy the part (Ctrl+C in Windows; Apple+C on the Mac). Then, paste the part (Ctrl+V in Windows; Apple+C on the Mac). This will create a duplicate part and place it to the right of the original part (see Figure 4.36). Paste in a couple more copies so that the bass line matches the length of the REX groove, as in Figure 4.37.

Figure 4.36
Copying and pasting parts.

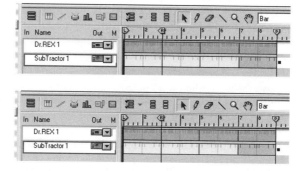

Figure 4.37
Now the parts are the same length.

8. Press play to hear how the bass line works with your drum loop. You might want to sweeten up the mix by adding a little delay to your bass groove; scroll to reMix and turn up the Aux 2 send on channel 2 to send a little bit of the bass track to the delay device.

Now you're off and grooving!

Adding a Pad

The next texture you'll add to the song is a pad line. A *pad* refers to a kind of ensemble sound that fills up the empty space, like playing chords on a guitar. The chords are held and sustained for generally long periods of time and add mysterious overtones and moods to any piece of music. A good example is a string section in an orchestra, which is used to play long sustained chords throughout film scores and symphonies.

You are going to add that texture into your groove here by creating another Subtractor synth, selecting a pad sound for it, and then drawing in some chords to give the song the mood it needs.

Create a new Subtractor synth. There should be a new MIDI track in the Sequencer window called Subtractor 2 and it should be routed to channel 3 in reMix.

To find an appropriate pad sound, again click on the Browse Patch button in the upper-left corner of the Subtractor to launch the browser window. This time, you will see all of the bass patches that you worked with in the previous tutorial.

You have to get back to the starting point in the browser, and the easiest way to do this is to click on the Find All ReFills button in the upper-right corner of the browser window. Reason will then find all available sound sets, or *ReFills* as they are called, within your computer. If this is your first time using Reason, you should see two different sound sets—the Reason Factory Sound Bank and the Orkester Sound Bank. Double-click on the Reason Factory bank and then double-click on the Subtractor Patches folder. Finally, double-click on the Pads folder to see the available pad patches for the Subtractor.

USERS OF REASON 2.0—READ THIS

If you are one of the many users of the previous version of Reason, you probably downloaded the 2.5 update from the Propellerhead website. If this is the case, when you click on the Find All ReFills button, there will be a third ReFill called the In Full Effect Sound Bank. This small ReFill contains patches for the RV-7000 Reverb and the Scream 4 Distortion.

For users who installed Reason 2.5 from the original CD-ROM, the patches from the In Full Effect Sound Bank are included within the Reason Factory Sound Bank.

Scroll down the list and select the patch called Omenous. It will load in the Subtractor window.

You're ready to draw in your pad part, so switch to Edit mode and use the Pencil tool to draw in a couple of chords. Keep in mind that you want your chords to be long and sustained. Here's how to accomplish that:

1. After switching to the Edit mode, create a four-bar loop so you can draw in two sustained chords that are each two bars long. Set the right locator to 5 on the Transport control.

2. Select the Pencil tool and locate the first note you want to draw in. Then click and hold on that note and drag your mouse to the right to bar 3. As shown in Figure 4.38, release the mouse and you will now have a sustained note. Repeat this a couple of more times on different notes, so you have a nice long, sustained chord, as in Figure 4.39.

Figure 4.38
Click and drag to draw in long, sustained notes.

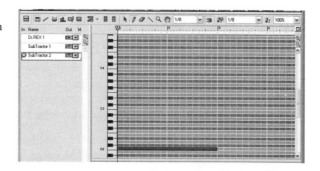

Figure 4.39
Here's a long, sustained chord.

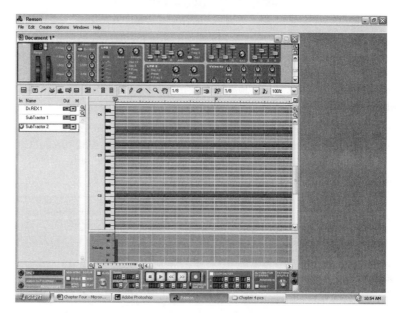

CHAPTER 4

3.   Repeat the previous step and draw in another chord that starts at bar 3 and extends out to bar 5. This will give you two long sustained chords.

You've created your four-bar pad track. Next, return to Arrange mode and use the Pencil to make a part out of your loop, as you did with the bass line. Now you need to duplicate this part one time only, so use the copy-and-paste trick that you learned in the bass tutorial and repeat the pad part once to make it equal the distance of the other two tracks.

Pads are like instant mood enhancers for music. They will set the tone and make your music sound much fuller than before. A handy tip to make the pad sound even larger than before is to add some reverb and delay to it. Scroll up to reMix and use the Aux knobs from channel 3 to send the pad to the reverb and delay devices. You can give your pad sound a very generous helping of the two effects and turn the Aux send up to twelve o'clock or even three o'clock.

Topping It Off with a Little Lead

You're doing great! So far you have created a grooving drum loop and sequenced in bass and pad lines. Now it's time to sprinkle a little auditory sugar on top by adding a lead line.

Throughout this tutorial, you've kept the overall tone of this song a bit on the mellow side. It's time to spice things up a bit, so you're going to use Malström and add a little acidy four-bar lead line on top of the mix. Click and drag the right locator to bar 5 in order to create a four-bar loop.

Let's start by creating a Malström. Click on the second Subtractor, and then select Create > Malström Graintable Synthesizer. The funky green machine will appear in your Device Rack below the second Subtractor synth. It will also show up as a track in the sequencer and should appear under channel 4 in reMix (see Figure 4.40).

You need to find an appropriate lead synth patch for the Malström, so click Malström's browse patch button, and then click the Find All ReFills button again. Double-click on the Reason Factory Sound Bank and you should see the Malström Patches folder. Double-click on this folder and open the Mono Synths folder. In the long list of mono patches, find the patch called RadioHammer. Highlight it and click Open.

Switch to the Edit mode and draw in a lead line that complements the bass and pad lines. When you are finished, your sequence should look something like Figure 4.41. If it sounds a little funky at first, read on; I will give you some tips to make your lead sing.

Figure 4.40
The Malström is my favorite virtual synth in Reason.

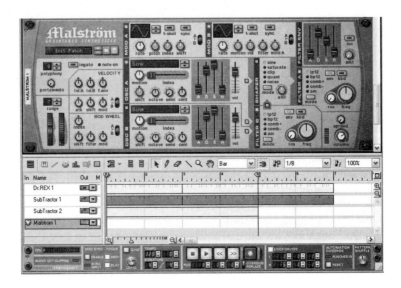

Figure 4.41
Sequencing the Malström
lead line.

CHAPTER 4

Although the RadioHammer patch is a dreamy, acid-drenched sound that will burn its way through your mix, I thought this would be a good time to show you a couple of tricks to make this patch sound even better. Follow along as I show you how to edit your first synth in Reason.

1. Begin by changing the Polyphony of the Malström setting to 1. If you recall from Chapter 3, polyphony refers to the number of notes that can be played simultaneously by a synth or sound module. With the polyphony set to 1, only one note can be played at a time. Malström's polyphony display is in the upper-left portion of the interface. Using the arrow pointers beside the display, change it to 1 (see Figure 4.42).

Figure 4.42
Polyphony is the secret
to changing any synth
into a lead line.

2. Below the polyphony control is a knob called Portamento. This controls the speed of the "sliding sound" you get between two notes. As in Figure 4.43, turn the knob until it reaches the eleven o'clock position. This will produce a very nice note sliding effect when you play your sequence back.

Figure 4.43
The more Portamento,
the more slide.

3. Next, scroll up the Device Rack to reMix; you're going to make a couple of volume adjustments to the Malström. If you play the sequence as it is now, the Malström is probably a little too loud for the mix, so first start by clicking and holding on the volume fader for the Malström (the fader on channel 4) and just slide it down to adjust the volume of your Malström track (see Figure 4.44).

Figure 4.44
A little level adjustment is just what the doctor ordered.

4. A neat effect that I like is to pan the synth either hard right or hard left and then use a lot of delay and reverb to create a stereophonic effect. This is done quite easily by adjusting the pan knob to the left or right, and then using the Aux knobs to send the Malström to the reverb and delay, as shown in Figure 4.45. Voila! Instant synthesized bliss!

Figure 4.45
Pan the Malström to the left, and top it off with some delay. It will give your track some needed ambience.

Putting the Pieces Together

There are two essentials for creating good dance music. First, you have to come up with some killer hooks and grooves with your synths. The second is that you must assemble them so that there is an intro, middle, and ending. At this point, you have accomplished step one with your first Reason song. As good dance music also depends on predictable beats and a generous dose of repetition, you must now assemble this tune to give it the final touch. In this section, I'm going to show you the quick-and-easy way to stretch your Reason song from four bars to 40. It won't be a long song, but it will be sufficient to help you understand how to arrange your pieces of music.

First, let's start with the REX loop.

1. Look at the REX track in Figure 4.46, and you will see that there are four two-bar loops lined up next to each other. First, you are going to combine all of these loops together in order to create one large eight-bar loop to make it easier to copy and paste.

Figure 4.46
At this point, you have four separate two-bar loops.

2. Select the Pencil tool and click at the far left of the REX track; drag your mouse to the right until you reach the end of the fourth two-bar loop. Release the mouse button and you will see just one eight-bar loop, as in Figure 4.47.

Figure 4.47
By using the Pencil tool, click and drag until both loops are drawn over.

3. Select the Pointer tool and click once on the REX loop to highlight it.
4. Copy the selection (press Ctrl+C in Windows; press Apple+C on the Mac).
5. Paste the selection (press Ctrl+V in Windows; press Apple+V on the Mac). This will place a new copy of the eight-bar loop immediately to the right of the original loop.
6. Because the copy that you made is still on your virtual Clipboard inside your computer's memory, just repeat the Paste key command three more times until the REX loop reaches bar 41 (see Figure 4.48).

Figure 4.48
Copy and paste your REX loop until it reaches bar 41.

7. Click and drag the right locator point to the beginning of bar 41, so that you can listen to the entire track in a constant loop.

Now that the drums are laid down and arranged, you can do the same with the bass track, which is being played by the first Subtractor synth.

1. Select the Pencil tool and click at the far left of the bass track. Drag your mouse to the right until you reach the end of the 42-bar loop. Release the mouse button and you will see just one eight-bar loop, as shown in Figure 4.49.

Figure 4.49
Use the Pencil to combine the four bass loops into a single eight-bar loop.

2. Using the Pointer tool, click on the bass part and drag it to bar 5. Release the mouse button and Reason will move the four-bar part to bar 5, as shown in Figure 4.50.

Figure 4.50
Click and drag is the name of the game when moving parts around.

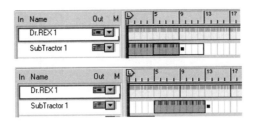

3. Using the same copy-and-paste method found in the last section, copy and paste the bass part until it reaches bar 37 (see Figure 4.51).

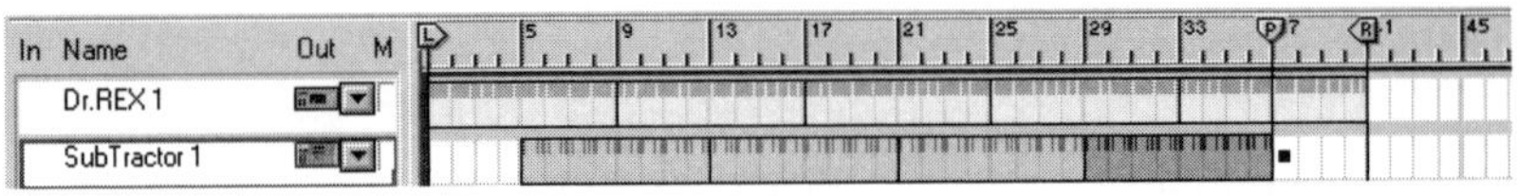

Figure 4.51
Copy and paste the bass part.

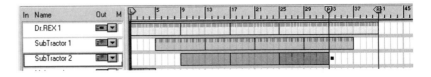

Next comes the pad part that you created with the second Subtractor synth.

1. Select the Pencil tool and click at the far left of the pad track. Drag your mouse to the right until you reach the end of the second four-bar loop. Release the mouse button and you will see just one eight-bar loop.

2. Select the Pointer tool; click and drag the pad track to bar 9.

3. Using the same copy-and-paste method that you used in the last two sections, copy and paste the pad track until it reaches bar 33, as shown in Figure 4.52.

Figure 4.52
Now for the pad track.

Last on the arrangement is the lead part that you created using the Malström synth. This is going to be a little different, because you probably wouldn't want this part to play constantly through the entire song. Instead, you are just going to drop it in here and there to flavor up the mix.

1. Click and drag the lead part to bar 13.

2. Hold down the Control key on your PC or the Option key on the Mac, and then click and hold on the lead part. Start to drag the part to the right and you will see that a copy has been made and is following your pointer. Drag the new copy to bar 21 and release the mouse. This will create a new part as seen in Figure 4.53.

3. Repeating the same step as before, create a new copy and drop it in at bar 37. After doing this, your lead part should look a lot like Figure 4.54.

Figure 4.53
Clicking and dragging a part while holding down the Control (Option) key will create a copy that can be placed elsewhere in your track.

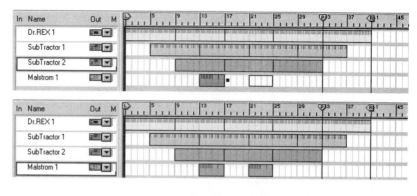

Figure 4.54
Because this is a lead part, you don't want to overdo it with the repetitions, but having it play back here and there is a good use of textures and moods.

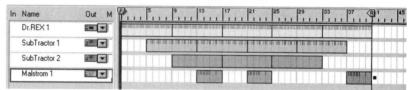

It's All in the Mix!

Last but not least are saving and mixing down your first song. Reason can create a stereo digital audio file of your song. You can then burn it onto a CD to listen to it wherever you like, or you can place it on the web so others can download it and groove along with ya. Mixdown is simple.

MIXES GALORE

Aside from the standard audio file mixdown, Reason features a few other unique mixing capabilities. These other features are examined in more detail in Chapter 18, "Mixing and Publishing Your Reason Songs."

When creating an audio mixdown, Reason exports the *entire* song, including all of the empty bars at the end. So, unless you like a lot of empty space at the end of your tune, you need to get rid of the empty bars by adjusting the endpoint position (E icon) of your song (see Figure 4.55). As in Figure 4.56, just click and drag the endpoint to the left until it is four bars after the right locator point. This ensures that the tail end of your real-time effects isn't unexpectedly cut off (see note below for more details).

Figure 4.55
The endpoint position dictates the end of a song file.

Figure 4.56
Click and drag the
endpoint within four
bars of the right locator
point.

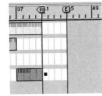

DON'T CUT OFF THE TAIL

Tail effect refers to the lingering sound of reverb or delay (or similar effect) after the
initial sound (the hit of a snare drum, for instance) has stopped. The tail eventually
dissipates to silence.

When mixing down, it's important that you extend the song beyond its ending
point long enough to capture any lingering effect tails. Notice, in Figure 4.57, how
abruptly the mix is cut off. Figure 4.58 shows the same mix with the tail in place;
the mix was extended long enough to capture the entirety of the fading effects.

Figure 4.57
This is an example of
cutting off the tail end of
your mix. It doesn't look
or sound good.

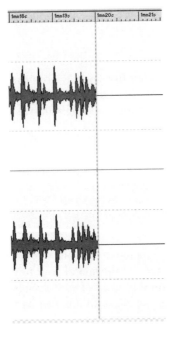

Figure 4.58
Here is the same mix
without the tail cut off.

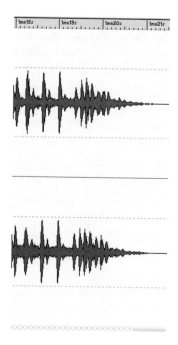

CHAPTER 4

Now you are ready to export your song into a digital audio file. Select File > Export Song As
Audio File. You will then be able to name your song, select between WAV or AIFF audio formats,
and click Save. A new window will pop up asking you to select your bit depth and sampling rate
(see Figure 4.59). Reason can create a 16-bit, 44.1kHz recording, which is the standard for all
commercial music CDs. Reason can also create very high-resolution digital audio files, for use in
pro audio programs or post-production. If this is your first time out, I recommend sticking with the
default setting of 16-bit, 44.1kHz.

After you select your bit depth and sampling rate, Reason will export your song as an audio file.
Depending on how fast your computer is and how many tracks you have in your song, this can
take a minute or two. After it's mixed, you can quit Reason and open your digital audio file in
your favorite digital audio jukebox program, such as Windows Media Player or iTunes.

Figure 4.59
Choose your mixdown
preferences and let 'er
rip!

Export Audio Settings	
Sample Rate: 44100 Hz	OK
Bit Depth: 16	Cancel
	Help

This chapter contained the step-by-step process of creating your first song in Reason. Propellerhead makes it so easy and fun to create music that it's infectious. And I'm sure you're anxious to learn more. From this point, the chapters give you an in-depth breakdown of every synth and sound module in Reason and show you how to use these creatively in ways that will set you apart from the average "Joe" Reason user.

5

The Reason Sequencer—
Close Up

The Reason sequencer (see Figure 5.1) can be thought of as the brain of the entire program. It is the compositional tool that makes it possible to record your performances, edit them, and then play them back with accuracy and precision. This chapter examines the individual parts of the Reason sequencer and discusses how to use the sequencer to its limits.

A sequencer is responsible for performing three tasks:

▶ Recording MIDI data

▶ Editing MIDI data

▶ Playing back MIDI data

Figure 5.1
The Reason sequencer—
The brain of your virtual
environment. The
sequencer is split into
three basic sections: the
Track window, the
Arrange/Edit views, and
the Transport Panel.

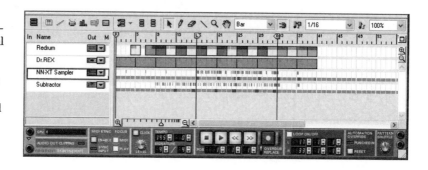

IMPORTING/EXPORTING MIDI FILES

The Reason sequencer can import and export MIDI files. This is a great feature for users who like to surf the Net and download MIDI files of their favorite songs. Additionally, you can export your songs in Reason as MIDI files for other users to download into their favorite MIDI sequencers.

To *import* a MIDI file, simply choose Import MIDI File from the File pull-down menu. Then locate the MIDI with your Windows or Mac file browsers and import it. Once imported, just keep these rules in mind:

▶ Imported sequencer tracks will not be routed to any Reason device. You will have to do this manually, and you will learn how later in this chapter.

▶ If the MIDI file contains multiple tempos and time signatures, Reason will disregard these and use only the first tempo and time signature. This is kind of a bummer for anyone wanting to import their favorite *Progressive Rock* song, for example, or other types of music that typically rely on time signature and tempo changes.

▶ All of the controller data, such as modulation wheel adjustments or pitch bend changes, saved within a MIDI file will be imported along with the rest of the data; however, in some cases this controller data might not work as intended with Reason devices. You might have to remove the controller information, which is covered toward the end of this chapter.

To *export* a MIDI file, first set your end (E) marker to the end of your song. Then simply choose Export MIDI File from the File pull-down menu and Reason will do the rest. Just remember the following:

▶ The tempo of the Reason song is stored in the MIDI file.

▶ All of the exported sequencer tracks are set to MIDI Channel 1 by default. This is because Reason is not a MIDI channel-dependent program, like Cubase SX and Logic are.

▶ All of the exported sequencer tracks will retain their given names from Reason.

The rest of this chapter explores every inch of the Reason sequencer, including the following topics:

▶ The basic layout

▶ The Sequencer toolbar

▶ The Track window

▶ The Transport Panel

▶ Sequencing a live performance

▶ Sequencing written data

The Basic Layout and Tools

Before you begin your exploration of the Reason sequencer, it's important to have a general understanding of the basic layout of its common and unique views and functions.

The Arrange/Edit View

When you first look at the sequencer, the Arrange view is probably the first point of interest you will notice. This is where all of the MIDI data for your Reason song is stored, arranged, and displayed.

Typically, a sequencer displays its MIDI data in a linear fashion, meaning that the information is read from left to right. With that in mind, a song begins on the far left and progresses to the right as the song plays. The timeline of the MIDI events in the sequencer is governed by the ruler, which is located at the top of the Arrange view and runs parallel to it. Looking at Figure 5.2, you can see that the ruler is displaying *bars*, or measure counts for every other bar. When you read through the next part of this section and use the Zoom tools, you'll find that the ruler can display much smaller and finer increments.

Two kinds of MIDI data are displayed in the Arrange view:

▶ Note information

▶ Controller information

If you open the Tutorial Song, which is located in your Reason program folder, and look at the Arrange view, you'll notice that the note information is displayed in two ways. Looking at the NN-XT tracking, you'll see that the note information is displayed on a white background. This can be thought of as ungrouped data (see Figure 5.3).

Looking at the Redrum track, you'll notice that the note information is displayed inside box frames of different colors. This can be thought of as grouped data (see Figure 5.4).

Figure 5.2
The ruler governs the timeline of your Reason song.

Figure 5.3
The NN-XT sequencer track is displaying ungrouped data.

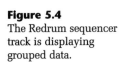

Figure 5.4
The Redrum sequencer track is displaying grouped data.

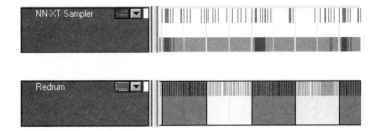

The Arrange view also has an alternate viewing mode, called the Edit view. In this view, all the MIDI data in a song can be edited and new data can be created (see Figure 5.5). As you read further in this chapter, you will find that there are many creative possibilities and different faces to the Edit view.

Figure 5.5
The Edit view is used to draw and edit MIDI data.

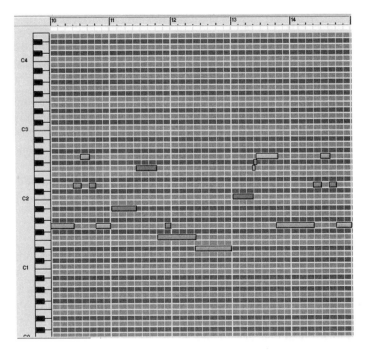

EVENTS—ALSO KNOWN AS NOTES

Throughout this book, I will be using two terms a lot: *notes* and *events*. These two terms can sometimes mean the same thing. For example, MIDI data can be thought of as notes, but really they are *events*—numeric bits of data that contain the note's pitch number, velocity, and length. Throughout this chapter, I refer to notes as events.

But I also use the term notes throughout this chapter as well, but only to refer to specifically named functions within Reason or to the length of the events, such as 8th notes or 16th notes.

The Zoom Tools

There are three pairs of Zoom tools in the Reason sequencer. These tools help you get a close-up look at any MIDI data in the Arrange or Edit views of a particular track. They also give you a better view of an overall song.

▶ The first pair of Zoom tools is located in the upper-right corner of the Track window. These are used to zoom in and out vertically on any selected sequencer track while in the Edit view (see Figure 5.6).

▶ The second pair of Zoom tools is located in the lower-left corner of the Arrange/Edit view. These are used to zoom in and out horizontally on any MIDI event(s) in the Arrange/Edit view (see Figure 5.7).

▶ The third pair of Zoom tools is located in the upper-right corner of the Arrange/Edit view. These are used to zoom in and out vertically on any MIDI event(s) in the Arrange/Edit view (see Figure 5.8).

Figure 5.6
The first pair of Zoom tools can be used while in the Edit view.

Figure 5.7
The second pair of Zoom tools can be used to horizontally zoom in/out on any MIDI event in the Arrange/Edit view.

Figure 5.8
The third pair of the Zoom tools is used to vertically zoom in/out on any MIDI event in the Arrange/Edit view.

Sizing Up the Sequencer

The size of the Sequencer window can be easily adjusted in two ways:

▶ By clicking on the Maximize button, located just above the Zoom tool found in the upper-right corner of the Sequencer window. Note that after maximizing the Sequencer window, the Maximize button becomes a Restore button, which is used to return the window to its default position.

▶ By clicking and dragging on the divider between the Sequencer window and the Reason Device Rack (see Figure 5.9).

Figure 5.9

You can manually resize the Sequencer window by clicking and dragging the divider between it and the Device Rack.

Drag the divider

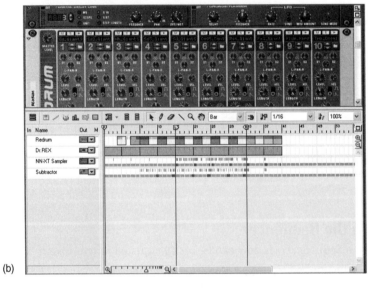

(a)

(b)

DETACHING THE SEQUENCER WINDOW

A relatively new feature in Reason is the capability to detach the Sequencer window from the Reason interface. If your computer supports dual monitors, you might find this a very useful feature. It allows you to use one monitor for the Reason devices and another for the sequencer.

To detach the sequencer, simply choose Detach Sequencer Window from the Windows pull-down menu. Once selected, the Sequencer window will separate itself from the Reason interface and appear in its own window. This window can then be dragged to another monitor and maximized in order to create an optimal dual monitor setup (see Figure 5.10).

At any time, if you want to close the separated Sequencer window, just click on the Close Window button in the Sequencer window. The sequencer will return to its default position.

Figure 5.10
Detaching the Sequencer window is great for users who own computers with dual monitors. Notice that the Transport Panel appears on both sides of the screen.

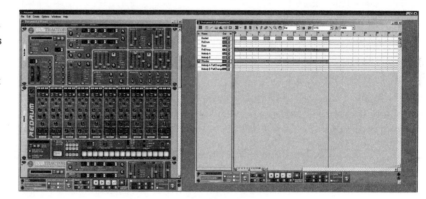

CHAPTER 5

The Sequencer Toolbar

The Sequencer toolbar is used to perform numerous tasks in the sequencer. This section discusses each of these tasks (see Figure 5.11).

Figure 5.11
The Sequencer toolbar provides all the tools and editors to sequence like a pro.

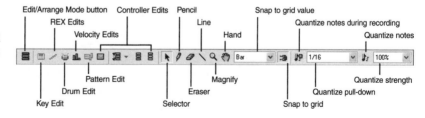

Start at the far left of the toolbar and work your way to the right.

Edit/Arrange Mode Button

This button is used to switch between the Arrange and Edit views of the sequencer (see Figure 5.12). Every time Reason is booted up and a song is loaded, the Arrange view is the default. Clicking on the switch button will allow you to view any MIDI data within a sequencer track.

Figure 5.12
The Edit/Arrange Mode button is used to toggle between the two viewing modes of the Reason sequencer. The top shows the button as it appears when the sequencer is in the Arrange view. The bottom shows the button as it appears in the Edit view.

The Lane Buttons

To the right of the Switch button are the Lane buttons. These are used to view and edit MIDI data from any sequencer track in a Reason song. Each of the six lane editors has a particular and unique purpose.

▶ **The Key lane**—This lane is used to edit the MIDI data related to the Subtractor, Malström, NN-19, and NN-XT devices (see Figure 5.13).

Figure 5.13
The Key lane is used to edit sequences for the Malström and Subtractor.

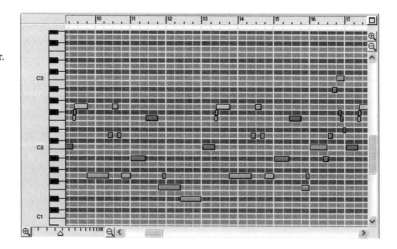

▶ **The REX lane**—This lane is used to edit the MIDI data of the Dr:rex Loop Player (see Figure 5.14).

Figure 5.14
The REX lane is used to edit sequences for Dr:rex.

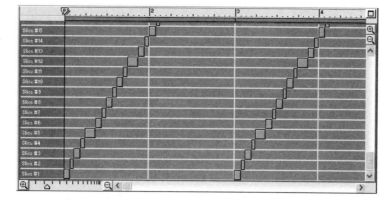

▶ **The Drum lane**—This lane is used to edit the MIDI data of Redrum (see Figure 5.15).

Figure 5.15
The Drum lane is used to edit sequences for Redrum.

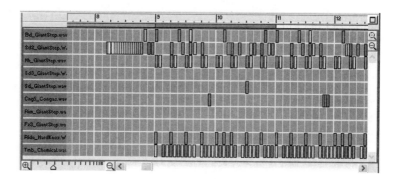

▶ **The Velocity lane**—This lane is used to edit the velocity of each MIDI event in either the Key, REX, or Drum lanes (see Figure 5.16). Additionally, the Velocity lane appears by default when switching to the Edit view.

Figure 5.16
The Velocity lane edits the velocities of each MIDI event.

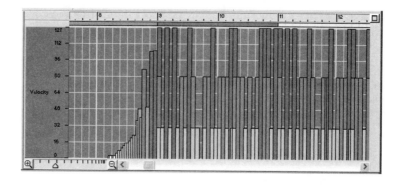

CHAPTER 5

▶ **The Pattern lane**—This lane is used to write and edit pattern data for pattern-driven Reason devices, such as the Matrix and Redrum (see Figure 5.17).

Figure 5.17
The Pattern lane is used to edit the Pattern Section of Redrum and the Matrix.

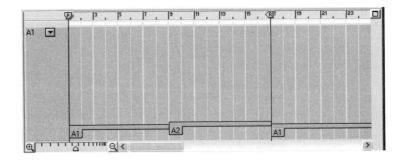

▶ **The Controller lane**—This lane is used to write and edit controller data for the individual parameters of each Reason device (see Figure 5.18). I'll be discussing this in-depth later in this chapter.

Figure 5.18
The Controller lane is used to draw in controller data for the individual parameters of each Reason device. Notice the additional controller buttons to the right of the Controller Lane button (refer to Figure 5.11). These buttons are used to display a list of individual controllers, display all of the controllers, and display only the controllers that contain active data within the selected sequencer track.

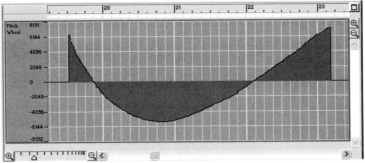

The Editing Tool Buttons

To the right of the Lane buttons are the Editing Tool buttons (see Figure 5.19). These six buttons are used to view/write/edit data in both the Arrange and Edit views.

Figure 5.19
The Editing Tool buttons can be used in the Arrange and Edit views.

▶ **Selector tool**—Also known as the *pointer*, this tool is used to select an individual MIDI event or group. It can also be used to select a group of MIDI events and groups by clicking and dragging a marquee box around a group of events and groups (see Figure 5.20).

Figure 5.20
To select a group of MIDI events, choose the Selector tool, and then click and drag over the group of events.

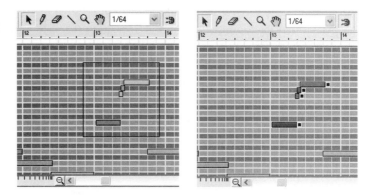

▶ **Pencil tool**—This tool is used to draw MIDI events and groups. Additionally, it can be used to draw in controller information and velocity information.

▶ **Eraser tool**—This tool is used to delete single MIDI events and groups. Additionally, it can also delete a group of MIDI events by clicking and dragging a marquee box around the events and groups, and then releasing the mouse.

▶ **Line tool**—This tool is used to draw straight and diagonal lines to edit the velocity and/or controllers of a series of MIDI events.

▶ **Magnify tool**—This tool is used to get a close-up look at a group or MIDI event.

▶ **Hand tool**—This tool is used to scroll through a Reason song. Select it, and then click and drag to the left or right while in the Arrange or Edit views. The song position will shift along with you.

Snap Controls

To the right of the Editing tools are the Snap controls (see Figure 5.21), which perform two tasks:

▶ Assign a note value to the Pencil tool.

▶ Assign a note value for shifting MIDI events.

Figure 5.21
The Snap controls are used for assigning note values.

Snap supports a wide variety of note values, ranging from bar (whole notes) to 64th notes (1/64). Once a note value is selected, you can then use the Pencil, Line, or Selector tools to draw, edit, or shift groups in the Arrange view or MIDI events in the Edit view.

It's important to understand how the Snap works, so try a couple of exercises. Get yourself ready by starting a new Reason song and creating an instance of reMix and Subtractor.

1. Click on the Switch to Edit Mode button. This will open the Key Lane Editor for the Subtractor. The Velocity lane should also be viewable by default.

2. Select a note value of 1/8 from the Snap pull-down menu.

3. Make sure the Snap to Grid button, located to the right of the Snap pull-down menu, is active.

4. Select the Pencil tool and click to create a few events in the Key lane. Notice that each note is an 8th note in length (see Figure 5.22).

5. After drawing in a few events, click on the Controller Lane button and select the Mod Wheel setting from the Controller Lane pop-up menu (see Figure 5.23).

Figure 5.22
The Pencil tool can draw in 8th-note resolutions, because 1/8 has been selected from the Snap pull-down menu. Note that you can click and drag to the right if you want to make the event longer than an 8th note.

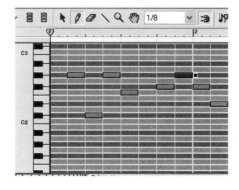

Figure 5.23
Select Mod Wheel from the list of controllers to draw in controller data for that parameter.

6. Select the Line tool and draw a diagonal line from the bottom-left of your sequence to the upper-right of the sequence and release the mouse. Because 1/8 is still the assigned note value, this also defines the resolution of the controller data, which is pretty choppy, as you can see in Figure 5.24.

7. In order to smooth out this controller data, select a smaller note value of 1/64 from the Snap pull-down menu.

8. Try drawing a diagonal line again. When you release the mouse, it should be a lot smoother (see Figure 5.25).

9. Click on the Switch to Arrange Mode button.

Figure 5.24
The Snap also determines the resolution when drawing in controller data.

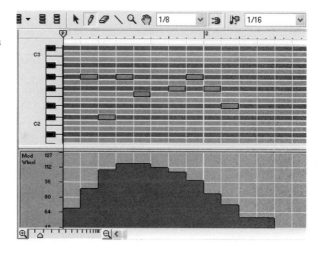

Figure 5.25
Once a smaller note value is selected, the newly drawn controller data looks a lot smoother.

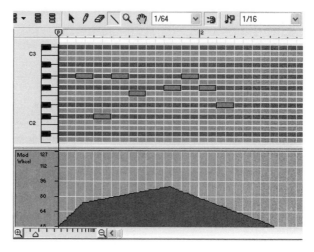

CHAPTER 5

In the next exercise, you'll try to use the Pencil and Selector tools in the Arrange view. Make sure that the Snap to Grid button is still active before you begin this exercise.

1. Switch to the Arrange view and choose 1/2 from the Snap pull-down menu. This assigns a half note value.

2. Select the Pencil tool and proceed to draw in a group on the Subtractor sequencer track. Notice that the group being drawn is a half measure in length (see Figure 5.26). Note that you can create larger groups by clicking and dragging to the right.

3. After you have drawn in a group or two, click the Selector tool. Now click and drag your drawn groups to the left or right and you will notice that the groups are moving in half-note increments.

4. Choose a smaller note value from the Snap pull-down menu, such as 1/8 perhaps.

5. Try moving the groups again and you will see that they move in much smaller increments than before.

Figure 5.26
The Snap determines the size of drawn groups. In this case here, the groups are a half note in length.

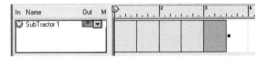

SNAP TO GRID VERSUS FREE WHEELIN' EDITS
Located just to the right of the Snap pull-down menu is the Snap to Grid button. This button turns the Snap function on and off. You have just seen how the Snap works when activated. Try turning off the Snap to Grid button and using the Selector tool to move around a few groups. You will notice that the moving groups are not governed by the Snap note value. Rather, you can move groups around freely, which is typically referred to as *free time*. This enables you to make very fine adjustments to a MIDI performance.

Quantize Tools

To the right of the Snap controls are the Quantize controls (see Figure 5.27). Quantization helps to correct timing problems. The easiest way to explain it is to think of quantizing as an invisible magnet that pulls and pushes MIDI events to a determined note value, which is assigned by the Quantization pull-down menu. It's an indispensable tool for rhythmically challenged people (like me) who need rhythms that are tight and punchy.

Figure 5.27
The Quantization tools help correct timing issues.

Because you are going to use these tools extensively later in this chapter, it's a good idea to review the individual controls:

▶ **Quantize Notes During Recording**—When activated, this button performs real-time quantization after the MIDI event has been recorded. The amount of applied quantization is determined by the selected note value and quantization strength.

▶ **Quantize Pull-Down Menu**—This pull-down menu determines the note value to use for quantization. Like the Snap pull-down menu, it has a range of bar to 1/64, and all points in between. However, unlike the Snap menu, there are a few additional quantization values that can be applied, which you'll read about later in this section.

▶ **Quantize Notes**—This button applies quantization to a batch of selected MIDI events and groups. It's governed by the assigned note value and strength.

▶ **Quantize Strength**—This pull-down menu determines the amount of quantization to apply to a batch of selected MIDI events or groups. It has a range of 5% to 100%.

SHUFFLE AND GROOVE

As you saw in the Quantize pull-down menu, there are five additional quantizing values: Shuffle, Grooves 1-3, and User. Take a closer look at these values:

▶ **Shuffle**—This value applies a shuffle or swing feel to a group or selected batch of MIDI events. The Pattern Shuffle knob in the Transport Panel determines the amount of the shuffling effect.

▶ **Grooves 1-3**—These are three prepared rhythmic grooves that Propellerhead included with Reason. Select a bar of MIDI events and try each one to hear the difference.

▶ **User**—If you have sequenced a performance and like the rhythmic feel of it, you can select its events and choose Get User Groove from the Edit pull-down menu. You can then apply this groove to another series of MIDI events by selecting them with the Selector tool and choosing User from the Quantize pull-down menu and then applying the quantization. Note that the User groove is not saved with your song; it is a temporary parameter that will be erased once you close the program.

Using these values in combination with Quantization Strength can lead to some very interesting rhythmic possibilities.

The Transport Panel

Although some might consider the Transport Panel a separate entity from the Reason sequencer, I disagree, because the sequencer is dependent on the Transport Panel in order to properly function. With that in mind, the next part of the tour is dedicated to the features and functionality of the Transport Panel (see Figure 5.28).

Figure 5.28
The Reason Transport
Panel is vital to the
functionality of the
sequencer.

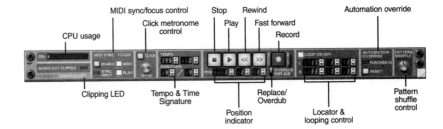

In the dead center of the Transport Panel are the Stop and Play controls of the Reason sequencer
(see Figure 5.29). They look very similar to the buttons on a tape machine or VCR, and there is
really no mystery to what each button does, but there are a few variations to each of these buttons
to make them more flexible to the Reason environment.

Figure 5.29
The Stop and Play
controls in the Transport
Panel work just like
standard controls on a
VCR or CD player.

▶ The Stop button stops the sequencer wherever it is playing within a sequence.
Additionally, if you click on the Stop button a second time, the song position
returns to the beginning of the sequence. This is called the *return to zero* function.

▶ The Play button makes the Reason sequencer begin playing. There are no
additional features on this button.

▶ The Rewind button shuttles the song position backward to any point in a Reason
song. The button can be used while the song is playing or when the sequencer is
stopped. When clicked once, the song position jumps back one bar, but when
clicked and held, the song position scrolls back even faster.

▶ The Fast Forward button shuttles the song position forward to any point in a
Reason song. Just as with the Rewind button, it can be used while the song is
playing or when the Reason sequencer has stopped. When clicked once, the song
position jumps forward one bar, but when clicked and held, the song position
scrolls forward even faster.

▶ The Record button triggers Reason's sequencer to record MIDI data. If the Record
button is clicked while the sequence is stopped, the sequencer is placed into a
Record Ready mode. This means that the Play button must be clicked in order to
start recording. Additionally, if the sequence is playing, you can also click on the
Record button to input MIDI data on the fly. This is also referred to as *punching in*.

KNOW YOUR KEY COMMANDS

The key to becoming a seasoned user of Reason is to learn the keyboard shortcuts that are linked to the graphical user interface controls in the program. Because I just went over the basic transport controls, here is a quick list of their corresponding key commands (see Figure 5.30).

▶ The Stop button can be accessed by pressing the 0 key on your keypad.

▶ Pressing the Enter key on your keypad, or the spacebar, accesses the Play button. Additionally, the spacebar can be used as a way to play and stop sequences.

▶ The Rewind button can be accessed by pressing the 7 key on your computer keypad.

▶ The Fast Forward button can be accessed by pressing the 8 key on your computer keypad.

▶ The Record button can be accessed by pressing the * (asterisk) key on your computer keypad.

Figure 5.30
Here is a layout of the Transport key commands on your computer keyboard. This layout works for PC and Mac users.

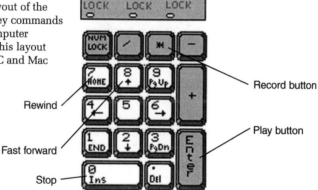

Record button

Rewind

Play button

Fast forward

Stop

WHAT'S YOUR POSITION?

Located just below the main Transport Panel is the Position Indicator. This is a numeric readout of where you currently are in your sequence. Click on Play and notice that the Position Indicator is constantly calling out position readings.

Replace or Overdub?

Located just below and to the right of the main Transport Panel is a toggle that places the Reason sequencer into either Record Replace or Overdub mode. These modes are defined as follows:

▶ **Record Replace mode**—In this mode, if you record MIDI data onto a track that already contains active data, the old data will be replaced with the new data.

▶ **Overdub mode**—In this mode, if you record MIDI data onto a track that already contains active data, the new data will be combined with the old data.

Tempo and Time

Located just to the left of the main Transport Panel is the window in which you can make adjustments to both the song tempo and time signature.

▶ *Tempo* refers to the speed of the song played by the sequencer. Tempo is measured in BPM, or beats per minute, and can be adjusted anywhere from 1–999.999. This gives you many possibilities when writing and recording songs within Reason. Note: You can adjust the tempo by using the + and – keys on your keypad.

▶ *Time Signature* specifies the beats per bar (such as 1, 2, 3, 4, and so on), and what counts as a beat (that is, half note, quarter note, 8th note, and so on).

Locators—the Key to Looping

To the right of the main Transport Panel are the locator points and looping controls. If you recall from Chapter 3, "Getting Started with Reason 2.5," you learned a little bit about Reason's locator points. Although there are many ways to describe them, the easiest way to explain locators is to think of them as a pair of bookends. Just like a shelf of books, locator points act as the virtual bookends of a sequence. You have a left locator, which is used as a starting position, and a right locator, which is used as an ending position.

These locator points can be used together to create a loop for a specific number of measures. Here's how:

LITTLE LATIN LOOPY LOU

The key to any electronic or dance music is the incorporation of loops and repetition. As you will read in future chapters, there are a few virtual sound modules in Reason that will help to easily create these loops for you. For now, let's just look at the basic idea of creating a loop in the Reason sequencer.

1. Set your left locator to measure 1 by using the arrow keys next to the numeric values or by double-clicking on the numeric value and typing the desired value.

2. Using the same method, set your right locator to measure 9.

3. Just above the locators in the Transport Panel is the Loop On/Off button. Click on it to activate the loop feature. This can also be done by pressing the / key on your keypad.

4. Click on Play and watch as the Position Indicator moves to the right. As soon as it reaches the right locator point, it jumps back to the left locator point.

Once a looping point has been created, you can listen to a specific part of your song over and over in order to edit the MIDI or audio data.

Automation Override

To the right of the locator window is the Automation Override button (see Figure 5.31). This LED glows a bright red whenever an automated parameter within Reason is overwritten.

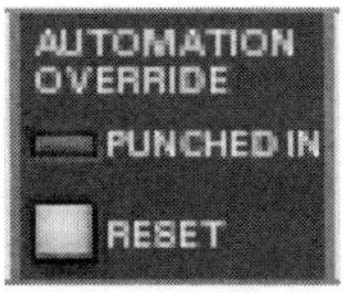

Figure 5.31
The Automation
Override is used to write
over already recorded
automation data.

The Pattern Shuffle Control

To the far right of the Transport Panel is the Pattern Shuffle control. This global control affects the creation of a swing feel within a song. It can be linked to control the amount of shuffle produced by the Reason virtual synths and sound modules that support it.

The Click Control

To the left of the Tempo and Time Signature portion of the Transport Panel is the Click Track control. When activated, this function provides a metronome sound that is accented on the first beat of every measure. Just clicking on the Click button can turn it on, and the volume of the click can be adjusted by using the knob below. The click sound itself is quite loud, so exercise caution when adjusting the volume.

MIDI Sync and Focus

Moving along to the left of the Transport Panel is the MIDI Sync and Focus control, which handles and regulates the activation and usage of synchronization within Reason.

Once the Sync button is activated, the Reason transport will not function until it receives sync information from an external source, such as an external sequencer or sound module.

The MIDI and Play Focus buttons relate to how incoming MIDI and MIDI sync is prioritized when several Reason songs are open at the same time. If the MIDI Sync is not active, the open song on top (the current song) receives MIDI priority over another song. But, if MIDI Sync is active, one of the following can occur:

▶ If the MIDI and Play Focus buttons are active in a song, that song will receive MIDI data and MIDI sync, whether or not that song is on top.

▶ If one song has MIDI active while another song has Play active, the first song will receive MIDI data, and the sync data will be received by the second song.

SYNC, WHAT?
Synchronization is covered in detail in Chapter 16, aptly called "Synchronization."

The CPU and Audio Clipping LEDs

To the far left of the Transport Panel are the CPU and Audio Clipping LEDs.

The CPU meter is a real-time indicator of how much of the computer's CPU is being used within a given Reason song. As you begin to accumulate more and more virtual synths, real-time effects, and equalizers within a song, this meter will tell you how much more CPU you have left until your audio "drops out."

The Audio Clipping LED is a warning light to alert you when the audio output of Reason is in danger of clipping or distorting. To demonstrate this, open the Reason Tutorial Song and turn up one of the volume faders until you see the clip LED shine a bright red. It is important to keep an eye on this, because you really don't want to clip in the digital domain. Trust me; it sounds terrible! Figure 5.32 shows a graphical example of digital clipping.

Figure 5.32
Both of these audio clips were taken from the Reason Tutorial Song. The image on the left is an example of digital audio that is not clipping. The image on the right is an example of digital audio that is clipping.

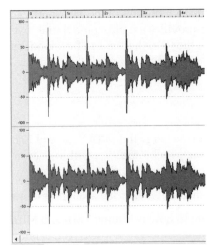
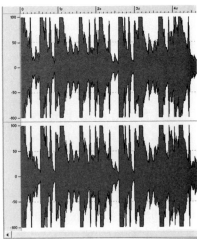

Creating and Managing Tracks

Now that you've covered the basics of the Transport Panel, you're ready to move to the left side of Reason's sequencer, called the Track window. This is where all the tracks in a song are created and maintained. If you are not new to the concept of sequencing, this section should look similar to other programs you have used. If you are new to this whole game, you'll be happy to know that understanding this portion of the sequencer is a snap.

Creating and Cutting Sequencer Tracks in Reason

There are a few ways to create a sequencer track in Reason:

- ▶ A sequencer track is automatically created whenever a Reason synth device is created.
- ▶ You can choose Sequencer Track from the Create pull-down menu.
- ▶ You can right-click (Windows) or Ctrl-click (Mac) anywhere in the sequencer or Device Rack and select Create Sequencer Track.

Once you have created a sequencer track, you can name it anything you want by double-clicking on the name of the sequencer track and typing (up to 30 characters). Note: If you already have your sequencer track routed to a synth module in the device rack, the new name that you give to the sequencer track will also be reflected on the side of the module as well as on the channel it is routed to in reMix.

If you want to cut a sequencer track from Reason, you also have a few choices:

▶ Highlight the sequencer track and press the Delete or Backspace key on your keyboard.

▶ Highlight the sequencer track and choose Cut from the Edit pull-down menu or use the keyboard shortcut Ctrl+X (Windows) or Apple+X (Mac).

DELETE, KEEP, OR CANCEL?

If you have created a sequencer track by first creating a synth module as described in this section of the chapter, this note is for you. When you want to delete this track, a window will appear informing you that the track that you want to delete is routed to a module in the device rack. At this point, you have three options.

▶ Delete both the sequencer track and the synth module.

▶ Keep the synth module but delete the sequencer track.

▶ Cancel the entire action.

The Track Columns

After creating a sequencer track, it's time to look at the different columns of the Track window.

▶ **In**—This column is used to connect a MIDI controller keyboard to any of the sequencer tracks. Select a track and click on the In column. An input symbol in the form of a MIDI jack will appear, signifying that the track is ready to receive MIDI from a keyboard controller (see Figure 5.33).

Figure 5.33
When you see the MIDI jack symbol, your sequencer track is ready to receive MIDI data.

▶ **Name**—This is where the name of the sequencer track is displayed.

▶ **Out**—This is where you route the MIDI data to any of the Reason devices. Note that when a synth device is created, such as a Subtractor, Redrum, or Dr:rex, a sequencer track is already created and routed to that device. If you want to send the output of this sequencer track to another device, simply click on the corresponding pop-up menu and select the Reason device to send it to (see Figure 5.34).

Figure 5.34
You can route MIDI data to any Reason device just by clicking on the pop-up menu of any sequencer track and routing it to that device.

▶ **Mute**—Known simply as "M," the Mute column is used to mute individual tracks from within the Track window (see Figure 5.35). You can also solo a track by holding the Alt key down while clicking on the track you want to solo (PC and Mac). Please note that the Alt key on the Mac is sometimes also known as the Option key.

Figure 5.35
When a track is not muted, it will display the playback of MIDI data as shown in the figure on the left. If a track is muted, a red "X" is displayed in the sequencer track, as shown in the figure on the right.

Moving and Duplicating Tracks

Once you begin to accumulate a few tracks, you might want to organize the tracks by moving them up and down in the track list. For example, I generally like to have my Redrum and Dr:rex tracks at the top of the track list, followed by the bass track and then the chord and lead tracks. This is very easy to do; check out the following exercise, using the Tutorial Song.

1.   Click on the sequencer track that you want to move.

2.   Click and drag with your mouse until you reach the desired position (see Figure 5.36).

3.   Release the mouse button. The track should drop into place.

Figure 5.36
Click and drag the bass track up or down until you reach the desired position.

After you have arranged your tracks in the order that you want, you might also want to duplicate one of the tracks to send it to another Reason device. Why might you want to do that? A little trick that I like to frequently use is to double my bass lines and chords, so that I can thicken up the sound of my mix. To demonstrate this idea, follow along with the next exercise. Use the Tutorial Song as in the last example.

1. Scroll to the bottom of the Device Rack and click anywhere in the blank area.
2. Select Malström from the Create pull-down menu.
3. Delete the Malström track, but click on the Keep option when the Delete window pops up.
4. Select the Subtractor track by clicking on it.
5. Choose Duplicate Track from the Edit pull-down menu. This will create a duplicate sequencer track right below the original. Note that the output of this new sequencer track is still set to the Subtractor (see Figure 5.37).
6. Click on the pop-up menu of the new track's output column and route it to the Malström (see Figure 5.38).
7. Click on Play. The bass line should now be played by both the Subtractor and the Malström.

Figure 5.37
. . . and then there were two.

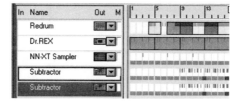

Figure 5.38
Route the output of the duplicated track to the Malström.

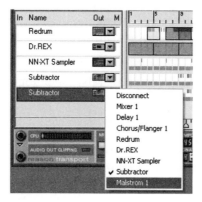

Sequencing a Live Performance

Now that you have taken your first detailed look at the sequencer interface, it's time to press forward and record your first live sequencer track. In this tutorial, you are going to:

▶ Create an instance of Redrum

▶ Record a drum pattern live

▶ Edit that pattern with quantization and dynamics

BEFORE YOU BEGIN

Before you start this tutorial, make sure that your MIDI keyboard is turned on and connected to your computer. Additionally, make sure that the keyboard has been selected by Reason as a MIDI input source. You can do this by selecting it from the MIDI page of the Preferences window (see Figure 5.39).

Figure 5.39
The M-Audio Ozone has been selected as the source of MIDI input. Note that if you are using a MIDI keyboard that is connected to computers with a standard MIDI interface (for example, MOTU MIDI Timepiece, or Steinberg MIDEX 8), the name of the MIDI input will be Port 1 or Port 2.

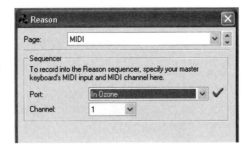

In this tutorial, you will record a drum pattern with Redrum.

1. Start a new Reason song with an empty Device Rack.

2. Create an instance of reMix by selecting Mixer 14:2 from the Create pull-down menu.

3. Create an instance of Redrum by selecting it from the Create pull-down menu. Note that a Redrum sequencer track has been created and is already armed to receive MIDI from your keyboard. Take a second to turn off the Enable Pattern Section in the Redrum interface. This will enable you to trigger and record live MIDI data from Redrum without using its pattern sequencer.

4. Load a Redrum kit into its interface by using its Patch Browser buttons.

5. Because Redrum is already armed to receive MIDI data, you can press the C1 key on your keyboard. This key should trigger the kick drum sample. Also note that C#1 is typically the snare drum sample in any Redrum kit.

6. In the Transport Panel, make sure that the Loop section is activated. Set the left locator to 2:1:1 and the right locator to 6:1:1. This will provide you with four empty measures to record a four-bar loop and one additional measure at the beginning (see Figure 5.40) that can be used as a "count off" (one, two, three, four, record!). Also make sure that the Click is turned on so that you will have a metronome to play against.

7. Click on the Stop button twice to send the Position Indicator back to measure 1. Now, click on the Record button to prepare the sequencer for recording. Click on the Play button. The Position Indicator should now begin moving to the right and will start recording MIDI data as soon as it reaches measure 2.

8. Once the sequencer starts recording data, play the kick drum sample on beats one and three until the Position Indicator reaches measure 6, at which time it will jump back to measure 2 and begin recording more MIDI data.

9. Once the Position Indicator jumps back to measure 2 and begins recording again, play the snare sample on beats two and four until it reaches measure 6, at which point it will jump back to measure 2 again.

10. Once the Position Indicator jumps back to measure 2 and begins recording again, play the hi-hat sample (typically found on the G#1 key) on beats one, two, three, and four until it reaches measure 6, at which point it will jump back to measure 2 again.

11. Click on Stop on the Transport Panel or use the spacebar on your computer keyboard to stop the recording. Notice that there is now MIDI data displayed on the Arrange view of the sequencer (see Figure 5.41).

Figure 5.40
One of Reason's small shortcomings is that it doesn't have a count off function in which the sequencer will give you one full measure to prepare yourself to record and then begin recording. The only way to get around this is to set your left locator one measure to the right, which in turn gives you all of measure 1 to prepare yourself for recording.

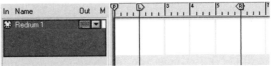

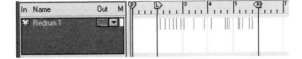

Figure 5.41
You have just sequenced your first live MIDI performance.

CREATE A GROUP

Now that you have recorded a MIDI performance, you should make it a group. By converting your performance to a group, you can easily move, cut, copy, or paste it anywhere in your song. It's easy to do and only takes a minute, so let's go.

1. Select the Pencil tool.

2. Set the Snap value to Bar.

3. Click and drag your Pencil tool over the sequence you want to convert to a group.

4. Once you have reached the end of your sequence, release the mouse. A group will now be created (see Figure 5.42).

Another way to do this is to select the events with the Selector tool and choose Group from the Edit pull-down menu, or use the Ctrl+G (Windows) or Apple+G (Mac) keyboard command. Additionally, once a group has been created, you can ungroup the MIDI events by selecting the group and choosing Ungroup from the Edit pull-down menu, or using the Ctrl+U (Windows) or Apple+U (Mac) keyboard command.

Figure 5.42
Converting your performances to groups makes it easy to move your sequences to any point in your song.

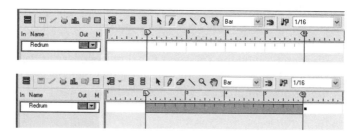

Editing Your Performance

At this point, you have recorded the performance. If this was your first time recording a live MIDI performance using a sequencer, the timing might not have been as tight as you wanted. In this next tutorial, you learn how to fix any timing problems and move events around by using the Editing tools.

Before you begin, make sure that you switch to Edit mode by clicking on the Switch to Edit Mode button. Because you are working with Redrum, the Redrum Lane Editor will be displayed by default (see Figure 5.43). Use the Zoom tools to close in on the Redrum group that you are going to work on.

Figure 5.43
The sequencer knows which lane editor to display when you switch to Edit mode. In this case, the Redrum Lane Editor is displayed.

Quantize—Timing Corrections

The first thing you are going to do is correct any timing problems by using the quantization function. If you recall from Chapter 4, "Creating Your First Reason Song," you used the quantize function to help correct rhythmic mistakes made while recording a performance.

1. Looking closely at the Redrum group, you can see many timing inconsistencies, because the events don't quite match up with the vertical lines (see Figure 5.44).

2. Use the Pointer tool to click and drag a box around the Redrum events in order to select them all. You can also use Crtl+A (Windows) or Apple+A (Mac).

3. Next, you need to select the note value used to quantize. Click on the Quantize pull-down menu and select 1/4. This means that Reason will nudge each note to its nearest quarter note (see Figure 5.45).

4. To the right of the Quantize pull-down menu is the Quantize Strength pull-down menu (see Figure 5.46). This option determines the amount of quantization that will occur when the process is performed. By default, it is set to 100%, which means that the events will be moved completely to the nearest quarter note. This is fine for this demonstration, but you can try different values to achieve a different effect. This feature can help to prevent your music from feeling too robotic or unnatural.

Figure 5.44
This is the drum group before quantization.

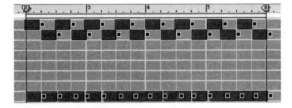

Figure 5.45
Select the correct quantize note value. Because this rhythm was written using only quarter notes, you should select 1/4 to have Reason nudge the selected events to their closest quarter note.

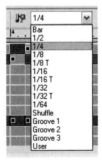

Figure 5.46
Select a desired percentage of quantize strength to apply to your performance.

5.   Click on the Quantize Notes button to apply your quantize setting to your performance. You can also use the Crtl+K key command on the PC, or the Apple+K key command on the Mac.

6.   Looking at the performance now, you can see the events have been nudged left and right toward their closest quarter note (see Figure 5.47). Click on Play and listen to the corrected timing.

Figure 5.47
The events have now been quantized.

QUANTIZE WHILE YOU RECORD

Quantizing can also be done while you are recording a performance. To the left of the Quantize pull-down menu is the Quantize Notes During Recording button, which, when activated, will automatically quantize your events while recording your performances.

To dig into this function a little more, try activating it and recording a new Redrum pattern like the one you created at the beginning of this tutorial.

Adding Velocity

Now that the timing has been corrected, you can add some dynamics to the performance by using the Velocity Lane Editor. Activate this editor by clicking on the Show Velocity Lane Editor button in the Sequencer toolbar. Once activated, it will appear below the Drum Lane Editor (see Figure 5.48).

Figure 5.48
Click on the Show Velocity Lane Editor button to activate and display it below the Drum lane.

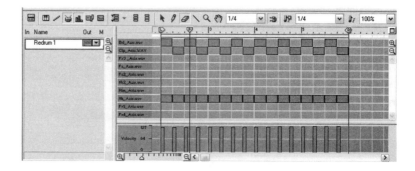

This editor can increase or decrease the amount of velocity assigned to a recorded MIDI note. It is a great tool to use if you find that you didn't press the keys hard enough when recording your performance. In this next tutorial, you are going to edit the velocity of your Redrum pattern with the Pencil and Line tools.

AN ADDED VELOCITY BONUS

In Chapter 7, "Redrum—Close Up," you'll learn about the benefits of using velocity to change the timbre and tuning of your Redrum sounds.

1. With the Velocity Lane Editor open, select the Pencil tool. Click and drag downward on the velocity of the first MIDI event. Notice that as you drag down, which decreases the velocity, the color of the MIDI event changes from a dark red to a light pink.

2. Use the Pencil tool on a couple of other MIDI events to alter their velocities. Try alternating between MIDI events to create a more interesting sequence (see Figure 5.49).

Figure 5.49
Use the Pencil tool to assign different velocities to the MIDI events.

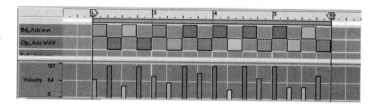

UNIVERSAL EDITS

Edits to the velocities of a performance are *universal*. This means that a velocity edit that you make to a MIDI event affects all of the other MIDI events that occur at that same time location. Let me show you exactly what I mean.

In Figure 5.50, you will see all of the MIDI events used to create the drum pattern. Notice how two separate MIDI events occur at the same time on each beat. For example, on the downbeat of bar one, you will see a kick drum MIDI event and a hi-hat MIDI event that are lined up vertically, which means that they will both trigger at the same time.

Now use the Pencil tool again to edit the velocity of the downbeat of bar one. As you make a change to the velocity, notice that both of the MIDI events change in color (see Figure 5.51). This means that the velocities of both the hi-hat and the kick drum are being altered simultaneously.

This can become a problem, because each drum sample's velocity should be independent of the other. So how does one combat this problem? Well, there are a few things that you can do:

▶ You can create separate sequencer tracks for each drum sound. For example, you can create one sequencer track dedicated to the kick drum and another for the snare, and so on.

▶ You can use the Velocity knobs on the Redrum interface to decrease each channel's sensitivity to different velocities. More information on this can be found in Chapter 7.

Figure 5.50
There are at least two MIDI events happening at the same time.

Figure 5.51
The velocities of both the MIDI events are being simultaneously altered.

Aside from the Pencil tool, the Line tool can also be used to edit the velocities of a performance. Try the following example:

1. Select the Line tool and proceed to click and drag horizontally across the velocities of a few events. Release the mouse and the velocities should change accordingly (see Figure 5.52).

2. Start at the beginning of the Redrum pattern, and then click and drag diagonally across the velocity lane until you reach the end of the pattern. Release the mouse and you have now created a fantastic crescendo (see Figure 5.53).

Figure 5.52
The Line tool can be used to alter the velocities of many events at one time.

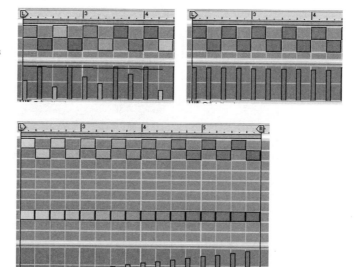

Figure 5.53
The Line tool can also be used to create crescendos, which are commonly found in dance music.

Sequencing Written Data

As you saw in Chapter 4, the sequencer can also be used to draw in events and MIDI data quite easily. This section shows you:

▶ How to draw/erase events with the Key and REX Lane Editors.

▶ How to draw in controller information using the Controller Lane Editor.

Drawing/Erasing Events

Drawing in events with the sequencer is quite easy. As an experienced sequencer jockey for the past 10 years, I frequently need to write complicated performances that I can't play due to my lack of skill as a keyboardist. It's also a handy way to write in performances when I do not have a MIDI keyboard handy, which is the case for so many traveling musicians. When inspiration hits, drawing in sequences is a real lifesaver.

Let's first begin by drawing in a Subtractor sequence with the Key Lane Editor. Get yourself ready by starting a new Reason song and creating an instance of reMix and an instance of Subtractor. Also, make sure that you set your right locator to bar two.

1. Click on the Switch to Edit Mode button. The Key Lane Editor should open by default (see Figure 5.54).

2. Use the horizontal zoom tools (found at the lower-left corner of the sequencer) to zoom in on the individual beats of bar one.

3. You are going to write in an 8th note sequence, so select 1/8 from the Snap pull-down menu (see Figure 5.55).

Figure 5.54
The Key lane is the assigned editor to the Subtractor, Malström, NN-19, and NN-XT Reason devices. Also notice that the Velocity lane is active.

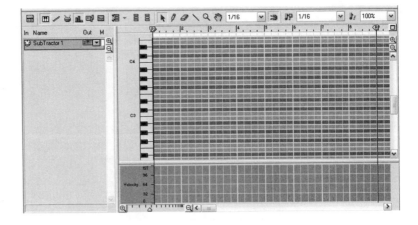

Figure 5.55
Select 1/8 from the Snap pull-down menu, so you can draw 8th notes.

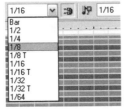

4. Select the Pencil tool and proceed to draw in an 8th-note sequence. For the sake of simplicity, you might want to try something as simple as a C major arpeggio (C-E-G), as shown in Figure 5.56.

5. Click on Play. You will hear the sequence play back in perfect time. At this point, you can try drawing in some different velocities for effect.

6. Click on the Switch to Arrange Mode button to switch modes.

Figure 5.56
Draw in an 8th note sequence. In this example, I have drawn an arpeggio line based on the C major scale. Notice that each drawn note has a default velocity of 100.

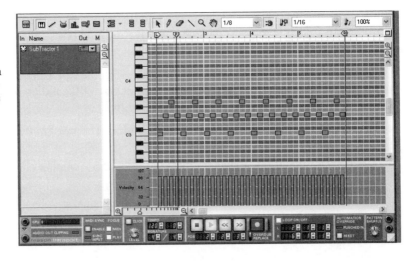

MOVING EVENTS

After writing your sequence, you can easily shift the events around by using the pointer tool. Try selecting it and then clicking and dragging on individual events to change their events and time locations. Notice when you're doing this that you can move the events left and right only by 8th-note increments. This is because the Snap is set to 1/8. If you want to make finer adjustments, try changing the Snap value to 16th notes (1/16).

DUPLICATING MIDI EVENTS

After performing or drawing in MIDI events, you can very easily duplicate those MIDI events in order to create a repetition. There are two ways to do this: use the Copy/Paste trick that you learned in the last chapter, or use the mouse and a key command to duplicate the events and place them anywhere you want.

Let's have a look at the first method by using the Tutorial Song, selecting the Subtractor track, and switching to the Edit mode.

1. Use the Selector tool to draw a marquee around a selection of MIDI events.

2. Choose Copy from the Edit pull-down menu (or use the Ctrl+C or Apple+C key command).

3. Select Paste from the Edit pull-down menu (or use the Ctrl+V or Apple+V key command). This will paste the copied events right after the original selection of events (see Figure 5.57).

Now let's look at the other way of doing this.

1. Use the Selector tool to draw a marquee around a selection of MIDI events.

2. Hold down the Ctrl key on your PC or the Option key on your Mac, and then click and drag the events to the right (see Figure 5.58).

3. Release the mouse button. The events should now be duplicated and placed where you released the button (see Figure 5.59).

When a selection of MIDI events has been duplicated, the new MIDI data is not grouped. If you switch back to Arrange view, you will see the new ungrouped data. You can easily remedy this by selecting the new data and choosing Group from the Edit pull-down menu.

CHAPTER 5

Figure 5.57
The MIDI events are now pasted after the original events.

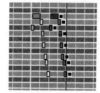

Figure 5.58
As you hold the Ctrl key
(Option key for the Mac)
and click and drag your
events to the right, the
pointer will display a +,
indicating that it is
copying the events.

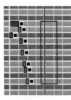

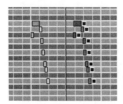

Figure 5.59
The events are now
copied and pasted.

For the next example, you'll use Dr:rex and the REX Lane Editor. Prepare for the example by
clicking on the Subtractor in the Reason Device Rack and selecting Dr:rex Loop Player from the
Create pull-down menu. This will place Dr:rex just below the Subtractor. Now, load a REX file by
clicking on the Dr:rex Patch Browser button and selecting a REX loop from the Reason Factory
Sound Bank. If you are not sure how to do this, refer back to Chapter 4, when you created your
first Reason song.

1.   After loading your REX loop into the Dr:rex device, click on the To Track button to
     send the loop to its sequencer track.

2.   Click on the Switch to Edit Mode button and you will see the REX Lane Editor.
     Notice that the Velocity lane is also open.

3.   Select the Eraser tool and erase a few REX slices by clicking on them (see Figure
     5.60).

4.   Time to draw in a few events. Set your Snap value to 1/16 so that you can draw
     16th notes.

5.   Select your Pencil tool and draw in a few REX slices in the same area that you
     erased earlier (see Figure 5.61).

6.   Click on Play. The REX loop should now sound rhythmically different.

Figure 5.60
Click on a few REX slices
with your Eraser tool to
delete them.

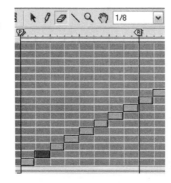
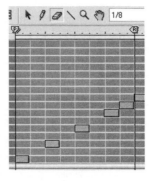

Figure 5.61

Use your Pencil tool and draw in a few REX slices. Notice that as with the previous example, a default velocity value of 100 is assigned to any drawn events.

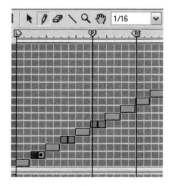

RESIZING EVENTS

Once you begin to edit your MIDI data in either of the different lanes, you might want to resize the events that you have either drawn in or performed live. This is very easy to do. Try the following exercise:

1. Open the Reason Tutorial Song and select the Subtractor track.

2. Click on the Switch to Edit Mode button and find some MIDI events in the Key lane.

3. Use the Selector tool to draw a marquee around a few of the events to select them (see Figure 5.62).

4. With the Selector tool still selected, navigate to the end of the selected MIDI events.

Notice that the Selector tool changes to an icon with two arrows pointing in opposite directions. This is used to resize the events.

1. Click and drag to the right. You'll see the MIDI events growing in length (see Figure 5.63).

2. Release the mouse. The events should now be resized (see Figure 5.64).

It's important to note that individual MIDI events can be resized as well as groups of events.

Figure 5.62

After drawing a marquee around a few events and releasing the mouse, the events have been selected. Notice that each of the selected events has a tiny black square.

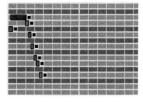

Figure 5.63

Click and drag to the right to resize the events.

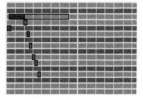

Figure 5.64
The events are now resized.

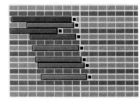

Change Events

For those of you who like to ask questions such as, "what would this chord progression sound like when it's transposed up a third?" or "I wonder what this synth line would sound like when sped up" the Change Events feature will probably become one of your best friends (see Figure 5.65). Change Events can be used in either the Arrange or Edit mode and is activated by selecting a group of events and choosing Change Events from the Edit pull-down menu.

Change Events is used to perform four tasks:

▶ **Transpose**—This function is used to transpose a group of MIDI events up or down by semitones, or as we musicians would call it *chromatically*. The Transpose has a very wide range of –127 to 127 and all points in between.

▶ **Velocity**—This is used to add or subtract velocity from a group of MIDI events. As you can see, it is split into two controls—Add and Scale. The Add control will add or subtract an assigned amount of velocity, whereas the Scale control is used to create a bigger or smaller gap between the hard and soft events. Using these two controls in combination can create some interesting dynamics in your synth lines.

▶ **Scale Tempo**—This is used to speed up or slow down the tempo of a group of selected MIDI events. If you are curious to hear your lead lines or chord progressions played back at half or double the original tempo, this is the feature made just for you. There are three ways to adjust the tempo—using the scroll buttons next to the percentage, using the *2 or multiplied by 2 button, or using the /2 or divided by 2 button. Figure 5.66 shows this feature in action.

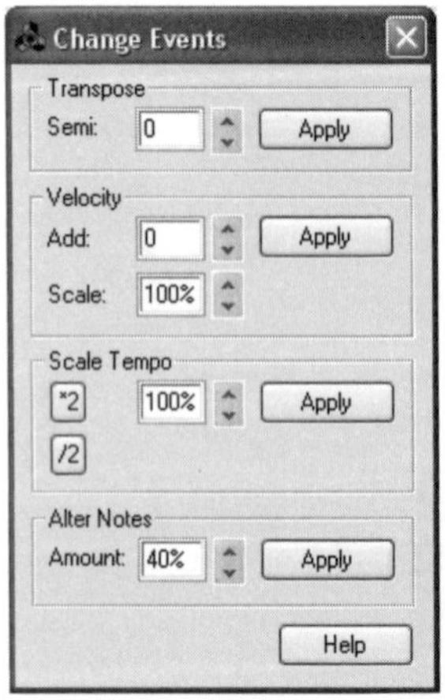

Figure 5.65
The Change Events window is used to alter MIDI events.

Figure 5.66
The figure on the left is a sequence of events playing back at their normal tempo. The figure on the right is that same sequence of events, but altered to play back at double the speed. It's important to note that although the speed of the events can be slowed down or sped up, the pitch of the events is not altered, because they are just MIDI events and not actual audio.

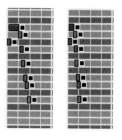

▶ **Alter Notes**—This is used to randomly alter the pitch, length, and velocity of a group of selected MIDI events. The trick to remember here is that this feature will only randomize the values assigned to the selected events, rather than just randomly generate events on its own. See Figure 5.67 for a better example.

Figure 5.67
For this example, I have selected a group of MIDI events that are used by Dr:rex. I have selected those MIDI events and chosen to alter them by 100%. On the right side of this figure, you can see the results of using the Alter Notes function. Note that the pitch of the MIDI events has not changed, but the rhythmic placement of the MIDI events has.

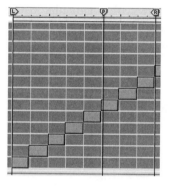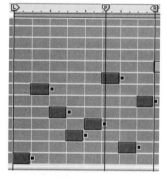

CHANGING EVENTS ON MULTIPLE TRACKS

When using the Change Events window, it's important to know that you can change the events of more than one track at a time. This comes in handy when transposing the chords and melody of a song. To do this, just open any Reason song and follow these simple steps:

1. Select the first group or groups of MIDI events that you are going to transpose by clicking on them in the Arrange mode.

2. Hold down the Shift key on your computer keyboard and click on the next group.

3. Choose Change Events from the Edit pull-down menu and adjust the transposition to any value you want.

4. Click on Apply and then play the sequence back. Both of the tracks should have transposed and should be in perfect tune with each other.

Drawing Controller Data

Reason's sequencer is also a great way to draw in data that controls the various parameters of each Reason device, which is done via the Controller Lane Editor. Although it's covered briefly in this chapter, you will find oodles of info on controller data and automation in Chapter 15, "Automation."

This tutorial continues to use the setup from the last tutorial and shows you how to draw in controller data for the Modulation Wheel of Dr:rex.

1. Select the Dr:rex sequencer track and click on the Switch to Edit Mode button to view the REX Lane Editor.

2. Click on the REX Lane Editor button to hide the REX lane from the Edit view. Click on the Velocity Lane Editor button to hide that lane, as well. This will leave you with a blank Edit view to work with (see Figure 5.68).

3. Click on the Show Controller Lane button (see Figure 5.69). This will appear to do nothing at first, because you have not yet selected a controller to edit.

4. To the immediate right of the Show Controller Lane button is the Controllers button. Clicking on this button will bring up a pop-up menu that lists all of the available controllers to view with a particular Reason device. In Figure 5.70, you will see a list of controllers for the Dr:rex device. Select Mod Wheel from the list. The corresponding lane will be displayed in the Edit view.

Figure 5.68
Hide the REX and Velocity Lane Editors by clicking on their corresponding buttons in the Sequencer toolbar.

Figure 5.69
The Show Controller Lane button is used to view the Controller lane.

Figure 5.70

Click on the Controllers button to view a list of available controllers for Dr:rex. Selecting Mod Wheel will cause the lane for that controller to appear in the Edit view.

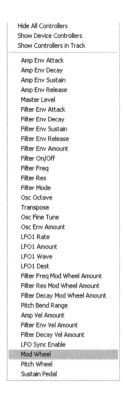

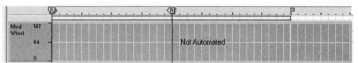

5. At this point, you are almost ready to write in your controller data. Before you begin, select 1/64 from the Snap pull-down menu, because this will allow you to make very fine changes to the controller data.

6. Select your Pencil tool and begin to draw in some controller data for the Modulation Wheel (see Figure 5.71). Notice a neon green box around the Modulation Wheel of Dr:rex, which means that automation data has been written to this parameter.

Figure 5.71

Use the Pencil tool to draw in controller data for the Modulation Wheel of Dr:rex.

SMOOTH IT OUT

Using the Pencil tool to write controller data is great, but you might find that it's not as precise as you would like. This is a good time to use the Line tool to write in controller data that contains smooth transitions. Try the following exercise:

1. Select the Line tool.

2. Click and drag diagonally up to the middle of bar one, and then release the mouse. This will produce controller data that will smoothly ramp upward (see Figure 5.72).

3. Click and drag diagonally downward from the middle to the end of bar one, and then release the mouse. This will produce controller data that will smoothly ramp down (see Figure 5.73).

Figure 5.72
Half of the controller data has been smoothed out with the Line tool.

Figure 5.73
All of the controller data has been smoothed out.

THE PATTERN LANE EDITOR

Included with the Key, REX, Drum, and Controller lanes, the Pattern Lane Editor is used to write and edit automation data to control the two pattern-based devices included with Reason—the Matrix and Redrum.

The Pattern Lane Editor is discussed in Chapter 13, "The Matrix—Close Up."

Throughout this chapter, you have witnessed the ins and outs of the Reason sequencer. I'm sure you'll agree that there is a lot under the hood of this baby. Be sure to read through Chapter 15, which takes an in-depth look at automation and revisits the sequencer.

Now, it's time to begin looking at the individual Reason devices, starting with reMix.

6

ReMix—Close Up

Reason's mixer, called *reMix*, is a compact yet versatile virtual mixer that allows numerous variations in signal routing. Or to put it another way, you fix it, and Reason will mix it. Because this book is for beginner and advanced users of Reason, this chapter covers the basic concepts of mixing as well as the more advanced features and concepts of reMix. In short, there is something in this chapter for every reader. So, stick around and let's mix!

What Is a Mixer?

A mixer enables you to gather a combination of signals (or sounds) from various sources, route those signals in a variety of ways, adjust their individual amplitudes (and other sonic characteristics), and sum it all to a single monophonic or stereophonic signal called *the mix*. As you can see in the mixing example in Figure 6.1, this mix is then routed to a master recording

Figure 6.1
Mixing, old school.

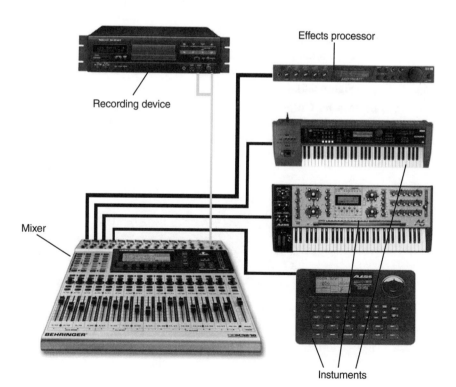

Effects processor

Recording device

Mixer

Instuments

device of some kind, such as a DAT recorder, in order to be mastered and archived. That is a very basic explanation of a mixer, but it will do nicely for now.

To get a better idea of what a hardware mixer looks like and how it works, see Figure 6.2. The Mackie 1604 hardware mixer is commonly found in hardware-based recording studios. The 1604 has 16 individual built-in inputs, which simply means that 16 different signals (drums, guitars, vocals, and so on) can be plugged in to it. After these signals have been plugged in, you can then make adjustments to various attributes—such as volume and equalization—on each signal. These signals are then sent, or "bussed" to the master output section of the 1604, and from there, the mix is sent to a pair of speakers and/or a hardware recording device.

Over the years, the mixer's interface has evolved into a relatively standard layout. Here are the primary components of just about any mixer:

▶ **Inputs**—Typically found at the top or rear of a mixer. This is where analog signals, such as a guitar or a microphone, are plugged in. Additionally, you will find a Trim knob that amplifies the signal.

▶ **Auxiliary Sends**—These knobs, shown in Figure 6.3, allow you to send a percentage of your dry signal to an external effects processor, such as a reverb for your snare drum, or a chorus for a vocal track. Typically you will find between two and four auxiliaries on a hardware mixer.

▶ **Equalization**—A mixer's EQ section is for boosting or cutting particular frequencies or ranges of frequencies within the signal flowing through a channel. As in Figure 6.4, you will likely find knobs to control the "High EQ," "Low EQ," and sometimes the "Mid EQ" as well. Some mixers offer more flexible EQing options.

▶ **Faders**—Faders dictate the volume, or amplitude, of the signal on a given channel. On a typical mixer, you'll find faders to control the volume of each individual signal as well as a master fader to control the master outputs of the signal (see Figure 6.5).

▶ **Master Output**—Located at the far right side of the mixer, from here the combined signals are sent to your speakers as well as some sort of recording device, such as a DAT machine or multi-track recording device.

Figure 6.2
The Mackie 1604 mixer is found in many project studios.

Figure 6.3
Auxiliary knobs send a
portion of a channel's
signal to outboard effect
processors.

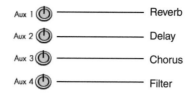

Aux 1 — Reverb
Aux 2 — Delay
Aux 3 — Chorus
Aux 4 — Filter

Figure 6.4
With a good equalizer,
you can boost or cut any
frequencies.

HIGH FREQ

HI MID FREQ

LO MID FREQ

LOW FREQ

Figure 6.5
The fader strip shown
here can adjust the
volume of the individual
and master signals.

Meet the reMix Mixer

Reason's reMix mixer shares many features with the standard hardware mixer. Propellerhead went to great lengths to give Reason a look and feel that would make the transition between hardware and software seamless. The signal flow in reMix is easy to understand. Start by working your way down a single channel strip.

Figure 6.6 shows a single channel strip—reMix's channel 1. At the top of the channel are four auxiliary sends. These knobs can send a selected amount of signal to one, two, three, and four real-time effects. These effects can be heard by adjusting the Return knobs, located at the far right side of reMix (see Figure 6.7).

Below the auxiliary sends (back to Figure 6.6 again) is a two-band equalizer. This is a very basic EQ that is activated by clicking on its power button and then adjusting the Treble and Bass knobs to boost and/or cut the treble or bass.

The last section of each channel, just below the EQ, controls the level and stereo placement of any mixed signal. This section contains Mute and Solo buttons (which allow you to temporarily shut off this particular channel or leave this channel on and shut off all the others), a pan control (which places the signal from this channel wherever you like in the stereo field), and the channel's fader (which controls the volume of this channel). The next section takes a closer look at each of these components.

CHAPTER 6

Figure 6.6
The reMix channel strip.

Figure 6.7
The Master section.
There are four knobs for
the returns and a master
fader, which controls the
overall signal of the mix.

Setting Levels

The first step to mixing in Reason is to set levels in your mix. To do this, start by opening the Tutorial Song, which can be found in the Reason folder. After opening it (see Figure 6.8), have a quick listen to it. I think you'll agree that the mix is a little on the flat or boring side, and this is a perfect place to start.

Look at the faders on the lower left side of reMix. As shown in Figure 6.9, there are four separate signals, or sounds, that you can mix in this song.

Press the spacebar on your Mac or PC to play the song. Keep your eye on the Dr:rex track to see where the level is in the mix. If you want to know the numeric value of the Dr:rex track volume, click on the fader once, and the Parameter Value tooltip (or tooltip for short) will open near your cursor to tell you what the value is (see Figure 6.10).

Figure 6.8
Reason's Tutorial Song—
a flat, dull mix.

Figure 6.9
There are four separate
active channels in this
song: Redrum, Dr:rex,
NN-XT, and the
Subtractor.

Figure 6.10
Navigate your mouse
over (or click on) any
parameter in reMix to
have the tooltip display a
numeric value of its level
or amount.

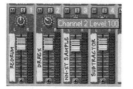

As the song is still playing, click and drag down on the Dr:rex fader and take notice of a few modifications (see Figure 6.11):

▶ The overall volume of the track has faded out of the mix.

▶ The track's graphic meter has dropped.

▶ The graphic meter of the master fader on the lower right of reMix has dropped.

As you can guess, raising the fader will raise the volume of the Dr:rex track. Experiment with some adjustments of the individual faders.

Figure 6.11
Just like a hardware mixer, reMix can visually display level changes.

RESETTING THE REMIX
If you hold down your Ctrl key (Apple Key for the Mac) and click on any of the faders or knobs on the reMix interface, that fader or knob will be reset to its default position (see Figure 6.12).

Figure 6.12
Ctrl-click will reset any knob in reMix to its default position. It's a real time-saver!

CLIPPING IS BAD

While you are honing your mix-master skills with the volume faders, you might occasionally notice a bright red LED flashing in the lower-left corner of the Reason Transport (see Figure 6.13). This indicates that the mixed signal in Reason has overloaded or "clipped."

In the analog world of reel-to-reel tape machines, clipping can be a useful effect for distorting guitars and grunging up the drums. Digital clipping, on the other hand, produces a very harsh and nasty distorted sound that can hurt your ears and damage your speakers.

In other words, digital clipping is bad. If you experience any clipping while mixing your signal in Reason, turn the levels down just a little bit. Your ears and sound card will thank you.

Figure 6.13
Clipping in the digital world is not a good thing, so watch your levels.

Mutes and Solos

After you experiment with the levels and achieve a mix that you are happy with, take a look at the reMix's Mute (M) and Solo (S) buttons (see Figure 6.14).

The Mute button is used to temporarily remove an individual signal from a mix. If you play the Tutorial Song and click on the Mute button over the Redrum track, you'll notice that you can no longer hear the drums playing, but the other instruments still play. You can also tell that the Mute button has been clicked, because the M button turns bright pink.

The Solo button is used to isolate an individual signal from an entire mix. If you play the Tutorial Song and click on the Solo button over the Redrum track, you'll immediately notice that the drums are the only instrument playing, and that the S button on the Redrum track is bright green. Another dead giveaway that the Solo function is in use is to look at all of the other channels on reMix, as they will be muted.

When it comes to the challenge of mixing, these two buttons are vital. The Solo button is one of my best friends, and I use it to isolate any particular instrument in my latest song. I typically give the drum and bass tracks the most priority, because they can very easily dominate the song and make everything sound muddy if they aren't properly mixed in. I can't say that this wouldn't be possible if the Solo button didn't exist, but the button sure makes this task a lot easier.

Figure 6.14
reMix's Mute and Solo buttons.

CHAPTER 6

Likewise, the Mute button is also important in both the songwriting and mixing stage. A Mute button can be used creatively in many ways, such as with automation (see the following tip), but it is also useful when you want to take a particular instrument out of a mix, so that you can hear the rest of the ensemble.

CREATIVITY AT WORK

Although the Mute and Solo buttons might not look it, they can help to create a very interesting mix through the art of automation. Check out Chapter 15, "Automation," which covers automation in depth. Furthermore, if you want to see some cool automation at work, be sure to review the other Reason demo songs that come with Reason 2.5.

Panning

Panning is a mixer function that allows you to assign a channel's audio signal to a particular position in the stereo field—whether hard left, hard right, or anywhere in between. When used creatively, panning can help bring out separate voices and elements that would otherwise be buried behind the heavy thump of the drum and bass.

Notice that in the Tutorial Song, the Dr:rex channel is panned slightly to the left (see Figure 6.15). Solo the Dr:rex track so you can hear the REX file by itself. If you click and hold the Pan knob, you can drag upward to send the Dr:rex track to the center of the mix, which is at the twelve o'clock position in reMix. Notice how the Master Level displays a balanced signal between the left and right channels.

Now click on the Solo button again (to release it) and try moving the Pan knob to the hard right and hard left positions. Listen to how it sounds in a full mix. Notice how heavy the REX track sounds when panned hard left or right. Propellerhead probably had it correctly panned from the start, but it never hurts to experiment or be creative with your panning.

Figure 6.15
Dr:rex is panned slightly to the left in the Tutorial Song.

STEREO SYNTHS AND MONO SYNTHS IN REASON 2.5

Press the Tab key on your keyboard to flip the Reason interface around, and have a look at the first synth, which is Redrum. In Figure 6.16, notice that there are distinct left and right outputs for this device (hence, it is a stereo synth). If you follow the cable, you will see that the Redrum outputs have been routed to two separate inputs on channel 1 of reMix. Next, scroll down the Device Rack until you see the outputs of Subtractor (see Figure 6.17) and you will notice that there is a single audio output jack on the back of it. Follow its output cable and notice that it is routed to channel 4 of reMix.

Press the Tab key again and notice that you have one pan control for the Redrum channel and one pan control for the Subtractor channel. This might seem a little strange to the veteran mix board jockeys out there, so let me explain.

Figure 6.18 shows how a stereo signal is routed into a hardware mixer. In a typical studio environment, a stereo signal will occupy channel 1 and channel 2. Additionally, channel 1 is panned hard left while channel 2 is panned hard right.

Why is reMix different? To save space in the interface, Propellerhead has combined both the left and right channels into one channel in reMix. Also, stereo signals are automatically panned hard left and right upon being routed into reMix. So, if you were to pan Redrum left, it would look something like Figure 6.19 in the analog-mixing world.

Let's now look at the typical routing of a mono synth with a hardware mixer. As seen in Figure 6.20, the pan control must stay at the twelve o'clock position in order for the signal to be heard equally in the left and right channels. The same goes for reMix in this case. Interestingly enough, the top or left input of every channel in reMix is labeled as the "Mono" input, so the synth will automatically be panned in the dead center when routed to reMix.

Figure 6.16
Redrum's outputs have both been routed to channel 1 in reMix.

Figure 6.17
The mono Subtractor
synth is routed to the left
input of channel 4.

Figure 6.18
Here is how a stereo
signal looks when routed
on a hardware mixer.

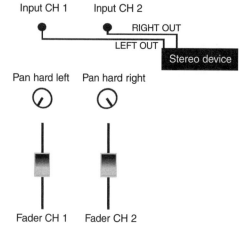

Figure 6.19
Playing with the stereo
field of a synth in Reason
looks a lot different from
a hardware mixer.

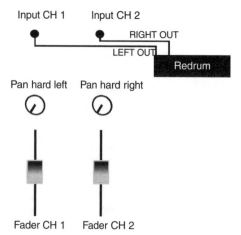

Figure 6.20
But the mono synths
look and act the same in
the software and
hardware realms.

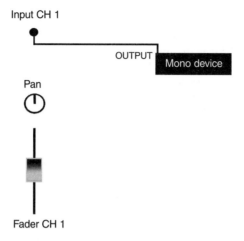

ITTY BITTY KNOB ADJUSTMENTS

If you find that the knobs and slider movements in Reason are not as precise as you would like, you can adjust this in the Preferences window (see Figure 6.21) located in the Mouse Knob Range pull-down menu. Here you can specify the desired accuracy by selecting Normal, Precise, or Very Precise.

Figure 6.21
How precise do you
want to be?

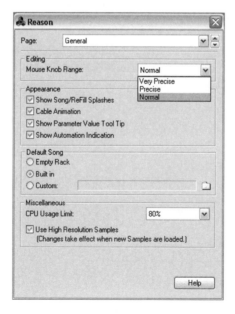

Equalization

Equalization (or EQ) is the process of adjusting (cutting or boosting) specific portions of the audio frequency spectrum within an audio signal. Equalization can help liven up a mix by adding punch to your bass tracks and by giving your leads and arpeggios an added crispness. Equalization can also be used to effectively remove unwanted frequencies to balance out a mix. To sum up, a good dose of EQ might be just what the doctor ordered when mixing a new track.

Although reMix's EQ section is fairly basic, it will be helpful to take a quick look at the various types of equalization that exist:

▶ **Shelving EQ** is the most common of all EQs. It's found on radios, entry-level audio mixers, and, more importantly, in reMix. This type of EQ is comprised of two shelving filters, called the Low Pass Filter and the High Pass Filter. As you might guess, the Low Pass filter is responsible for either boosting or cutting the low end of the frequency spectrum, whereas the High Pass filter handles the high end of the spectrum, as shown in Figure 6.22. On certain hardware mixers that use Shelving EQs, you might find a Mid Pass Filter, which is responsible for cutting/boosting midrange frequencies and makes for a somewhat more accurate EQ section than the typical high-pass/low-pass setup.

▶ **Graphic EQs** are found in mid-level hardware mixers and in many pro audio software plug-ins. Graphic equalization incorporates a number of separate filters, each of which controls a specific slice of bandwidth within the frequency spectrum. These filters have controls (knobs or sliders) that can either boost or cut their assigned slice of bandwidth. Although they are a bit more complicated than Shelving EQs, the Graphic EQ (see Figure 6.23) is a step in the right direction toward accurately shaping your sound.

▶ **Parametric EQs** are the big daddy of equalizers, because they are the most accurate equalizers available. As opposed to Shelving and Graphic EQs, Parametric EQs allow you the flexibility of setting the center frequency, range, and the amplitude of each band. Parametric EQs are found within the virtual mixing consoles of most pro audio software, such as Cubase or SONAR (see Figure 6.24), and although they take a little more practice to understand, you can be sure to achieve much better results with them.

Figure 6.22
A Low Pass and High Pass shelving EQ.

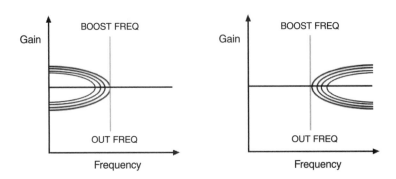

Figure 6.23
A graphic equalizer is a lot more complicated, but can achieve great results.

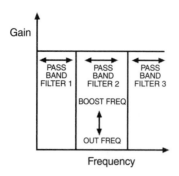

Figure 6.24
The parametric EQ, shown here in Cubase SX, is an eye-catching marvel that really works well.

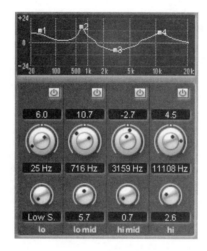

EQ REASON HAS A PARAMETRIC EQ

Reason has a two-band Parametric EQ called the PEQ2 that can be used as a send or insert effect. Learn all about it in Chapter 14, "Effects—Close Up."

The Shelving EQ in reMix is simple and easy to use. Just follow these steps while playing the Tutorial Song:

1. Select any channel with a signal and activate the EQ section of the reMix channel strip by clicking on the EQ button, found just above the Bass and Treble knobs (see Figure 6.25).

2. As the song is playing, make adjustments to either the Bass or Treble knobs to adjust either the low or high frequencies, respectively (see Figure 6.26).

3. If at any time you want to bypass the equalizer, just click on the EQ button again to turn it off.

Figure 6.25
Activate the EQ section
of reMix.

Figure 6.26
Have some fun and make
EQ adjustments to any of
the active channels in
the Tutorial Song.

LESS EQ, LESS CPU

As long as I have been using virtual studio programs such as Cubase or Pro Tools, I have never seen a program as CPU-optimized as Reason. Even back when I was using a really slow G3 laptop running at a then-blistering 233MHz, I could get a lot more performance out of Reason than any other virtual studio program in my arsenal. That said, Reason's EQs and effects do require a certain amount of CPU resources in order to be used effectively. Located in the lower-left corner of the Transport Control is Reason's CPU meter, which indicates how much of your computer's CPU is being used in your song, much like the temperature gauge on your car. If you happen to notice that your CPU meter is starting to run a little on the high side, temporarily turning off an EQ or two might save some precious CPU speed.

Auxiliary Sends and Returns

As you will see in coming chapters, Reason has a full supply of real-time effects to cater to any electronic musician's needs. In order to use the real-time effects in Reason, you must first understand the mixing basics of *sends* and *returns*, also called *auxiliaries*.

The sends are the four knobs found on the reMix console just above the Equalizers on every channel, as shown in Figure 6.27. They are responsible for sending a specific amount of dry signal from the channel to a real-time effect, such as a delay or reverb. If you have the Tutorial Song still open, look directly below reMix and you will see a delay and a chorus/flanger loaded (see Figure 6.28). If you press the Tab key on your computer keyboard, the Reason interface will swing around

Figure 6.27
reMix has four auxiliary
sends and returns.

and you will see that the auxiliary sends are routed to the inputs on both of the effect units. You will also notice that the virtual outputs of the effect units are routed back to reMix. These are called the returns.

The returns are located in the upper-right corner of reMix. They are responsible for returning a specific amount of the processed signal back into the channel strip. See Figure 6.29 to get a better idea of how this process works.

You can use up to four auxiliary effects per instance of reMix. If that isn't enough for you (it rarely is in my case), you can create another reMix and route additional effects to that device, and connect the two mixers together, in a process called *chaining*. Chapter 14 covers some creative effect routing options in Reason.

Figure 6.28
Follow the cables in the back of the Device Rack to see how the send effects are routed in reMix.

Figure 6.29
Shows how a send and return work within a mixer.

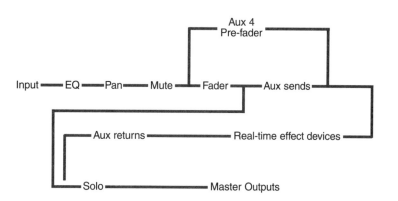

PRE-FADER, POST-FADER

The button labeled P in the Aux send section of reMix is the pre-fader button for auxiliary send 4. When it's clicked on, any signal currently routed through Aux send 4 will be sent to the effect before it goes to the channel fader.

By using an effect in pre-fader mode, you are essentially using it as an insert effect without any additional routing. There are a couple of real-time effect devices in the Reason arsenal that can be used as pre-fader or post-fader effects, such as the Comp-01 Compressor, or possibly the PEQ2 parametric EQ.

To see how it works, create a Comp-01 compressor on auxiliary 4, activating the pre-fader button on its channel. Next, assign an amount of signal to the real-time effect. You can now turn down the fader of that channel and you will hear just the effect. Then you can turn up the fader to hear the mix of both the dry signal and the affected signal.

As you can see, reMix is a compact and versatile mixer that offers many creative possibilities. It also has a few more tricks up its sleeve, which you will discover in future chapters.

7

Redrum—Close Up

Redrum is Reason's drum machine, with features and capabilities that go far beyond most software drum machines (see Figure 7.1). Propellerhead Software designed Redrum to perform both as an independent, pattern-based drum machine and as a sequencer-driven powerhouse.

A Guided Tour of the Redrum Interface

At first sight, the Redrum interface might look a little confusing if you're new to computer music, but as you start to look at the interface from left to right, you are going to find it's quite easy to understand and use. With its extensive feature set and originality in design, it'll get your creative juices flowing.

Figure 7.1
Redrum is the groove
machine that could.

In order to become acquainted with Redrum, you're going to work through some tutorials in this chapter. To follow along, set up your Reason song using these steps:

1. Load an empty Reason song (see Figure 7.2).
2. Create a reMix module (see Figure 7.3).

Figure 7.2
Create a new empty
Reason song.

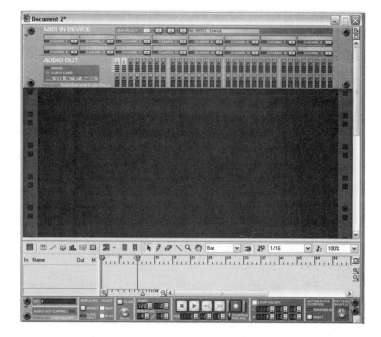

Figure 7.3
Create a reMix 14:2
mixer.

3.   Create a few real-time effects, such as a reverb and delay (see Figure 7.4).

4.   Create a Redrum. Notice that Redrum is already routed to channel 1 of reMix and a sequencer track has been created and armed for MIDI input (see Figure 7.5).

Now you are ready to begin your lesson on this rhythmic marvel!

Figure 7.4
Now you need a couple of real-time effects. For this chapter, create a reverb and a delay.

Figure 7.5
Create a Redrum module. Notice that it is already routed to channel 1 in reMix.

Browsing and Loading Patches

When you first load a Redrum module there is no drum kit loaded. Of course, this will simply not do for this tutorial, so navigate to the lower-left corner of the interface, where you can browse the drum patches (see Figure 7.6).

Either click on the browser window or on the folder button located directly below it to open the Patch Browser window (see Figure 7.7).

At this point, you should see the Reason Factory Sound Bank ReFill. However, if this is your first time using Redrum or Reason for that matter, the ReFills might not be displayed in your browser window. If this is the case, just click on the Find All ReFills button, located at the upper-right corner of the browser window (see Figure 7.8). At this point, you should then see all three of the installed ReFills available in the browser window.

Figure 7.6
Redrum's Patch Select area is where you access the drum patches.

Figure 7.7
The Patch Browser window is where you locate and load Redrum kits.

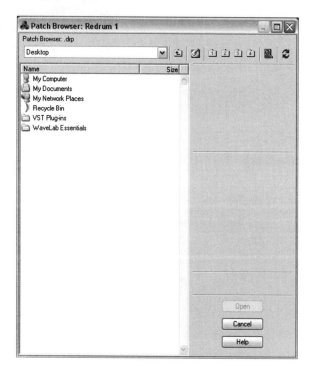

Figure 7.8
The Find All ReFills
button locates every
installed ReFill on your
computer.

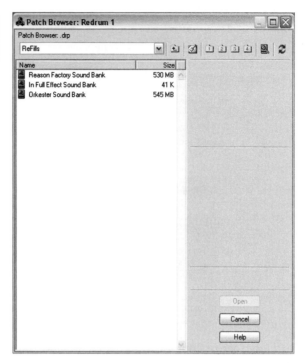

Double-click on the Reason Factory Sound Bank ReFill and you will then find a series of folders dedicated to each Reason module. The folder that you are interested in is the Redrum Drum Kits folder; double-click on it to display the contents.

You should now see 14 alphabetized folders with different styled drum kits within each one. Double-click on the Rock Kits folder to display five rock-style drum kits. Load the first kit, called Groovemasters Rock Kit 1.drp. Because each loaded Redrum kit contains 10 individual samples, loading can take five to ten seconds, depending on how fast your computer is and how much installed RAM you have.

MORE IS BETTER

As stated in Chapter 2, "Installing and Configuring Reason," Redrum is one of several RAM-dependent synths found in Reason (like the NN-XT and NN-19). The samples and drum kits that you load into these modules will perform only as well as your computer allows.

It is wise to consider upgrading your computer with another stick of RAM. You wouldn't believe the performance boost that can be achieved with another 256MB or possibly 512MB of RAM—and RAM is relatively affordable these days.

TIME-SAVER

Here's a quick tip that will not only save you time, but will also impress your friends. Once a patch is loaded into the Redrum interface, you can quickly change to the next drum kit of that same style by clicking once in the Patch Name window. A pull-down menu will appear (see Figure 7.9) with all of the other available kits within the same genre. In this case, because you already loaded a Groovemasters drum kit, once you click on the Patch Name window, you can choose from the five included kits of this style. Additionally, you can use the up and down arrow buttons located below the Patch Name window.

Figure 7.9
By clicking on the Patch Name window, you can quickly select another kit.

Just below the patch selection window are the two global setting options for Redrum (see Figure 7.10). They both are important to the overall sound quality and playability of Redrum.

High Quality Interpolation can greatly improve the sound quality of the sample playback in Redrum. When activated, this function employs a very advanced interpolation algorithm, which results in better audio playback, especially with samples that contain a lot of high frequencies, such as hi-hat sounds or Latin percussion.

Figure 7.10
Redrum's global settings.

ALGORITHMS? INTERPOLATION?

An *algorithm* is a term used to describe the step-by-step mathematical process of problem solving. *Every* functioning part within your computer is algorithmically related, right down to the language code that was used to conceive and create the Reason program.

In digital sampling terms, algorithms are used to capture, store, and play back audio. As audio is not a constant, there are many variables (such as frequency and amplitude) needed to accurately capture an analog signal and then convert it to digital bits. Using interpolation algorithmically solves these variables.

Interpolation is a key building block for algorithms in the sense that it is a calculation that estimates numerical values of a function (or action) between two or more known values. When the High Quality Interpolation function is selected in Redrum, new sets of calculations are used to determine a more precise algorithm.

The Channel 8&9 Exclusive button produces a virtual link between the eighth and ninth sound channels of the Redrum interface (see Figure 7.11). When activated, sound channel 8 works as a cutoff for channel 9 and vice versa. For example, an open hi-hat sample is loaded on channel 9 and a closed hi-hat sample is loaded on channel 8. If channel 9 is playing its sample, it will be immediately silenced when channel 8 is triggered, much as a hi-hat would behave in an acoustic drum kit.

Figure 7.11
Use the Channel 8&9
Exclusive button to make
your hi-hat parts sound
realistic.

The Drum Sound Channels

Next, let's take a look at the drum sound channels. As you proceed, note that there are a lot of creative editing features that can add interest to your rhythms.

Let's begin with drum sound channel 1, which is typically where the kick drum sample is loaded. (See Figure 7.12.)

Across the top of channel 1 are the Mute, Solo, and Trigger buttons, defined as follows:

▶ The Mute (or "M") button works similarly to the mute buttons on the reMix mixer; it silences the particular channel on which it is active. For example, if you have a full pattern playing that includes a kick, snare, and a hi-hat, clicking on the kick channel's Mute button will allow you to hear just the snare and hi-hat without the kick.

▶ The Solo (or "S") button works in the opposite way, because it will isolate just the drum sample that you want to hear on its own. If you have a full Redrum kit playing and you just want to hear the kick drum, select the kick channel's Solo button. All of the other drum sounds will be muted (see Figure 7.13).

▶ The Trigger button (shaped like a right-pointing arrow) works as a sample preview button; when it is clicked, the corresponding channel will play the drum sample that is loaded within. If you click on channel 1's Trigger button, you will hear the kick drum sample.

Figure 7.12
Drum sound channel 1 is
typically where the kick
drum sample is loaded.

Figure 7.13
When a Solo button is clicked on a Redrum channel, all other channels are muted.

TWO WAYS TO TRIGGER SAMPLES

There is a second way to trigger samples from Redrum without having to click on each trigger on the interface. You can set up your MIDI controller keyboard to trigger each sound.

First, make sure that you have selected your controller keyboard as your MIDI input device (covered in Chapter 2).

Next, select the sequencer track that is connected to Redrum (see Figure 7.14). Make sure that the track is armed and ready to receive input from your controller keyboard.

If you press the C1 note on your MIDI keyboard, you should now hear the kick drum play.

At this point, you will also be able to trigger all of the different drum samples loaded in your Redrum kit, as they are mapped out between notes C1 and A1 on your controller keyboard.

Figure 7.14
Highlight your Redrum sequencer track and make sure that it is armed to receive MIDI input from your controller keyboard.

MAPPED SAMPLES EXPLAINED

From time to time, you will hear the term *mapped out* used to describe how samples are assigned to specific keys on your MIDI keyboard. In the case of Redrum, this is a very easy concept to understand, because there are only 10 possible keys that your drum samples can be assigned to.

First, you need to understand that there are 10 available octaves in a MIDI sequencer, just as there are 10 octaves on an 88-key piano. Each octave uses the C key as its starting point. Additionally, every note on your MIDI keyboard has a corresponding numeric value. With this in mind, the octaves on a MIDI keyboard are identified as follows:

▶ C-2 to B-2 (MIDI notes 0-11)—The lowest octave on a keyboard

▶ C-1 to B-1 (MIDI notes 12-23)

▶ C0 to B0 (MIDI notes 24-35)

▶ C1 to B1 (MIDI notes 36-47)

▶ C2 to B2 (MIDI notes 48-59)

▶ C3 to B3 (MIDI notes 60-71)—This is the center note of a keyboard, also called Middle C

▶ C4 to B4 (MIDI notes 72-83)

▶ C5 to B5 (MIDI notes 84-95)

▶ C6 to B6 (MIDI notes 96-107)

▶ C7 to B7 (MIDI notes 108-119)

▶ C8 to B8 (MIDI notes 120-127)—The highest octave on a keyboard

Drum machine samples are typically mapped out in the C1 octave of a MIDI keyboard. Figure 7.15 shows how the individual drum samples of Redrum are mapped out within this octave.

Figure 7.15
Here is how the samples of Redrum are mapped out in the C1 octave of a MIDI keyboard.

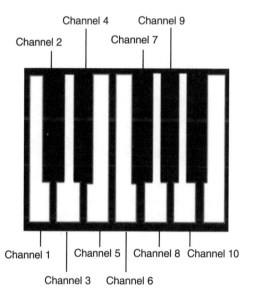

Selecting Your Drum Sounds

A major limitation of hardware drum machines is that most of them can't change their sounds. Once you buy the drum machine, you are stuck with the sounds, which, over time, will become less and less interesting.

Thankfully, this is not the case with Redrum, because each channel's sample can be changed and customized. It is all done in the sample browser portion of the Redrum channel strip, located just below the Mute, Solo, and Trigger buttons. In the display window of this section is the filename of the currently loaded sample. If there is no sample loaded, this window remains blank. Because you have already loaded a Redrum kit, the kick drum file is listed here as BD1 1 OHS.

Located just below the display window are the scroll and browser buttons. These are the tools you will use to change the kick drum sample loaded on drum sound channel 1.

The scroll buttons will allow you to manually navigate through your available samples one by one. Try clicking on the Scroll Down button once and notice that a new kick drum sample will load almost instantly. Also try clicking on the Scroll Up button to return to the original kick drum sample.

CHECK YOUR LIST

Redrum offers a quicker method of locating samples. Just click once on the display window and a very long list of available samples should pop up (see Figure 7.16). As you can see, there are many kick drum samples to choose from.

Additionally, you will find that a lot of these listed samples can be musically categorized by their filenames. For example, the kick drum sample named Bd2_Abused.wav would suggest that this kick drum is suitable for industrial-style music, whereas Bd2_Chemical.wav would be used in big beat Fatboy Slim type music.

Figure 7.16
Redrum is chock full of samples to fill every channel.

Open browser...

BD1 1 OHSH.aif
BD1br.aif
BD1Dub.aif
Bd2_Abstract.wav
Bd2_Abused.wav
Bd2_Anarchy.wav
Bd2_Artefact.wav
Bd2_Beltram.wav
Bd2_Brat.wav
Bd2_Bricks.wav
Bd2_Cheese.wav
Bd2_Chemical.wav
Bd2_CutCodes.wav
Bd2_Dentaku.WAV
Bd2_DubHead.WAV
Bd2_FatBoy.wav
Bd2_GiantStep.wav
Bd2_HardKnox.wav
Bd2_HotValve.WAV
Bd2_Jeepkeys.wav
Bd2_Kru.wav
Bd2_MaryJ.wav
Bd2_Monk.wav
Bd2_NeonLights.WAV
Bd2_NextStep.wav
Bd2_One2.wav
Bd2_Optical.wav
Bd2_Rabotnik.WAV
Bd2_Rarest.wav
Bd2_RawDirt.wav
Bd2_RawFunky.wav
Bd2_RiteHere.wav
Bd2_Rollers.wav
Bd2_Sexy.wav
Bd2_SoleSide.wav
Bd2_SupaDupa.wav
Bd2_SupaFunky.wav
Bd2_Trent.wav
Bd2_Vintage.wav
Bd2_Xfile1.WAV
Bd2_Xfile2.wav

The Sample Browser button located to the right of the scroll buttons opens a browsing window. From that window, you can search your computer for an entirely new sample to import to any of Redrum's 10 channels. For example, if you don't want a kick drum on channel 1, click on the Sample Browser button to find and import a new sample (see Figure 7.17).

Figure 7.17
The Redrum Sample Browser window is where you import new samples.

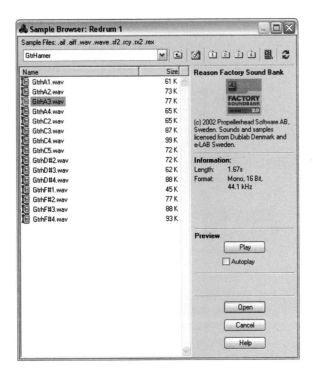

FILE FORMATS

Redrum supports a great many file formats that can be imported into its individual channels. This leaves the playing field wide open for users who own a lot of sample CDs, because they can be used at will in Reason.

Redrum supports these audio file formats:

▶ `.aif`—A commonly used format for the Macintosh platform.

▶ `.wav`—The standard file format for the Windows platform.

▶ SoundFonts or `.sf2`—A file format developed and implemented by EMU and Creative Labs.

▶ REX file slices—A format developed by Propellerhead and implemented in a program called ReCycle!. Read more about it in Appendix B, "ReCycle! 2.0."

Additionally, Redrum supports multiple bit depths and sampling rates, and works with both mono and stereo files, so you can import your pristine quality drum samples in a flash. Just keep in mind that these samples are stored and used internally in 16-bit format.

Sends and Pans

Located just below the Sample Browser controls are the Sends and Panning knobs for each Redrum channel. These knobs perform a function similar to that of the Sends and Panning knobs on reMix—they control both the amount of signal that is sent off to a real-time effect and where the signal is placed within the stereo field.

As you read further in this book, you'll find that every module has a couple of neat but subtle tricks up its sleeve, and Redrum is certainly no exception to the rule.

The Sends knobs, or "S1" and "S2," as they are labeled, are directly linked to the same effect sends as reMix. If you recall from Chapter 4, "Creating Your First Reason Song," reMix has four auxiliary knobs, or "sends" that send the desired amount of dry signal to one of the loaded real-time effects that are virtually routed to it. In this example, you should have a reverb and a delay effect routed to reMix that can be accessed by using auxiliary sends 1 and 2. This is the same setup for Redrum, because the "S1" and "S2" knobs have access to these effects as well. In Redrum terms, this means that you can assign individual drum samples to their own real-time effects, which in turn can create a much more dynamic and creative mix. (See Figure 7.18.)

Figure 7.18
Both reMix and Redrum have access to auxiliary effects one and two.

The Pan knob controls where each drum sample is placed within the stereo field of a mix. Creatively using all 10 of these knobs can produce a very realistic drum mix that mirrors an acoustic drum kit. For example, give this drum mix idea a spin:

- ▶ Pan the kick dead center at the 12:00 position.
- ▶ Pan the snare slightly off to the left or right at either the 10:00 or 2:00 position.
- ▶ Pan the hi-hat (closed and open) to the left or right at either the 9:00 or 3:00 position.
- ▶ Pan the high tom to the 11:00 or 1:00 position.
- ▶ Pan the low tom to the 10:00 or 2:00 position.

Try varying the panning to come up with your own interesting combination. It's important to experiment with every aspect of mixing if you want to produce a song that is truly original and attention grabbing. Stereo was invented for a reason, so use it!

One additional point of interest to note here is the LED located just above the knob that indicates whether the loaded sample is a mono or stereo sample. The LED lights up when the sample is stereo and stays dark when the sample is mono.

Advanced Redrum Routing with ReMix

Being the meticulous person that I am, I like having as much control over virtual synths and sound modules in Reason as possible. When it comes to Redrum, I like to be able to make reMix faders available to each sound Redrum can produce. That way, I have total volume and panning control at my disposal, and many additional virtual routing possibilities—for example, using a compressor as an insert effect on the kick sound channel.

This can be very easily accomplished using Reason's virtual routing. You're going to create a submixer for Redrum which will give you close control over each Redrum channel and leave plenty of room for other virtual synths.

1.   Click once on the Delay unit (see Figure 7.19) to select it. Next, choose Mixer 14:2 from the Create pull-down menu. This will create another reMix device between the real-time effects and Redrum. Also notice that Redrum is still routed to channel 1 on the primary reMixer.

Figure 7.19
Select the Delay real-time effect and create a reMix device.

2. Rename the second reMix Redrum Submix by clicking on the virtual tape at the left of reMix (see Figure 7.20).

3. Press Tab. You will see that the Redrum submix has automatically been routed to the primary reMix by way of the Chaining Master inputs (see Figure 7.21).

4. Scroll down the Device Rack and find Redrum, which should be the bottom device. Click and hold on the outputs to bring up the routing pull-down menu. Now select Disconnect to virtually disconnect Redrum from the primary reMix (see Figure 7.22).

5. Using your mouse, click and drag each individual Redrum output to an input on the Redrum Submix, as shown in Figure 7.23.

Figure 7.20
Rename the second reMix Redrum Submix.

Figure 7.21
Reason has already routed the Redrum Submix to the primary reMix by using the Chaining Master inputs.

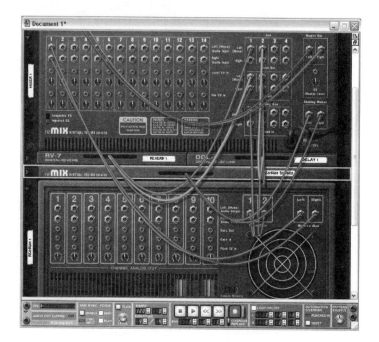

Figure 7.22
Disconnect Redrum from
the primary reMix so you
can start with a clean
slate.

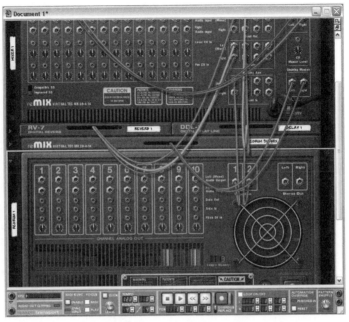

Figure 7.23
Route each Redrum
sample to its own reMix
channel.

6. After completing this, press the Tab key again. You should now see each Redrum
   sample routed to its own fader on the Redrum Submix (see Figure 7.24).

If you now trigger any sample in Redrum, you will have total control over its volume and
placement in the stereo field with the help of your handy submixer.

Figure 7.24
Now Redrum has its own mixer.

Redrum Levels and Dynamics

Continuing down Redrum's channel 1 strip, below the Panning knob you will see Level and Velocity knobs. These help to introduce a dynamic element to your Redrum kits. These help keep your drum patterns from sounding as though they were played by Robby the Robot.

▶ The Level knob controls the volume of each channel in the Redrum interface.

▶ The Velocity, or VEL knob, affects the impact of the Level knob by introducing a dynamic element to the mix.

VEL MEANS DYNAMICS

The VEL knobs in Redrum can be used to effectively produce a realistic and dynamic drum performance, which sets Redrum apart from many other drums machines, whether they are software- or hardware-based.

As previously stated, the Level knob affects the volume of any Redrum channel. The Dynamic switch of the Pattern Programmer (you'll look at it later in this chapter) introduces different velocities (or dynamics) to the Redrum channels, which can then alter these volumes.

The VEL knob determines how much the volume is affected by different velocities. For example, if the VEL knob has a positive value, the volume of a Redrum channel will become louder with increasing dynamics. If the VEL has a negative value, the volume will decrease as the dynamic increases, which is called *inverting*.

Later in this chapter, when you begin to write your own patterns, be sure to add different velocities to each note. Try experimenting with the VEL knob to create a realistic drum groove.

DYNAMICS MEANS CREATIVE MIXES

Along with melody, harmony, and rhythm, *dynamics* is an important element needed to give any form of music its edge or character. Such character makes the song more interesting. It is a governing element that cannot be ignored, but only better understood by listening to numerous styles of music as examples.

For example, because this chapter discusses drums and drum machines, consider jazz music as a blueprint to define a good use of dynamics. Check out some of jazz's greatest artists, such as Miles Davis, Buddy Rich, or Dave Brubeck. Notice how the drummer plays with the mix by introducing both loud and soft dynamics simultaneously. This alone helps make the drums and percussion pop out of the mix.

If you need something that rocks out a little more, listen to something with more of an edge, such as hard rock or alternative. You can hear that even steady rock such as music by Rush or Pearl Jam needs good dynamics to make the song memorable.

Believe it or not, even good old "four-on-the-floor" techno music has dynamics. Check out CDs by Moby or Orbital and listen for the variations in dynamics.

Think of your audio mix like a good painting—it can't be just one color, so mix it up!

Length, Decay, and Gate

Up to this point, you've looked at controls that affect the mix of the Redrum channels. As you continue down channel 1, the following sections discuss controls that will alter the actual sound of the sample.

The Length knob sets the playback length of the drum sample. In the case of channel 1, this knob controls the playback length of the kick drum. If you click and drag on the knob to decrease the length, you will hear the sample get shorter.

The Decay/Gate switch (see Figure 7.25) sets the playback mode of the drum sample. When the switch is in the down position, it's set to Decay mode, which allows the sample to play with a decay (or sustain). Additionally, when using Redrum in Decay mode with the main Reason sequencer, the sample will play the same length of time, no matter how long or short the MIDI note is held.

When this switch is set to Gate mode the sample will play for a determined amount of length, and then cut off without a sustain. When using Redrum in Gate mode with the main Reason sequencer, the sample will abruptly cut off as soon as it either reaches its determined length or its MIDI note is released (whichever comes first).

Figure 7.25
The Length knob and Decay/Gate switch set the playback mode of the loaded drum sample.

Try an example of this with sound channel 1 to see its effectiveness. Make sure the Decay/Gate switch is set to Decay mode before you begin.

1. Turn the Length knob down to about its middle position, until the tooltip reads 56.

2. Play the sample using either the Trigger button or your MIDI keyboard. You will hear the slight decay effect.

3. Switch to Gate mode.

4. Play the sample again with either the Trigger button or your MIDI keyboard. It should now sound much more beefy, because it contains no sustain or decay at the end. It is simply playing the sample until it reaches its determined length.

Pitch

The Pitch knob alters the playback pitch of any Redrum sample. The range of the available Pitch is +/– one full octave and all points in between. Notice the LED above the Pitch knob lights up whenever a value greater or less than zero is selected.

RETURN TO ZERO
Remember, holding down the Ctrl key (or Apple Key on the Mac) on your computer keyboard and clicking on a knob such as Pitch will reset its value to zero.

Tone

The Tone knob controls the "brightness" of the sample assigned to the Redrum channel. Lowering the Tone value will "darken" and muddy up the sample as it plays back, whereas increasing its value will make your samples quite bright and brittle sounding.

Velocity

To the right of the Tone knob is its corresponding Velocity knob, which applies the effect of the Tone knob based on the velocity values of the sample playback. The end of the chapter contains tutorials to show you how this process works in detail.

Selecting Your Channels

Beneath the Tone and Velocity knobs on every channel is the Select button. When clicked on, this button selects the channel for use with the Redrum pattern sequencer.

Not All Channels Work Alike

As you look over the other channels of Redrum, you will notice that there are channels whose parameters are similar to those of channel 1 and others whose parameters are altogether different (see Figure 7.26). Let's have a look at these other parameters and see what they do.

Let's Get This Sample Started

Available on Redrum channels 3, 4, 5, 8, and 9, the Start knob sets the point at which the loaded sample will begin to play back. In other words, when the Start knob is adjusted, Redrum will play that sample back not at the beginning, but rather in accordance to the position of the Start knob. See Figure 7.27 for a graphical example of this function.

Figure 7.26
Redrum is certainly not a one-trick pony by a long shot.

Figure 7.27
These waveforms were captured in WaveLab and graphically show at which point Redrum began to play the sample. Using a snare drum sample as an example, in the top figure, the sample is played from start to finish, as the Start knob is set to zero. In the bottom figure, the sample is played well after its original starting point, as the Start knob has been set to 9:00.

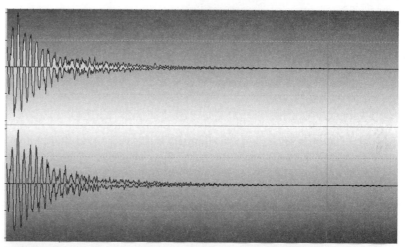

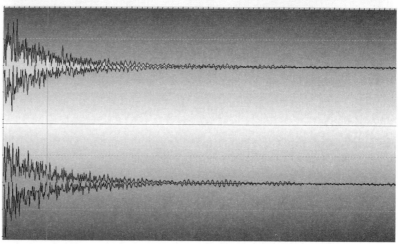

To the right of the Start knob is its corresponding Velocity control. This knob determines where the starting point of a sample will be in relation to its played velocity. Notice the LED above this knob that will light up whenever a value of greater or less than zero is selected.

When used together, the dynamic possibilities are virtually endless. I will show you some examples later in this chapter when you use the Pattern Sequencer.

Bend That Pitch

Moving along to channels 6 and 7, you will find what I kindly refer to as the *disco effect*. You'll understand why in a minute. Seriously though, these parameters are used to create a pitch bend effect (see Figure 7.28).

Figure 7.28
Channels 6 and 7
produce a disco-like
pitch bend to your toms.
Sorry, but the Mirror Ball
is not included.

On channels 6 and 7, you will see the Pitch knob that works as it does on the other Redrum channels. The difference on these channels is the additional Bend knob.

CREATING A PITCH BEND

You can use either channel 6 or 7 for this example. Without altering the position of the Pitch knob, turn the Bend knob by clicking and dragging upward.

Now use your MIDI keyboard or the Trigger button to hear the results. Notice how the pitch starts at the top and slides down.

Now adjust the Pitch knob to either a positive or negative value and listen to the sample again.

Like I said . . . Disco! Disco! Disco!

Below the Pitch and Bend controls are the Rate and Velocity knobs for further editing of the pitch bend effect.

The Rate knob controls the bend time of the pitch bend effect. Setting this knob to a negative value decreases the bend time and speeds it up, whereas setting it to a positive value increases the bend time, which slows the effect down.

Its Velocity knob controls the amount of the pitch bend effect according to the velocity at which the sample is played. Try increasing the value and notice how much wider a range the pitch bend effect has when triggered.

The Redrum Pattern Programmer

Aside from great sounds, Redrum includes a fantastic pattern-based programmer (see Figure 7.29). Although this composition tool is much different from the main Reason sequencer, they can be used together at the same time, which creates a virtual drummers' paradise.

Figure 7.29
The Redrum pattern
programmer is Redrum's
composition tool.

Before you begin to explore the interface in depth, you need to understand what a pattern-based
programmer is.

What Is a Pattern-Based Programmer?

A pattern-based programmer is comprised of a series of step programmed drum patterns that are
compiled and stored within a saved song. Redrum offers four pattern banks, each of which can
store eight separate patterns (see Figure 7.30). This adds up to 32 individual drum patterns that
can be created, saved, and used within one song. Believe me, that's a lot of patterns.

Figure 7.30
With 32 individual
possible patterns to
choose from, your song
won't run out of creative
rhythms by a long shot.

All of these patterns are *step programmed,* which means that each drum sound in the Redrum
module must be manually programmed with your mouse one step (or beat) at a time. This might
sound a little tedious to the beginning Redrum programmer, but the immediate benefit of using a
pattern programmer like this is that you have meticulous control over every dynamic of each of
the 10 samples in Redrum. Better yet, there are even a few add-ons of a sort that will make your
drums sound even more expressive.

Run Those Patterns

I can't think of a better place to begin this tour than with the Run button, located to the far-left side
of the pattern section (see Figure 7.31).

The Run button starts and stops the pattern section. Click on it once, and then look to the step
section and notice the "running lights" as the pattern plays through. Click on it again and the
sequencer will stop. The pattern programmer can also be started and stopped from the Transport
Panel of the Reason sequencer. Press your computer's spacebar and notice how the Redrum
sequencer starts right up.

Figure 7.31
Redrum's step pattern
controls are used to
change patterns and
stop/start patterns.

Located just above the Run button is the Enable Pattern Section button. This links the Redrum pattern section to the main Reason sequencer. Click on it once to turn it off and then start up the main Reason sequencer again. Notice that the Redrum pattern section does not start up. Additionally, as the Reason sequencer is playing, try clicking on the Run button again. You will see that the Redrum pattern section will not start up unless the Enable Pattern Section button is active.

To the right of the Run and Enable buttons is the Pattern section. As mentioned, there are four banks: A, B, C, and D, with eight patterns assigned to each bank. This gives you 32 available patterns to program. In order to change patterns manually, just click on either a numeric pattern or one of the four banks followed by a pattern number. This will bring up the pattern stored in that location. Of course, you will not see any available patterns, because you have not written any yet. Clicking on the Pattern button located just above the numeric pattern buttons will deactivate the pattern section entirely. Even with the Run button active, the patterns will not play again until you reactivate the Pattern button. This can be useful when you are using the Reason sequencer to program Redrum rather than using patterns.

Climbing the Steps of Pattern Programming Success

To the right of the Pattern section is the Redrum Step-Programming Interface (see Figure 7.32). This is where your step patterns will be written and edited. You won't believe how easy and creative it really is!

Figure 7.32
The Redrum pattern programmer interface is where you write and edit your step patterns.

Before you learn about the specific parameters that can be edited, you'll program your first pattern to get your feet wet.

1. Select the channel 1 kick drum by clicking on its Select button (see Figure 7.33).

2. Look at the 16-step pattern in front of you and decide which steps you will place your Redrum sample on. By default, each step is a single 16th note, so for the sake of simplicity, you may want to just place the sample on steps buttons 1, 5, 9, and 13 for starters (see Figure 7.34). Just click on the step buttons to light them up.

Figure 7.33
Select the Redrum channel that you want to program. For this tutorial, I have selected a kick drum sample on channel 1.

Figure 7.34
Select the steps that you want to use to write in your pattern. Because a kick drum is selected, this example uses steps 1, 5, 9, and 13.

3. Now select another Redrum channel and write in a pattern for that sample as well. Try a snare drum on steps 5 and 13 or a hi-hat on steps 1, 3, 5, 7, 9, 11, 13, and 15 (see Figure 7.35).

Figure 7.35
Now select another Redrum channel and sequence that sample. I have selected channel 8, which is a hi-hat sample, and placed it on steps 1, 3, 5, 7, 9, 11, 13, and 15.

4. Now press the spacebar on your computer keyboard, or click on the Run button in the Redrum pattern section. You should hear the sample you programmed played in time with the tempo of your Reason song.

CLICK AND DRAG

If you want to write in a drum roll or 16th note pattern in Redrum, you have two choices. One way is to click on the individual notes, which is kind of a drag when you are writing in a long string of 16th notes in a row.

The other way is to select the sound that you want and simply click and drag along the steps (see Figure 7.36). This will allow you to write in a 16-step hi-hat pattern in no time.

Figure 7.36
Click and drag across the step buttons to activate all of the 16th steps.

Now let's have a look at the specific parameters that can be used in the Redrum pattern programmer.

How Many Steps Do You Need?

Although working with 16 steps is a lot of fun, as time goes on you might come to find that your patterns and song require more than 16 steps. With this idea in mind, I give you the Steps Spin control (see Figure 7.37).

Figure 7.37
The Steps Spin can assign up to 64 steps to your Redrum patterns.

The Steps Spin control assigns a specific number of steps to your patterns. Any value between 1 and 64 steps can be assigned using this control. Assigning specific step values to your Redrum programmer makes it possible to sequence different time signatures. For example, if you want to create a "waltz" feeling in 3/4 time, just set the number of steps to 12. Just keep in mind that the Reason sequencer must also be set to 3/4 time (look back at Chapter 5, "The Reason Sequencer—Close Up," to review). The number of steps can be increased and decreased by either clicking on the scroll buttons to the right of its display, or by clicking and dragging up or down in the display.

To the right of the Steps Spin control is the Resolution knob (see Figure 7.38). This knob assigns note values to your steps in the Redrum programmer. By default, the Resolution knob is set to 1/16 or 16th notes, which simply means that each step is a 16th note. Aside from 16th notes, there are many other available resolutions, such as the 16th note "triplet" setting, which produces a triplet feeling against a 4/4 time signature. There are also extremely high resolutions, such as the 1/64 or 64th note resolution, and lower values such as the 1/4 or quarter note resolution. The Resolution knob is there for your experimenting and creativity; just remember that the resolution is linked to the tempo of the Reason sequencer, so higher resolutions can sound strange at fast tempos.

Figure 7.38
The Resolution knob assigns different note values to each step.

As the saying goes, "It don't mean a thing if it ain't got that swing," and Redrum has the perfect tool for giving it to you. Located to the right of the Resolution knob, the Shuffle button applies a swing or shuffle feel to your drum patterns (see Figure 7.39). Once activated, this shuffling effect can be intensified by using the Pattern Shuffle knob located at the far right of the Transport Panel of the Reason sequencer.

Figure 7.39
The Shuffle button is directly linked with the Pattern Shuffle knob in the Reason Transport Panel.

Give the Shuffle a test drive by following these steps:

1. Wipe the slate clean by selecting Edit > Cut Pattern.

2. Select the Redrum channel that has a closed hi-hat sound. Now write in a 16th note pattern by clicking and dragging across the steps. Make sure that the Resolution knob is set to 16th notes or 1/16 (see Figure 7.40).

3. Activate the Shuffle button and set the Pattern Shuffle knob to the 10:00 position.

4. Click on the Run button in Redrum, or start the Reason sequencer and listen to the shuffling effect. Be sure to make changes with the Pattern Shuffle knob to hear the different shuffling feels you get with this function. Also try adding in kick and snare patterns against it.

If you increase the number of steps in your patterns, you will certainly need a way to view and edit the additional steps. The Edit Steps switch is located to the right of the Shuffle button (see Figure 7.41) and addresses this very need. Click and drag the switch up and down to view and edit all of the 64 available steps.

Figure 7.40
Write a 16th note hi-hat pattern and add some swing to it by activating the Shuffle button and turning up the Pattern Shuffle knob.

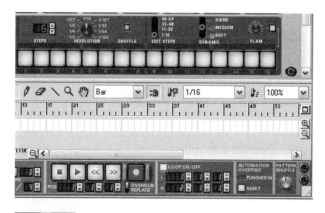

Figure 7.41
View and edit all of the steps in your Redrum pattern by using the Edit Steps switch.

Dynamics and Flam

As I stated earlier, dynamics are the key to creating a great sounding track, no matter what instrument is used. Redrum has several features to help make control of dynamics easy.

The color-coded Dynamic switch is used to assign different velocities to each step in a pattern (see Figure 7.42).

Figure 7.42
The Dynamic switch creates a much-needed element for any pattern programmed in Redrum.

Have a look at how you can use this to create some interesting effects with just a hi-hat sound.

1. Just as before, delete the current pattern by choosing Cut Pattern from the Edit pull-down menu, or by using the Ctrl+X (Windows) or Apple+X (Mac) keyboard command.

2. Select the closed hi-hat channel in Redrum and set the Dynamic switch to Soft.

3. Using your mouse, create a hi-hat pattern by clicking on steps 1, 2, 5, 6, 9, 10, 13, and 14. Notice that these selected steps are light green.

4. Now switch the Dynamic switch to Medium by clicking and dragging upward.

5. Click on steps 1, 5, 9, and 13. Notice how the colors of these steps change to a shade of orange.

6. Press the Run button on Redrum and listen to how the dynamics change with the hi-hat. You can also click on the Shuffle button to hear the dynamics along with a shuffling feel.

7. Click and drag upward on the Dynamic switch to change the value from Medium to Hard.

8. Click on steps 1, 5, 9, and 13 while the sequencer is still running so you can hear the effect in real time. Notice that the color of these steps has changed to a shade of bright red.

To the right of the Dynamic switch are the Flam controls. In drumming terms, flam describes what it also known as a *double strike* on a percussion instrument. This double strike creates a very slight drumroll sound and the Flam controls are used to re-create that effect (see Figure 7.43).

Figure 7.43
Use the Flam controls to create a realistic double strike sound on any channel.

A flam can be applied to any step or sound in a Redrum pattern by activating the Flam button and clicking on any step. After you select a step to affect, you can control the speed of the flam by adjusting its knob. Let's look at an example.

1. Cut the current pattern.

2. Click on the Run button, select your kick drum channel, and set your dynamics to Medium. Write a kick pattern on steps 1 and 9.

3. Select your closed hi-hat channel, set the dynamics to Soft, and write a simple 8th note pattern on steps 1, 3, 5, 7, 9, 11, 13, and 15.

4. Select your snare drum channel, set the dynamics to Medium, and write a syncopated rhythm on steps 5, 8, 11, and 14.

5. Activate the Flam button by clicking on it. Click on step 14 of the snare drum pattern. Listen to the immediate effect and notice the red LED above step 14 stays lit.

6. Use the Flam knob to control the speed of the effect. I suggest setting it at the 3:00 position to make the snare pattern sound realistic.

Building the Redrum Groove with the Pattern Programmer

By now, you should have a pretty firm grasp on the Redrum interface and how to navigate through the step sequencer. Now is as good a time as any to start using Redrum as a power user should!

Because you have been probably using the same Redrum kit throughout this tutorial, I think it's high time that you find another Redrum kit to have some fun with. Click on the Patch Browser folder to bring up the browser window.

Ideally, you need a drum kit that can be used at fast and slow tempos effectively, so I suggest double-clicking on the Heavy Kits folder. You'll see seven Dublab Redrum kits at your disposal. Select the first kit and let's get cracking!

Listen to each Redrum channel by clicking on the Trigger buttons or by using your MIDI keyboard. There are good solid drum sounds that you can use effectively with the Redrum pattern programmer in order to create some interesting patterns. Let's start by writing out a simple pattern with the programmer using just a kick, snare, and hi-hat. Make sure that you have Bank A, Pattern One selected for this tutorial, and set the song tempo to 90 BPM.

1. Select the kick drum Redrum channel, set its dynamic to Medium, and write in a simple kick drum pattern on steps 1, 4, 8, and 12. Click on the Run button to start the pattern so you can hear the changes as you are making them.

2. Select one of the snare drum Redrum channels, set its dynamics to Medium as well, and write in a quick pattern line on steps 5, 10, and 13. Notice that the pattern sounds rather empty. This is where you fill in the blank space with the hi-hat.

3. Select the closed hi-hat Redrum channel, set its dynamics to Soft, and write in a quarter note pattern on steps 1, 5, 9, 13, and 16 for some variation. Notice that the groove is starting to take shape nicely as all of the blank space is filled.

HONING YOUR DRUMMING SKILLS

If drums are not your primary instrument, you might soon find yourself running out of rhythmic ideas for Redrum. Not to worry, because you can take a quick trip to your local sheet music store and pick up a book of drum patterns for $10-20. These books are full of pattern ideas that are sure to provide an ample source of material for months and years to come.

If you are short on funds, you might also search the Internet for drumming web pages that offer free drum patterns.

This is a good starting point, because a basic groove has been set up. Now is the perfect time to add some real-time effects using the S1 and S2 knobs on each Redrum channel.

Start by giving the snare drum some reverb, which is accessible by using the S1 knob. Because the reverb is most likely set to its default of Hall, it's a good idea to not overdo it with the effect on the snare drum, as it will sound too saturated. Try assigning a send value of 40 to the snare channel. You should now hear a nice, smooth echoing reverb underneath the snare sample. Also notice that the signal meter for the reverb effect should be lit up (see Figure 7.44).

Figure 7.44
The RV-7 real-time reverb is lit up with delight as it now has a dry signal to process.

You should have the delay effect loaded and ready to be used with the S2 knob. It's time to add some delay to the hi-hat track in order to create an interesting 16th note feeling. Select the closed hi-hat Redrum channel and set the S2 knob to a value of 80. At this point, you should now hear a very smooth, syncopated pattern with the hi-hat. You might consider panning the hi-hat a little off to the left or right to create a stereo effect that sounds good in a drum mix.

Altering and Randomizing Your Redrum Patterns

You should now have a drum pattern that can be used as a good, solid rhythm. But this shouldn't be the only drum loop you will use in your entire song, so now you are going to create a few new patterns by using some of Reason's handy pattern edits.

1.   Start by selecting Copy Pattern from the Edit pull-down menu. You can also use the Ctrl+C (on a PC) or Apple+C (on Mac) key command. This will copy all of the written steps from Pattern 1, and allow you to move them to Pattern 2 to begin editing.

2.   Select Pattern 2 by clicking on it and choosing Paste Pattern from the Edit pull-down menu. You can also use Ctrl+V on a PC or Apple+V on a Mac. This will paste the copied pattern into Pattern 2.

3.   At this point, click on the Edit pull-down menu and notice how many pattern edits you have available. For starters, try something simple, like the Randomize Pattern. This can be done by choosing it from the Edit pull-down menu, or using the key command of Ctrl+R for the PC or Apple+R for the Mac. Reason will now randomize your original pattern and also add in new Redrum channels. Notice that the dynamics will also randomize, giving you a very different pattern that can be used as a fill.

4.   You can repeat the randomization as many times as you like in order to find the pattern that you like best.

Upon closer inspection of the Edit pull-down menu, you will see many other pattern alterations you can perform on your patterns, so let's take a moment to discuss their functions.

►   **Shift Pattern Left**—This will shift all of the active Redrum channels one step to the left. In Figure 7.45, you can see the kick drum pattern before and after selecting this option. Notice how the kick on step 1 shifted all of the way to step 16, as it had no space to move on the left.

►   **Shift Pattern Right**—This shifts the pattern one step to the right.

►   **Shift Drum Left**—This will shift an individual Redrum channel's sequence one step to the left. In Figure 7.46, I have selected and edited the hi-hat channel.

▶ **Shift Drum Right**—This shifts one channel's sequence one step to the right.

▶ **Randomize Pattern**—As you read in the previous section, this will randomly generate an entirely new pattern by adding new sounds and dynamics.

▶ **Randomize Drum**—This will randomize an individual Redrum channel while still adding new dynamics.

▶ **Alter Pattern**—This function will alternate the active pattern entirely without adding any new sounds or dynamics. If the Randomize Pattern effect is a little too much for your song, this is a good alternative.

▶ **Alter Drum**—This function performs the same task as Alter Pattern, but will alter a single Redrum channel.

Figure 7.45
Selecting Shift Pattern Left will move the entire pattern one step to the left.

Figure 7.46
Selecting Shift Drum Left
will move just the active
Redrum channel
sequence one step to the
left.

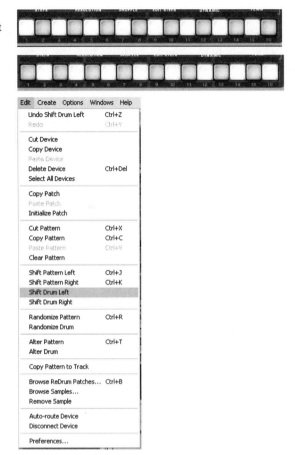

Using Dynamics to Alter Velocities

After creating a few patterns, you can now begin to alter the actual sound and timbre of the
Redrum channels themselves by working with the dynamics and individual velocities.

For this example, let's start with the kick drum and create a dynamic pattern that will modify the
tone of the kick drum as the pattern plays. Make sure that you have selected Pattern 3 so you have
a clean slate to start with.

1. Select Redrum channel 1, which is the kick drum. Set your dynamic to Soft and
    write an 8th note pattern on steps 1, 3, 5, 7, 9, 11, 13, and 15. Click on the Run
    button to hear the pattern.

2. Switch the dynamic to Medium and click on steps 3, 7, 11, and 15 to alter their
    dynamics.

3. Switch the dynamic to Hard and click on steps 5 and 13 to alter their dynamics.
    You should now have a kick pattern that has a very distinctive loud and soft
    characteristic to it.

4. Locate the Level and Velocity knobs on channel 1 strip. Leave the Level knob alone, but try different values for the Velocity to hear the enhancements that it produces.

5. Now locate the Tone and Velocity knobs on channel 1. Set the Tone knob to –42, which will make the kick drum sound very "lo-fi" and muddy. Now set the Velocity to a positive value, such as 45. You will hear the immediate change in the tone of the kick drum. Listen to how the tone of the kick alters with the change in dynamics.

In the next example, you'll have a go with the Start and Velocity knobs on channel 3.

1. Select channel 3, which is a snare drum sample. Set your dynamic to Soft and write a 16th note pattern on steps 3, 4, 5, 7, 8, 9, 11, 12, 13, 15, and 16. Click on the Run button to listen to the pattern.

2. Switch the dynamic to Medium and click on steps 4, 8, 12, and 15 to alter their velocities.

3. Switch the dynamics to Hard and click on steps 5, 9, and 13 to alter their velocities. You should now hear a very driving snare drum pattern.

4. Locate the Start and Velocity knobs at the bottom of channel 3. Adjust the Start knob to a value of 38. To really hear this effect, select the Solo button at the top of channel 3. Listen to the effect and notice how soft it sounds, as the starting point of the sample has been altered.

5. Now, adjust the Velocity knob to a value of -20. The snare drum line now sounds much more realistic; the snare sample is reacting in much the same way as a real snare drum would.

6. Click on the Solo button again, so you can hear both the snare and kick playing together. For added effect, you might also activate the Shuffle to swing it a little bit.

In this last example, you'll use the low tom channel and create a pitch bend effect by using a combination of dynamics and velocities.

1. Select channel 7, which is the low tom sample. Set your dynamic to Soft and write a quick 16th note pattern on steps 3, 4, 11, 12, and 16. Click on the Run button to listen to it.

2. Switch the dynamic to Medium and click on step 16 to alter its dynamic.

3. Switch the dynamic to Hard and click on steps 4 and 12 to alter their dynamics.

4. Locate the Pitch knob for channel 7 and set it to a negative value of 24. Set the Bend knob to a maximum positive value of 55. Listen to the sequence and notice how there is now a slight pitch bend effect on the tom as it plays.

5. Locate the Rate knob and set it to a positive value of 88. Set the velocity to a positive value of 28.

6. Now listen to the tom sample and notice how it changes pitch according to the dynamics and velocity.

You've come a long way in this section—from a simple four beat pattern, to an all out cacophony of drumming thunder.

Using Redrum with the Reason Sequencer

After you have completed your rhythmic bits and pieces in Redrum, you need to use the Reason sequencer to string your patterns together in order to create a full composition. There are a couple of ways to do this.

▶ You can program an automation to switch between patterns in a song.

▶ You can copy the patterns into the Reason sequencer for further editing.

Let's take a closer look at each of these.

Shifting Between Patterns with Automation

Automating the patterns of the Redrum sequencer is probably the quickest way to compose your overall song structure and it is surprisingly quick and easy to do.

In this next tutorial, you will need to have at least two or three patterns already programmed into the Redrum programmer, because you will be shifting between them during your automation recording.

1. Make sure the Redrum track in the Reason sequencer is armed to receive MIDI data, as shown in Figure 7.47. Also make sure that the Enable Pattern Section option of the Redrum programmer is activated and ready to go, and that Pattern 1 is selected in the Redrum sequencer.

2. Click on Record in the Reason sequencer. This will place the sequencer into Record Ready mode.

3. Click on Play. Both the Reason and Redrum sequencers should start playing. Because you previously selected Pattern 1 in the Redrum programmer, this is what you should be hearing.

4. Let Pattern 1 play for a measure or two, and then get ready to shift patterns by just clicking on Pattern 2. As soon as the next measure starts to record in the Reason sequencer, you should hear Pattern 2 playing. Be sure to notice the automation that has been recorded on the Redrum track in the Reason sequencer (see Figure 7.48).

5. Now switch to Pattern 3. It should start playing as the new measure starts in the Reason sequencer.

6. Click on Stop. Notice that there is now a neon green box around the Pattern section of the Redrum programmer (see Figure 7.49). This means that automation has now been written within this section.

Figure 7.47
Make sure your Redrum track is ready to receive MIDI.

Figure 7.48
The Reason sequencer displays automation data as it is being recorded.

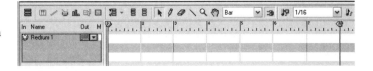

Figure 7.49
When you are finished recording your automation, a neon green box will appear around the parameter that has been automated.

7. Click on Stop again to return to the first measure of the Reason sequencer. Click on Play to listen to the Redrum pattern playback. Notice that the patterns are changing on their own, as they have been automated.

CLEARING YOUR AUTOMATION

After listening to your recording, you might find that you don't like the way the patterns came together, so you will probably want to redo your recording. Chapter 15, "Automation," covers automation extensively, but for now here is a quick tip on resetting the automation.

Find any parameters that have an automation written in by looking for the neon green box around it. Right-click on the parameter (or Control-click on the Mac). At this point, a menu will appear and you should see an option to Clear Automation. Choose this option, and the automation will be erased from that parameter.

Copying Patterns to the Reason Sequencer

After programming your patterns into Redrum, you might decide that you want to rework them with a bit more precision than a step-programmed sequencer allows. This is where the Reason sequencer comes in handy.

1. Select the Redrum pattern that you want to copy to the Reason sequencer.
2. Set the left and right locators in the sequencer to where you want the pattern to start and stop. For example, set the left locator to measure one and the right locator to measure two and the Redrum patterns will be copied in between.
3. Click once on the Redrum interface to select it.
4. Choose Edit > Copy Pattern to Track.
5. You should see the MIDI events for the Redrum pattern you selected in the sequencer.
6. Click on Play. You should now hear the pattern play back from the Reason sequencer.
7. If you want to copy more patterns to the Reason sequencer, you must reset the left and right locators to the starting and end points that you want.

TURN IT OFF

After you have copied your patterns to the Reason sequencer, make sure that you deactivate the Enable Pattern Section button in the Redrum programmer. If you forget to do this and click on Play, both sequencers will begin to play again, but this time, Redrum will be playing the notes in its own sequencer as well as what it is receiving from the Reason sequencer. This will produce a very strange *flange* effect that doesn't sound very good and will most certainly cause the Audio Out Clipping LED in the Reason Transport Panel to glow a bright red, which is not a good thing.

After you have copied your tracks to the Reason sequencer, you should click on the Switch to Edit Mode button in the Reason sequencer to see how Redrum information is displayed.

As shown in Figure 7.50, the MIDI events for Redrum look a little different from the standard Edit mode that you might remember from Chapter 5. Each drum sound has its own lane that can be edited in various ways. For example, you can now draw and erase notes, or you can re-quantize the whole sequence to create an entirely new groove.

Figure 7.50
Redrum MIDI events as displayed in the Reason sequencer.

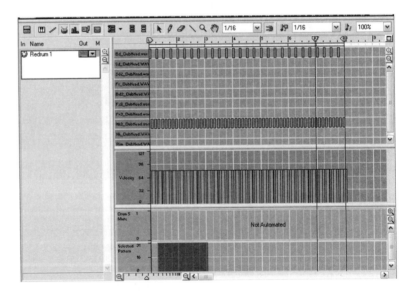

You can now have access to different controllers and edit automated parameters with more accuracy and precision. The possibilities are virtually endless.

8

Dr:rex—Close Up

One of the most unique devices in the Reason Device Rack is the Dr:rex Loop Player (see Figure 8.1). Dr:rex is a RAM-based sample playback device based on the ReCycle! technology created by Propellerhead Software. Dr:rex can import specially prepared digital audio loops, called REX files, and play them back at just about any tempo.

▶ **.rex**—A mono file format supported by the Mac platform.

▶ **.rcy**—A mono file format supported by the PC platform.

▶ **.rex2**—A *stereo* file format supported by both Mac and PC platforms.

A New Reason to ReCycle!

Propellerhead Software began to make its mark in the audio industry in 1996 by releasing a sample-editing software product called ReCycle! This program gave musicians the ability to import digital audio loops into their computers, slice them up, and then send these individual slices back to the sampler (see Figure 8.2). This gave musicians the ability to use an audio loop within varying tempos while not affecting the pitch. It was a real breakthrough, because musicians could now use the same loops in different songs and styles and keep it all in the original pitch and tempo.

And just when musicians were starting to comprehend the concepts and possibilities that ReCycle! had to offer, Propellerhead again broke new ground in 1997 by introducing its own digital audio format, called REX. A REX file is a single audio file that contains a number of smaller separate audio files, or slices. The REX file could then be imported into a digital audio/MIDI sequencing program, and the audio loop would instantly work at any tempo. Not only this, but if you were to change the tempo of your song, the REX files would instantly speed up or slow down to match that new tempo. It was just like the original concept of ReCycle!, but without the need for an external sampler.

Figure 8.1
The Dr:rex Loop Player is based on Propellerhead's REX technology.

Figure 8.2
ReCycle! will breathe
new life into your audio
loops.

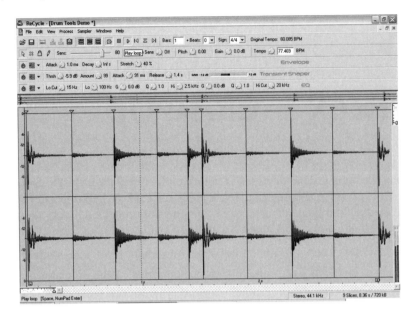

REX files could be created within ReCycle! and became an adopted format for many digital audio programs such as Cubase VST and Logic Audio. Since the introduction of the REX format, many companies have begun releasing new REX format titles and re-issuing older audio loop titles as well. At the time of this writing, there are literally thousands of audio loops available in the REX format.

ROLL YER OWN

In Appendix B, "ReCycle! 2.0," you can learn how to create your own REX files from an audio loop.

In 2000, when Reason 1.0 was announced, it seemed only right that Propellerhead would incorporate its REX technology into this program, because it's all about remixing and loops. With that, I give you the subject of this chapter, Dr:rex!

A Guided Tour of Dr:rex

Now that you have a basic idea of what Dr:rex is and the technology behind it, let's begin your tour of the Dr:rex interface.

Getting Sound into Dr:rex

In the upper-left corner of the Dr:rex interface is its file browser (see Figure 8.3). If you have not loaded a REX file yet, the Patch Browser display will be empty, so you'll want to start by clicking on the folder icon (see Figure 8.4). Either way, this will bring up the Patch Browser, so you can begin to audition and load sounds (see Figure 8.5).

Figure 8.3
Dr:rex's file browser is
used to load REX loops
into Dr:rex.

Figure 8.4
The folder icon.

Figure 8.5
The Patch Browser
window.

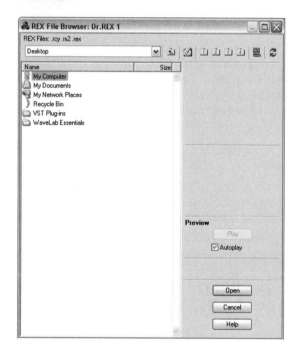

When the browser opens, you might not see any sound files to audition. If this is the case, click on the Find All ReFills button, located in the upper-right corner of the browser (see Figure 8.6). This will give you a list of all ReFill files on your computer. Double-click on the Reason Factory Sound Bank, and then double-click on the Dr:Rex Drum Loops folder or the Music Loops folder. From either of these folders, you can select a REX file to import into your Dr:rex device. For example, I have opted to go with the Dub style drum loop, which sounds like reggae. Also, notice that the Autoplay option is selected in the lower-right corner of the Patch Browser window. This lets you audition the loop before you bring it in by clicking the Open button, which in turn saves a lot of time.

THE AUDITION TEMPO
The auditioning feature plays loops at their assigned natural tempos, not at the tempo your Reason song is set to. This might change in future updates of the program.

Figure 8.6
After clicking the Find
All ReFills button,
Reason will display a list
of all available ReFills on
your computer.

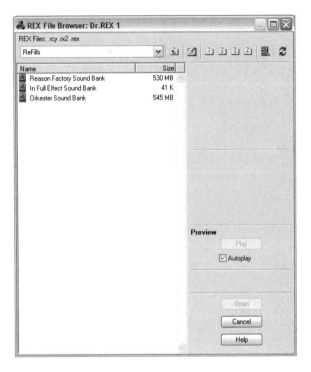

Once you have selected your loop, click the Patch Browser's Open button or just double-click
the file to load it into Dr:rex (see Figure 8.7). Notice also that the name of the REX file is now
displayed in the Dr:rex waveform display.

Once a REX file is imported into Dr:rex, the slices that make up the REX file are mapped out over
the C1 octave of your keyboard. This enables you to preview each slice of a loaded REX file by
arming the sequencer track and playing any keys within the C1 octave of your keyboard (C1, C#1,
D1, D#1, E, and so on).

Figure 8.7
The REX file has now
been loaded into Dr:rex.

Audio Quality in Dr:rex

Just below the browser window are two parameters that affect the quality of your loops (see Figure 8.8).

Figure 8.8
These controls affect the audio quality of Dr:rex.

▶ **HIGH QUALITY INTERPOLATION**—When activated, Dr:rex plays the REX file back with a more advanced interpolation algorithm, resulting in a higher-quality audio signal. The difference is most noticeable in loops containing a lot of high-frequency data, such as a hi-hat track.

▶ **LO BW**—This stands for low bandwidth, and it removes some of the high end from the playback of a REX file in order to relieve the burden on your CPU. The difference is very evident in loops with a lot of hi-hat or Latin percussion. If, on the other hand, your loops are mostly low-frequency data, or if they've been put through a Low Pass filter, you'll be less likely to hear the difference.

Polyphony

To the left of the interpolation control is the Polyphony parameter (see Figure 8.9), which determines the number of REX slices your MIDI keyboard can play simultaneously. Dr:rex contains a large polyphony potential that ranges from 1 to 99. You can change the polyphony by clicking on the increase/decrease controls to the right of the display or by clicking and dragging within the display itself.

Figure 8.9
The Polyphony control assigns the number of voices that can be played simultaneously.

Adjusting the polyphony allows for some very interesting loop-editing possibilities. Because each slice in a REX file is assigned to a key on your MIDI keyboard, you can re-sequence loops using the REX Lane Editor in the Reason sequencer. This will give you a chance to reinterpret the loop by introducing a new groove and feel that includes playing different voices simultaneously. You'll learn more about this later.

The Synth Parameters

In the middle of the Dr:rex interface is the main display, where REX loops can be edited with ease. Here you can accomplish everything from transposition to pitching and panning each slice within a loaded REX file.

Just to review, a REX file contains a number of different slices of audio, which are compiled and seen as one file. The sliced nature of the REX files makes them ideal for easy editing.

The Waveform Display

In the Dr:rex waveform display (see Figure 8.10), you can see the REX file split in a slice-by-slice view along with the original tempo of the loop. Below the waveform and to the left, Dr:rex displays the default pitch of the REX file. The default pitch for any REX file loaded into Dr:rex is C. Every aspect of the REX file can be edited, though, with the help of the parameter knobs above and below the waveform display. Let's take a look at them.

Located just above the waveform display are a few of Dr:rex's play parameters (see Figure 8.11).

▶ **Select Slice Via MIDI**—This button allows you to select each REX slice with a MIDI controller, such as a keyboard or drum machine. If you activate this button and click on play, you'll see the slice selector move across the loop from left to right in accordance to the MIDI note that is being played. Above this is the Note On indicator light, which will let you know when Dr:rex receives any kind of MIDI signal, whether from a controller or a keyboard.

▶ **Preview**—The Preview button will allow you to listen to the REX file before you send it to the sequencer track. While previewing your REX file, you can make all of the real-time changes that you want, such as transposing, pitching, panning, and filtering slices.

▶ **To Track**—After using the Preview to listen and edit the REX file, To Track sends the MIDI notes that are assigned to each slice to its sequencer track. If you select the Dr:rex sequencer track and click on the Switch to Edit Mode button, you will see each of these MIDI notes displayed in the REX Lane Editor.

▶ **Osc Pitch**—The Oscillator section can adjust the overall pitch of the REX as well as assign a selected amount to the Dr:rex Filter Envelope. The OCT knob will transpose the entire REX file up or down an octave at a time. As with the Pitch knob, the OCT knob has an eight-octave range. The Fine knob will adjust the overall pitch of the REX file in cents, which are hundredths of a semitone. With a range of +/– 50 cents, this is for making extremely minor adjustments to the overall pitch. The Env Amount knob is used to assign a determined amount of the Dr: rex oscillator over to the Filter Envelope. This will produce a pitch shifting effect based on the amount of filter applied to the oscillator.

Figure 8.10
The Dr:rex waveform display shows a graphic representation of the loaded REX file.

Figure 8.11
These play parameters are used to preview your REX file and alter its pitch.

Below the waveform display, you'll find the following parameters to edit the REX file (see Figure 8.12).

Figure 8.12
Below the waveform display are the available parameters to alter the entire REX file and individual slices of the REX file.

▶ **Transpose**—This knob will move the center key of the loop down or up by half step increments, also called *semitones*. By clicking and dragging the mouse up or down, you can move the center key up or down. Because this is a real-time process, you can do this while the loop is playing and hear the effect immediately.

▶ **Slice**—This knob allows you to select each slice in the waveform view, by clicking and dragging the mouse up or down.

▶ **Pitch**—The pitch knob transposes each slice within a REX file. Each slice can be adjusted either up or down, giving you a possible pitch range of eight octaves. This is great for creating some interesting rhythmic ideas or mapping the pitches in a chromatic effect. I'll cover some neat uses for this later in the chapter.

▶ **Pan**—The pan knob adjusts the stereo position for any slice within the REX file. For example, you can set slice number one to –64 or hard left, while setting slice number three to 63 or hard right. This can create a very cool stereophonic effect, especially when you combine it with the pitch knob.

▶ **Level**—This knob changes the volume of an individual slice in a REX file. By default, each slice is set to 100, which is moderately loud. This allows for some very interesting dynamic changes that can affect the overall feel of the REX file when used creatively.

▶ **Decay**—The Decay knob adjusts the length of each slice in a REX file. By default, each slice is set to 127, which is the maximum length. When adjusted, each slice can be shortened to create a "gate" effect of sorts.

The Filter Section

To the right of the waveform display lies Dr:rex's Filter section (see Figure 8.13). By shaping the overall tone of the REX file, you can generate incredible filter sweeps that hurt the ears and shatter speakers. The filter can then be modified with an envelope and finally be assigned to the

Figure 8.13
The Dr:rex Filter section is used to shape the character of the REX file.

CHAPTER 8

Modulation Wheel for dynamic control. Do I sound excited or what? But I am getting too far ahead of myself, so let's have a look at the filter.

Whenever a Dr:rex is loaded into the Reason Device Rack, the filter is already activated. It can be turned off and on by simply clicking on the Filter power button located at the top of the Filter section.

Once the filter is activated, you can select one of five filter modes by either clicking on the individual names or simply clicking on the Mode button:

> ▶ **Notch**—This filter can be thought of as the opposite of a Band Pass filter. It will reject the mid-frequencies while allowing the high frequencies and low frequencies to pass through. Although not the most dramatic filter effect, it still has a place in the mix for making minor changes to a sample.

> ▶ **HP 12**—This will filter out the low frequencies while letting the high frequencies pass through. It has a roll off curve of 12 decibels per octave.

> ▶ **BP 12**—This filters out both the high and low frequencies, leaving the mid frequencies alone to be toyed with. With a roll off curve of 12 decibels per octave, the BP 12 can be used effectively on instrument loops such as a guitar loop or possibly hi-hat heavy percussion loops.

> ▶ **LP 12**—This filter is similar to the 24dB low pass, but the roll off curve is not as strong, because it has a range of 12 decibels per octave. This makes the LP 12 a perfect solution for creating a filter sweep that is low but not low enough to blow up your speakers.

> ▶ **LP 24**—This filter allows low frequencies to pass through, whereas high frequencies are filtered out. To top it off, this low pass filter has an intense roll off curve (approximately 24 decibels per octave), which produces a greater emphasis on the low frequencies.

A filter typically has two controls: *cutoff frequency* and *resonance*. The cutoff frequency (or filter frequency or cutoff filter as it is also called) is used to specify where the filter will function within the frequency spectrum. It is a popular parameter used to create the "sweeping" effect that we hear so often in electronic music. When the frequency is used to alter a filter, it opens and closes the filter within a specific frequency range. For example, if the cutoff frequency is set to the highest position possible and is in LP 12 mode, the entire frequency spectrum will pass through. Likewise, if the cutoff is set to a lower position and the cutoff frequency is set in the LP 12 mode, say between the middle and bottom, the resulting sound will contain a majority of low end signal, because only the lower end of the frequency spectrum can pass through.

Resonance on the other hand is a parameter that modifies the filter's sound. It is used to emphasize different frequencies around the cutoff slider. When used within different positions, the resonance slider can filter out different frequencies or create fantastic "bell tones." For example, if the cutoff slider is set to the maximum potential and the resonance is set to the minimum potential, the resulting sound will be extremely treble heavy with minimal bass. However, if the resonance slider is in the middle position, the bass will be filtered out even more. If the resonance is set to its highest potential while the cutoff is set to its lowest potential and the filter is in LP 12 mode, the resulting signal will be extremely bass heavy. As the cutoff filter moves up, the bass frequencies will be dynamically enhanced by the resonance and the resulting sound will have the neighbors pounding at your door immediately afterward.

WATCH YOUR LEVELS

As I have stated, make sure to keep an eye on the Audio Out Clipping LED, at the bottom left of the Transport Panel, especially when you start fiddling with the filters found on just about every synth and sound module in Reason. Not only can you distort your signal, but you also run the risk of damaging your speakers and, more importantly, your ears.

To the right of the Filter modes is the Filter Envelope (see Figure 8.14). An envelope is used to modify specific synth parameters, including pitch, volume, and filter frequencies. By using an envelope creatively, you can control how these parameters are modified over a specific amount of time. But before you get ahead of yourself, take a look at the essential controls of the Filter Envelope.

Figure 8.14
The Dr:rex Filter Envelope affects the overall impact of the filter.

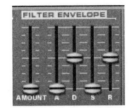

- ▶ **Amount**—This slider assigns a specific amount of the filter section to the envelope. By default, the Amount slider is set to 0 and will not produce any noticeable changes as it is moved up and down. This will change drastically if adjustments are first made to the Filter section itself.

- ▶ **Attack**—When a sound's envelope is triggered, the Attack parameter determines the length of time before the envelope reaches its maximum value.

- ▶ **Decay**—Once the maximum value is reached, the Decay parameter determines the length of time until the value begins to drop.

- ▶ **Sustain**—After the value begins to drop, the Sustain determines the level at which the falling value rests.

- ▶ **Release**—Once the value has been set at its rested value, the Release parameter determines how long it will take for the value to fade to 0 after the key has been released, or in this case, after audio has passed through the filter.

A FILTER EXERCISE

The following is a filter exercise that should start a few ideas brewing. Before you begin, start a new Reason song, and create an instance of reMix and Dr:rex.

1.   Load a REX loop with a lot of kick drum in it. For example, choose something from the House folder. After loading the REX loop into Dr:rex, click on the Preview button so you can listen and edit at the same time.

2.   Select the LP 12 Filter mode and adjust the Frequency Filter slider to a numeric value of 25 and the Resonance to about 75. This should produce a very low end, bass-heavy sound.

3.   Raise the Filter Envelope's Amount slider to about 50. This should start to change the timbre of the sound immediately.

4.   Now, try working with a different combination of Filter Envelope parameters. For example, to create a percussive loop, have the Attack, Decay, and Release set to 0. Then move the Sustain slider up and down until you reach a desired effect. Click on the Preview button to stop playing the loop.

5.   To make this loop appear in the Reason sequencer, click on the To Track button. The corresponding MIDI notes should appear in the Dr:rex track. Click on Play in the Reason sequencer to hear your loop.

The LFO (Low Frequency Oscillator)

Directly beneath Dr:rex's filter you will find the LFO, or Low Frequency Oscillator (see Figure 8.15).

Figure 8.15
The Dr:rex Low Frequency Oscillator can be used to alter different Dr:rex parameters.

▶   An LFO is capable of generating waveforms with a low frequency, hence the name LFO.

▶   An LFO's purpose is to modulate a parameter, such as a filter or another oscillator. That means that the LFO itself is never actually heard, just its effect on other synth parameters.

In order to hear the effect of the LFO, you must first adjust the Amount knob, located to the right of the Rate knob. Once this parameter is turned up, you can start to explore the other functions of the LFO.

Keeping It in Sync

No "boy band" jokes, please. The LFO has the capability to modify the main oscillator in either free time or synchronized time that is determined by the master tempo of the Transport Control. To activate the synchronization, click on the Sync button, located directly above the waveform selector (see Figure 8.16). This will sync the Dr:rex LFO with the Reason master tempo. At this point, you can follow this up by assigning both a waveform shape and a destination to the LFO.

Figure 8.16
Activating the Sync option will synchronize the LFO with the tempo of your Reason song. As shown here, when the Sync button is activated, the Rate knob adjusts the rate of the LFO in note values.

Waveforms—Take Your Pick

There are six types of waveforms that can be applied to your LFO. They can be selected by clicking on them with the mouse or by using the WAVEF. button at the bottom of the waveform list.

Let's discuss the differences between these individual waveforms.

▶ **Triangle**—Creates a smooth up and down vibrato.

▶ **Inverted Sawtooth**—Creates a cycled ramp up effect.

▶ **Sawtooth**—Creates a cycled ramp down effect.

▶ **Square**—Makes abrupt changes between two values.

▶ **Random**—Creates a random stepped modulation. Also known as sample and hold.

▶ **Soft Random**—Exactly as the previous waveform but with a smoother modulation curve.

Destination, Anywhere

Once a LFO waveform and rate/amount has been selected, it is now time to choose which parameter will be modulated by the LFO. LFO modulation can be applied to three destinations. Again, you can either click directly on each one or cycle through them by clicking the DEST button.

▶ **Osc** will send the LFO modulation effect to the overall pitch of the REX loop. Depending on which waveform is selected and how much LFO is assigned to the oscillator, it can produce a very neat "up and down" effect.

▶ **Filter** will send the LFO modulation to the filter section of Dr:rex. This can produce a tempo-based filter sweep effect if the Sync button is activated.

▶ **Pan** sends the LFO modulation to the pan controls of Dr:rex. When synced, this will create a tempo-based stereophonic effect.

The Amp Envelope

It takes two basic actions to create an audible sound—the generation of the sound and its amplification. This chapter has spent a great deal of time focusing on the generation of sound in Dr:rex. The amplification aspect is covered by Dr:rex's Amp Envelope feature (see Figure 8.17).

Figure 8.17
The Dr:rex Amp
Envelope is used to affect
the overall amplitude of
Dr:rex.

▶ **Level**—This slider controls the volume of Dr:rex.

▶ **Attack**—When a sound's envelope is triggered, the Attack parameter determines the length of time before the envelope reaches its maximum value.

▶ **Decay**—Once the maximum value is reached, the Decay parameter determines the length of time until the value begins to drop.

▶ **Sustain**—After the value begins to drop, the Sustain parameter determines the level the falling value rests at.

▶ **Release**—Once the value has been set at its rested value, the Release parameter determines how long it will take the value to fade out after releasing the key.

The Velocity Section

The Velocity section (see Figure 8.18) allows you to assign certain filter and amplification parameters to be modified according to the velocity at which each note (or slice) is played at. Remember, the term *velocity* refers to how hard the note is played on your keyboard. Whether you play it hard or soft, these assignable parameters will respond according to their settings.

If you are not using a controller keyboard, you can draw the velocity data in via the Reason sequencer.

Figure 8.18
Different Dr:rex
parameters can be
modified by velocity.

▶ **F.Env**—When set to a positive value, different velocities will control the Amount knob of the Filter Envelope. A negative value will have the opposite effect.

▶ **F.Decay**—When set to a positive value, different velocities will control the Decay parameter of the Filter Envelope. A negative value will have the opposite effect.

▶ **Amp**—When set to a positive value, the velocity will control the amount of volume. A negative value will have the opposite effect.

Pitch and Modulation

The Pitch and Modulation controls are located on the left side of the Dr:rex interface (see Figure 8.19).

Figure 8.19
Pitch and Modulation controls are just what any good synth needs.

Get It in Pitch

The Dr:rex pitch control is similar to pitch controls on hardware synths—it bends the pitch of the whole loop up or down. The range of the pitch bend is controlled by the Range parameters just above the Bend wheel (see Figure 8.20). You can click on the up and down buttons, or just click and drag in the dialog box itself to change the range. For kicks, try selecting 24, which is the equivalent of 24 semitones, or two octaves. Now click on the Preview button. While the file is playing, use a keyboard controller with a pitch shifting wheel or just click and drag up or down on the Bend wheel to hear the pitch shifting at work.

Figure 8.20
Use the Range controls to assign the amount of pitch bend to your REX files.

Modulation

To me, modulation is the "secret sauce" or essential ingredient in any form of artistic electronic music. It can be used to effectively change the timbre of a signal. The common Modulation Wheel found on most typical synthesizers can be assigned to a number of different synth parameters. When assigned, the Modulation Wheel then makes modifications in real time to the played note according to the selected parameter and its assigned value.

To the right of the Modulation Wheel are three parameters that can be assigned to it (see Figure 8.21).

Figure 8.21
Assign different parameters to your Modulation Wheel.

▶ **F.Freq** is assigned to the cutoff filter of the Dr:rex filter section. When a value is assigned to this knob, the cutoff filter's value will either decrease or increase as the Modulation Wheel is used.

▶ **F.Res** is assigned to the resonance control of the filter section. Depending on where it is set, the resonance control will either increase or decrease while the Modulation Wheel is in use.

▶ **F.Decay** is assigned to decay slider of the Filter Envelope. Depending on where it is set, the envelope decay will increase or decrease.

The whole point of electronic music is to experiment and deviate from the norm. The Modulation Wheel is a useful tool for accomplishing that goal.

MAKE IT PUNCHY!

Here's a quick DIY tutorial on using the Modulation Wheel with the three parameters. Before beginning this exercise, start a new Reason song and create instances of reMix and Dr:rex. Finish off by loading a REX file into Dr:rex.

1. In the Filter section, activate the filter. By default, the filter mode should be set to LP 12 mode, which is fine for this exercise. Now set the Filter Frequency slider to about 25 and set the Resonance slider to 75.

2. Click on the Preview button to hear your REX file in action with the active filter.

3. In the Filter Envelope, set the amount slider to 100%. Then set the Attack, Decay, Sustain, and Release to 0.

4. In the Modulation Wheel section, set the F.FREQ knob to 32, the F.RES knob to −32, and the F.DECAY to −64.

5. Now use the Modulation Wheel with your mouse or MIDI keyboard and notice how the filter opens up as it is activated. Also notice how the decay amount increases.

Creative Uses for Dr:rex with the Reason Sequencer

The key to enjoying a long, creative, and fruitful future with Dr:rex and Reason is to try different combinations and ideas. Remember, anything can be routed into anything within Reason. This section goes through a few tips and tricks to fire up the synapses and get the creative juices flowing.

Before you begin these exercises, make sure that you start a new Reason song and create instances of reMix and Dr:rex. Finish preparing yourself by locating a new REX file from the Reason Factory Sound Bank and loading it into Dr:rex.

Cut It Out!

Although many folks like a good predictable four-on-the-floor beat in dance music, it is a good idea to introduce some variations from time to time. One of those variations includes the deletion of different slices from a REX file in order to give it an entirely different feel.

Recall that a REX file contains two file formats in order to do its magic. The first format is a digital audio format, which you see in the waveform view of Dr:rex as a series of slices. The other format is the corresponding MIDI notes that accompany each digital audio slice. When you click on the To Track button on the Dr:rex interface, it copies the MIDI notes to its track on the sequencer. Once the MIDI tracks have been recorded, you can simply open the appropriate editor in the sequencer and remove a few of the MIDI notes, so that the corresponding audio slices will not play back.

Start by clicking on the Switch to Edit Mode button on the Reason sequencer. Because this is a Dr:rex track, the sequencer will automatically know which editor to open, in this case the REX Lane Editor. At this point, you should see all of the MIDI notes lined up in zipper fashion (see Figure 8.22), as they move upward diagonally from left to right. To the far left of the notes is a list of numeric names for each slice. Depending on the length of the loop, there can be up to 92 slices displayed here. Navigate your mouse to Slice 1 of the Slice List and notice that the Selector tool has now become a Speaker tool, which enables you to preview a slice by clicking on the slice name. You can also click and hold on the name of any slice in the list and drag your mouse up and down to preview the slices one by one.

At this point, listen to each slice and decide which sound you want to remove from your loop. For example, you will probably want to keep the kick drum in order to keep a steady beat, but you can remove the snare or hi-hat sounds. Locate each of the sounds that you want to remove, and then highlight them. Click Delete to get rid of them or use the Eraser tool. You can also highlight each note and use the Cut key command.

When you're finished, play the loop and see how you like the results. Getting a sound you like might take a lot of experimenting. Remember, you can always go back to the original loop by using the To Track button in Dr:rex, or by using the unlimited levels of Undo.

Figure 8.22
The REX Lane Editor is the default editor used to modify the sequence of REX files.

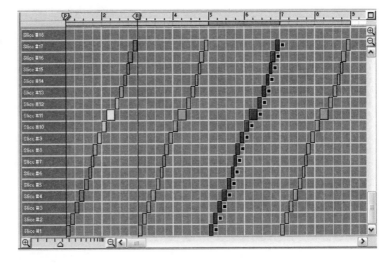

Write Your Own Grooves

Aside from erasing MIDI notes, you can also rewrite your REX file groove in a couple of ways.

▶ Draw in a new sequence using the slices

▶ Use a MIDI controller to record a new sequence

By using the Pencil tool, you can redraw the MIDI notes that are connected to the different slices in your Dr:rex module. It's easier than it sounds, but it will take a little practice.

Before you begin this exercise, start a new Reason song and load instances of reMix and Dr:rex. Load a new REX file into Dr:rex and click on the To Track button to send the MIDI notes of the REX file to the Reason sequencer. Then click on the Switch to Edit Mode button. You should now see the REX Lane Editor.

Select the Pencil tool from the toolbar and find the sounds that you want to draw notes for. Choose Edit > Select All to highlight each MIDI note in the editor. Now press the Delete key to erase all of the notes. As you can see in Figure 8.23, you have a clean palette to work with.

Next, create a two-bar loop, so that you can work quickly. In the Transport Panel, set your left locator to bar one and the right locator to bar three. Make sure that the loop function is on by clicking on the Loop On/Off button in the Transport Panel. Click on the Stop button twice in the Transport Panel to send the Position Indicator back to the beginning of the sequence. Click on Play. You should now have a two-bar template to work with.

Next, choose the note value that you want to draw in. Because this is probably your first time doing this, I suggest using something simple like an 8th note. To do this, just select it from the Snap pull-down menu of the Sequencer toolbar (see Figure 8.24). Select the Pencil tool and you can now begin to draw in your MIDI notes.

Figure 8.23
Erase all of your notes and start with a clean slate.

 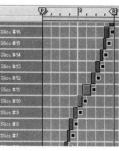 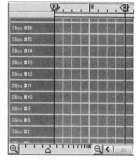

Figure 8.24
Select your note value using the Snap pull-down menu.

Start with Slice #1 and draw in an 8th note on each downbeat of bar one (1, 2, 3, and 4) (see Figure 8.25). Click on Play. You should now hear the first slice play four times. Now choose a few more slices and draw them in. As you can see in Figure 8.26, I have made a very simple yet effective rhythm with just four slices. Try it on your own with different note values and you are on your way to a groove.

Figure 8.25
Using Slice #1, draw in a few 8th notes.

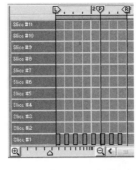

Figure 8.26
Draw in more note slices to create your new REX groove.

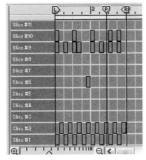

OLD SCHOOL STYLE

If you've sequenced in other programs, you might be accustomed to seeing a Key edit window that looks more like Figure 8.27. As you learned in Chapter 5, "The Reason Sequencer—Close Up," Reason also has a Key edit window, called the *Key lane*. You can draw your new REX grooves in using either the REX Lane Editor or the Key Editor, by selecting them in the upper-left corner of the sequencer (see Figure 8.28).

Figure 8.27
Any kind of recorded event can be viewed in any of Reason's editors. In this case, the REX slices are viewed in Key editor.

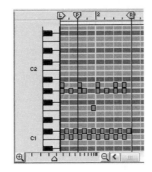

CHAPTER 8

Figure 8.28
Select the editor you
want to work in. The left
button is the Key editor
and the button on the
right is the REX editor.

You can also input data into the Reason sequencer live, as covered in Chapter 5. Just make sure
that your Dr:rex track is activated and ready to accept live MIDI data. You do so by clicking on the
MIDI In section of the track (see Figure 8.29). Using your MIDI keyboard, you can now play your
Dr:rex in much the same way that you would play a drum machine with a MIDI keyboard. Any
REX file loaded into Dr:rex is mapped across a MIDI keyboard starting with C1 on your keyboard,
because this is Slice #1 in Dr:rex.

Just click on Record followed by Play. You can record a new performance of the REX file.

Figure 8.29
Arm your Dr:rex
sequencer track so you
can input MIDI data.

Drawing in Automation

The last trick in the bag is to draw in some automation for the individual controls of Dr:rex, which
is done using the Controller Lane Editor. As shown in Figure 8.30, you can use the Pencil tool to
draw in an automation movement for any controller found on the Dr:rex interface. This example
shows how to draw in some Modulation Wheel data with the Controller lane.

To select the Controller lane, click on the blue envelope button in the Editor toolbar (see Figure
8.31). Hide the other editors by clicking on their buttons in the Editor toolbar.

Because you're going to draw in some Modulation Wheel data, you'll start by bringing that
controller to the forefront. To do this, click on the Controller's pull-down menu and choose the
Mod Wheel controller. This lane will then appear in the Controller Editor (see Figure 8.32).

Because this is a controller that will require a lot of data in order to create a realistic effect, it is a
good idea to turn off the Snap To Grid function (see Figure 8.33).

Figure 8.30
Reason's Controller Lane
Editor is used for
drawing and editing
automation data.

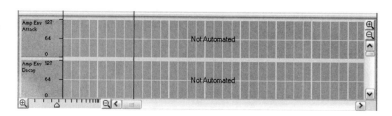

Figure 8.31
The Controller toolbar is
used to activate the
Controller Lane.

Figure 8.32
Select the Modulation
controller to draw in an
automation movement.

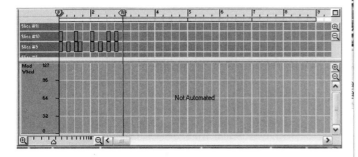

Figure 8.33
Turn off the Snap to Grid
button so you can draw
in a smooth automation
curve.

Next, select the Pencil tool and draw some modulation data in the controller lane. Notice that as
you draw this data in, the Modulation Wheel in the Dr:rex interface has a neon green frame
around it, signifying that there is automation present (see Figure 8.34). If the pencil isn't accurate
enough, you can also use the Line tool to click and drag a more accurate depiction of the kind of
controller data you would like to see.

Figure 8.34
Select the Pencil tool and
draw in some
automation. The neon
green frame around the
Modulation Wheel
indicates that automation
has been written.

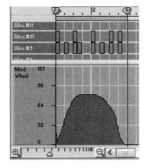

When you're finished drawing, click on Play to hear what Dr:rex sounds like with the Modulation Wheel moving and creating a very cool filter sweep. Of course, this is just scratching the surface of the different controllers that you can create data for. Just have another look at that list of controllers and you'll see.

As you have seen in this chapter, the Dr:rex is a Reason device that takes looping to a whole new level. Next, you are going to delve into the first of Reason's two virtual synths—the Subtractor!

9

Subtractor—Close Up

The Subtractor Analog Synthesizer is Reason's workhorse synth (see Figure 9.1). Its usefulness is virtually boundless, because it can be used for many different textures and elements in electronic music, including leads, pads, FX, and percussion. It is also a great synth to help you learn to create your own great-sounding patches.

This chapter explores and explains the inner workings of this wunderkind, covering such topics as:

- ▶ The basics of subtractive synthesis
- ▶ The Subtractor interface
- ▶ Programming your own patches
- ▶ Advanced programming with the Matrix Pattern Sequencer

Figure 9.1
The Subtractor Analog
Synthesizer is a software
emulation of a classic
hardware analog synth.

Subtractive Synthesis Explained

Subtractive synthesis is a form of analog synthesis, in that it relies on non-digital means to generate sound. Subtractive synthesis requires three active elements in order to generate sounds:

- ▶ **Oscillator**—The module that generates a continuous sound, determined by a waveform (more on this later).
- ▶ **Filter**—A device that alters the timbre of the oscillator's waveform by filtering out, or *subtracting*, various frequencies from the waveform (or combination of waveforms).
- ▶ **Amplifier**—This module receives the altered signal from the filter and amplifies it.

Of course, this is a simplified explanation of a complex synthesis process. Understanding and using subtractive synthesis with hardware synthesizers was a constant challenge for those who desired the ambience and textures that were possible. In the old days of synthesizers, a musician would have all of the required synth parts (oscillator, filter, and amplifier) in separate hardware devices encased in a modular apparatus, and the signal had to be physically "patched" or routed from one hardware device to another. As an example:

1. You began with the oscillator by selecting a waveform.

2. That signal would then be routed to a filter to manipulate the frequencies of the oscillator.

3. That output of the manipulated signal could then be patched to an envelope that could adjust the Attack, Decay, Sustain, and Release of the filter.

4. The output of the envelope would then be routed to an amplifier with an envelope that would adjust the Attack, Decay, Sustain, and Release of the amplitude.

5. That signal would then be routed to a hardware mixer.

There are many other factors and modifications that can be introduced along the signal flow, all of which make analog synthesis a lot more fun to program than it sounds on paper. Additionally, you will find that Subtractor does a good job of taking away the mystery of patch programming.

PHYS ED 101

When I was new to this whole game of virtual synths, I was quite confused by the use of the term *analog synthesis* within the confines of the digital realm. Think about it. How can anything "analog," which is comprised of physical parts and patches, such as a Moog or Oberheim synthesizer, exist in the digital world, which relies on just 0s and 1s? The answer is physical modeling.

Physical modeling is a form of programming that uses sets of equations to emulate the inner workings of an instrument. In the case of subtractive synthesis, physical modeling is used to emulate the oscillators, filters, and amplifiers. The benefit of physical modeling is that the performance characteristics of the modeled instrument can be accurately reproduced. A good example of this is a guitar string that's picked too hard, causing the produced tone to play sharp. Physical modeling is a simple enough concept to understand, but a lot of thought must go into formulating and creating the equations, and then they must be programmed.

If you want to learn more about the inner workings of physical modeling, you can read all about it at this website:

www.harmony-central.com/Synth/Articles/Physical_Modeling/converter

A Guided Tour of Subtractor

It's time to take a look under the hood of this powerful synth. After the tour has finished, be sure to read on and learn how to create your own customized Subtractor patches and learn how to use the Subtractor with the Matrix Pattern Sequencer.

The Oscillator Section

The Subtractor is the only virtual synth inside of Reason that actually generates sound by pure oscillation (see Figure 9.2). As you read further in this book, you will find that the term "oscillator" is associated with just about every one of the other virtual synths, but this is not precisely accurate. For example, the NN-19 and NN-XT generate sounds by using digital audio samples stored in RAM. Yet they both have an "oscillator" section in their interface. The same is true for the Malström, which is a virtual synth that generates sound by a completely unique form of synthesis called *graintable*, which you'll take a closer look at in the next chapter.

Figure 9.2

The Subtractor has two oscillators, which have 32 individual waveforms each.

An oscillator generates sounds by producing a combination of two characteristics:

▶ A selected waveform.

▶ An assigned pitch. This is done by pressing a key down on your MIDI keyboard.

Oscillator 1

Oscillator 1 is the Subtractor's primary source of generating sound. You'll soon see that Osc 1 has plenty of choices to offer when it comes to variable waveforms. First, take a look at the main parameters of Osc 1.

▶ **Waveform Selector**—There are 32 waveforms available in each oscillator. A waveform is a "sound shape" that is generated by the oscillator, which determines the character of the sound.

▶ **Octave Selector**—This shifts the frequency of the waveform up and down in pitch by octaves. When an instance of a Subtractor is created, the octave is set to 4, but the actual range of this parameter is 0-9, providing a 10-octave range in total.

▶ **Semitone Selector**—This parameter shifts the frequency of the waveform up and down in 12 semitone steps, equaling one octave.

▶ **Cent Selector**—This parameter is also commonly known as *fine-tuning*. It is used to make very small tuning adjustments and has a range of 1 semitone.

▶ **Keyboard Tracking**—This button is used to change the pitch of the oscillator as it receives different MIDI notes. If this button is not activated, the pitch of the oscillator will remain constant, no matter what incoming note messages it receives. This is ideal for programming sounds that are not pitch specific, such as percussion sounds.

CHAPTER 9

As mentioned, each oscillator has 32 individual waveforms, listed as follows. The first four are typically found on any hardware analog synth. The remaining 28 are unique and exclusive to the Subtractor.

▶ **Sawtooth**—The most complete of all waveforms because it contains all harmonics. The resulting sound is full and very bright in character.

▶ **Square**—This waveform contains odd numbered harmonics and has a very present hollow timbre to it.

▶ **Triangle**—This waveform contains a few harmonics and has a slight hollow sound to it.

▶ **Sine**—The simplest of all waveforms because it contains no harmonics (overtones). It is a very smooth and soft tone.

▶ **Waveform 5**—This waveform features the high harmonics. Not quite as bright as a sawtooth wave.

▶ **Waveform 6**—This waveform contains several harmonics and can be used to emulate an acoustic piano.

▶ **Waveform 7**—This waveform is very smooth and sounds similar to an electric piano.

▶ **Waveform 8**—This waveform has a very sharp sound and can be used to emulate percussive keyboards like a clavinet.

▶ **Waveform 9**—This waveform can be used for bass sounds.

▶ **Waveform 10**—This waveform sounds very similar to a Sine wave and can be used for sub-bass sounds (a la Drum n' Bass).

▶ **Waveform 11**—This waveform is formant heavy and perfect to use for voice patches.

▶ **Waveform 12**—This waveform has a metallic ring to it, making it perfect for xylophone type sounds.

▶ **Waveform 13**—This waveform is very full sounding and sounds similar to a pipe organ.

▶ **Waveform 14**—This waveform is also very organ-like but is not as bright as waveform 13.

▶ **Waveform 15**—This waveform can be used to emulate bowed string instruments.

▶ **Waveform 16**—This waveform is similar to 15 but contains a higher set of overtones.

▶ **Waveform 17**—This waveform is also similar in texture to 15 but contains a lower set of overtones.

▶ **Waveform 18**—This waveform can be used for steel string guitar sounds.

▶ **Waveform 19**—This waveform has harmonic qualities similar to bass instruments.

▶ **Waveform 20**—This waveform can be used to emulate muted brass instruments, like trumpet or trombone.

▶ **Waveform 21**—This waveform can be used to emulate saxophone sounds.

▶ **Waveform 22**—This waveform is yet another that can be used to emulate brass instruments but with a little more character.

▶ **Waveform 23**—This waveform is great for creating mallet percussion instruments.

▶ **Waveform 24**—This waveform is similar to 23, but it contains a higher set of overtones.

▶ **Waveform 25**—This waveform has a plectrum attack and can be used to program guitar patches.

▶ **Waveform 26**—This waveform is similar to 25, but it contains a higher set of overtones.

▶ **Waveform 27**—This waveform is similar in tone to 23 and 24, but it has a bell-like tone.

▶ **Waveform 28**—This waveform is similar to 27, but it contains fewer overtones.

▶ **Waveform 29**—This waveform has a complex harmonic structure and can be used to program organ and metallic pad patches.

▶ **Waveform 30**—This waveform can be used with frequency modulation and Osc 2 to create noise patches.

▶ **Waveform 31**—This waveform is similar to 30, but it contains fewer overtones.

▶ **Waveform 32**—This waveform is similar to 30, but it contains more overtones.

Oscillator 2

Oscillator 2 functions in the same way as Osc 1, but it has a few surprises up its sleeve. Adding a second source of oscillation to the mix can lead to an endless amount of modulation possibilities without a lot of extra programming.

To the right of Osc 2 is the Oscillator Mix knob. This knob is used to mix the amplitude of the two oscillators. Turning it clockwise will increase the volume of Osc 2 and decrease the volume of Osc 1. Turning the knob counter-clockwise will do the opposite.

Try the following example:

1. Set the waveform of Osc 1 to the Square Wave and the waveform of Osc 2 to the Triangle Wave.

2. Set the octave of Osc 1 and 2 to 2 for a very bass-heavy sound.

3. Turn the Mix knob clockwise until it reads 100.

4. Adjust the fine-tuning of Osc 1 to 20 Cent.

5. Arm the Subtractor sequencer track to receive MIDI from your keyboard and play a low note to hear the very solid bass sound and the wavering out of tune mix between Osc 1 and 2, which sounds pretty cool too.

Phase Offset Modulation

Along with generating a single waveform, the Subtractor oscillators can also generate a second identical waveform within the same oscillator. That second waveform's phase is then offset and modulated. Very complex new waveforms can be created with this process, which is called *phase offset modulation.*

To begin offsetting the phase of an oscillator, you must first select one of three modes to activate this function.

▶ **X**—Waveform multiplication

▶ **–**—Waveform subtraction

▶ **0**—No phase offset modulation

To better see how these waveforms look once phased, see Figure 9.3. In the first image, you will see a single Sawtooth waveform that contains no phase modulation at all. In the second image, you will see that same Sawtooth waveform, but this time it has been multiplied and a new waveform has been created. In the third image, you will see that same waveform again, but this time it has been subtracted and another new waveform has been created.

To the left of the phase mode sectors is the Phase knob, which controls the amount of offset between the two waveforms within a single oscillator.

Figure 9.3
Three graphical examples of phase offset modulation.

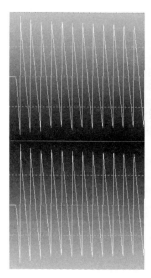 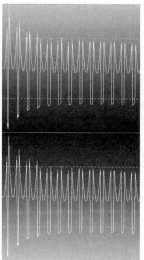 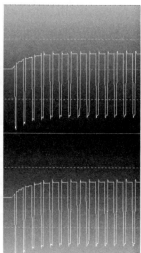

LEARN BY EXAMPLE

Phase offset modulation can be a difficult concept to grasp. As a personal preference, I generally find using a Subtractor patch that features this function is the best way to learn and better understand how it works. Browse through the various patches in the PolySynth folder and you will find several examples. A good patch to demonstrate phase offset is "The Plague" or possibly "Synced Up."

Noise Generator

The Noise Generator can be thought of as another oscillator. But this oscillator does not generate a pitched waveform. Rather, it generates noise that can be used for several sound design and instrumental possibilities, such as "wind noises" and percussion sounds.

To activate the Noise Generator, click the power button located in the upper-left corner of its interface. Let's have a look at the main parameters of the Noise Generator:

▶ **Noise Decay**—This parameter determines the length of time the noise will last when a note is played. Unlike Osc 1 and 2, the Amp Envelope does not govern the Noise Generator's parameters, so you can create a short burst of noise at the beginning of a sound using just this parameter.

▶ **Noise Color**—This parameter controls the character of the noise. The easiest way to think of it is like a single band of EQ. If you turn the knob to the right, the noise becomes brighter. If you turn the knob to the left, the noise becomes muddier sounding and bass heavy.

▶ **Level**—This parameter controls the volume of the Noise Generator.

Let's try an example of the Noise Generator.

1. Choose Initialize Patch from the Edit pull-down menu to reset the Subtractor. Note that Osc 2 should be turned off.

2. Activate the Noise Generator by clicking on its power button.

3. Play a note on your MIDI keyboard to hear the mix between Osc 1 and the Noise Generator. Turn the Oscillator Mix knob clockwise to hear just the Noise Generator.

4. Experiment with the three main parameters of the Noise Generator. Once you find a setting you like, turn the Oscillator Mix knob counter-clockwise to hear Osc 1 mix back in.

THE NOISE GENERATOR OUTPUTS

The outputs of the Noise Generator are internally routed through Osc 2. Even if Osc 2 is not active, as was the case with the previous exercise, the Noise Generator can still be heard.

If you turn on Osc 2, you will hear the output of Osc 2 mixed in with the Noise Generator.

Frequency Modulation

Frequency modulation (FM) is a form of synthesis that requires two separate signals in order to generate a new sound:

▶ **The Carrier**—Produced by Osc 1, the carrier is used as a basic sound that will be modulated.

▶ **The Modulator**—Produced by Osc 2, the modulator is used to modulate, or modify, the output of the carrier. How much it is modulated is determined by the amount of FM assigned.

CHAPTER 9

This is a fantastic effect that can be best explained by example:

1. Initialize the Subtractor patch. Select the Sine Wave for Osc 1.

2. Activate Osc 2 and select the Triangle Wave for Osc 2.

3. Turn the FM knob to 50 and start playing some notes on your keyboard to hear the FM effect.

4. Turn the Osc Mix all the way to the left so you can just hear Osc 1.

5. Change the semitone settings on Osc 2 and notice that you can still hear the FM effect, even though you are listening to just Osc 1. As Osc 2 is a modulator when using FM, its modulation effect is still heard, even though the actual output of the oscillator is inaudible.

Because the Noise Generator is routed through the output of Osc 2, it can also be used to modulate Osc 1 through FM.

Try the following example. Make sure that you are playing a sequence of some kind to hear the effect:

1. Turn off Osc 2 and turn on the Noise Generator.

2. Turn the Osc Mix completely to the right so you will just hear the Noise Generator.

3. Play a sequence.

4. Set the Level knob of the Noise Generator to 64.

5. Set the FM knob to 24.

6. Turn the Osc Mix to the left to mix the two signals. The resulting generated sound should sound tight and nasal.

Frequency modulation is just one of those effects that has its own unique niche in electronic music. I suggest trying it on a sequenced arpeggio; it produces a killer staccato sound.

Ring Modulation

A ring modulator is used to multiply two audio signals, thus creating a new signal that contains additional frequencies. It is a unique sound that can be used to generate frequencies that are smooth and bell-like or jarring frequencies dripping with dissonance.

As you can see in Figure 9.4, the ring modulator is quite simple to show in diagram form. However, the sounds that you can create with it can be surprisingly complex in tone and texture.

Figure 9.4
Osc 1 is multiplied by Osc 2 to create a completely original sound, which is the magic of ring modulation.

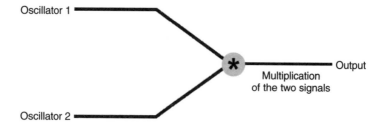

Try this exercise to see how ring modulation works:

1. Initialize the Subtractor patch before you begin.

2. Activate the ring modulator. Note that you won't hear any difference yet, because Osc 2 is still not active.

3. Activate Osc 2. You will now hear the ring modulator in action. At this point, the ring modulator should sound like it is playing one octave above Osc 1.

4. Turn the Osc Mix knob clockwise to the right to hear just the ring modulator.

5. Play some notes on your MIDI keyboard or play a sequence of notes in the Reason sequencer.

6. Make a few adjustments to the semitone controls of either Osc 1 or 2 to start hearing the dissonant effect created by the ring modulator.

7. At this point, you can now turn the Osc Mix knob to the left in order to bring Osc 1 back into the mix.

The Filter Section

As you read earlier in this chapter, a filter is one of the three elements needed to shape your sounds. The Subtractor is certainly up to the challenge, because there are two filters included that can run independently of each other or be linked (see Figure 9.5).

Figure 9.5
Subtractor has two filters that can be used individually or linked.

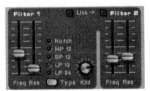

Filter 1

Filter 1 is the Subtractor's primary filter. It has many available filter types and a Keyboard Tracking parameter, which is discussed later in this section. For now, take a look at the different kinds of filters.

▶ **Notch**—This filter can be thought of as the opposite of a Band Pass filter. It will reject the mid-frequencies while allowing the high and low frequencies to pass through. Although not the most dramatic filter effect, it has a place in the mix for making minor changes to a sample.

▶ **High Pass**—HP 12 is the opposite of the Low Pass filters, in that it will filter out the low frequencies while letting the high frequencies pass through. It has a roll-off curve of 12 decibels per octave.

▶ **Band Pass**—Labeled as BP 12, this filters out both the high and low frequencies, leaving the mid frequencies alone. With a roll-off curve of 12 decibels per octave, the BP 12 can be used effectively on instrument loops such as a guitar loop or possibly hi-hat heavy percussion loops.

CHAPTER 9

▶ **12dB Low Pass**—Also called LP 12, this filter is similar to the 24dB low pass, but the roll-off curve is not as steep, because it has a range of 12 decibels per octave. This makes the LP 12 a perfect solution for creating a filter sweep that is low, but not low enough to blow up your speakers.

▶ **24dB Low Pass**—Also called LP 24, this filter allows low frequencies to pass through, while high frequencies are filtered out. To top it off, this low pass filter has a very intense roll-off curve (approximately 24 decibels per octave), which produces a greater emphasis on the low frequencies.

The Filter Frequency, or *cutoff filter,* as it is also called, is used to specify where the filter will function within the frequency spectrum. It is a very popular parameter used to create the "sweeping" effect that often occurs in electronic music. When the frequency is used to alter a filter, it opens and closes the filter within a specific frequency range.

1. Load a PolySynth patch from the Reason Factory Sound Bank. Try the Analog Brass patch, which is located in the PolySynth folder.

2. The Filter is already activated. Set the Filter mode to the LP 24 setting and make sure the Resonance slider is set to 0. Also make sure the Filter Frequency slider it set to its maximum setting of 127.

3. Arm the Subtractor sequencer track to receive MIDI and play a sustained chord with your left hand. With your right hand, click on the Filter Frequency and drag the control down, so you can hear the filter close as it decreases in value. Once the Filter Frequency is set to 0, all of the high frequencies have been filtered out. Try this same exercise with other filter modes, such as the Notch or Band Pass, to hear the effect.

The Resonance slider is used in combination with the Filter Frequency. It emphasizes the frequencies set by the Filter slider, which thins the sound out but also increases the sweep effect mentioned earlier. In order to better understand how the Resonance slider works with the Filter Frequency, try the following exercise.

At the far right of Filter 1 is the Keyboard Tracking knob. It can be used to bring the higher notes to the forefront in a mix.

Filter 2

Filter 2 brings an *additional* 12dB Low Pass filter to the table. Although it might not have all of the bells and whistles that Filter 1 has, it can produce many interesting timbres that are not possible with most hardware-based synths.

To activate Filter 2, just click on its power button. Once this is done, the outputs of Filter 1 are virtually routed through Filter 2.

Filter 2 can be used in two ways:

▶ The Frequency slider of Filter 2 can be used independently of Filter 1, meaning that any changes you make to this parameter will only affect Filter 2.

▶ The Frequency slider of Filter 2 is linked to the Frequency slider of Filter 1, meaning that any changes you make to this parameter will affect both Filter 1 and Filter 2.

Let's have a look at an example of frequency independence:

1. Load the Singing Synth patch from the Monosynth folder in the Reason Factory Sound Bank.

2. Once it is loaded, notice that Filter 1 is set to BP 12. Arm the Subtractor sequencer track and play a couple of MIDI notes. Notice the vowel-like texture of the patch.

3. Notice that Filter 2 is activated but it is not linked, so its Frequency slider is running independently.

4. Try turning off Filter 2 to hear the difference between using one and two filters. When Filter 2 is deactivated, the patch really loses its originality and sounds like a standard run-of-the-mill synth patch.

Let's look at an example of linking up the Frequency sliders of both filters:

1. Load the Fozzy Fonk patch from the PolySynth folder in the Reason Factory Sound Bank.

2. Notice that Filter 1 is set to Notch mode. Arm the Subtractor sequencer track and play a couple of MIDI notes. Listen to the sound that is being generated from the Subtractor. There is no way a Notch filter could sound that way on its own, because it has a very nasal timbre to it and has far too many mid-frequencies in the mix.

3. Notice that the Filter 2 Link button is now activated. This means that the Frequency slider of Filter 1 will affect the Frequency slider of Filter 2 as well. Note also that as there is an offset between the two frequencies, that offset will remain as the Frequency slider changes on Filter 1.

4. To demonstrate the Filter 2 Link, try making some adjustments to the Frequency slider of Filter 1. Also try deactivating Filter 2 and making those same adjustments to the Frequency slider of Filter 1 to hear the difference.

The Envelope Section

The Subtractor has three envelopes, and although they share some common parameters, you'll find that the purpose and functionality of the envelopes are quite different (see Figure 9.6).

Figure 9.6
The Subtractor has three envelopes: Modulation, Filter, and Amplitude.

There are four basic parameters that all the Subtractor envelopes share:

▶ **Attack**—When an envelope is triggered, the Attack parameter determines the length of time before the envelope reaches its maximum value.

▶ **Decay**—Once the maximum value is reached, the Decay parameter determines the length of time before the value begins to drop.

▶ **Sustain**—After the value begins to drop, Sustain determines at what level the falling value should rest.

▶ **Release**—Once the value has been set at its rested value, the Release parameter determines how long it will take the sound to drop to silence after you release the key.

The following sections take a look at each of the available envelopes.

Filter and Amplitude Envelopes

The Filter Envelope is used to modify the Frequency parameter of Filter 1. When using it in combination with the Filter Frequency and Resonance sliders, the Filter Envelope can be used to create long, sustained filter sweeps and percussive filter powered stab sounds.

To the right of the Filter Envelope are two additional parameters that can be used in combination with it.

▶ The Invert button is used to invert the functions of the individual envelope parameters. For example, say you are using the Attack parameter of the Filter Envelope and have assigned a positive value of 80, which produces a very slow attack. Activate the Invert button and the attack parameter is inverted, which means the attack will be much faster now.

▶ The Amount knob determines how much the filter will be affected by the envelope. Increasing the value of this parameter directly affects the set value of the Filter Frequency, which in turn will affect the Filter Envelope, resulting in some very intense filter combinations.

To demonstrate the capabilities of the Filter Envelope, try the following exercise. Make sure that your Subtractor sequencer track is armed to receive MIDI signals.

1. Load the Desiree patch in the PolySynth folder of the Reason Factory Sound Bank. Notice the filter settings of this patch.

2. Use your mouse to increase the value of the Attack parameter to 55. Play a chord on your keyboard and notice the sweeping effect it produces. Because the Filter mode is set to LP 24, using the envelope with a slow attack causes the filter to first play the lower frequencies, followed by the higher frequencies. Additionally, if you increase the Amount knob, this sweeping effect will dramatically intensify.

3. Now decrease the value of the Decay parameter to 24. Play a chord and notice how the filter abruptly closes as soon as the Attack reaches its maximum value. Also notice how there is still a long sustain after the filter closes.

4. Now increase the value of the Sustain parameter to 101 and listen to how fast the filter opens and decays, but the Filter Frequency still remains open for a long while.

5. With the Decay set to such low values, the Release parameter will have virtually no effect on this patch.

The Amplitude Envelope is used to shape the volume characteristics of the Subtractor patch. This is useful for creating very long sustained patches (such as pads), or medium to short sustained patches (such as bass synths or percussion). The same types of parameters are available here (Attack, Decay, Sustain, Release). The included Level slider located just above the Amplitude Envelope is used as a Master Level for the Subtractor.

To experiment with the Amplitude Envelope, try using the previous exercise as a road map to guide you through the different envelope parameters.

Modulation Envelope

The Modulation Envelope works in the same way as the Filter Envelope, but it has a different use. The Modulation Envelope sends the standard set of envelope parameters to one of six destinations, including:

▶ **Osc 1**—This destination will alter the pitch of Oscillator 1.

▶ **Osc 2**—This destination will alter the pitch of Oscillator 2.

▶ **Osc Mix**—This destination will control the Oscillator Mix knob.

▶ **Frequency Modulation**—This destination will control the amount of FM.

▶ **Phase**—This destination will control the amount of Phase Offset between Osc 1&2.

▶ **Filter Frequency 2**—This destination will control the amount of Filter Frequency for Filter 2.

The Amount and Invert knobs work in the same way as they did with the Filter Envelope, so there is no need to waste time on that. Instead, try the following exercise to better understand the functionality of this envelope.

Make sure that your Subtractor sequencer track is armed and ready to receive MIDI.

1. Load the GlassOrgan patch from the PolySynths folder in the Reason Factory Sound Bank. Notice that the Modulation Envelope is not being used at all; its Amount parameter is set to 0.

2. Set the Amount knob to 127 so that the envelope will be triggered with its maximum potential.

3. Set the Attack to 85 for a very slow attack.

4. Play a note or chord on your keyboard and listen to the pitch of Osc 1 slowly rise and quickly decay.

The LFO Section

The Subtractor sports two independent Low Frequency Oscillators, or LFOs (see Figure 9.7). In some ways, an LFO can be thought of as a standard oscillator, as it is capable of generating a waveform and frequency. However, the purpose of an LFO differs greatly from that of a standard oscillator in two ways:

▶ The LFO can only generate waveforms with low frequencies.

▶ The LFO's purpose is to modulate a specific parameter of a patch, such as a filter or another oscillator. That means that the LFO itself is never actually heard, only its effect on other synth parameters.

Figure 9.7
Subtractor has two LFOs.

LFO 1

LFO 1 has many waveform choices and destinations. It is also capable of synchronizing the LFO effect to the tempo of your Reason song. Let's first look at the different available waveforms:

▶ **Triangle**—Creates a smooth up and down vibrato.

▶ **Inverted Sawtooth**—Creates a cycled ramp up effect.

▶ **Sawtooth**—Creates a cycled ramp down effect.

▶ **Square**—Makes abrupt changes between two values.

▶ **Random**—Creates a random stepped modulation. Also known as sample and hold.

▶ **Soft Random**—Exactly as the previous waveform but has a smoother modulation curve.

The Amount knob assigns the amount of LFO effect to your patch. It's fairly easy to get carried away with this parameter, so easy does it.

The Rate knob increases and decreases the rate of the LFO effect.

The Sync button synchronizes the LFO effect to the tempo indicated on the transport bar. Also note that once Sync is active, the Rate knob displays its amount by note values rather than numerically.

Once you have selected your rate, amount, and waveform, you must next decide where to send the LFO signal. There are six possible destinations to choose from:

▶ **Osc 1&2**—This destination will alter the pitch of Oscillators 1 and 2.

▶ **Osc 2**—This destination will alter the pitch of just Osc 2.

▶ **Filter Frequency**—This destination will control the Filter Frequency Filter 1 (and Filter 2 if they are linked).

▶ **Frequency Modulation**—This destination will control the amount of FM.

▶ **Phase**—This destination will control the amount of Phase Offset for Osc 1 and 2.

▶ **Oscillator Mix**—This destination will control the Oscillator Mix knob.

LFO 2

Although the LFO 2 might not be as complex and versatile as its bigger brother, it is a welcome addition to the Subtractor interface. LFO 2 does not sync to tempo. Instead, it is *key triggered*, which means that the LFO will trigger every time a note is played on your keyboard.

The Rate and Amount knobs perform exactly the same task as they do with LFO 1, minus the Sync feature, of course.

The Delay knob is used to create an offset between playing a note and then hearing the LFO modulation. It can be used to mimic the vibrato effect of a wind or stringed instrument, which calls for long sustained notes followed by a vibrato.

The Keyboard Tracking knob can be used to increase the frequency of the LFO the farther up on the keyboard that you play.

Once you have set the individual parameters of LFO 2, you can send the effect to one of four destinations.

▶ **Osc 1&2**—This destination will control the pitch of Oscillators 1 and 2.

▶ **Phase**—This destination will control the amount of phase offset for Osc 1 and 2.

▶ **Filter Frequency 2**—This destination will control the Filter Frequency Filter 2.

▶ **Amplitude**—This destination will control the overall volume of the Subtractor.

The Play Parameters

Once you have familiarized yourself with the ins and outs of programming the Subtractor, it's time to take a look at the parameters that involve the performance side of this virtual synth (see Figure 9.8). You'll find that there are a lot of interesting and creative choices that you will enjoy playing with.

Figure 9.8
Subtractor's Play parameters are used to add expression to your performance.

Velocity Control

The Subtractor is a *velocity-sensitive* virtual synth. Although this might not be as impressive to those of you who have oodles of digital synths lying around your studio, this is a significant feature to vintage synth connoisseurs; velocity-sensitive keyboards were not available in the early days of subtractive synthesis. If you played a note on, say a vintage Moog or ARP synth, that note would be generated at its maximum velocity, regardless of how hard or soft the note was played.

Located in the lower-right corner of the Subtractor is the Velocity Control section, where different parameters can be made velocity-sensitive and will react according to how hard or soft a note it played (see Figure 9.9). The velocity data can be received from a live performance with a MIDI keyboard or played from the Reason sequencer or the Matrix sequencer. After you read through this section, be sure to read the programming tutorial later in this chapter. There, you'll use a few of these parameters.

Figure 9.9
The Velocity Control section is a big part of the Subtractor's Play parameters.

The different parameters that can be modified by velocity are as follows:

▶ **Amplitude**—This parameter controls the overall volume of the Subtractor. When set to a positive value, a harder velocity will increase the volume. When set to a negative value, a harder velocity will decrease the volume.

▶ **Frequency Modulation**—When set to a positive value, a harder velocity will increase the Frequency Modulation parameter. A negative value will have the opposite effect.

▶ **Modulation Envelope**—When set to a positive value, a harder velocity will increase the Modulation Envelope's Amount parameter. A negative value will have the opposite effect.

▶ **Phase Offset**—This parameter controls the phase offset of oscillators 1 and 2. When set to a positive value and the phase offset is activated, a harder velocity will increase the amount of phase offset. A negative value will have the opposite effect.

▶ **Filter Frequency 2**—This controls the Frequency slider of Filter 2. When set to a positive value, a harder velocity will increase the amount of filter frequency. A negative value will have the opposite effect.

▶ **Filter Envelope**—When set to a positive value, a harder velocity will increase the Filter Envelope's Amount parameter. A negative value will have the opposite effect.

▶ **Filter Decay**—This controls the Decay parameter of the Filter Envelope. When set to a positive value, a harder velocity will increase the Filter Decay parameter. A negative value will have the opposite effect.

▶ **Oscillator Mix**—This knob controls the Oscillator Mix. When set to a positive value, a harder velocity will increase the amount of Osc 2 in the mix. A negative value will have the opposite effect (Osc 1 will be more present).

▶ **Amp Attack**—This controls the Attack parameter of the Amplifier Envelope. When set to a positive value, a harder velocity will increase the Amp Envelope Attack parameter. A negative value will have the opposite effect.

Pitch Bend and Modulation

The Pitch Bend Wheel is an emulation of a standard pitch wheel found on most MIDI keyboards. Simply put, it is used to bend the pitch of the played notes up and down. The Range parameter, located just above the Pitch Bend Wheel, controls the range of pitch by up to +/− two octaves.

The Modulation Wheel is used to control a number of different available parameters:

▶ **Filter Frequency**—When set to a positive value, the Modulation Wheel will increase the Filter Frequency parameter. A negative value will have the opposite effect.

▶ **Resonance**—When set to a positive value, the Modulation Wheel will increase the Resonance. A negative value will have the opposite effect.

▶ **LFO 1**—When set to a positive value, the Modulation Wheel will increase the Amount knob of LFO 1. A negative value will have the opposite effect.

▶ **Phase**—This knob controls the Phase Offset parameter of Oscillators 1 and 2. When set to a positive value, the Modulation Wheel will increase the amount of Phase Offset. A negative value will have the opposite effect.

▶ **Frequency Modulation**—When set to a positive value, the Modulation Wheel will increase the Frequency Modulation parameter. A negative value will have the opposite effect.

Legato/Retrig

Retrig is thought of as the "normal" setting for the Subtractor, because it is the commonly used parameter for playing polyphonic patches. When Retrig is selected, the Subtractor envelopes are triggered when you press and hold down a note and then retriggered when another note is played.

Retrig can be used with monophonic patches as well. Try pressing a note and holding it while pressing a new key. Release the new key and the first note will retrigger.

Legato is a commonly used parameter for playing monophonic patches, such as leads or bass lines. With the polyphony set to 1, press and hold down a note, and then press and hold another note. Notice that the new note has no attack, as the Subtractor's envelopes have not been retriggered, as would be the case when Retrig is selected. If you add some portamento to this patch, you will get a retro vintage mono synth glide sound.

It is also possible to use Legato with a polyphonic patch. Set the Polyphony of a patch to a low number of voices, such as 3. Hold down a three-note chord and then play another note. Notice that the new note will be played with a legato effect (no attack), but it will cease to play the highest note of the chord you are playing, because it is "stealing" that note in order to play the new note.

Portamento

Portamento is used to create a sliding effect between played notes. The knob determines the amount of time it will take to slide from one note to another. It can be used with either monophonic or polyphonic patches and is a great tool for creating some interesting effects. Try loading a polyphonic patch, such as the Glass Organ patch found in the Poly Synths folder. Set the Portamento to a value of 45 and play some chords. You will hear a slight sliding effect that makes the patch sound a little funny, but try adding some real-time effects.

Polyphony

Polyphony assigns the number of voices that can simultaneously played at one time. The Subtractor has a wide range of polyphony, from 1 to 99 voices, offering a wide range of creative possibilities. For example, when set at 1, the Subtractor becomes a monophonic instrument, which is perfect for creating scorching lead lines.

External Modulation

The Subtractor is capable of receiving common MIDI controller messages and then routing that data to a number of available parameters. When used effectively, this can create performances with a great deal of additional expression.

CHAPTER 9

The three MIDI messages that can be received are:

> ▶ **Aftertouch**—Also known as *channel pressure*. This is when a note is held down on a keyboard. Additional pressure can be applied to this note, which sends additional MIDI data. Many keyboards support this feature, so check your manual.

> ▶ **Expression Pedal**—Looks a lot like a sustain pedal. If your keyboard has an input for it, you can buy an expression pedal at your local music instrument shop.

> ▶ **Breath Control**—This external source is found mostly on older Yamaha keyboards, but it enables you to mimic the attack of wind instruments.

Once you have selected the external source, you can then route the MIDI data to any or all of these parameters.

> ▶ **Filter Frequency**—When set to a positive value, an External Control message will increase the Filter Frequency parameter. A negative value has the opposite effect.

> ▶ **LFO 1**—When set to a positive value, an External Control message will increase the LFO amount knob. A negative value has the opposite effect.

> ▶ **Amplitude**—When set to a positive value, an External Control message will increase the amplitude of the Subtractor. A negative value has the opposite effect.

> ▶ **Frequency Modulation**—When set to a positive value, an External Control message will increase the Frequency Modulation parameter. A negative value has the opposite effect.

Your First Subtractor Patch

Now that you have a pretty firm idea of what makes the Subtractor tick, it's time to dig in and create your first customized Subtractor patch. This tutorial takes you through a step-by-step process of programming a pad patch that will be perfect for any ambient occasion.

Setting Up a Start Point

Before you begin to program your first Subtractor patch, it's important to find a good starting point to begin your synthetic experimentations. As a guitar player, I find it frustrating to play my keyboard while making adjustments to the Subtractor, so I use the Reason sequencer to get around it. By writing in a sequence that is related to the kind of patch I am going to create, the programming process is much quicker and more efficient. Confused? Consider these examples.

If I am planning to program a bass synth patch to be used in techno music, I typically write in a standard techno bass line in the Reason sequencer. Then I set the sequencer to play the bass line over and over again in a loop (see Figure 9.10). I can make real-time adjustments to the patch as the sequence is playing and program the patch to complement the style of music I am going to create with the patch.

Figure 9.10

I have written a techno-styled bass line into the Reason sequencer in order to program a bass synth patch in the Subtractor.

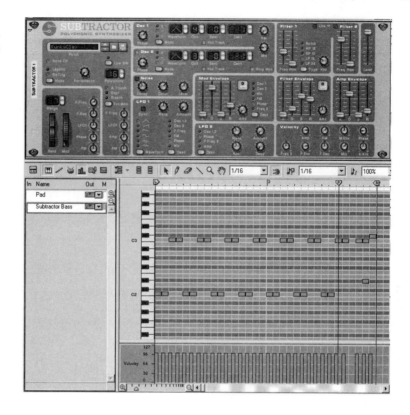

For this programming tutorial, you are going to create a pad patch, which is typically used for long, sustained chords. This is a perfect place to set up the Reason sequencer with a few sustained chords so that you can loop the sequence and make changes to the Subtractor in real time.

1. Click on the Switch to Edit Mode button to display the Key Lane Editor.

2. Set the Snap value to 1 bar. This will allow you to draw in measure-long notes.

3. Using your Pencil tool, draw in an E major chord at measure one using the notes E1, B1, E2, G#2, B2, and E3.

4. Using your Pencil tool, draw in an A major chord at measure two using the notes A1, E2, A2, C#3, and E3.

5. Activate the Loop mode on the Transport Panel. Set the left locator to measure one and the right locator to measure three. This will give you a two-bar loop (see Figure 9.11).

Figure 9.11
A two-bar loop has been
created.

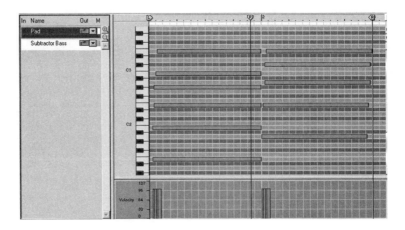

Programming Your Subtractor Patch

In this tutorial, you are going to build a pad patch by working with each section of the Subtractor interface. This will serve as a good review of everything you have learned about the functionality of the Subtractor throughout this chapter.

Programming the Oscillators

Let's start things off simple by working with Oscillator 1, and then adding in Oscillator 2. To hear the changes in real time, click on Play on the transport bar. The two-bar loop should start playing continuously.

1. Set the waveform of Osc 1 to a Sine Wave. Notice the organ-like bell tone that is produced.

2. Set the Octave box of Osc 1 to 3. Notice how the tone still retains its bell tone quality but sounds very dark and muddy.

3. Next, set the Phase Offset to Waveform Multiplication or X, and set the Amount knob to 44.

At this point, the patch sounds very dull, so let's add another timbre to the mix by using Osc 2. Before activating Osc 2, make sure that you turn the Mix knob counter-clockwise until it reaches a value of 44. This will allow Osc 1 to be the dominant voice in the patch.

And now, on to Osc 2.

1. Activate Osc 2 and set its waveform to a Square Wave.

2. Next, set the Cent control to a positive amount of 20. This will fine-tune Osc 2 a little higher than Osc 1, which will sound much cooler later on in this tutorial.

3. Set the Phase Offset to the Waveform Subtraction or –, and set its Amount knob to a value of 123. If you want to experiment with this setting a little bit, try making adjustments between the values of 0 and 127 to hear how Osc 2 will fade out from the mix when set to a low value.

4. Activate the ring modulator. Notice all of the new frequencies and timbres that are introduced to the patch.

AD TERMINOLOGY

In many cases, the computer chip that does the digitizing also handles the analogizing. Hence, you'll see DAC/ADC or ADC/DAC or DA/AD or even AD/DA. You'll also see both types of converters referred to as simply an "A/D converter."

BRING IN THE NOISE

When creating a pad, I like to add a little noise to the mix to give the patch a little grit on top of the synthetic smoothness of Oscillator 2. If you want to add this element to your patch, try these settings:

1. Activate the Noise Generator.

2. Set the Decay knob to its maximum value.

3. Set the Color knob to a low value; this will dull the tone of the digital noise.

4. Set the Level knob to a mid value. I suggest starting with a value of 30 and working from there.

BRING THE NOISE

Throughout the rest of this tutorial, you can choose to turn the noise off or leave it on. It's not an essential texture to this patch that you are creating, but it never hurts to add a little gravy now and then.

Programming the Filters and Envelopes

You now have a much more interesting sound to work with. It's time to manipulate it further by using both of the filters.

1. Change the mode of Filter 1 to LP 24.

2. Set the value of the Filter Frequency to a low amount—around 30 or so. The patch should now have a very abrupt Attack and Decay, but you should also be able to hear a very low sustained timbre underneath it.

3. Activate Filter 2 and set the Resonance slider to a high value of 90.

4. Activate the Link button. This will connect the Frequency Filter slider of Filter 1 with the Frequency slider of Filter 2.

Upon listening to the patch at this point, it might sound a little strange, because it is not quite a pad sound. That's all about to change as you introduce the Filter Envelope to the patch.

Before you begin this part of the tutorial, set the Amount knob of the Filter Envelope to a value of 67. Now set the Attack, Decay, Sustain, and Release to the following values:

▶ **Attack**—Set to 80 to create a slow rising attack.

▶ **Decay**—Set to 80 as well, so the envelope will remain at its peak value.

▶ **Sustain**—Set to 37. This will create a fast drop off from the peak value.

▶ **Release**—Set to 37 as well. This will introduce a slight sustain to the envelope, but not too much.

WATCH THOSE LEVELS

Because you are using an LP 24 filter on this patch, you will surely notice how much fuller and louder the patch is getting. That said, you might want to turn down the Level slider of the Subtractor to avoid any potential digital clipping.

Now the patch should sound much more like a pad than before. Notice how the filters fill out the sound nicely by using a slow attack on the envelope. Another texture to note is the "wavering sound" between the two oscillators, courtesy of the fine-tuning Cent value of 20. Try changing the Cent value to 0 and notice the difference.

Let's continue working with the envelopes by using the Amplitude Envelope. Set this envelope to the following values:

▶ **Attack**—Set to 60 for a slow attack.

▶ **Decay**—Set to a high value of 100 for a prolonged peak level.

▶ **Sustain**—Set to 60 for a slower drop off from the Decay.

▶ **Release**—Set to a low value of 0.

SAVE YOUR WORK

Don't forget to occasionally save your patch by clicking on the Save button at the top-left corner of the Subtractor interface.

The last envelope to program is the Modulation Envelope, which is going to modulate the FM knob of the Subtractor. Set the Envelope Destination mode to FM, and adjust the parameters of this envelope to the following values:

▶ **Attack**—Set to 0 for a fast attack.

▶ **Decay**—Set to 70 for a long, sustained peak level.

▶ **Sustain**—Set to 10 for a fast drop off from the Decay.

▶ **Release**—Set to 0 for a fast release.

Programming the LFOs

Adding the LFOs to this patch is what will help give it originality and character. As you know, there are two LFOs in the Subtractor. In this tutorial, you will start by creating a tempo-synced LFO for the Filter Frequency; and you will then use the second LFO to modulate the phase of the two oscillators.

Let's begin with LFO 1.

1. Activate the Sync button to synchronize LFO 1 to the tempo of your Reason song.

2. Set the Rate knob to a value of 1/8. This will cause the Filter Frequency to modulate on every 8th note.

3. Set the Amount knob to a low value of 12. You will still hear the effect of the LFO, but it will not become too dominant in the patch.

4. Set the Destination mode to F.Freq or Filter Frequency. Note that as you are using both filters, the LFO will modulate both Frequency Filter sliders.

5. Select the Square Waveform from the waveform mode. This will produce an abrupt modulation between the maximum and minimal potential of the square waveform that will sound great when synced to tempo.

Next, let's introduce LFO 2 and have it modulate the phase of Oscillators 1 and 2.

1. Set the Destination mode of LFO 2 to Phase.

2. Set the Rate knob to a value of 30.

3. Set the Amount knob to a high amount of 90.

4. Set the Keyboard Tracking to 100.

ADD A DASH OF VELOCITY

In this tutorial, you're not making much use of the Velocity section, so I want to point out a parameter or two in this section that you can use if you want.

▶ **Filter Envelope**—Using this knob will increase or decrease the amount of the Filter Envelope according to the velocity at which your notes are played. Try adding a positive amount, such as 25, and notice how much more present the filter effect becomes.

▶ **Filter Frequency 2**—Using this knob will increase or decrease the amount of Filter Frequency from the second filter. Try using a negative amount such as −34 and notice how the Filter Frequency changes with velocity. Now imagine that with some delay on it.

Programming the Play Parameters

You're in the homestretch; you can finish this patch by making a few adjustments to the Play parameters of the Subtractor.

▶ **Polyphony**—By default, the Subtractor has polyphony of 8, and this won't do for those really large, sustained ambient chords. Begin by assigning a higher polyphony count of 16.

▶ **Modulation Wheel**—Assign a negative value to the Filter Frequency so it will decrease in value as the Modulation Wheel is used. Assign a positive amount to the LFO 1. This will increase the amount of LFO as the Modulation Wheel is used.

▶ **Portamento**—Assign a positive amount to this parameter. This will create a sliding effect that sounds great with pads and bass synths.

Another additional parameter you might want to adjust is the range of the Pitch Bend Wheel. As a personal preference, I like to assign a value of 24 to the Pitch Bend Wheel to create wild pitch bent notes and chords.

Using the Subtractor with the Matrix

This section gives you a little taste of the kind of fantastic sounds you can get from the Subtractor, when using it along with the Matrix Pattern Sequencer. Although you dig into the Matrix later in this book, I thought it might be fun to show you how to make the Subtractor sound like Robby the Robot.

What Is the Matrix?

The Matrix is a software emulation of what is called a *control voltage sequencer* (see Figure 9.12). This was a hardware device that was used to sequence synthesizers back in the days of "Switched on Bach" and Emerson, Lake, and Palmer. Essentially, a control voltage (or CV) sequencer sends out controlled amounts of voltage that are read by the synthesizer and interpreted as pitch and length of notes.

Figure 9.12
The Matrix Pattern Sequencer is used to write synth patterns for the Subtractor.

The Matrix does this as well, but takes it a step further by sending pattern data, note data, gate data, and parameter control data. The Matrix is capable of storing up to 32 individual patterns that can each be up to 32 steps long, and it supports many different note values, including the ability to shuffle.

For much, much more on the Matrix, be sure to turn to Chapter 13, "The Matrix—Close Up."

Connecting the Matrix

The first thing you need to do here is create a Matrix sequencer and route it to the Subtractor, and this can be done in just a couple of steps.

Make sure that you have initialized your Subtractor patch, so you can begin with a clean slate.

1. Click anywhere on the Subtractor to highlight the interface. Doing this before creating a Matrix will create a Matrix directly below the Subtractor and automatically route it to the Subtractor inputs.

2. Select the Matrix Pattern Sequencer from the Create pull-down menu. An instance of the Matrix will appear below the Subtractor. Click on the Tab key and the Device Rack will swing around. You will see that the Matrix has indeed been automatically routed to the sequencer controls of the Subtractor (see Figure 9.13).

Figure 9.13
The Matrix has been
automatically routed to
the sequencer controls of
the Subtractor.

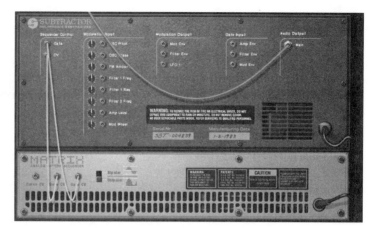

Creating a Curve Pattern with the Matrix

Now that the Matrix has been routed to the Subtractor, let's use the Matrix to draw in a curve
pattern, which will affect the pitch of Oscillator 1.

1. Route the Curve CV output of the Matrix to the Osc Pitch Modulation Input of the
    Subtractor (see Figure 9.14). This will allow the Matrix to control the pitch of
    Oscillator 1.

2. Press the Tab key to flip the Device Rack around again.

3. Switch from Keys to Curve mode in the Matrix by clicking on the switch located
    in the upper-left corner of the interface.

4. Click on Play in the Transport Panel of Reason. The Matrix sequencer should begin
    to run as well.

Figure 9.14
Route the Matrix Curve
CV to the Osc Pitch
Input of the Subtractor.

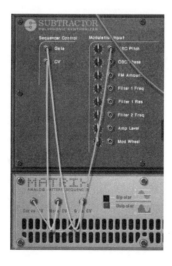

5. In order to hear the Subtractor, you will need to draw in a Gate pattern, which is done at the bottom portion of the Matrix grid section (see Figure 9.15).

Figure 9.15
Draw in a Gate pattern in order to hear the Subtractor in the next step.

6. Draw in a Curve pattern for the Matrix by simply clicking in the grid section. As the pattern recycles, you should be able to hear random notes play from the Subtractor. Giving each grid a different value, as shown in Figure 9.16, can change these notes.

Figure 9.16
Drawing in a curved pattern with the Matrix is easy and sounds great when you need some interesting elements for your electronic masterpiece.

I'm sure at this point you can see that the Subtractor is a synth of many creative possibilities. It has certainly earned a welcome place in my virtual studio due to its very useful sounds and endless routing potential.

For those of you looking for even more wild synth sounds and swirls, get ready for Chapter 10, "The Malström—Close Up," where you'll take a guided tour of Reason's other synth, the Malström.

10

The Malström—Close Up

When Reason 2.0 hit the market in 2002, Propellerhead introduced a new virtual synth, based on a completely original form of synthesis, called the Malström (see Figure 10.1). Immediately drawn to its handsome graphical interface and unbelievable synthesis prowess, I have made it a permanent fixture in my Reason songs.

Graintable Synthesis

Malström's uniqueness stems from the method by which it generates sound, called *graintable synthesis*, which is essentially a combination of granular and wavetable synthesis. To better understand how this works, you need to understand these two forms of synthesis.

In *granular synthesis*, sound is generated by a specific number of short, adjacent audio segments, called grains. Grains can be generated either by using a mathematical formula or by using a sample. These grains are usually 5-100 milliseconds long and are spliced together in order to form a sound. Altering the order of slices or modifying the individual properties of each slice can change the overall sound.

A good example of granular synthesis is found in the Native Instruments Reaktor 3.0 virtual synth.

Wavetable synthesis is based on the playback of sampled waveforms. Wavetable synthesis offers a few key benefits, such as the capability to sweep through the wavetable at any speed without affecting the pitch, and isolating and looping specific points of the wavetable. For a modern-day example of wavetable synthesis, check out the Waldorf PPG virtual synth.

Figure 10.1
The Malström is a virtual synth unlike any other, software or hardware.

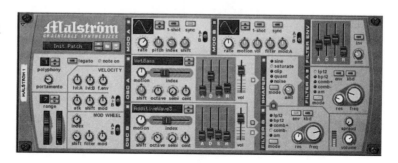

As stated, graintable synthesis is a combination of these two forms of synthesis and works in the following way:

1. The oscillators of the Malström play sampled sounds that have been pre-processed in a complex manner and cut into individual grains. From this point on, these converted samples are now called graintables.

2. These graintables are made up of periodic sets of waveforms that, when combined, play back the original sounds.

3. At this point, the graintable is treated in the same way as a wavetable. You have the ability to sweep through the graintable and single out any nuance of the graintable that you would like to manipulate. For example, you could extract a vowel out of a voice graintable. Additionally, the graintable can be manipulated further by incorporating the ability to "shift" the frequency region or "formant" without altering the pitch, which is a granular synthesis quality.

Tour the Malström

Now that you have learned the fundamentals of graintable synthesis, load up an instance of the Malström and take a tour of the interface. Before you begin this section, start a new Reason song and load an instance of reMix and the Malström.

The Oscillator Section

The Malström has two oscillators from which to generate sound (see Figure 10.2). As mentioned in the last chapter, the Subtractor is the only virtual synth that generates sound through pure oscillation; the Malström's oscillators are meant to perform two tasks:

▶ Play the loaded graintable

▶ Generate a pitch

Upon first loading an instance of the Malström, Oscillator A is activated by default. To activate/deactivate Oscillator B, simply click on its power button, located at the top-left corner of the OSC B section.

Figure 10.2
The Malström has two
built-in oscillators.

At this point, you can click on the Patch Browser located in the upper-left corner of the Malström interface and load patches from the Reason Factory Sound Bank. As was the case with the Subtractor, Malström patches are organized by their intended use, including the following:

- ▶ Bass
- ▶ FX
- ▶ Mono synths
- ▶ Pads
- ▶ Percussion
- ▶ Poly synths
- ▶ Rhythmic

Of course, none of these presets is set in stone, so to speak. You can modify a poly synth patch to be used as a pad, or a mono synth patch to be used as a bass synth. You just have to learn your way around the Malström interface and understand how each part of the interface works. With that thought in mind, continue onward by touring the individual sections of the Malström. You will not load a preset at this time.

After activating either of the oscillators, the next task is to select a graintable from the display just to the right of the OSC A and OSC B power buttons. You can select a graintable either by using the scroll buttons of the graintable display or by clicking on the display itself. If you click on the display, a pop-up menu will appear, displaying a very long list of available graintables to choose from (see Figure 10.3).

Figure 10.3
The Malström includes many available graintables. Notice that they are categorized by type (for example, Guitar: AcousticGuitar and FX:Drip).

ORGANIZATION OF THE GRAINTABLES

As you begin to explore the long list of over 80 graintables, it's refreshing to see that Propellerhead has categorized these graintables by type. This makes it much easier when beginning to build a new patch from scratch or when editing a patch.

The graintable list is organized as follows:

- Bass—6 graintables
- FX—10 graintables
- Guitar—5 graintables
- Misc—3 graintables
- Perc—5 graintables
- Synth—22 graintables
- Voices—11 graintables
- Wave—10 graintables
- Wind—10 graintables

Setting the Oscillator Frequency

Once a graintable has been selected, you can then alter the frequency of the oscillators by using a combination of three parameters (see Figure 10.4).

Figure 10.4
Alter the frequency of the oscillators by using the Octave, Semi, and Cent parameters.

- **Octave**—This parameter alters the frequency of a graintable by octaves and has a range of seven octaves.
- **Semi**—This parameter alters the frequency of a graintable by semitones and has a range of 12 semitones, or one full octave.
- **Cent**—This parameter alters the frequency of a graintable by cents. With a range of one semitone, it is used to make very fine adjustments to a loaded graintable.

Altering the Oscillator Playback

After setting the frequency of a graintable, you can alter the playback of the oscillators by using the Motion, Index, and Shift parameters (see Figure 10.5).

Figure 10.5
The Index, Motion, and Shift controls allow you to tweak the selected graintable to the max.

▶ **Index**—This slider is used to set the start point for the playback of the graintable. It has a range of 0-127.

▶ **Motion**—This parameter is used to set the speed at which a graintable is played, according to its motion pattern. Turning the knob to the left slows the motion of the graintable down, whereas turning it to the right will speed it up.

▶ **Shift**—This parameter alters the timbre or formant spectrum of a graintable. The formant spectrum is the overview that determines the overall character of a graintable. This is done by a procedure known as re-sampling. Using this parameter effectively creates a pitch shift effect on the oscillator.

MOTION PATTERN

Each graintable in a patch has a preset motion pattern and speed. If you're setting the Motion parameter to any value higher than −63 or hard left, the graintable loops and follows one of two motion patterns:

    ▶ **Forward**—The graintable is played from beginning to end, and then loops back to the beginning.

    ▶ **Forward/Backward**—The graintable is played from beginning to end, and then from the end to beginning. It then starts over.

As stated before, the Motion parameter can change the speed of the graintable, but not the actual graintable itself.

The Amplitude Envelope

Each of the Malström oscillators has an individual envelope and volume knob to alter its amplitude (see Figure 10.6).

Figure 10.6
The Amp Envelope of each oscillator allows for precise amplitude control.

▶ **Attack**—When an envelope is triggered, the Attack parameter determines how long it takes for the envelope to reach its maximum value.

▶ **Decay**—Once the maximum value is reached, the Decay parameter determines how long it stays at the level before the value begins to drop.

▶ **Sustain**—After the value begins to drop, the Sustain parameter determines the level the falling value should rest at.

▶ **Release**—Once the value has been set at its rested value, the Release parameter determines how long it will take for the value to return to zero after the keys have been released.

Routing and Output

Once you have set the oscillator parameters, you can then route the output of those signals to a combination of four filter destinations. Looking at Figure 10.7, you can see that each oscillator points to the right, with a corresponding "routing" button that looks a lot like the standard power buttons you have been looking at throughout this chapter. To route the oscillators to their corresponding filters, just click on the available routing buttons.

Figure 10.7
The oscillators point to the right, which means that they can be routed to the filter sections. Notice that OSC A points to both filters, which means that the output signal of OSC A can actually be split and routed to two destination filters.

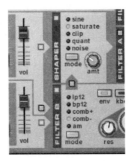

The Output section of the Malström is very simple and has only two adjustable parameters (see Figure 10.8).

Figure 10.8
The output of the Malström can control the amplitude and panning assignment for both oscillators.

▶ **Spread**—This parameter is used to adjust the panning width of OSC A and B. Turning this knob hard right creates a very wide stereo field, in which OSC A is heard only in the left channel, whereas OSC B is heard in the right.

▶ **Volume**—This adjusts the overall volume of the Malström.

The Filter Section

As you have read in previous chapters, a filter is used to alter the overall character of a sound. The Filter section of the Malström does this tenfold, by including additional filters and parameters that deviate significantly from most other filters (see Figure 10.9).

Figure 10.9
The Malström Filter section provides many creative filtering possibilities that differ greatly from those of most other synths.

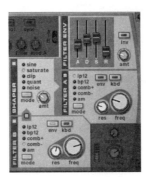

To activate either Filter A or Filter B, click on their power buttons, found in the upper-left corner of each filter. Also, make sure that the appropriate oscillator is assigned to the desired filter.

Filter Types

Before altering the Resonance and Cutoff Frequency parameters, you must choose one of five filter types (see Figure 10.10).

Figure 10.10
Each of the Malström filters offer five filter types.

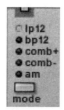

▶ **LP24**—This filter allows low frequencies to pass through it, while high frequencies are filtered out. This low pass filter has a very intense roll-off curve (approximately 24 decibels per octave), which produces a greater emphasis of the low frequencies.

▶ **BP12**—Filters out both the high and low frequencies, leaving the mid frequencies alone to be toyed with. With a roll-off curve of 12 decibels per octave, the BP 12 can be used effectively on instrument loops such as a guitar loop or possibly hi-hat heavy percussion loops.

▶ **Comb +/−**—A comb filter is essentially a series of delays with very short delay times assigned to each delay instance, resulting in a detuned sound. The feedback of these delays is controlled by the Resonance parameter in each filter. The difference between the Comb+ and Comb− is the position of the delay peaks within the spectrum.

▶ **AM (Amplitude Modulation)**—This filter produces a sine wave, which is then multiplied by the output of either OSC A or B. The resulting sound contains additional frequencies that are a result of the sum and difference of the two frequencies. Note that the Resonance knob controls the mix between the two signals. If this sounds familiar, another way to think of this is as a *ring modulator*.

The Filter Controls

Once a filter type has been selected, you can then use the main controls of the filter to alter the character of the Malström patch (see Figure 10.11).

Figure 10.11
The main parameters of the Malström filters.

▶ **Kbd (keyboard tracking)**—When this parameter is activated, it will enable the filter to react differently the higher you play on the keyboard. If this parameter is deactivated, the filter effect will remain constant.

▶ **Env (envelope)**—When this parameter is activated, the filter will then be modulated by the Filter Envelope.

▶ **Freq (Cutoff Frequency)**—This parameter has two purposes, depending on which filter type is selected. When LP24, BP12, or Comb+/− is selected, this parameter acts as a cutoff frequency knob that specifies where the filter will function within the frequency spectrum. When the AM Filter Type is selected, the Frequency knob will control the frequency of the ring-modulated signal generated by the AM filter.

▶ **Res (Resonance)**—This parameter has two purposes depending on which filter type is selected. When LP24, BP12, or Comb+/− is selected, this parameter emphasizes the frequencies set by the Freq knob. When the AM Filter Type is selected, the Resonance knob regulates the balance between the original and the modulated signal.

The Filter Envelope

The Filter Envelope is used to alter the characteristics of Filter A, Filter B, or both. The main parameters of the envelope match those of the Oscillator Envelopes, so there is no need to review how Attack, Decay, Sustain, and Release work (see Figure 10.12). The additional parameters for the Filter Envelope are as follows:

Figure 10.12
The Filter Envelope can be used to create long, sweeping effects for pad sounds, or bubble-like sweeps for bass synths.

▶ **Inv (Inverse)**—This button is used to invert the individual parameters of the Filter Envelope. For example, say you are using the Attack parameter of the Filter Envelope and have assigned a positive value of 80, which produces a very slow attack. Activate the Invert button and the attack parameter is inverted, which means the attack will be much faster now.

▶ **Amt (Amount)**—This knob is used to assign the amount of envelope to the filters.

The Shaper

Aside from the obvious auditory goodies that the Filter section provides, my favorite part has to be the Shaper. The Shaper is a *waveshaper*, which alters the waveform shape itself. This results in either a more complex, rich sound or a truncated distortion that rivals Industrial Music on a good day.

The Shaper is activated by clicking on its power button, located in the upper-left corner of the Shaper interface. Once activated, you can edit the waveshaping effect by selecting a mode and assigning an amount.

Let's have a look at the different shaping modes. They can be selected by using the Mode button, or by just clicking on the name of the desired mode itself (see Figure 10.13).

Figure 10.13
The Shaper is capable of beefing up your synth patches with saturation, or creating a synthetic meltdown with ultra distortion.

▶ **Sine**—This creates a smooth sound.

▶ **Saturate**—This saturates the original signal, resulting in a rich, lush sound.

▶ **Clip**—This adds digital distortion to the signal.

▶ **Quant**—This truncates the signal and can be used to create a grungy 8-bit sound.

▶ **Noise**—This multiplies the original signal with noise.

USING THE SHAPER WITH FILTER B
Located at the top of Filter B is a routing button that allows that filter to be sent to the Shaper, creating a very interesting combination of sounds. For example, you can send OSC A to the Shaper, while at the same time split and send OSC A to Filter B. OSC B will also be sent to Filter B and then routed to the Shaper as well. After both signals are combined and processed by the Shaper, the signal is then sent to Filter A and sent along to the outputs of the Malström.

The Modulator Section

Located above the Oscillator section are a pair of modulators, which are used to alter the character of the synth sound (see Figure 10.14). If this sounds a little familiar, another way to think of these modulators is as low frequency oscillators, which were discussed in the last two chapters and will be discussed again in future chapters. However, because the Malström is a synth unlike anything else in Reason, it's safe to say that these modulators go way above and beyond the call of duty when it comes to modulating the oscillators.

Figure 10.14
The Malström modulator section is actually a pair of LFOs.

THE SOUNDS OF SILENCE
As with the Subtractor and Dr:rex, the Malström modulators do not produce sound on their own. Although they do generate a waveform and frequency, they are assigned to alter the character of OSC A and B.

When an instance of the Malström is created, modulators A and B are active and ready to use. To deactivate either of these, click on their power buttons, which are located at the upper-left corner of each modulator.

Take a look at the source parameters of the Modulator section.

▶ **Curve**—This parameter is used to select a modulating waveform. You can either use the scroll buttons to select different waveforms or click and drag up and down on the display. There are over 30 waveforms to choose from, so it should keep you busy for a long time to come.

▶ **Rate**—This parameter controls the speed of modulation. Turn the knob to the left to slow the frequency down, or to the right to speed it up. Also note that if the Sync button is activated, the rate indicator is measured in note values (that is, 1/4, 1/8, and 1/16).

▶ **1-Shot**—When activated, the 1-Shot will play the modulation waveform a single time.

▶ **Sync**—This parameter makes the modulator synchronize with the tempo of your Reason song.

▶ **A/B Selector**—This parameter is used to select which oscillator the modulator will affect. You can select OSC A, OSC B, or both.

Once a modulation waveform, rate, and source have been selected, you can choose a destination parameter to be modulated. Note that both modulators have different destination parameters, so I will point those out along the way.

BIPOLAR PARAMETERS

The destination parameter knobs are bipolar. This means that when the knob is in the middle position, there is no modulation effect, but turning the knob to the left or right will increase the amount of modulation. To make it even more interesting, when the knob is turned to the left, the waveform of the modulator is inverted.

▶ **Pitch (Mod A)**—Modulates the pitch parameter of OSC A, B, or both.

▶ **Index (Mod A)**—Modulates the index start position of OSC A, B, or both.

▶ **Shift (Mod A)**—Modulates the harmonic content of OSC A, B, or both.

▶ **Motion (Mod B)**—Modulates the motion speed of OSC A, B, or both.

▶ **Vol (Mod B)**—Modulates the output amplitude of OSC A, B, or both.

▶ **Filter (Mod B)**—Modulates the cutoff filter of OSC A, B, or both.

▶ **Mod:A (Mod B)**—Alters the amount of modulation from Mod A.

The Play Parameters

The parameters covered in this section affect the overall sound of the Malström based on the way that you play the synth (see Figure 10.15).

Figure 10.15
The Malström Play parameters are used to give your synth performance more expression.

Polyphony

Polyphony assigns the number of voices that can be played at one time. The Malström has a polyphony range of 1 to 16 voices, which is not a lot by comparison to the Subtractor or NN-19/XT synths. However, it is important to keep in mind that the Malström is a much more CPU-intensive virtual synth, and every voice takes up a little more CPU power.

NO LOW BANDWIDTH

One feature that the Malström is missing is a Low Bandwidth button. There is no explanation why this feature is not included with the Malström, but my take on it is that the technology behind this synth wonder makes it impossible to support such a feature.

But I have run Malström with no problems on a pair of fairly slow computers. However, the slower first edition G3/G4 Macs or Pentium II computers might not be able to run the Malström.

Portamento

Portamento creates a sliding effect between played notes. The knob determines the amount of time it will take to slide from one note to another. It can be used with either monophonic or polyphonic patches and is a great tool for creating some interesting effects.

Legato

Legato is a commonly used parameter for playing monophonic patches, such as leads or bass lines. With the legato parameter activated and the polyphony set to 1, press and hold down a note, and then press and hold another note. Notice that the new note has no attack, as the Malström envelopes have not been retriggered.

Velocity Controls

The Malström is a velocity-sensitive synthesizer, as are the other Reason synths. The Velocity Controls are used to affect different parameters of the Malström according to how much velocity is applied to individual notes.

> ▶ **Level A**—This parameter velocity controls the output of OSC A.

> ▶ **Level B**— This parameter velocity controls the output of OSC B.

> ▶ **Filter Envelope**—This parameter assigns the velocity control of the Filter Envelope.

> ▶ **Attack**—This parameter velocity controls the Attack parameter of OSC A, B, or both.

> ▶ **Shift**—This parameter velocity controls the Shift parameter of OSC A, B, or both.

> ▶ **Modulation**—This parameter velocity controls the amounts of Modulator A, B, or both.

Pitch Bend Wheel

The Pitch Bend Wheel is an emulation of a standard pitch wheel found on most MIDI keyboards. Simply put, it is used to bend the pitch of the played notes up and down. The Range parameter, located just above the Pitch Bend Wheel, controls the range of the pitch bend by up to +/– two octaves.

Modulation Wheel

The Modulation Wheel is used to control a number of available parameters:

> ▶ **Index**—This parameter affects the graintable index of OSC A, B, or both.

> ▶ **Shift**—This parameter affects the Shift parameter of OSC A, B, or both.

> ▶ **Filter**—This parameter affects the Frequency Filter of Filter A, B, or both.

> ▶ **Modulation**—This parameter alters the amount of modulation from Modulator A, B, or both.

CV Connections

Press the Tab key to flip the Device Rack around, and you'll see that the Malström has many connections that can be used to sequence with the Matrix, modulate other devices, or be modulated by other devices (see Figure 10.16).

Figure 10.16
The back of the Malström offers many routing possibilities.

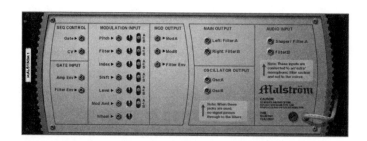

Audio Outputs

These connections are used to output the signal from the Malström to reMix. There are a couple of options.

▶ **Main Outputs**—These are the main audio outputs of the Malström. They are taken from the outputs of the Filter section.

▶ **Oscillator Outputs**—This second pair of outputs is taken directly from the outputs of OSC A and B. If you connect these outputs to reMix, the main outputs will no longer work.

Audio Input

Another of the many lesser known, yet equally mind-blowing, features of the Malström is the audio input capabilities. These inputs make it possible to route the audio output of any Reason device into the audio inputs of the Malström, which are then directly fed into Filters A and B. Essentially, this makes the Malström an audio effect that is perfect for laying down some intense filter work on your loops, synths, and samples.

For kicks, try the following exercise:

1. Create a new Reason song.
2. Create instances of reMix, Malström, and the NN-19. Load a sample patch into the NN-19 and arm the sequencer track to receive MIDI.
3. Press the Tab key to flip the interface.
4. Disconnect the NN-19 from reMix by selecting it and choosing Disconnect Device from the Edit pull-down menu.
5. Route the audio outputs of the NN-19 to the audio inputs of the Malström (see Figure 10.17).
6. With the NN-19 sequencer track selected and armed to receive MIDI, play a note on your MIDI keyboard and you will hear the sample patch played through the filters of the Malström.

Figure 10.17
Connect the audio outputs of the NN-19 to the Malström.

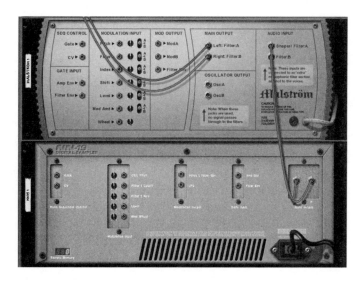

Sequencer Controls

The Sequencer Control inputs are used to connect the Malström to a pattern-controlled device, such as the Matrix or Redrum.

> ▶ **Gate**—This input is typically connected to the Gate CV output of the Matrix or Redrum in order to receive Note On/Off messages.

> ▶ **CV**—This input is typically connected to the Note CV output of the Matrix in order to receive note information.

SEE CHAPTER 13

For more information on using the Matrix, be sure to check out Chapter 13, "The Matrix—Close Up," where you will find some interesting tutorials on how to connect the Matrix to the Subtractor. These tutorials also work great with the Malström.

Gate Input

These inputs are used to receive Gate information from either the Matrix or Redrum in order to trigger the following envelopes.

> ▶ Amp Envelope
> ▶ Filter Envelope

Modulation Input/Output

To the right of the Sequencer controls and Gate input are the Modulation inputs and outputs. The Modulation inputs can receive modulation output signals from any Reason device. The Curve CV output on the back of the Matrix is a good example of this. The Modulation outputs send out modulation information to any Reason device. A commonly used connection is to connect any of the Modulation outputs of the Malström to the Modulation inputs of the Subtractor.

Let's have a look at the various inputs.

> ▶ **Pitch**—This input is used to affect the pitch of Modulator A, B, or both.

> ▶ **Filter**—This input is used to affect the filter frequency of Modulator A, B, or both.

> ▶ **Index**—This input is used to affect the index of Modulator A, B, or both.

> ▶ **Shift**—This input is used to affect the shift of Modulator A, B, or both.

> ▶ **Level**—This input is used to affect the amplitude of Oscillator A, B, or both.

> ▶ **Modulation Amount**—This input is used to affect the amount of modulation.

> ▶ **Wheel**—This input is used to affect the Modulation Wheel.

And now, let's have a look at the outputs.

> ▶ **Mod A**—This connection routes the output of Modulator A to the modulation inputs of any other Reason device. Try connecting it to the FM Amount parameter of the Subtractor.

▶ **Mod B**—This connection routes the output of Modulator B to the modulation inputs of any Reason device.

▶ **Filter Envelope**—This connection routes the output of the Filter Envelope to the modulation inputs of any Reason device.

Your First Malström Patch

Now that you have a pretty firm idea of how the Malström works, it's time to dig in and create your first customized Malström patch. This tutorial takes you through a step-by-step process of programming a bass synth patch that will be perfect for any ambient occasion.

Setting Up a Start Point

Before you program your first Malström patch, it's important to find a good starting point. Writing in a sequence that's appropriate for the kind of patch you are going to create will make the programming process quicker and more efficient. For example, if I were going to create a pad sound, I would typically write in a sequence of long, sustained chords, so I could hear the pad sound properly.

If you are planning to program a bass synth patch to be used in techno music, it's a good idea to write in a standard techno bass line in the Reason sequencer. Then set the sequencer to play the bass line over and over again in a loop (see Figure 10.18). Then you can make real-time adjustments to the patch as the sequence is playing and program the patch to complement the style of music you are going to create with the patch.

Figure 10.18
I have written a techno styled bass line into the Reason sequencer in order to program a bass synth patch in the Malström.

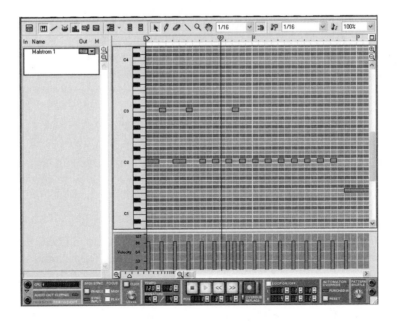

For this programming tutorial, you are going to create a bass patch, which is used to establish the rhythm section along with Redrum or Dr:rex. This is a perfect place to set up the Reason sequencer with a punchy bass line so that you can loop the sequence and make changes to the Subtractor in real time. Before you begin, start a new Reason song and create instances of reMix and the Malström.

1. Click on the Switch to Edit Mode button to display the Key Lane Editor.

2. Set the Snap value to 1/16. This will draw in 16th notes.

3. Using your Pencil tool, draw in a bass line in any key that you want.

4. Activate the Loop mode on the Transport Panel. Set the left locator to measure 1 and the right locator to measure 3. This will give you a two-bar loop (see Figure 10.19).

Figure 10.19
A two-bar loop has been created.

LEARN BY EXAMPLE

Although this tutorial is a good hands-on learning experience, it might not answer all of your questions pertaining to the Malström. You might find yourself wanting to program a pad or a solo instrument of some kind. My best suggestion for you is to use the Patch Browser and locate Malström patches that are similar to the type of patch you want to program. Experiment with the different parameters of a particular patch until you get a feel for how each one works and how they can be used in creating your own custom patch.

Make no mistake about it; the Malström is a tough nut to crack when it comes to programming, because there are so many directions to channel your creativity. Give it time and try to learn by example.

Programming Your Malström Patch

In this tutorial, you are going to build a bass patch by working with each section of the Malström interface. Just as in the last chapter, this tutorial serves as a good review tool to help you remember everything that you have learned about the functionality of the Malström.

Programming the Oscillators

Let's start things off simple by working with OSC A, and then add OSC B later. To hear the changes in real time, click on Play on the transport bar. The two-bar loop should start playing continuously.

1. By default, the graintable of OSC A is set to a Sine Wave. Notice the organ-like tone that is produced.

2. Use the scroll buttons or click on the graintable box to display a list of available sounds. Choose the Wet Bass graintable.

3. Next, use the Index slider to set the start point of the graintable. Set it to 40 and notice how dramatically the overall tone and timbre of the graintable changes.

Let's also make a few adjustments to the Amplitude Envelope of Osc A. Set the parameters to the following values:

▶ **Attack**—Set to 0

▶ **Decay**—Set to 65

▶ **Sustain**—Set to 0

▶ **Release**—Set to 14 for a short release

And now, on to OSC B.

1. Activate OSC B and set its graintable to Additive Wave 3.

2. Set the Motion to 7.

3. Set the Oct parameter to 3.

4. Set the index slider to 48.

Let's make a few adjustments to the Amplitude Envelope of Osc B. Set the parameters to the following values:

▶ **Attack**—Set to 12

▶ **Decay**—Set to 25

▶ **Sustain**—Set to 16

▶ **Release**—Set to 10

Upon listening to the patch at this point, it lacks a uniqueness. You can introduce such a quality by way of the modulators.

Programming the Modulators

As you read earlier in this chapter, the modulators are actually two separate LFOs. In this section of the tutorial, you are going to assign the modulators to manipulate Osc A and B.

1. Activate Mod A and select the Sync button. This will lock the modulation effect up with the tempo of the Reason sequencer.

2. By default, the waveform of Mod A should be set to a Sine Wave. Leave it at this setting and set the Rate knob to 1/4, which means that the modulation effect will take place every quarter note.

3. Set the destination of Mod A to OSC A&B by using the A/B selector to the right of the Mod A interface.

4. Assign a negative value of –24 to the Index knob. This should then cause the Shift of OSC A&B to open and close in tempo.

Programming the Filter and Shaper

In this section of the tutorial, you are going to add the Shaper to Osc A to introduce a little distortion to the bass sound.

1. Activate both the Route Oscillator A to Shaper and Activate Shaper buttons.

2. Select the Saturate Shaper mode by using the Mode button or by clicking on the name. You should immediately hear a strong distorted signal applied to Osc A.

3. Set the Shaper Amount knob to 39 to turn down the distortion effect.

Next, let's route Osc B to Filter B and do some more damage.

1. Activate the Route Oscillator B to Filter B button. Filter B should already be activated and ready to use. Also note that the Env button is already active, which means that the Filter Envelope can be used at this time.

2. Set Filter mode to Comb– by using the Mode button or by clicking on the name.

3. Set the Resonance knob to 70.

4. Set the Frequency Filter knob to 99.

You can also assign Osc A to Filter B by clicking on the Route Osc A to Filter B button. I would suggest not activating it for this tutorial, because Osc A has a very strong signal of its own.

Additionally, you can route Filter B to the Shaper by clicking on the Route Filter B to Shaper button, which is located in between Filter B and the Shaper sections. This will add a pleasant distortion to Filter B, which sounds pretty cool.

To finish with the Filter and Shaper sections, use the Filter Envelope on Filter B. Set the envelope parameters to these values:

▶ **Amount**—Set to 32

▶ **Attack**—Set to 38

▶ **Decay**—Set to 59

▶ **Sustain**—Set to 64

▶ **Release**—Set to 10

Programming the Play Parameters

You're in the homestretch; you can finish this patch by making a few adjustments to the Play parameters of the Malström, as follows:

▶ **Polyphony**—By default the Malström has a polyphony of 8, and this is fine for a bass synth sound. You might even want to assign a polyphony of 1 so that you can make this a monophonic synth.

▶ **Modulation Wheel**—Set the A/B Selector to its default position. Assign a negative value to the Shift knob so it will decrease in value as the Modulation Wheel is used. Assign a positive amount to the index.

▶ **Portamento**—Assigning a positive amount of 34 to this parameter will create a sliding effect that sounds great with monophonic bass synths.

After all is said and done, your new bass patch should sound pretty awesome and work well with just about any form of electronic music. Just make sure to click on the Save Patch button to save your work.

The next chapter covers the first of Reason's two virtual samplers, called the NN-19.

11

NN-19—Close Up

Introduced with Reason in version 1.0, the NN-19 (see Figure 11.1) is a software sampler that looks and functions a lot like the classic Akai hardware samplers of the past decade. If you are new to the concept of sampling and samplers, the NN-19 is a perfect tool for learning all about this interesting technology.

Figure 11.1
The NN-19 emulates a hardware sampler, but with a few tricks and treats to fuel creativity.

A SAMPLER—DEFINED

Classifying the NN-19 and its big brother NN-XT as samplers is not quite accurate. By musical instrument standards, a *sampler* is a piece of hardware capable of recording and playing back selected bits of digital audio.

Such is not the case with the NN-19; it fits only half of that definition. The NN-19's primary purpose is to play back bits of recorded digital audio (called *samples*), such as guitars, basses, and voices. However, the NN-19 *cannot* record or capture digital audio as a hardware sampler would, so they are more correctly called sample *players*.

If you want to create your own samples for the NN-19, there are many fine digital audio-editing applications that will meet your needs. Check out Steinberg's WaveLab or Sonic Foundry's Sound Forge for the PC; if you are on the Macintosh, Bias' Peak or TC Worx's Spark will certainly do the job.

Basic Sample-Creation Principles

A great advantage to using software samplers is that they support a number of audio file formats, unlike their hardware counterparts (for example, Akai and EMU), which are format specific. The NN-19 supports several digital audio formats, including:

▶ NN-19 sample patches (.smp)

▶ WAVE (.wav)

▶ AIFF (.aif)

▶ SoundFonts (.sf2)

▶ REX files and individual REX slices (.rex2, .rex, and .rcy)

Using Single Samples

Using a single sample with the NN-19 is accomplished by loading a sample into its interface. This sample is then *mapped*, or spread out over the entire length of the virtual keyboard of the NN-19 interface. Once a sample is loaded into the NN-19, you can then arm its sequencer track and press a key on your MIDI controller keyboard to trigger the sample. Additionally, the loaded sample's original pitch (or *root key*) is automatically assigned to the C3 key (see Figure 11.2).

The next sections show how to accomplish this by first importing a standard AIFF or WAV file and then loading an individual REX slice.

Loading AIFF and WAV Files

Loading AIFF and WAV files into the NN-19 is done almost exactly the same way as loading REX slices.

1. Create a new NN-19 and click on the Sample Browser button to open the browser window.

2. Double-click on the Reason Factory Sound Bank to display the contents.

3. Double-click on the folder called Other Samples to open it.

4. Double-click on the folder called Chords-Phrases-Pads-Stabs to open it.

5. You will see a long list of available AIFF files. Double-click any one of them to import it into the NN-19.

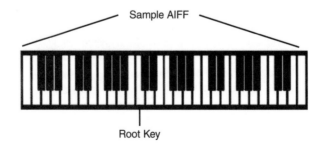

Figure 11.2
In this diagram, a single sample has been loaded into the NN-19 sampler and automatically mapped out over the entire keyboard. By doing this, the loaded sample will trigger no matter which key is pressed on your MIDI keyboard.

Loading REX Slices

As mentioned earlier, the NN-19 can import and use REX files. This can be done from the standard patch-browsing interface in the upper-left corner. Once imported, the REX file is mapped out chromatically on the NN-19 interface starting at the C1 key.

The NN-19 can also import individual REX file slices. This is a great feature, because it can lead to several creative possibilities. For example, by importing individual slices from different REX files, you can build your own custom drum kit and save it as an NN-19 patch, or possibly a kit of different sound effects taken from different REX files. It really is up to you and your creativity!

In order to import a REX slice, you must use the Browse Sample tools, found in the upper-middle portion of the NN-19 interface (see Figure 11.3). Click on the folder icon to launch the sample browser window, which is identical to the patch browser window. Let's get in a little practice importing a REX slice.

1. Use the sample browser window to find the Reason Factory Sound Bank ReFill.

2. Open the ReFill and navigate to (and open) the Dr Rex Drum Loops folder. Open the first folder in the list, called Abstract Hip Hop.

3. Double-click the first REX file, SoleSide. The sample browser window will then display all of the 17 individual slices within the SoleSide REX file (see Figure 11.4). Notice that, just like the patch browser window, you have the Autoplay option in the lower-right corner to audition each slice.

Figure 11.3
Use the Browse Sample button and its scroll buttons to import individual samples.

Figure 11.4
The sample browser window is used to locate and load individual audio samples into the NN-19.

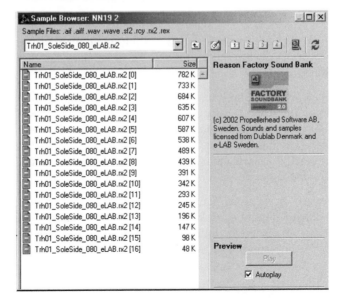

CHAPTER 11

4. Select the first slice and double-click on it to load it into the NN-19 interface (into note #C3). If you have a MIDI keyboard, arm the NN-19 sequencer track and play the C3 key on your keyboard to hear it play back.

5. You can now create a few more key zones and add more REX slices or other AIFF/WAV files to create your first drum kit. When you're finished, save it as an NN-19 patch (an .smp file).

Although single samples are incredibly easy to work with, they have a serious drawback. A single-sampled note sounds natural only within a very limited range. For example, if you load one piano sample into the NN-19 and play the root note (C3), that note will sound fine. Now try playing that sample a half-octave from the root note; you will hear digital noise in the playback, and you'll notice that the sample is playing faster or slower depending on where you are playing in relation to the root note.

Another way to demonstrate this effect is to use a sample of a person talking. When you play this sample above its root note, the person's voice will sound too fast, just like a tape machine that is playing faster than normal. You will get the opposite effect when playing the same sample below its root note.

The whole point of using a sampler is to make your performance sound just like the real instrument you are attempting to emulate. This is accomplished using a technique called multisampling, discussed next.

DELETING SAMPLES
To delete a loaded sample, select the sample by clicking on it in the virtual keyboard and selecting Delete Sample from the Edit pull-down menu.

Multisampling

Multisampling is a process in which several samples of a specific instrument are loaded into assigned parts of the sampler keyboard. The resulting sound is usually an accurate representation of the instrument you are attempting to emulate. There are many multisampled NN-19 patches included with Reason, but this can also be done on your own.

To begin the process of multisampling, you must first divide the sampler's virtual keyboard into sections. This is accomplished by using key zones. As shown in Figure 11.5, *key zones* are assignable portions of the virtual keyboard that contain a defined range of notes. For example, a key zone can have a specified low note of C3, and a specified high note of E3, giving you a five-note range. Additionally, a sample that has a root note within this range (C3 for instance) can then be loaded into this zone and played, and it will sound very natural.

Creating a key zone is very simple. You simply choose Split Key Zone from the Edit pull-down menu of Reason, at which point a marker is placed on the keyboard display of the NN-19. This marker can be moved to the left or right in the virtual keyboard. After the zone has been created, you can then load a sample into it by clicking on the Sample Browser button, located just above the virtual keyboard. Once the sample is loaded, you can then create and select another zone to load another sample.

Figure 11.5
In this diagram, the sampler keyboard has been split into specified sections, known as key zones. Once these zones are created, individual samples can be loaded into each zone.

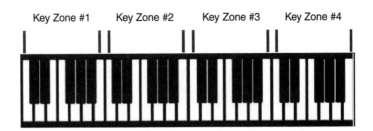

Key Zone #1   Key Zone #2   Key Zone #3   Key Zone #4

DELETING KEY ZONES

If you need to delete a key zone, just select it in the virtual keyboard. Then choose Delete Key Zone from the Edit pull-down menu.

HANDS-ON MULTISAMPLING

At the end of this chapter, you'll find a step-by step tutorial showing how to multisample an acoustic guitar.

ANOTHER USE FOR MULTISAMPLING

Another way to use multisampling is to load multiple sample loops to the virtual keyboard. This will enable you to play different sampled loops at the same tempo within one sampler (see Figure 11.6). This is done by creating numerous key zones and setting each of them up with a range of one note. For example, C3 to C3 would be the range of one key zone, and C#3 to C#3 would be the range of the next key zone.

CHAPTER 11

Figure 11.6
When using multiple sampled loops, you can create numerous key zones and load a loop into each one.

Loop 02.aiff   Loop 04.aiff

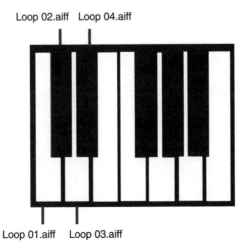

Loop 01.aiff   Loop 03.aiff

A Guided Tour of the NN-19

It's time to begin an in-depth tour of the NN-19. Toward the end of this chapter, you can further enhance your NN-19 education by following the step-by-step tutorial for creating your own sample patches.

Loading Patches

At the top-left corner of the NN-19 interface is the patch-browsing interface. This functions in exactly the same way as all of the other Reason devices.

USING HI-RES SAMPLES

The NN-19 supports just about every bit depth and sampling rate in the book. By default, it will import these various bit-depth files, but it will dither the file to 16 bits upon playback unless told otherwise, which might sound good enough to some, but not to others (myself included).

This can be easily remedied by checking the Use High Resolution Samples check box in the General Preferences window (see Figure 11.7). Once you select this option, the NN-19 as well as Reason's other RAM-based sound modules will play high-resolution samples at their original bit depth.

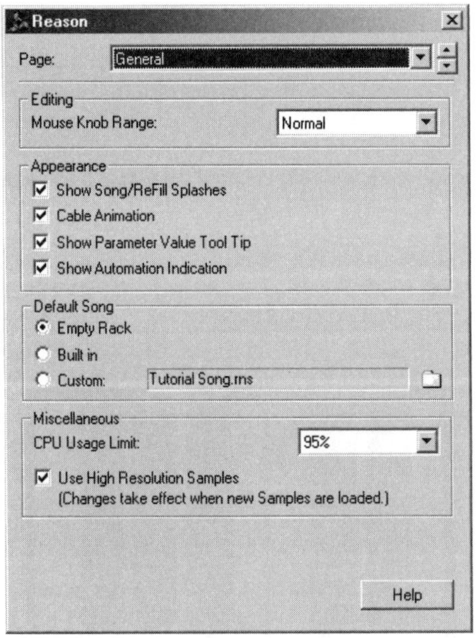

Figure 11.7
Choose the Use High Resolution Samples check box to have the NN-19 play files back at their original bit depth.

AUDITIONING LOADED PATCHES

Once a patch has been loaded into the NN-19 interface, you will want to audition it before using it in your song. This can be done by using a MIDI keyboard, or by using the key editor in the Reason sequencer.

There is a third way to accomplish this, using your computer keyboard and mouse. Hold the Alt key down (or Option key on the Mac) and navigate your cursor to the keyboard display of the NN-19 interface. The pointer icon will change to a speaker symbol, which you can then use to click on the different keys of the keyboard display to trigger the samples.

The NN-19 Virtual Keyboard Display

In the center of the NN-19 interface, the virtual keyboard is where all of the preferences are set for the loaded samples (see Figure 11.8).

Figure 11.8
The NN-19 virtual keyboard is used to load and assign samples.

Once a sample has been loaded into the NN-19, it can then be selected and given specific parameters. You can see how this works by loading up a basic NN-19 patch and looking at the individual parameters. For this tour, use a basic patch, such as the Didgeridoo patch, which can be found in the Mallet and Ethnic folder of the NN-19 folder.

Selecting and Editing Key Zones

In the upper-left and upper-right corners of the virtual keyboard are the scroll tools to help you navigate to the right and left sides of the keyboard. Use these tools to navigate to the lowest key zone so it can be selected. Once you locate it, click on it to display its information just below the virtual keyboard.

SELECT A KEY ZONE VIA MIDI

Another way to select a key zone is to activate the Select Key Zone Via MIDI button, located just above the virtual keyboard. Once this is selected and the NN-19 sequencer track is armed to receive MIDI, you can use a MIDI keyboard to select the different key zones of any loaded patch.

The following key zone parameters can be edited:

▶ **Low Key**—Sets the lowest possible note in a selected key zone. Note that it cannot have a value greater than its high key value.

▶ **High Key**—Sets the highest possible note in a selected key zone. Note that it cannot have a value less than its low key value.

▶ **Sample**—If you are using a patch with multiple samples and key zones, you can use this knob to select a sample for a particular key zone.

▶ **Root Key**—Displays the root or original pitch of the loaded sample. Use the Root Key knob to move the original pitch up or down the keyboard.

▶ **Tune**—This knob is used to correct the pitch of a sample and has a range of +/– 50 semitones.

▶ **Level**—Sets the amplitude for a selected sample.

▶ **Loop**—Sets the loop mode for the sample. You can select Off (no looping), FW (constant looping between two points), and FW-BW (plays loop from start to end, and then end to start).

SETTING LOOP POINTS

A *loop point* occurs when a sample is prepared to continuously loop from left to right in order to give the illusion that the sample is sustaining. Loop points are commonly used on sample patches such as pianos or guitars, to make the patch act more like the actual instrument. Another use for loop points are with drum loops that need to repeat cleanly without pops and clicks.

These loop points are created in audio-editing programs such as WaveLab, Sound Forge, and Peak. Once the loop points have been established, the audio-editing program saves them with the audio file. NN-19 will use them when the Loop mode is activated in the virtual keyboard.

Selecting Key Zones and Soloing Samples

Located just above the key zone display are two additional parameters.

▶ **SELECT KEYZONE VIA MIDI**—When activated, this parameter links the key zone display to your MIDI keyboard. Whenever you press a key on your MIDI keyboard, the relevant key zone will display in the Key Zone editor.

▶ **SOLO SAMPLE**—This parameter will solo a sample within a key zone and hear it mapped throughout the virtual keyboard. This is used primarily to make sure that the root note is set correctly. Note that SELECT KEYZONE VIA MIDI must be disabled prior to activating this parameter.

The NN-19 Synth Parameters

Once you have loaded your samples into the NN-19 interface, you can begin to manipulate, twist, and contort them to your heart's content by using the synth parameters. As shown in Figure 11.9, the synth parameters of the NN-19 bear a striking similarity to those in the Subtractor and Dr:rex. If you are familiar with these aforementioned Reason devices, the NN-19 synth parameters should be a walk in the park.

Figure 11.9
The NN-19 synth parameters.

 THESE PARAMETERS ARE GLOBAL

It's important to note that all of the parameters in the NN-19 are *global*, meaning that they affect the playback of the entire loaded sampler. Those of you who want to edit the individual parameters of each sample will be glad to know that the NN-19's big brother, the NN-XT, can handle it easily. When you've finished this chapter, move to Chapter 12, "NN-XT—Close Up," to learn how individual manipulation is done.

CHAPTER 11

The Oscillator Section

Although the name suggests that the NN-19 has an oscillator, that's not quite true. Yes, the NN-19 does make sounds, but not with the help of an oscillator, like the one found in the Subtractor. A sampler produces sounds by using digital audio as its catalyst, rather than using oscillation (see Figure 11.10).

The Sample Start knob alters the starting position of a loaded sample. As you increase the value of the Sample Start knob, the start position moves further and further toward the end of the sampled sound. This can be used, for example, to remove unwanted silence before a sample or to trigger a specific part of a sample, rather than the whole sample itself.

To make a little more sense out of this parameter, see Figure 11.11. I prepared a sequence using the Pizzicato string sample patch found in the NN-19 sample directory. On the left side of this figure, you can see the waveform of the sequence playing but the Sample Start knob is set to 0. The waveform on the right side of the figure shows the same sequence with the Sample Start knob set to 50, or 10:00. Notice how much more abruptly the sample played back.

Figure 11.10
The NN-19 Oscillator section is used to specify when a sample starts and is also used to tune the sample.

Figure 11.11
These waveforms show the same sequence with the Sample Start knob at different positions.

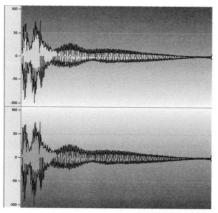
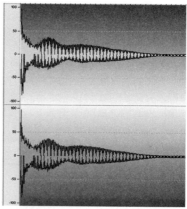

SAMPLE START VIA VELOCITY

For added effect, the Sample Start feature is linked to the Velocity section of the NN-19 Play parameters. By using the Velocity section to control your Sample Start, it is possible to achieve a wide variation of dynamics with percussive samples.

Below the Sample Start knob is the High Quality Interpolation button. This button is used to optimize the sound quality of the loaded samples. This button was discussed in past chapters. To review how it works, see the note in Chapter 7, "Redrum—Close Up," called "Algorithms? Interpolation?" for more information.

To the right of the Sample Start knob are the NN-19 pitch controls. These manipulate the pitch of your sample patches using any of the three main parameters:

▶ **Oct**—Shifts the sample pitch by octaves. It has an 8-octave range with a default setting of 4.

▶ **Semi**—Shifts the sample pitch by up to 12 semitones, equaling one octave.

▶ **Fine**—Shifts the sample pitch by 100ths of a semitone and allows for very precise pitch adjustments. This knob has a range of −50 to 50.

Located in the lower-right corner of the main pitch parameters are two additional controls that can be used with them.

The KBD.Track button specifies whether the sample patch you have loaded contains variable pitches or a constant pitch. For example, a violin has many pitches, so you would want to make sure that the keyboard tracking button is active. But if you are using a sample that is not pitch specific, such as a snare drum, you can turn this button off, and the pitch of the snare drum will remain constant, no matter what key you play on your keyboard.

The Env Amt knob links the pitch of your sample patches to the Filter Envelope, which is discussed later in this chapter. When assigned a positive amount, the pitch of the sample will raise according to the settings of the F. Envelope parameters. When assigned a negative amount, the pitch will lower according to the same parameters. You're going to have a little fun with this knob later on.

The Filter Section

The NN-19 Filter section is used to shape the timbre of the loaded samples (see Figure 11.12). Its functionality is akin to the filter sections of Dr:rex and Subtractor, because it is a multimode filter with five available filters.

- ▶ **Notch**—This filter can be thought of as the opposite of a Band Pass filter. It will reject the mid-frequencies, yet allow the high frequencies and low frequencies to pass through. Although not the most dramatic filter effect, it still has a place in the mix for making minor changes to a sample.

- ▶ **High Pass**—HP 12 is the opposite of the Low Pass filters; it will filter out the low frequencies, yet allow the high frequencies to pass through. It has a roll-off curve of 12 decibels per octave.

- ▶ **Band Pass**—Labeled BP 12, this filters out both the high and low frequencies, leaving the mid frequencies alone to be toyed with. With a roll-off curve of 12 decibels per octave, the BP 12 can be used effectively on instrument loops such as a guitar loop or possibly hi-hat heavy percussion loops.

- ▶ **12dB Low Pass**—Also called LP 12, this filter is similar to the 24dB low pass, but the roll-off curve is not as strong, because it has a range of 12 decibels per octave. This makes the LP 12 a perfect solution for creating a filter sweep that is low but not low enough to blow up your speakers.

- ▶ **24dB Low Pass**—Also called LP 24, this filter allows low frequencies to pass through, yet filters out the high frequencies. To top it off, this low pass filter has an intense roll-off curve (approximately 24 decibels per octave), which produces a greater emphasis on the low frequencies.

To the left of the mode buttons are the controls for the Resonance and Filter Frequency parameters.

The Filter Frequency, or *cutoff filter* as it is also called, is used to specify where the filter will function within the frequency spectrum. It is a very popular parameter used to create the sweeping effect heard so often in electronic music. When the frequency is used to alter a filter, it opens and closes the filter within a specific frequency range. In order to better understand what the Filter Frequency does, try the following exercise.

Figure 11.12
The NN-19 Filter section. You can select the different filter modes by either clicking on the Mode button at the bottom of the filter or by just clicking on the desired filter mode.

1. Load a "pad" patch from the Reason Factory Sound Bank. A good one for this example is the Big Strings patch, located in the Strings folder.

2. The Filter is already activated. Set the filter mode to the LP 12 setting and make sure the Resonance slider is set to 0. Also make sure the Filter Frequency slider is set to its maximum setting of 127.

3. Arm the NN-19 sequencer track to receive MIDI and play a sustained chord with your left hand. With your right hand, click on the Filter Frequency and drag the control down, so you can hear the filter close as it decreases in value. Once the Filter Frequency is set to 0, all of the high frequencies are filtered out. Try this same exercise with other filter modes, such as the Notch or Band Pass, to hear the effect.

The Resonance slider is used in combination with the Filter Frequency parameter. It emphasizes the frequencies set by the Filter slider, which thins the sound out, but also increases the sweep effect mentioned earlier. In order to better understand how the Resonance slider works with the Filter Frequency, try the following exercise.

1. Using the same sample patch as before, set the filter mode to LP 12, and set both the Filter Frequency and Resonance sliders to 0.

2. Arm the NN-19 sequencer track to receive MIDI and play a sustained chord with your left hand. With your right hand, click and drag the Resonance slider until it reaches a value of 70. Release the mouse and listen to the emphasis on the lower frequencies.

3. Now click and drag the Filter Frequency slider until it reaches a value of 52. This should create a grand sweeping sound, because the higher frequencies of the sample patch have now been re-introduced into the mix.

4. Try this with other filter modes to hear the different filter sweeps you can create when using the Filter Frequency and Resonance sliders together.

Located above the filter modes, the Filter Keyboard Track knob (labeled KBD) is used to compensate for the loss of high frequencies as you play higher notes on the keyboard, bringing those higher notes to the forefront in a mix. To demonstrate how this works, try the following exercise.

1. Using the same sample patch as before, set the filter mode to LP 12; set the Resonance to 86 and the Filter Frequency to 60. Also make sure that the Filter Keyboard Track knob is set to 0.

2. Play a sustained chord and include some high notes. Notice that the low notes are very loud and present in the mix.

3. Increase the amount of Keyboard Track knob by clicking and dragging on the knob until it reaches 70 or 12:00. Play the chord again; the high notes should now be much more present in the mix.

4. Increase the Keyboard Track knob to its maximum setting and play the chord again. This time, the high notes should be the dominant voices in the chord. This is not an ideal setting, because you do not want to lose the low frequencies, so it is important to find that happy medium.

The Envelope Section

To the right of the Filter section are the NN-19 envelope generators (see Figure 11.13). An envelope generator is used to modify specific synth parameters, including pitch, volume, and filter frequencies. By using an envelope creatively, you can control how these parameters are to be modified over a specific amount of time. The NN-19 includes two envelope generators. One is assigned to the Filter section whereas the other is assigned to Amplitude.

As you read in Chapter 9, "Subtractor—Close Up," an envelope generator has four basic parameters; Attack, Decay, Sustain, and Release (collectively called ADSR).

Let's very briefly recap what these parameters do.

- ▶ **Attack**—When a sound's envelope is triggered, the Attack parameter determines the length of time before the envelope reaches its maximum value.
- ▶ **Decay**—Once the maximum value is reached, the Decay parameter determines the length of time until the value begins to drop.
- ▶ **Sustain**—After the value begins to drop, Sustain determines the level at which the falling value rests.
- ▶ **Release**—Once the value has been set at its rested value, the Release parameter determines how long it will take until the value will fade out after releasing the key.

Now that you have reviewed these parameters, let's discuss what each of the envelope generators does.

The Filter Envelope modifies the Filter Frequency and Sample Pitch. When used in combination with the Filter Frequency and Resonance sliders, the Filter Envelope can create long, sustained filter sweeps and percussive filter-powered stab sounds. To the right of the Filter Envelope are two additional parameters that can be used in combination with it.

- ▶ The Invert button is used to invert the functions of the individual envelope parameters. For example, you are using the Attack parameter and have assigned a positive value of 74 to it, which produces a very slow attack. Activate the Invert button and the attack parameter is inverted, which means the attack will be much faster. Essentially, the Invert button reverses the effect of the envelope parameters.
- ▶ The Amount knob determines how much the filter will be affected by the envelope. Increasing the value of this parameter directly affects the set value of the Filter Frequency, which in turn affects the Filter Envelope, which results in some very intense filter combinations to use.

Figure 11.13
The NN-19 Envelope section includes two envelope generators.

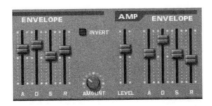

To demonstrate the capabilities of the Filter Envelope, try the following exercise. Make sure that your NN-19 sequencer track is armed to receive MIDI signals.

1. Use the patch browser window to locate and load a good patch to work with. I suggest the Bright Piano patch in the Piano folder of the Reason Factory Sound Bank. Once it is loaded, notice the filter settings of this patch.

2. Use your mouse to increase the value of the Attack parameter. Play a chord on your keyboard and notice the sweeping effect it produces. Because the Filter mode is set to LP 12, using the envelope with a slow attack causes the filter to first play the lower frequencies, followed by the higher frequencies of the sample. Note that the Filter Frequency slider determines the higher frequencies.

3. Now decrease the value of the Decay parameter. Play a chord and notice how the filter abruptly closes as soon as the Attack reaches its maximum value. Also notice how there is still a long sustain after the filter closes.

4. Now decrease the value of the Sustain parameter and listen to how fast the filter opens and closes.

5. With both the Decay and Sustain set to such low values, the Release parameter will have virtually no effect on your sample. Let's change that by increasing both the Decay and Sustain parameters to their maximum values. Now set the Release to 0 and play a chord on your keyboard, and then release the notes. Notice how quickly the envelope closes.

The Amplitude Envelope (AMP ENVELOPE) is used to shape the volume characteristics of the sample. This is useful for creating very long sustained patches (such as pads), or medium to short sustained patches (such as bass guitars or drums). The same types of parameters are available here (Attack, Decay, Sustain, and Release). The included level knob to the left of the Amplitude Envelope is used as a Master Level for the NN-19.

To experiment with the Amplitude Envelope, try using the previous exercise as a road map to guide you through the different envelope parameters.

The LFO Section

No synth would be complete without an LFO, or Low Frequency Oscillator (see Figure 11.14). Like a standard oscillator, LFOs can generate a waveform and frequency, but there are two distinct differences between them:

▶ An LFO is capable of generating waveforms with a low frequency, hence the name LFO.

Figure 11.14
The NN-19 LFO section is used to adjust the Low Frequency Oscillator.

▶ An LFO's purpose is to modulate a parameter, such as a filter or another oscillator. That means that the LFO itself is never actually heard, just its effect on other synth parameters.

The Waveform Selector (WAVEF.) is used to choose a desired waveform for modulating one of three available parameters. Because the NN-19 Waveform Selector functions exactly as the one found on the Subtractor, this section briefly recaps the available waveforms.

▶ **Triangle**—Creates a smooth up and down vibrato.

▶ **Inverted Sawtooth**—Creates a cycled ramp up effect.

▶ **Sawtooth**—Creates a cycled ramp down effect.

▶ **Square**—Makes abrupt changes between two values.

▶ **Random**—Creates a random stepped modulation. Also known as sample and hold.

▶ **Soft Random**—Exactly as the previous waveform but with a smoother modulation curve.

Once you have selected a waveform, you then need to specify which parameter the LFO will modulate. This is done using the LFO Destination (DEST) button. There are three parameters available to modulate.

▶ **Osc**—This assigns the LFO to modulate the sample pitch of the NN-19.

▶ **Filter**—This assigns the LFO to modulate the Filter Frequency. This is great for creating tempo-controlled filter sweeps.

▶ **Pan**—This assigns the LFO to modulate the panning position of the samples. By using this, you can create a tempo-controlled stereo vibrato effect.

Located just above the Waveform Selector, the Sync button assigns the frequency of the LFO to synchronize to the song tempo. Once activated, the Rate knob then assigns one of 16 possible time divisions to the LFO. If the Sync button is not active, the Rate knob has a range of 0-127.

After the Sync and Rate are sorted out, the Amount knob is then used to assign a specific amount of LFO to the desired destination (Osc, Filter, or Pan). There is a lot of room to work with when using this parameter. How much you use depends on how much you think the sample needs to be modulated.

READ THE TUTORIAL

Near the end of this chapter, I have written a step-by-step tutorial for creating your own NN-19 patch from scratch. Also included in this tutorial is a section devoted to editing the patch using the featured sections just covered. Be sure to check it out!

CHAPTER 11

The NN-19 Play Parameters

After using the NN-19 synth parameters to shape and mold your samples, the play parameters are fantastic for giving your samples some character (see Figure 11.15). These parameters are meant to be used during a live performance; they modify your samples on the go.

Figure 11.15
The NN-19 Play parameters are best used during a live performance.

Low Bandwidth

The Low Bandwidth (LOW BW) button will remove some high frequencies of the loaded NN-19 patch. This is a play parameter that should be used on slower computers with less RAM, because it will help conserve your computer resources.

Voice Spread

Located just below the Patch Name window, Voice Spread (SPREAD) is used to create a stereo effect by placing the separate voices of the loaded samples in different parts of the stereo field. The intensity of this effect is controlled by the knob and then panned according to one of the three pan modes.

▶ **Key Mode**—As you start from the low part of the keyboard and work your way up, the panning position will change gradually as you move from left to right.

▶ **Key 2 Mode**—This functions in the same way as the previous key mode, except the panning will shift from left to right every eight steps on the keyboard and then repeat.

▶ **Jump Mode**—Panning will alternate from left to right for each note played. This function is not note specific, so you can play the same note in succession and the panning position will still change.

Polyphony and Portamento

Polyphony assigns the number of voices that can simultaneously be played. The NN-19 has a wide range of polyphony, from 1 to 99 voices, offering a wide range of creative possibilities. For example, when set at 1, the NN-19 becomes a monophonic instrument, which is perfect for use with a flute or clarinet sample, because they are monophonic instruments.

Portamento is a parameter that creates a slide effect between the notes you play. The Portamento knob assigns the amount of time needed to slide from one note to another. When used in combination with Polyphony, the Portamento feature can be used to create a sliding monophonic synth, much like the retro classic Moog or ARP synths, or a slide effect ideal for a chord progression. Near the end of this chapter, you will work through an in-depth tutorial using these parameters.

Retrig and Legato

Retrig is thought of as the "normal" setting for the NN-19, because it is the commonly used parameter for playing polyphonic patches. The NN-19 envelopes are triggered when you press and hold down a note, and then they are retriggered when another note is played.

Retrig can be used with monophonic patches as well. Try pressing a note and holding it while pressing a new key. Release the new key and the first note will retrigger.

Legato is a commonly used parameter for playing monophonic patches. With the polyphony set to 1, press and hold down a note, and then press and hold another note. Notice that the new note has no attack, because the NN-19's envelope has not been retriggered. If you add some Portamento to this patch, you will get a retro vintage mono synth glide sound. Note that the NN-19 envelope *will* retrigger if you release all of the keys and play a new one.

It is also possible to use Legato with a polyphonic patch. Set the Polyphony of a patch to a low number of voices, such as three. Hold down a three-note chord and then play another note. Notice that the new note will be played with a legato effect (no attack), but it will cease to play the highest note of the chord you are playing, because it is "stealing" that note in order to play the new note.

The Controller Section

The NN-19 is capable of receiving three commonly used MIDI controller messages, and then sending those messages to three available parameters:

▶ **A.Touch**—Also known as *channel pressure*. If your keyboard supports it, while holding a note down you can apply a little more pressure to the key to send additional MIDI data.

▶ **Expr**—This is an external piece of gear that works a lot like a sustain pedal on a piano. If your MIDI keyboard has an input for an expressional pedal, you can buy one at your local music instrument shop, plug it in, and use it to send MIDI data to the NN-19.

▶ **Breath**—This is also an external piece of gear that is found on Electronic Wind Instruments, or EWI. This is used to give your patches a woodwind effect by emulating the attack of a woodwind instrument.

If you have any of these external devices, you can use them to send MIDI data to any or all of these three parameters:

▶ **F.Freq**—When set to a positive value, the additional MIDI data will increase the Filter Frequency parameter. A negative value has the opposite effect.

▶ **LFO**—When set to a positive value, the additional MIDI data will increase the LFO amount knob. A negative value has the opposite effect.

▶ **Amp**—When set to a positive value, the additional MIDI data will increase the amplitude of the NN-19. A negative value has the opposite effect.

Pitch and Modulation

The Pitch Bend Wheel is an emulation of a standard pitch wheel found on most MIDI keyboards (see Figure 11.16). Simply put, it is used to bend the pitch of the played notes up and down. The Range parameter, just above the Pitch Bend Wheel, controls the range of pitch by up to +/– two octaves.

CHAPTER 11

Figure 11.16
The Pitch and
Modulation wheels and
corresponding
parameters.

The Modulation Wheel is used to control a number of available parameters. One of my personal favorite play parameters, the Modulation Wheel can be used to give your sequences a very realistic and emotional performance.

The Modulation Wheel can control the following parameters:

▶ **F.Freq**—When set to a positive value, the Modulation Wheel will increase the Filter Frequency parameter. A negative value has the opposite effect.

▶ **F.Res**—When set to a positive value, the Modulation Wheel will increase the resonance. A negative value has the opposite effect.

▶ **F.Decay**—This knob controls the Decay parameter of the Filter Envelope. When set to a positive value, the Modulation Wheel will increase the amount of decay. A negative value has the opposite effect.

▶ **Amp**—When set to a positive value, the Modulation Wheel will increase the amplitude of the NN-19. A negative value has the opposite effect. It's very cool for creating a crescendo with your sample patch.

▶ **LFO**—When set to a positive value, the Modulation Wheel will increase the LFO amount knob. A negative value has the opposite effect.

Velocity Control

The Velocity section of the play parameters gives you control over multiple parameters according to how hard the notes are played. This is a feature not commonly found on hardware synths and samplers (see Figure 11.17).

Figure 11.17
The Velocity controls can
make your samples
sound more lively and
add expression by
making specific
parameters sensitive to
varying velocities.

The Velocity controls can modify the following parameters:

▶ **F.Env**—When set to a positive value, different velocities will control the Amount knob of the Filter Envelope. A negative value has the opposite effect.

▶ **F.Decay**—When set to a positive value, different velocities will control the Decay parameter of the Filter Envelope. A negative value has the opposite effect.

- ▶ **Amp**—When set to a positive value, the velocity will control the amount of volume. A negative value has the opposite effect.

- ▶ **A.Attack**—When set to positive value, the velocity will control the Attack parameter of the Amplitude Envelope. A negative value has the opposite effect.

- ▶ **S.Start**—When set to a positive value, the velocity will modify the starting time for the sample patch. A negative value has the opposite effect.

Creating Your First NN-19 Sample Patch

Now that you have learned all there is to learn about the functionality of the NN-19, it's time to put your knowledge to the test and create your first sample patch from scratch. In this section, you'll use a few samples of single guitar notes. You will then proceed to map these notes over the NN-19 key zones. You will top it off by using the filters and envelopes to end up with a unique guitar sound that can then be saved as an NN-19 patch.

GET THE SAMPLES

Before you begin this tutorial, take a quick trip to the Course Technology website (**www.courseptr.com**) to download the sound files needed. They are in a ZIP compressed file that can be automatically opened from Windows XP. If you are using a Mac or an earlier Windows operating system, you will need to download the appropriate version of Stuff-It by visiting the Aladdin Software website (**www.aladdinsys.com**).

Once you download and decompress the Guitar Samples folder, place it in the Reason application folder on your computer's hard drive. Note that I have prepared these samples specifically for this tutorial, meaning that the individual guitar samples have been processed with loop points and assigned a root note. There is no need to process these in another audio-editing program.

THESE SAMPLES ARE COPYRIGHT SAFE

After going through the steps of this tutorial and creating your first NN-19 sampler patch, you might get the urge to use these samples in a song you're working on. This is perfectly fine to do, because these samples are *copyright safe*. These samples were not taken from a sample collection. I created these samples sitting in front of my computer with a guitar over the course of an hour *specifically* for this tutorial. So I encourage you to use these guitar samples freely in any songs you write with Reason and the NN-19 or NN-XT sampler.

Setting the Key Zones

Before you can begin to import the guitar samples, you must first create a few key zones, so that the samples will reside in their proper mapped locations. This is an acoustic guitar, which has six natural tones (E, A, D, G, B, E). To make the upper register of the acoustic guitar sound more realistic, I have also added a high A and a high D to the Guitar Samples folder. So here are the key zone assignments these samples are going to use:

▶ **Low E**—Will be mapped out over the lowest portion of the map and have an assigned range of C2 to G#1.

▶ **Low A**—Will have an assigned range of A1 to C#2.

▶ **Low D**—Will have an assigned range of D2 to F#2.

▶ **Low G**—Will have an assigned range of G2 to A#2.

▶ **Low B**—Will have an assigned range of B2 to D#3.

▶ **High E**—Will have an assigned range of E3 to G#3.

▶ **High A**—Will have an assigned range of A3 to C#4.

▶ **High D**—Will be mapped out over the highest portion of the map and have an assigned range of D4 to G8.

This means that you will need to have eight key zones, so let's get cracking!

STARTING FROM SCRATCH

Make sure you're starting this tutorial on the right foot by initializing the NN-19. This way, the NN-19's memory is cleared and you are ready to press on. From the Edit pull-down menu, choose Initialize Patch and that's it.

Start by creating the key zone for the Low E sample:

1. Choose Edit > Split Key Zone. This will split the map in half and create a marker point that looks a lot like the left and right locators in the Reason sequencer (see Figure 11.18).

2. Select the left key zone and look below the virtual keyboard. You will see that the low key is set to C2 and the high key has been set to D#3 (see Figure 11.19). Click and drag the high key knob down until it reads G#1.

Figure 11.18
You've just split the key zone.

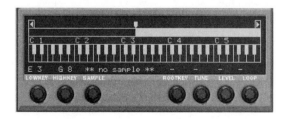

Figure 11.19
The high note of the first key zone must be set to G#1.

3. Once this is accomplished, click on the folder icon, located above the virtual keyboard. This will bring up the sample browser window. Locate the Guitar Samples folder, which should be located in your Reason program folder. Once you have it open, select the Low E.wav file and click Open to import that sample into your first key zone.

4. Look in the key zone display and you will see all of the sample details on display. Notice that the root key has been automatically set to E1 and that the Loop mode has been set to FW.

5. Next, you need to create another key zone. Select the empty key zone on the right. Now, choose Split Key Zone from the Edit pull-down menu again. Select your new key zone. Adjust the low key to A1 and the high key to C#2.

6. Click on the folder icon and locate the Low A.wav file. Import it into the new key zone.

7. Repeat the same steps until you have eight separate key zones with the proper sample imported into each zone. When you are finished, your map should look like Figure 11.20.

After you have inserted your samples, make sure to increase the Polyphony to a higher value than its default setting of 6. For this tutorial, try a value of 12.

If your NN-19 sequencer track is armed to receive MIDI, try plunking a few keys to hear how the guitar samples sound. Try holding down some chords to hear the richness of an open E major (the notes are E1, B1, E2, G#2, B2, and E3).

Before you proceed, make sure to save your newly created acoustic guitar patch by clicking on the Save button in the upper-left corner of the NN-19 interface. Be sure to save it in the Reason program folder and call it Acoustic Guitar.

Figure 11.20
The key zones have now been created and there is a guitar sample loaded into each zone.

Editing Your Sample Patch

Now that your patch has been created, it's time to make your patch unique by using the NN-19 filters, envelopes, and play parameters. This is where the real fun begins.

WRITE IN SOME CHORDS

Before you begin editing your guitar patch, take a few minutes to create a loop of guitar chords. That way, you can play the loop over and over again while making adjustments to the individual NN-19 parameters without having to play a chord on your MIDI keyboard. It makes it a lot more fun to tweak!

If you are not a guitar player, try this chord progression:

▶ **E major**—E1, B1, E2, G#2, B2, and E2

▶ **A major**—A1, E2, A2, C#3, and E3

▶ **G major**—G1, B1, D2, G2, B2, and G3

▶ **D major**—D2, A2, D3, and F#3

You are going to create a guitar pad sound, so I suggest creating an eight-bar sequence in the Reason sequencer. Each of these chords should be two bars in length.

Using the Amp and Envelope

Because you are going to create a pad patch, the first place to start making adjustments is to the Amp and its Envelope parameters. Set the Amp slider to 82; this will prevent the NN-19 from clipping when you make adjustments to the filter and LFO.

Make the following parameter adjustments to the Envelope:

1. Set the Attack to a high value. 70 is a good place to start; this will create a very slow attack on the pad patch.

2. Set the Decay to an even higher value, such as 105.

3. Set the Sustain to a mid-to-high value, such as 70.

4. Set the Release to a slightly smaller value than the Attack, such as 54. This will allow the pad patch to really sustain and ring out.

Click on Play and listen to the guitar chord progression as it plays through these adjustments you've just made. The chords should sound very long and dreamy, making it a perfect place to start adding a filter.

Using the Filter and Envelope

Like any good synth-o-holic, the first or second parameter I start editing is the Filter section. In this part of the tutorial, you are going to use the filter to complement the full sound of the guitar samples when played in a chord by making it into a pad sound.

You are going to use a Band Pass filter so that you can still hear the original guitar sample, while introducing a sweep filter effect to the mix. Select the BP 12 filter mode and make sure the Keyboard Tracking knob is set to 0.

Next, you need to create a sweeping filter effect, and the first step toward making this happen is using the Filter Frequency and Resonance sliders. Set the Filter Frequency slider to a low-to-mid value, such as 48. Now set the Resonance slider to a much greater value, such as 100. Click on Play on the sequencer and listen to the sweeping effect that has been created. Notice that the original timbres of the acoustic guitar samples are still present, but now a dreamy filter sweep had been added.

To further enhance the filter sweep, make the following adjustments to the Filter Envelope:

1.   Set the Attack to a very high value, such as 84. This will cause the filter sweep to begin playing the lower frequencies and then introduce the higher frequencies as it progresses.

2.   Set the Decay to an even higher value, such as 95.

3.   Set the Sustain to a mid-to-high value, such as 66.

4.   Set the Release to a high value that's less than or equal to the Attack parameter, such as 81.

Now increase the intensity of the filter by setting the Filter Amount knob to 42. Click on Play and listen to how the filter sweep has dramatically changed with the help of the Filter Envelope.

Before you go any further, make sure that you save your newly created patch. Click on the Save icon in the upper-left corner of the NN-19 and give your new patch a name, such as AcGuitar Pad, for example.

Using the LFO

It's time to add a little LFO and create a tempo-controlled filter sweep. Start by making sure that the Sync button is active and that the Amount knob is set to a low value, such as 24.

Next, select a waveform for your LFO to use. For this tutorial, try a square or random waveform. Personally, I am opting to use the square waveform, because I like the abrupt changes between the two values.

After you have selected your waveform, make sure to select the proper destination assignment for the LFO. Set the destination to Filter, and this will send the LFO effect to the Filter section. Just for kicks, you might try assigning the LFO to Pan in order to create a tempo synced panning effect.

Last, but not least, you must select a proper time division for your Rate knob. Because this is a pad sound, you might begin experimenting with a low division setting to complement the slow ominous sound of the pad patch.

Click on Play to hear your new Acoustic Guitar Pad patch!

Additional Parameters

After you have adjusted the parameters of the Filter and Envelopes, you can further enhance your new pad patch by adding in a few of the Play parameters.

You can use the Spread knob to create a very realistic stereophonic effect with your pad. Try setting the Spread knob to a high value and experimenting with the different types of spread available to you (Key, Key 2, and Jump). Click on Play and you will hear your pad in a stereo field, which sounds awesome.

CHAPTER 11

Although the Portamento knob is typically used for mono synth instruments, it can also be used for pad sounds. Try setting the Portamento knob to a low to middle setting, such as 67. Click on Play and notice how the chords slide into each other as the progression plays.

As soon as you have made your final tweaks and adjustments, be sure to save your work.

Throughout this chapter, I have shown you the ins and outs of the NN-19 sampler. Although it might be considered a very basic sampler, it is easy to use in creative ways.

But if you find yourself begging for more, go to the next chapter and meet the NN-19's big brother, the NN-XT.

12

NN-XT—Close Up

The NN-XT is the sampler that picks up where the NN-19 leaves off. After using the NN-19 as a learning tool, you might want to move up to the NN-XT. It's a big step toward more functionality, compatibility, and of course creativity (see Figure 12.1).

What Makes the NN-XT Different?

Aside from the extreme graphic face-lift, there are many other differences between the NN-XT and NN-19.

▶ **Multilayered sampling**—The NN-XT can trigger samples according to their assigned velocity.

▶ **More outputs**—The NN-XT has eight stereo outputs.

▶ **More sample formats**—The NN-XT can import a wider range of sample formats.

▶ **More control**—The NN-XT allows individual control over each sample in a patch.

Figure 12.1
The NN-XT is a two-panel Reason device. The main panel handles the global controls. The Remote Editor controls the individual parameters of the loaded sample patches.

A Guided Tour of the NN-XT

It's time to begin your guided in-depth tour of the NN-XT. Toward the end of this chapter, you can further enhance your NN-XT education by following the step-by-step tutorial for creating your own multilayered sample patches and learn how to expand your sample library by using Reload.

The NN-XT Main Display Panel

When you first create an instance of the NN-XT, Reason does not automatically expand the device's entire interface, because it takes up a lot of room and might seem a little intimidating to the novice sampling artist (see Figure 12.2). Rather, the NN-XT main display panel is the first part of the device that you will see. The main display includes all of the global controls of the NN-XT.

Figure 12.2
When the NN-XT is created, you will first see the compact version.

Loading Patches

As with all of the Reason devices, the patch browsing interface is available to locate and load patches, scroll through them, and save them. Because you already know how to browse for patches, you're ready to consider the various formats the NN-XT can import.

▶ **.sxt**—This is the standard NN-XT patch format extension name.

▶ **.smp**—This is the standard NN-19 patch format extension name.

▶ **.sf2**—This is the common file extension name for Sound Fonts. Unlike the NN-19, the NN-XT can import an entire Sound Font patch instead of just single Sound Font files.

▶ **.rcy, .rex, and .rx2**—These are the commonly known file extensions for REX files. As with the NN-19, when the NN-XT imports a REX file, it chromatically maps the individual REX slices, starting from the C1 note.

Just below the patch browser window is the High Quality Interpolation button and the Note On indicator, which lights up whenever a MIDI message is received.

Global Controls

To the right of the patch browsing interface are the global controls for your loaded patches.

▶ **Filter Controls**—These knobs are used to control a parameter of the Filter found on the NN-XT Remote Editor. Note that the Filter must be turned on before you can use these knobs.

▶ **Amp Envelope Controls**—These knobs are used to control the Amp Envelope on the Remote Editor.

▶ **Modulation Envelope**—This knob is used to control the Decay parameter of the Modulation Envelope in the Remote Editor.

▶ **Master Volume**—Controls the amplitude level for the NN-XT.

Pitch and Modulation

Located to the far left of the main display, the Pitch and Modulation controls are common to just about every Reason synth.

▶ **Pitch Wheel**—This wheel is used to bend the pitch of the sample up and down. The potential range of the pitch bend effect is determined by its corresponding controls found in the Remote Editor.

▶ **Modulation Wheel**—This wheel is used to control and modify a number of parameters, such as Filter Frequency, Resonance, and Level. When used effectively, modulation is a key tool for adding expression to your sampled instruments. Note that the Modulation Wheel is called the Wheel or simply "W."

External Control

To the right of the Modulation Wheel is the External Control Wheel. The External Control Wheel can receive three MIDI controller messages and then send that data to any of its assigned parameters in the NN-XT Remote Editor.

▶ Aftertouch

▶ Expression

▶ Breath

Additionally, the External Control Wheel can be used to send these three MIDI controller messages to the Reason Sequencer, should your MIDI keyboard not support these parameters.

Also note that the External Control Wheel is labeled as "X" in the main display, just as the Modulation Wheel is labeled as "W."

The NN-XT Remote Editor

As previously stated, when an NN-XT is first created in the Reason Device Rack, its main display is the only visible element. Just below the main display is the collapsed Remote Editor. To expand the Remote Editor, click on the arrow icon located on the far left of the Remote Editor (see Figure 12.3).

At first sight, the Remote Editor looks very complex. But as you read through the guided tour of this beauty, you will soon see that the Remote Editor is quite possibly one of the most well thought out and versatile devices in Reason 2.5.

There are several sections to the Remote Editor. Here's a rundown of what this chapter covers:

▶ **The Synth Parameters**—The parameters in this section are used to edit and manipulate your sample patches using filters, envelopes, and two LFOs.

▶ **The Group Parameters**—These parameters are used to enhance the performance or playing style of the NN-XT. They are very similar to the Play parameters of the NN-19.

▶ **Key Map Display**—This area is used to map samples across the NN-XT. Any sample information you need to know can be found in this section.

▶ **The Sample Parameters**—These parameters are used to set the key zones, root keys, play modes, and more for each sample loaded into the key map.

Figure 12.3
To expand the NN-XT
Remote Editor, click on
the arrow icon.

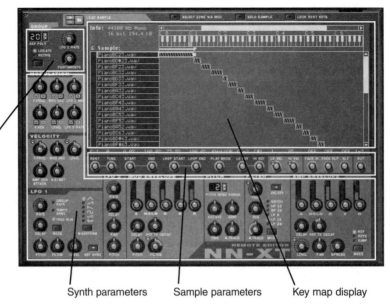

Group parameters

Synth parameters   Sample parameters   Key map display

THESE PARAMETERS ARE NOT GLOBAL

While touring through the Remote Editor, it's important to remember that, with the exception of the Group parameters, all of the remaining parameters you will be using are not global. When you select a single sample from the key map and make any change to the pitch, filter, or modulation, you are affecting just that single sample zone, not the rest of the sample patch.

However, if you want to make global changes to the entire sample patch, you can do so in several ways. Here's one:

1. Choose Edit > Select All Zones.

2. Click on one of the samples in the key map. Then hold the Shift button down and click on the additional samples.

3. Click the group of samples you want to make changes to in the Group column. This will select all of the samples in that particular group. If there are additional groups, you need to hold the Shift key down and select the next groups as well.

The Synth Parameters

The NN-XT synth parameters are used to edit and manipulate the characteristics of your samples with ease and precision. To make it easier to understand, I break these parameters into the following groups:

▶ The Modulation section

▶ The Velocity section

▶ The Pitch section

▶ The Filter section

▶ The Envelopes

▶ The LFOs

The Modulation Section

The Modulation section of the NN-XT is one of the most versatile of its kind (see Figure 12.4). There are six parameters that can be used on an individual basis or grouped together. Additionally, these parameters can be assigned to either the Modulation Wheel, by selecting the "W" button under each knob, or the External Control Wheel by selecting the "X" button under each knob. Better yet, the parameters can be assigned to both wheels simultaneously by selecting both the "W" and "X" buttons.

Figure 12.4
The NN-XT Modulation section is used to assign modulation to different parameters.

Take a look at what each of these parameters does:

▶ **F.Freq**—This parameter assigns the Filter Frequency parameters to the Modulation section. When assigned a positive value, the filter will open as the Modulation Wheel's value is increased. Assigning a negative value has the opposite effect.

▶ **Mod Dec**—This parameter assigns the Decay parameter of the Modulation Envelope to either the Modulation or External Control Wheel.

▶ **LFO 1 Amt**—This parameter determines the amount of modulation of LFO 1 that is affected by the Modulation Wheel.

▶ **F.Res**—This parameter assigns the Filter Resonance parameter to the Modulation section.

▶ **Level**—This parameter assigns the Level or amplitude of a single or several zones to the Modulation section.

▶ **LFO 1 Rate**—This parameter assigns the rate of LFO 1 to the Modulation section.

The Velocity Section

The Velocity section is used to modify a combination of five parameters according to the velocity of notes played by a MIDI keyboard (see Figure 12.5).

Figure 12.5
The NN-XT Velocity section is used to assign velocity to different parameters.

▶ **F.Freq**—When set to a positive value, different velocities will control the Amount knob of the Filter Envelope. A negative value has the opposite effect.

▶ **Mod Dec**—When set to a positive value, different velocities will control the Decay parameter of the Filter Envelope. A negative value has the opposite effect.

▶ **Level**—When set to a positive value, the velocity will control the amount of volume. A negative value has the opposite effect.

▶ **Amp Env Attaack**—When set to positive value, the velocity will control the Attack parameter of the Amplitude Envelope. A negative value has the opposite effect.

▶ **S.Start**—When set to a positive value, the velocity will modify the starting time for the sample patch. A negative value has the opposite effect.

The Pitch Section

The Pitch Bend Range is used to assign a bend range to the Pitch Wheel of the main display (see Figure 12.6). By default, a value of 2 semitones is selected whenever a NN-XT is created in the Reason Device Rack, because this is the standard pitch bend range found on most hardware synths. However, the Pitch Bend Range has a potential range of 24 semitones, or two octaves. To increase or decrease the bend value, you can click on its scroll buttons, or simply click and drag on the display itself.

Figure 12.6
The NN-XT Pitch section is used to make tuning adjustments to the Pitch Bend Wheel.

Below the Pitch Bend Range are three parameters used to modify the pitch of individual samples within a patch. Take a look at what each of these parameters does:

▶ **Octave**—This parameter shifts the pitch of a selected sample in octave increments. The range of the Octave knob is +/– five octaves.

▶ **Semi**—This parameter shifts the pitch of a selected sample by semitone increments. The range of the Semi knob is +/– 12 semitones, or two octaves.

▶ **Fine**—This parameter is used to make minimal adjustments to selected samples by cent increments. The range of the Fine knob is +/– 50 cents, or half a semitone.

The Keyboard Track knob is a parameter used to control the keyboard tracking of the NN-XT pitch. It's a fairy unique and unusual parameter that is best explained when having a patch loaded ready to listen to the resulting effect.

Load up a bass patch from the Reason Factory Sound Bank and try the following exercise.

1. Select all of the samples in the patch by choosing Edit > Select All Zones.

2. Navigate to the Keyboard Track knob and turn it all the way down by clicking and dragging with your mouse.

3. Arm the NN-XT sequencer track so you can play your MIDI keyboard to hear the effect. All the keys should now be the same pitch.

4. Now turn the Keyboard Track knob all the way up. Play the C3 note on your MIDI keyboard, followed by C#3 and D3. You should hear the same pitch played in different octaves.

The Filter Section

As with most of the other Reason devices, the Filter uses a combination of resonance and cutoff frequencies to shape the sound and timbre of a sample (see Figure 12.7). Take a look at the available parameters.

Figure 12.7
The NN-XT Filter section can be used to alter the timbre of individual samples or an entire selection of samples.

To activate the Filter, just click the On/Off button located at the top-right corner of the Filter section. Once activated, you can also use the Filter controls in the NN-XT main display.

After activating the Filter section, you can then select one of six filter modes by clicking on the Mode button, or by clicking on the filter's name. Here's a brief rundown of the available filter modes and the additional parameters.

▶ **Notch**—Rejects the mid-frequencies while allowing the high frequencies and low frequencies to pass.

▶ **HP 12**—Filters out the low frequencies while allowing the high frequencies to pass through with a roll-off curve of 12dB per octave.

▶ **BP 12**—Filters out both the high and low frequencies, while allowing the mid frequencies to pass with a roll-off curve of 12dB per octave.

▶ **LP 6**—Unique to the NN-XT, the LP 6 is a Low Pass filter that filters out the high frequencies while allowing the low frequencies to pass with a gentle roll-off curve of 6dB per octave. The LP 6's effect can only be heard when changing the value of the Frequency Filter knob, because it has no resonance.

▶ **LP 12**—Filters out the high frequencies while allowing the low frequencies to pass with a roll-off curve of 12dB per octave.

▶ **LP 24**—Filters out the high frequencies while allowing the low frequencies to pass with a steep roll-off curve of 24dB per octave.

CHAPTER 12

The Filter Frequency, or *cutoff filter* as it is also called, is used to specify where the filter will function within the frequency spectrum. Once the Filter section is activated, just click on the Filter Frequency knob and drag your mouse up or down to increase or decrease the cutoff effect.

The Resonance knob is used in combination with the Filter Frequency. It emphasizes the frequencies set by the Filter knob, which thins the sound out but also increases the sweep effect.

The Keyboard Track knob is used to compensate for the loss of high frequencies as you play higher notes on the keyboard. It can be used to bring the higher played notes to the forefront in a mix.

The Envelopes

An envelope generator is used to modify specific synth parameters, including pitch, volume, and filter frequencies. By using an envelope creatively, you can control how these parameters are to be modified over a specific amount of time. The NN-XT includes two envelope generators. One is assigned to Modulation and the other is assigned to Amplitude (see Figure 12.8).

Figure 12.8
The NN-XT has envelopes for Modulation and Amplitude.

Here are the standard envelope parameters:

▶ **Attack**—When an envelope is triggered, the Attack parameter determines how much time passes before the envelope reaches its maximum value.

▶ **Hold**—Unique to the NN-XT, this parameter is used to determine how long the envelope remains at its maximum potential.

▶ **Decay**—Once the maximum value is reached and held for a determined Hold time, the Decay parameter determines how much time passes before the value begins to drop.

▶ **Sustain**—After the value begins to drop, the Sustain determines at which level the falling value should rest.

▶ **Release**—Once the value has been set at its rested value, the Release parameter determines how long it will take until the value will begin to drop to 0.

▶ **Delay**—This parameter determines the amount of delay between playing the note and hearing the effect of the envelope. The Delay knob has a range of 0-10 seconds.

▶ **Key to Decay**—This creates an offset of the Decay parameter which is determined by where you play on your MIDI keyboard. If assigned a positive value, the Decay parameter will increase. The opposite effect will occur when assigned a negative value.

The Modulation Envelope is used to alter specific parameters over time. Aside from the common parameters that are found on both the Mod and Amp Envelopes, the Modulation Envelope also contains a few additional parameters:

▶ **Pitch**—This parameter causes the envelope to control the pitch of the notes played. If assigned a positive value, the pitch will bend up. The opposite effect will occur when assigned a negative value.

▶ **Filter**—This parameter causes the envelope to modulate the Filter Frequency. When assigned a positive value, the value of the Filter Frequency will increase. The opposite effect will occur when assigned a negative value.

The Amplitude Envelope is used to alter the volume of a patch over time. Aside from the common parameters shared by both the Mod and Amp Envelopes, the Amplitude Envelope also has a few additional parameters:

▶ **Level**—Controls the volume level of a selected zone in the key zone map. This parameter can also control the volume of an entire patch by selecting all of the zones.

▶ **Pan**—Controls the panning of a selected zone in the key zone map. This parameter can also control the panning assignment of an entire patch by selecting all of the zones.

▶ **Spread**—This parameter creates a stereo effect by placing single notes played in various places within the stereo field. The knob determines the amount of Spread whereas the type of Spread is determined by the Spread modes, which are located just to the right. For a detailed explanation of these different modes, please refer to Chapter 11, " NN-19—Close Up," where they are discussed in detail.

The LFOs

The NN-XT includes two independent *Low Frequency Oscillators*, or LFOs (see Figure 12.9). As you have read in previous chapters, LFOs do not actually produce audible sound on their own. Rather, an LFO is used to modulate the main oscillators of a synthesizer. The NN-XT's LFOs are designed to modulate the samples themselves.

Figure 12.9
The NN-XT has two separate LFOs.

If you look at both of the LFOs, you'll notice that they share common knobs, but there are some key differences between LFOs 1 and 2.

▶ Although LFO 1 supports a number of waveforms, LFO 2 supports only the triangle waveform.

▶ LFO 1 can modulate the NN-XT filter, whereas LFO 2 modulates the pan.

▶ LFO 2's play mode is *always* set to Key Sync. This means that the waveform of LFO 2 will always trigger whenever a note is pressed on your keyboard.

The Rate knob determines the frequency of the LFO. To increase the modulation rate, turn the knob to the right. For a slower modulation, turn the knob to the left.

It is important to note that LFO 1 has three Rate modes, as follows.

▶ **Group Rate Mode**—When this mode is selected, the rate of LFO 1 is controlled by the LFO 1 Rate knob in the Group parameters of the Remote Editor. This ensures that all of the zones in the NN-XT will modulate at the same rate.

▶ **Tempo Sync**—When this mode is selected, the rate of the LFO is controlled by the tempo of the Reason sequencer. If you activate this mode and then begin to make changes to the Rate knob, a tooltip will display the different time divisions.

▶ **Free Run**—When this mode is selected, the LFO runs continuously at the rate set by the Rate knob. If the Key Sync is activated, the LFO will trigger every time a note is played. Also note that LFO 2 *always* runs in the Free Run mode.

The Delay knob is used to set a delay between playing the note on your keyboard and hearing it. Both LFO 1 and LFO 2 Delay knobs have the same capability and range of 0-10 seconds.

Although LFO 2 always uses the triangle waveform, LFO 1 has six waveform choices for modulation. These modes can be selected by clicking on the Waveform Mode button, or by just clicking on the desired waveform.

▶ **Triangle**—Creates a smooth up and down vibrato.

▶ **Inverted Sawtooth**—Creates a cycled ramp up effect.

▶ **Sawtooth**—Creates a cycled ramp down effect.

▶ **Square**—Makes abrupt changes between two values.

▶ **Random**—Creates a random stepped modulation. Also known as sample and hold.

▶ **Soft Random**—Exactly like the previous waveform but has a smoother modulation curve.

After a rate, delay, and waveform mode have been selected, it's time to choose a modulation destination. Although LFO 1 and LFO 2 contain different destinations, I placed them all in a single list to discuss them.

▶ **Pitch**—This parameter modulates the pitch of the loaded sample patch. It is commonly used for trills and vibrato, but that is just a couple of many sound design possibilities. The Pitch knob has a range of −2400 to 2400 cents (up to four octaves), and is available in both LFO 1 and LFO 2.

▶ **Filter**—This parameter modulates the Filter Frequency. It is a great tool for creating a filter sweep that can open upward (when set to positive) or downward (when set to negative). Note that this parameter is available only on LFO 1.

▶ **Level**—This knob is used to modulate the output level of the NN-XT for creating a tremolo effect. Note that this is available only with LFO 1.

▶ **Pan**—This parameter is used to modulate the panning of a single or multiple zones. It is a great effect to use on orchestral percussion, such as xylophones or glockenspiels. When turned to the left, the panning effect will move from left to right in the stereo field. When the knob is turned to the right, the panning effect will move from right to left in the stereo field. Note that this parameter is available with LFO 2.

The Group Parameters

Located in the upper-left corner of the NN-XT interface, the Group parameters apply to all of the zones within a selected group (see Figure 12.10).

Figure 12.10
The NN-XT Group parameters apply to all tones within a selected group.

Polyphony

Polyphony determines how many notes can be played simultaneously from the NN-XT. When set to a value of 1, the NN-XT becomes a monophonic instrument, which is perfect for playing lead synth lines or mimicking monophonic instruments, such as a flute or clarinet. When set to a greater polyphonic value, the NN-XT becomes the perfect device for mimicking instruments that are capable of producing many voices at one time, such as a piano, guitar, or a choir.

The NN-XT has a Polyphony range of 1-99 voices, so that should give you plenty of room to work with.

Legato and Retrig

Legato is the play mode of choice for monophonic sounds. While in Legato mode, play a note and hold it. Now play another note and you will notice that the NN-XT will not retrigger the envelope, but rather just change the pitch. If you combine this with a good portion of Portamento, you can create a fantastic sliding synth sound.

Legato will also work with polyphonic patches. Set the Polyphony to 3 and play a three-note chord on your MIDI keyboard. Now, press and hold another note and you will hear that the new note will be played legato style, but it steals one of the original notes of the chord.

Retrig is thought of as the "normal" preference for polyphonic patches. While in Retrig mode, the NN-XT envelopes are triggered every time a note is played on your MIDI keyboard, which differs greatly from the legato effect.

Retrig can also be used with monophonic patches. Press a note, hold it, and then play another note and release it. Notice that the NN-XT will now retrigger the sample of the first note, unlike the Legato mode.

CHAPTER 12

LFO 1 Rate

The LFO 1 Rate knob is used to control the frequency of modulation within the LFO 1. This knob is active only when the Group Rate mode is selected in the LFO section of the synth parameters.

Portamento

Portamento is used to create a sliding effect between played notes. The knob determines the amount of time it will take to slide from one note to another. It can be used with either monophonic or polyphonic patches and is a great tool for creating some interesting effects. Try loading a polyphonic patch, such as a string section or piano. Set the Portamento to a value of 45 and play some chords. You will hear a slight sliding effect that makes the patch sound a little funny, but try adding some delay and reverb. After a while, you'll have an ambient masterpiece on your hands.

The Key Map Display

Occupying the majority of the Remote Editor, the Key Map display is where all the action happens when it comes to importing, grouping, and creating sample patches (see Figure 12.11). There are a few similarities to the NN-19 as you will see, but the NN-XT key map is a much more diverse and mature interface that is intuitive and shouldn't take too long to master.

The Key Map display is split up into seven areas:

> ▶ **The Info Area**—The Info Area is used to display the sampling rate, bit depth, and file size of a selected sample.

> ▶ **The Sample Area**—The Sample Area is used to list the filenames of the loaded samples in a patch.

Figure 12.11
The Key Map display is where samples are imported and sorted in a very easy-to-understand interface.

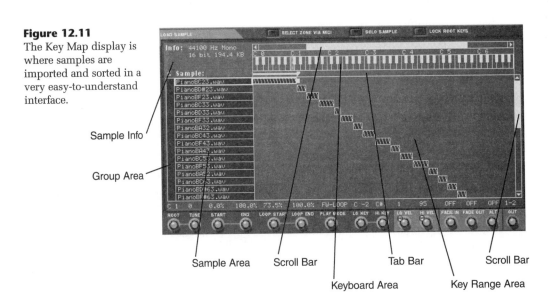

Sample Info

Group Area

Sample Area   Scroll Bar   Tab Bar   Scroll Bar

Keyboard Area   Key Range Area

▶ **The Group Area**—The Group Area does not display information. Rather, it is used to select a compilation of sample zones that are assigned to a group.

▶ **The Keyboard Area**—The Keyboard Area is used to display key ranges, audition loaded samples, and set root keys.

▶ **The Tab Bar**—The Tab Bar is located just below the Keyboard Area and is used to display the key range of a selected sample zone. It is here that you can resize a sample zone's key range.

▶ **The Key Range Area**—The Key Range Area is used to display the sample zones within a patch. Zones can be moved and resized in this area.

▶ **The Scroll Bars**—There are vertical and horizontal scroll bars that allow you to view any key range (vertical) or position on the keyboard (horizontal).

Aside from the Info Area and scroll bars, which are pretty self explanatory, let's have an in-depth look at these areas.

The Sample Area

All the files that are used to create a sample patch for the NN-XT are displayed in the Sample Area as a list. The Sample Area can also be used as a tool to load samples into a zone. To get better acquainted with the Sample Area, try this quick exercise.

1. If you have a patch loaded into the NN-XT, clear it by choosing Edit > Initialize Patch. This will give you a clean slate to work with.

2. Next, you need to add a zone to your key map so you can load a sample. Choose Edit > Add Zone to create an empty zone into which a sample can now be loaded. Notice that in the Sample Area the newly created zone is labeled **No Sample**.

3. To load a sample into the zone, you can either click on the Load Sample button at the upper-left corner of the Remote Editor or double-click on the **No Sample** label to open the sample browser window. At this point, you can select a sample and load it into your new zone.

The Group Area

After you have created a number of zones and loaded samples into them, you can compile these zones into a group. Once you do this, a number of zones can be selected and modified at one time, making it a big time-saver.

To create a group, try this quick exercise.

1. Using the previous exercise as an example, create several zones and load samples into them.

2. Once you have created a number of zones, select them all by either choosing Select All from the Edit pull-down menu or using Ctrl+A (or Apple+A on the Mac).

3. Choose the Group Selected Zones option from the Edit pull-down menu. This will place all the zones into one group.

The Keyboard Area

The Keyboard Area is a graphical representation of the virtual keyboard within the NN-XT. It is here that key ranges can be viewed, root notes can be set, and loaded samples can be auditioned without the use of a MIDI keyboard.

The *key range* refers to the lowest and highest key that will trigger a loaded sample. For example, let's suppose that you've imported a snare drum sample into a newly created zone in the key map. As a snare drum is a sample that does not have a specific pitch, you will not need more than one or two keys on your keyboard to trigger the sample. By using a key range, you can specify that the snare sample will be heard only by pressing the D1 or D#1 notes on a MIDI keyboard.

A *root note* specifies the original frequency at which a sample was recorded. If you record a piano played at Middle C, C3 is its root note. It is very important to specify a sample's root note, as you want to make sure that the recorded sample retains its realism and natural timbre.

LATER IN THE SHOW

In the next main section of this chapter, called "The Sample Parameters," you will read about root notes in more detail. You will also get an opportunity to work with root notes again in a tutorial that helps you create your first NN-XT patch.

It is very easy to audition loaded samples in the NN-XT by using your computer keyboard and mouse. If you are on the PC, just hold the Alt key and click on a key in the virtual keyboard. Notice that the mouse icon becomes a Speaker icon as you press the Alt key. This can also be done on the Mac by using the Option key.

The Tab Bar

The Tab Bar is one of several ways to adjust the key range of a zone. Start by selecting a sample zone in the key map. Once selected, the zone's Tab Bar will display the zone's key range and supply boundary handles to make adjustments. Just drag the handles to the left and right to make adjustments to the key range.

The Tab Bar can also be used to adjust the key range of several zones at one time and shift the positions of several zones at once. In order for this to work, the zones must share at least one common key range value.

The Key Range Area

The Key Range Area is used to adjust the key range of a selected zone and also to shift the position of a zone up and down the keyboard area. The main difference between the key range and the Tab Bar is that the key range will make adjustments on an individual basis. If there are two zones that share the same key ranges, adjustments to the key range are still made individually.

Zones can also be shifted in the Key Range Area on a singular or multiple basis if they are both selected.

The Sample Parameters

Located in the bottom portion of the Key Map display, the Sample parameters are used to edit any selected zone in the key map (see Figure 12.12). Whereas the synth parameters are used to alter the timbre and tone of a selected zone, the Sample parameters are used to set up loop points, root notes, route outputs, and simply do things that most samplers can't do.

Figure 12.12

The Sample parameters include 15 ways to edit your samples and enhance your sample performance.

Root Notes and Tune

The Root knob is used to adjust the original pitch of a loaded sample. When a sample is loaded into the NN-XT, it is necessary to assign a root as the original frequency of the recorded sample. For example, if you recorded a piano's C3 note and then imported it into the NN-XT, you will need to tell the NN-XT that the original pitch of the sample was C3. This is done with the Root knob.

Once a sample is imported into the key map, you can click and drag on the Root knob until you reach the desired root note. Another way to change the root note is to hold the Ctrl key (Apple key for Mac users) on your computer keyboard and click on the root note you want.

LOCK IT DOWN

Once you have set a root note, activate the Lock Root Keys button at the top of the Key Map display. Once active, you can still make adjustments to the root note with the Root knob, but if you want to shift the position of the sample zone, the root note will remain in place.

The Tune knob is used to make fine adjustments to your samples. It is used to make sure that the pitch of the samples matches the tunings of your other imported samples as well. For example, if you import a piano sample with a root note of C3 and then import another sample with a root note of E3, you might need to make fine-tuning adjustments to ensure that the piano samples will play in tune with each other as you make the transition from C3 to E3.

The Tune knob has a range of +/– half a semitone.

If you are not sure what the root note of your sample is or which way to tune it, Reason has a solution to help you out. Reason can automatically detect the root note of any imported sample with a perceivable pitch. Here's how it works.

1. Select the zone of the sample you want to use.
2. Choose Edit > Set Root Notes from Pitch Detection. Within a second, Reason will detect and assign a root note to your sample and will also make any fine-tuning adjustments.

CHAPTER 12

AN ALTERNATIVE ROOT

If you plan on doing in-depth sampling with the NN-XT, you might consider purchasing a dedicated audio-editing program. Recall Chapter 11, in which you were provided acoustic guitar samples to use in creating your own NN-19 sample patch. All of those samples were recorded and prepared in an audio-editing program called WaveLab, which I have mentioned previously.

The immediate benefit to the budding sampling geek is that an audio editor will give you access to various processors and plug-ins to make your recorded samples sound better. WaveLab, for example, supports both VST and DirectX formatted plug-ins, making it an ideal platform to make your samples sound as good as possible.

Most audio-editing programs also have the capability to establish clean loop points in a sample and can automatically detect a root note and make tuning adjustments automatically. This additional information is stored in the sample and recalled when the file is imported into the NN-19 or NN-XT.

Sample Start and End

The Sample Start knob is used to offset the start position of a loaded sample in the NN-XT. This function can be used for many purposes, such as:

▶ Removing unwanted noise at the beginning of a sample.

▶ Creating different versions of one sample. For example, if you have a sample of a person speaking the phrase "one, two, three, four," you could use the sample start and end knobs to isolate each word and map it on its own key without having to perform this task in an audio-editing program.

▶ Creating very realistic and dynamic performances perfect for percussion and drums samples, using the Sample Start knob in the Velocity section along with the Sample Start knob.

The Sample End knob is used to offset the end position of a loaded sample in the NN-XT. This is useful for removing unwanted sample portions from the end of a sample, such as noise or hiss.

To make changes to the Sample Start and End knobs, you can click and drag up or down with your mouse to move the offsets by percentages. If you want to make very fine changes to these knobs, hold the Shift key down while making adjustments to the start and end knobs.

Loop Start and End

In sampling terms, a loop is used to prolong the *sustain* of a note that is held down on your MIDI keyboard. For example, if you play a piano sample and hold the key down, notice that like a real piano, the note sustains as long as you hold it (see Figure 12.13). This is accomplished by finding a portion of the sample that can be looped continuously to sound like a sustain. Figure 12.13 shows a loop point that will occur toward the end of the sample. This loop point was created for this acoustic guitar sample using WaveLab. The loop that has been created occurs in an area where the loop start and end differ very slightly in amplitude. By creating a loop there, the loop is not noticeable and sounds very natural when used.

Figure 12.13
A loop is used to prolong the sustain of a note that is played on your keyboard.

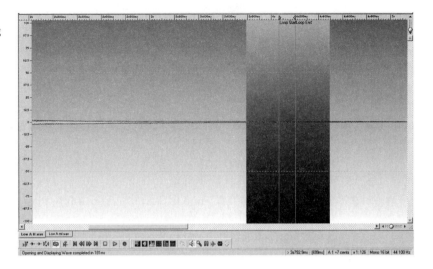

All of the samples in the Reason Factory Sound Bank and Orkester Sound Bank have already been assigned loop points, and you will find that this is the case for any sample collection that is commercially available.

The Loop Start knob shifts the offset of the loop starting point to the right in a sample. The Loop End knob shifts the offset of the loop end point to the left in a sample.

Play Mode

After a pair of loop points has been established, the Play Mode knob determines how the loop will be played. The Play Mode knob offers five choices:

▶ **FW**—The sample will play through once, without looping.

▶ **FW-LOOP**—The sample will play from the sample start to the loop end, and then it will jump back to the loop start and proceed to loop continuously between the loop points until the note is released.

▶ **FW-BW**—The sample will play from the sample start to the loop end. At this point, the sample will then play backward from the loop end to the loop start and finally play from the loop start to the loop end. This process will loop continuously until the note is released.

▶ **FW-SUS**—The sample will play from the sample start to the loop end, and then it will jump back to the loop start and proceed to loop continuously between the two loop points. After the note is released, the sample will play to the absolute end of the sample that reaches beyond the loop boundaries.

▶ **BW**—The sample will play backward once, without looping.

Low Key and High Key

These knobs are used to assign boundaries to the loaded samples. The *low key* assigns the lowest note that a sample can be played at, whereas the *high key* does exactly the opposite. You'll get a better idea of how this works later in the chapter when you will build your own sample patch.

Low Velocity and High Velocity

These knobs are used to assign velocity ranges to the loaded samples. *Low velocity* assigns the lowest velocity at which a sample can be played, whereas *high velocity* does the opposite.

Understanding these knobs and how they work is essential when creating a multilayered sample patch. For example, you can create sample zones and assign them all to the same key but give them different velocities. Here's an example of how you would velocity map four snare drum samples to the D1 note. Please note that this will include all of the other sample parameters that you have read about up to this point.

1. **Snare 1.aif**—Root D1, Tune 0, Start 0%, End 100%, Play Mode FW, Low Key D1, Hi Key D1, Lo Vel 1, Hi Vel 32

2. **Snare 2.aif**—Root D1, Tune 0, Start 0%, End 100%, Play Mode FW, Low Key D1, Hi Key D1, Lo Vel 33, Hi Vel 64

3. **Snare 3.aif**—Root D1, Tune 0, Start 0%, End 100%, Play Mode FW, Low Key D1, Hi Key D1, Lo Vel 65, Hi Vel 99

4. **Snare 4.aif**—Root D1, Tune 0, Start 0%, End 100%, Play Mode FW, Low Key D1, Hi Key D1, Lo Vel 100, Hi Vel 127

Fade In and Fade Out

These knobs are for assigning velocity crossfades to overlapping zones. As discussed in the Key Map display section, it is possible to have two zones that share the same range, root note, and velocity. The Fade In and Fade Out knobs can be used to smooth the transition between these two samples, making for an interesting dynamic effect.

The Fade In knob is used to create a velocity threshold that will trigger a sample when that threshold is reached via velocity. Once the threshold is reached, the sample will fade in, rather than abruptly trigger.

The Fade Out knob performs the same function, except when the threshold is reached the sample will fade out.

Here's an example of how to use these knobs:

1. Create two zones and load a sample into each one. Set the low velocity of both zones to 1 and their high velocities to 127.

2. Use the Fade Out knob on the first zone and set it to 40. This will tell the NN-XT to play that zone at its full level when the velocity is played under 40. Once the velocity has reached 40 and over, the sample will fade out.

3. Use the Fade In knob on the second zone and set it to 80. This will tell the NN-XT to play that zone with a fade in effect when the velocity equals 80. After the played velocity has surpassed 80, the sample will then play at its full level.

Alternate

To give your sample performance a realistic sound, the Alternate knob is used to semi-randomly trigger different sample zones during playback. For example, if you have a sample of a guitar chord playing with a down stroke and a sample of that same chord playing with an upstroke, you can use the Alternate knob to create a pattern where the NN-XT will determine when to alternate between the two samples.

Here's how you set up the Alternate function:

1. Create two zones and load a sample into each.
2. Select both zones.
3. Set the Alt knob to the On position. The NN-19 will now determine when to alternate between the two samples.

Output

The Output knob is used to assign your sample zones to one of eight stereo pairs of outputs. This comes in handy when you work with a sample patch that has many samples loaded in it. Each of these samples can be routed to any of these outputs by selecting the zone that the sample is loaded on and using the Output knob.

ROUTE THE OUTPUTS

Before you reassign all of the samples in your patch to different outputs, press the Tab key to flip the Device Rack around and route the additional outputs of the NN-XT to reMix (see Figure 12.14). This will help avoid any confusion you might encounter when you want to listen to all of the samples in your patch.

Figure 12.14
Route all of the outputs of the NN-XT to reMix before assigning your samples to different outputs.

Here's an example of how you would use the Output knob:

1. Use the Patch Browser to locate the Perc Set A.sxt patch in the Percussion folder of the Orkester Sound Bank. Load it and you will see that there are many sampled instruments here, including bass drum, snare, toms, castanets, cowbell, and a gong.

2. Select all three bass drums by clicking on its Group column. Notice that the Output is set to 1-2, which are the main outputs of the NN-XT.

3. Select the snare samples by clicking on the appropriate Group column. Set the output of the snare samples to 3-4.

4. Select the Tom samples by clicking on the appropriate Group column. Set the output to 5-6.

5. Repeat this for all of the other grouped samples until they all have their own outputs.

Creating a Multilayered NN-XT Patch

Now that you have all the ins and outs of the NN-XT down, it's time to put your knowledge to work and create your first NN-XT sample patch. In this tutorial, you are going to build a patch step by step by using guitar samples supplied by my trusty axe and me.

Unlike the sample patch that you created in Chapter 11, this guitar patch has different elements to it:

▶ The Samples are multilayered. There is a mezzo forte, forte, and double forte for each single note.

▶ There are samples of major chords played with an up stroke and a down stroke.

▶ There are FX samples, including a string slap and string slide sounds.

BEFORE YOU BEGIN

Before you begin this tutorial, take a moment to download the necessary samples from the Course Technology website at **www.courseptr.com**. Because there are more samples used this time around, it might take some time to download the archived file (it's around 11MB). If you are using a dial-up connection, go downstairs and make a cup of coffee (or beverage of choice) to pass the time.

After completing the download, you will need to unzip the archive file using either WinZip or Stuff-It Expander. Once the archive is expanded, place the NN-XT Guitar Samples folder into the Reason Program folder on your Mac or PC.

Importing Single Note Samples

Let's start the tutorial by working with the single note samples. Make sure you are working with a blank NN-XT and that there are no samples loaded into it. You can do so by choosing Initialize Patch from the Edit pull-down menu.

1. Click on the Load Sample button. This will bring up the Sample Browser. Navigate to the NN-XT Guitar Samples folder, open it, and double-click on the Single Notes folder to display the list of single note samples.

2. Locate the Low E samples, as these will be your starting place. There are three Low E samples available with three different dynamic levels.

3. Highlight the Low E mf.wav file first and click on the Open button to import it into the key zone area of the NN-XT.

4. As Yours Truly has already prepared these samples, all you have to do is set the key range and velocity for each sample. Begin by setting the key range of the Low E mf.wav file, which is Lo Key D1, High Key G#1.

5. Now set the velocity of the Low E sample as Lo Vel 1, Hi Vel 69. Notice as you do this, the zone that contains the sample is no longer solid shaded as before. Rather, a series of diagonal lines appears through the zone. This symbolizes that a velocity has been assigned to this zone.

6. Now, click anywhere in the key zone area to deselect the first Low E sample. Click on the Load Sample button again and import the Low E f.wav file.

7. Set the key range of the second Low E sample to the same values as the first sample. Set the velocity of this sample as Lo Vel 70, Hi Vel 99.

8. Click anywhere in the key zone area to deselect the first Low E sample. Click on the Load Sample button again and import the Low E ff.wav file.

9. Set the key range of the second Low E sample to the same values as the first and second samples. Set the velocity of this sample as Lo Vel 100, Hi Vel 127. You should now have three samples with different velocities stacked vertically, as shown in Figure 12.15.

10. Arm the sequencer track and use your MIDI keyboard to trigger the samples at different velocities. Notice the differences in dynamics between the three samples.

Figure 12.15
The three Low E samples have been imported and set up with different velocities.

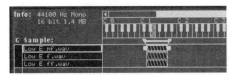

SAVE FOR A RAINY DAY

A reminder: You should save your patch periodically as you go through this tutorial. Click on the Save Patch button and save the patch in the NN-XT Guitar Samples folder. You can choose your own name of course, but keep it simple so you can easily find it.

CHAPTER 12

At this point, the first three single note samples have been imported into the NN-XT and have been assigned different velocities. It's time to move on to the next batch of guitar samples, so here is a list for each sample of the remaining strings.

▶ **Low A mf.wav**—Lo Key A1, Hi Key C#2, Lo Vel 1, Hi Vel 69

▶ **Low A f.wav**—Lo Key A1, Hi Key C#2, Lo Vel 70, Hi Vel 99

▶ **Low A ff.wav**—Lo Key A1, Hi Key C#2, Lo Vel 100, Hi 127

▶ **Low D mf.wav**—Lo Key D2, Hi Key F#2, Lo Vel 1, Hi Vel 69

▶ **Low D f.wav**—Lo Key D2, Hi Key F#2, Lo Vel 70, Hi Vel 99

▶ **Low D ff.wav**—Lo Key D2, Hi Key F#2, Lo Vel 100, Hi 127

▶ **Low G mf.wav**—Lo Key G2, Hi Key A#2, Lo Vel 1, Hi Vel 69

▶ **Low G f.wav**—Lo Key G2, Hi Key A#2, Lo Vel 70, Hi Vel 99

▶ **Low G ff.wav**—Lo Key G2, Hi Key A#2, Lo Vel 100, Hi 127

▶ **Low B mf.wav**—Lo Key B2, Hi Key D#3, Lo Vel 1, Hi Vel 69

▶ **Low B f.wav**—Lo Key B2, Hi Key D#3, Lo Vel 70, Hi Vel 99

▶ **Low B ff.wav**—Lo Key B2, Hi Key D#3, Lo Vel 100, Hi 127

▶ **High E mf.wav**—Lo Key E3, Hi Key G#3, Lo Vel 1, Hi Vel 69

▶ **High E f.wav**—Lo Key E3, Hi Key G#3, Lo Vel 70, Hi Vel 99

▶ **High E ff.wav**—Lo Key E3, Hi Key G#3, Lo Vel 100, Hi 127

▶ **High A mf.wav**—Lo Key A3, Hi Key C#4, Lo Vel 1, Hi Vel 69

▶ **High A f.wav**—Lo Key A3, Hi Key C#4, Lo Vel 70, Hi Vel 99

▶ **High A ff.wav**—Lo Key A3, Hi Key C#4, Lo Vel 100, Hi 127

▶ **High D mf.wav**—Lo Key D4, Hi Key A4, Lo Vel 1, Hi Vel 69

▶ **High D f.wav**—Lo Key D4, Hi Key A4, Lo Vel 70, Hi Vel 99

▶ **High D ff.wav**—Lo Key D4, Hi Key C#2, Lo Vel 70, Hi Vel 99

When you're finished, you should have a key map chock full of samples like the one in Figure 12.16. As a finishing touch, select all of the notes and then choose Group Selected Zones from the Edit pull-down menu. Also make sure that you have assigned a high amount of polyphony to the patch, such as 12.

Figure 12.16
All of the single-note guitar samples have been imported and configured.

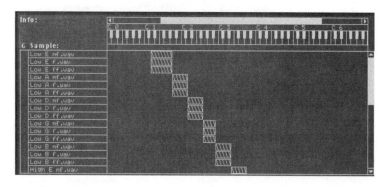

Importing Chord Samples

Now that the single notes have been imported and set up, it's time to import the chord samples. All the chords that were recorded for this tutorial are major triad chords and were recorded with up strokes and down strokes, providing an opportunity to use the Alternate feature.

1. Click on the Load Sample button. This will bring up the sample browser window.

2. Select the E Major Down.wav audio file and import the sample.

3. Because these chord samples were not assigned a root note, the NN-XT will assign the root note to C3 by default. Change the root note to E5, which can be done using the Root knob in the Sample Parameter area.

4. Now that the sample has been assigned the correct root note, you will need to assign the correct key range. Use the Lo Key knob to set the lowest note of the key range to D5. Use the Hi Key knob and set the highest note of the key range to F#5. This will give your E major chords a few extra notes to play.

5. Click in the empty part of the key map to deselect the newly created zone and click on the Load Sample button again. The sample browser window should still be pointed at the Chords folder. Import the E Major Up.wav audio file and the NN-XT will create a zone and import the sample as before.

6. Following the same steps as 1–5 , make the root key E5, the lowest note D5, and the highest note F#5.

7. At this point, you can preview the samples when played together by using the Alt key on your PC, or the Apple Key on your Mac, and clicking in the correct key range, which is D5-F#5. It should sound a little strange, because there are clearly different timbres and textures resulting from the way both samples were recorded.

8. Select both sample zones and turn on the Alternate function by using the Alt knob in the Sample Parameters area. Preview the samples again. The NN-XT should now alternate between the two samples.

Now that the E major sample has been imported and properly set up, you can proceed to do the same with the other chord samples. Use this list as a guide for setting up the correct root notes and key ranges.

▶ **G Major Up/Down**—Root Key G5, Lo Key G5, Hi Key G#5, set the Alt to On.

▶ **A Major Up/Down**—Root Key A5, Lo Key A5, Hi Key B5, set the Alt to On.

▶ **C Major Up/Down**—Root Key C6, Lo Key C6, Hi Key C#6, set the Alt to On.

▶ **D Major Up/Down**—Root Key D6, Lo Key D6, Hi Key D#6, set the Alt to On.

After you import and configure each sample, select all of the chord samples and choose Group Selected Zones from the Edit pull-down menu. This will group all of the chord samples together, so they can be edited and selected at one time.

Importing FX Samples

The single notes and chords are finished, so now it's time to top it off with a couple of guitar effect samples. I have included two types of effects that are commonly used when playing acoustic guitar:

▶ A string slide down the neck of the guitar on the Low E and A strings

▶ A slap of the guitar strings against the guitar frets

Unlike the chord samples you just imported and configured, these effects are going to be mapped at the C0 key. Use this list as a guide for setting up the correct root notes and key ranges.

▶ **Low E String Slide.wav**—Root Key E0, Lo Key D0, Hi Key G#0

▶ **Low A String Slide.wav**—Root Key A0, Lo Key A0, Hi Key C1

▶ **String Slap.wav**—Root Key C#1, Lo Key C#1, Hi Key C#1

KEEPING IT REAL

The Reason sequencer is an excellent tool for making your samples sound and act like the actual instrument. Let's use the acoustic guitar patch that you just created as an example. When a player strums a chord on an acoustic guitar, the strings are stroked either down or up. This means that the attack of each string is heard individually, because all six strings cannot be played simultaneously.

By using the Snap pull-down menu in the Reason sequencer, you can create a realistic guitar performance by making a few tiny adjustments.

Here's how to make the guitar patch sound like the real thing:

1. Plan out a chord progression that would be suited for an acoustic guitar. For example, E major to A major to G major to D major.

2. After planning the chord progression, determine the correct notes for each chord. For example, E major would traditionally be played using the notes E1, B1, E2, G#2, B2, and E3.

3. Using the Reason sequencer, switch to Edit mode and set the Snap value to Bar.

4. Write an E major chord using the notes listed in Step 2. Make sure that the notes are a full measure long (see Figure 12.17).

5. Once this is done, click on Play to hear how the guitar chord sounds. The actual sounds of the acoustic guitar are fine, but the attack of the chord sounds very unreal.

6. Now, set the Snap to a much finer resolution of 1/64.

7. Using your mouse, select the second note of the chord (B1) and move it to the right by a 64th note.

8. Select the next note (E2) and move it to the right by two 64th notes.

9. Continue to do this to the other remaining notes in the chord until you see each note of the chord on its own beat in the measure (see Figure 12.18).

10. Click on Play and listen to the chord. It now sounds like the actual strumming of an acoustic guitar.

Figure 12.17
The E major chord has been written in as whole notes.

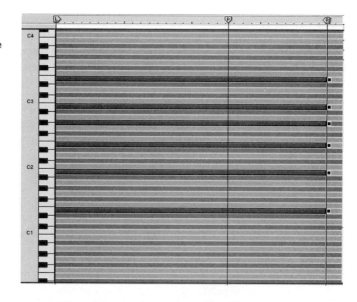

Figure 12.18
Each one of the notes in the chord has been moved to the right in 64th note increments.

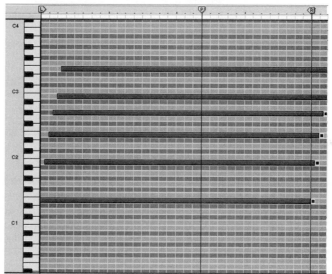

Expanding Your Sample Library with Reload

There is no doubt in my mind that a lot of you might have an Akai sampler or two lurking in your studio somewhere. I would also go so far as to say that there are quite a few of you who have invested a pretty penny into purchasing many Akai sample titles. There are many Akai titles in my library that I was just dying to use in Reason 1.0. It seemed that if the NN-19 looked like an Akai sampler, surely it could import Akai formatted samples. Sadly, this was not the case, and I found myself feeling a little misty-eyed. As though they read my mind, Propellerhead wrote two important free utility programs for Reason that brought hope back to my cause.

The *ReFill Packer* is a program written to compress and compile all of your programmed Reason samples and patches into one file that is accessed from the patch browser window. Although this utility is not covered in this part of the chapter, it is still required for the Reload program to run properly, so make sure you download it along with Reload. For a detailed tutorial on how to use this wonder, see Appendix C, "ReFills."

Reload is a program made to convert your Akai S1000 and S3000 samples to a format compatible with the NN-XT (see Figure 12.19). It is a simple single screen interface that leads you by the hand into converting your samples with ease and versatility. This section takes you through a quick-and-easy tutorial of the Reload interface and process.

Figure 12.19
Reload is a utility to convert Akai S1000 and S3000 samples to NN-XT patches. And it's free!

GET REGISTERED—GET HAPPY

Although ReFill Packer and Reload are free utility programs, they are available only to users who have registered Reason 2.0 or 2.5. In order to register your products quickly, visit the Propellerhead website (**www.propellerheads.se**) and proceed to the Users section. You will be prompted to log in with a username and password, which you can create within minutes.

Once you register Reason and any other Propellerhead programs you own, you can download Reload and install it. After you download Reload, the Propellerhead website will assign you a registration code that you will need to write down and use the first time you launch Reload.

Converting Akai to NN-XT

This tutorial shows you how to convert an Akai CD to NN-XT patches using Reload.

1. Start Reload. If this is your first time using this program, you need to enter your registration code (see the note entitled "Get Registered—Get Happy").

2. Reload will prompt you for an Akai CD. Open the CD tray on your PC or Mac and pop the CD in. Because an Akai CD is not Mac formatted, Reload must be running when you insert the Akai CD, or your Mac will automatically eject the disc.

3. Once Reload detects the Akai CD, it will give you two conversion choices (see Figure 12.20). You can convert your Akai CD to NN-XT patches, or you can have Reload convert the Akai CD to NN-XT patches and then create a ReFill of those samples. For this tutorial, select the NN-XT option.

4. Reload will then ask you to select a directory in which to place your converted samples. In Figure 12.21, I have created a folder on the desktop of my Mac and called it Hans Zimmer.

5. Once you select your directory, click Choose. Reload will proceed to make the conversion (see Figure 12.22). Depending on the size of the CD, this can take anywhere from 2-10 minutes.

6. When the procedure is finished, look at the contents of your converted folder. As you can see in Figure 12.23, Reload has split the samples into their own partitioned folders and created an HTML document that lists all the available samples and their locations.

Figure 12.20
Once Reload detects the Akai disc, it will give you two conversion choices.

Figure 12.21
Create a directory in which to place your converted samples.

Figure 12.22
Reload can convert your
Akai CDs to the NN-XT
format within minutes.

Figure 12.23
The contents of the
converted Akai CD.

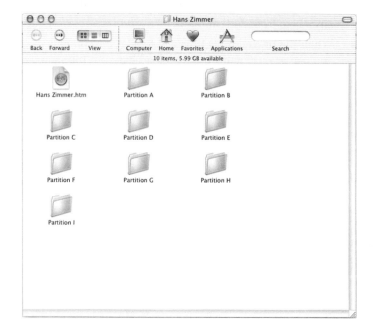

YOU'RE INVITED, BUT YOUR FRIENDS CAN'T COME

Although you might be tempted to copy these converted samples onto a CD and give them to another Reason buddy of yours, this is not a cool thing to do.

Speaking from personal experience, a lot of time and hard work goes into the development of these sample CDs. It's only right that the creators get their fair share of the profit pie; so don't contribute to the growing piracy problem. Be part of the solution and make your friends buy their own sample CDs.

Converting Akai to ReFill

This tutorial shows you how to convert an Akai CD to NN-XT patches using both Reload and the ReFill Packer.

GET REFILL PACKER

Before you can do this part of the tutorial, make sure that you get the ReFill Packer utility at the Propellerhead website. Just as a convenience, Reload will remind you if the ReFill Packer has not been installed every time Reload boots up (see Figure 12.24).

Figure 12.24
Reload will remind you if ReFill Packer is not installed.

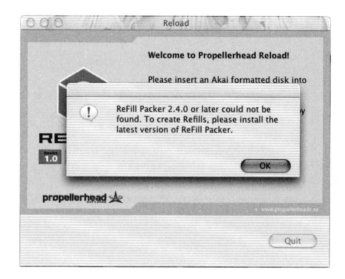

1. Start Reload.
2. Once the program launches, pop in an Akai CD. Once Reload detects the Akai CD, select Convert Akai Samples to ReFill.
3. Reload will then ask you to select a directory to place your ReFill in. As with the last tutorial, I have opted to use the Hans Zimmer folder that I created on my desktop.
4. Reload will now proceed to convert the Akai samples to the NN-XT format. This can take anywhere from 2-10 minutes, depending on the size of the CD.
5. After Reload is finished converting the Akai samples, ReFill Packer will automatically launch and begin to compile and compress the NN-XT samples into a single ReFill.
6. Once the process is complete, you will find a ReFill file and an HTML file in the folder in which you chose to place the converted files (see Figure 12.25).

Figure 12.25
After it's all said and
done, you get a ReFill
file, and an HTML file
that works as a listing of
all the available samples.

Whew! That's a lot of sampling information. After reading through these last two chapters, I'd
venture to say that you probably know more about sampling now than many seasoned
professionals! But don't let that stop you from continuing your sampling education. Try your hand
at sampling drums, pianos, basses, voices, or a few unique noises from a creaky bedroom door to
see how you can twist and turn those samples into music with the NN-XT!

13

The Matrix—Close Up

This chapter takes an in-depth look at the Matrix Pattern Sequencer, shown in Figure 13.1.

What Is the Matrix?

The Matrix is a pattern-based sequencer that can be used to write lead lines for the various Reason devices. As you might have guessed, it is not a sound module itself. Rather, it is a device that controls Reason's other sound-generating devices.

Essentially, the Matrix Pattern Sequencer generates three kinds of data:

▶ **Note**—This is pitch-based data that is assigned from within the Pattern window of the Matrix.

▶ **Gate**—This data is used to send Note On, Note Off, and Velocity data to the Reason device it is routed to.

▶ **Curve**—This data is used to send controller information to different modulation parameters of any Reason device.

The Matrix is capable of producing 32-step pattern sequences with many different note resolutions available. Once patterns are written, they can be stored in the Pattern section of the Matrix interface. Note, though, that written patterns are saved within a Reason song and cannot be stored individually for later use in another song.

Figure 13.1
The Matrix Pattern Sequencer is used to sequence any Reason device, such as the Subtractor and Malström.

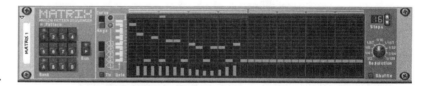

ENDLESS ROUTES

The possibilities for using the Matrix within Reason are just about endless. Create any Reason device, press the Tab key to flip the Device Rack around, and you will find an input of some kind that can be used with the Matrix. For example, you can use the Matrix to alter the panning and volume of any channel in reMix. Or you can use the Matrix to alter the individual parameters of any real-time effect.

Now that you have a basic understanding of what the Matrix does, it's time to consider its individual functions and features.

THE PATTERN SECTION AND RUN BUTTONS

As you read through this chapter, you will see many similarities between the Matrix pattern section and the pattern section of Redrum, most notably, the Run button. The controls are the same in the pattern sections of both devices, so please refer to Chapter 7, "Redrum—Close Up," to review.

Edit Mode

At the top-left corner of the Matrix interface is the Edit Mode selector. This selector switches between the two available edit modes—Key and Curve.

▶ **Key Edit**—When this edit mode is selected, the Matrix Pattern window displays note information and note on/off/velocity values for each note. This is the view that you use to write a sequenced pattern.

▶ **Curve Edit**—When this edit mode is selected, the Matrix Pattern window displays curve information and displays the note on/off/velocity values for each note. Curve Edit allows you to create patterns that can control various parameters on any of the Reason devices.

BIPOLAR OR UNIPOLAR CURVES

If you press the Tab key to view the back of the Matrix, you will see a switch in the middle of the interface that offers two curve types—Bipolar and Unipolar.

A *unipolar curve* has values starting from zero, which is the lowest setting. It is the default curve setting when an instance of the Matrix is created. See Figure 13.2 for a better look at a unipolar curve.

A *bipolar curve* is divided in the middle, where the middle value equals zero. When you begin to draw in a bipolar curve, it looks much different than the unipolar curve, because both positive and negative values can be drawn in (see Figure 13.3). This presents a number of possibilities for using the bipolar curve to control other Reason device parameters that contain positive and negative values.

Figure 13.2
A unipolar curve's values begin at its lowest numeric value of zero.

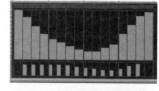

Figure 13.3
The bipolar curve setting allows the Matrix to control device parameters containing positive and negative values, such as the pan controls for reMix, or possibly the OSC phase controls for the Subtractor.

Octaves and Ties

Just below the Edit Mode switch are the Octave switch and the Tie button.

▶ **Octave**—This switch is used to view and edit notes within a five-octave range. When an instance of the Matrix is created, the Octave switch is set to 3 by default, which is approximately Middle C.

▶ **Tie**—When activated, this Tie button makes it possible to increase the length of your sequenced notes by tying them together. For example, tying two 16th notes together in order to create an 8th note. This button is covered in the Subtractor tutorial section later in this chapter.

The Matrix Pattern Window

The centerpiece of the Matrix device is the Pattern window. This is where your notes, velocities, and curve patterns are drawn, edited, and stored into the Pattern Selector within a saved Reason song. All three types of output information are viewable here—Note, Gate, and Curve.

The Pattern window is split into two sections. The majority of the window is dedicated to drawing in note and curve patterns, whereas the lower portion of the interface is used to draw in the note on/off/velocity of the sequence (see Figure 13.4).

Steps, Resolution, and Shuffle

To the right of the Matrix Pattern window are three important controls that assign the number of steps, note value, and shuffle feel to your Matrix sequences (see Figure 13.5).

▶ **Steps**—This parameter assigns the number of steps to your Matrix sequences. It has a range from 1-32 steps, offering a wide variety for creating patterns based on common and odd time signatures. This parameter is set at 16 by default whenever an instance of the Matrix is created.

▶ **Resolution**—This parameter is used to assign the overall note value of your pattern sequences. There are many note values to choose from. For example, you can use quarter notes (1/4) to draw in a slower pattern, or something much faster, like 32nd notes (1/32). This parameter is set to 16th notes by default whenever an

Figure 13.4
The Matrix Pattern window is used to draw and edit sequences for all three types of output information.

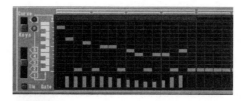

Figure 13.5
The Steps, Resolution, and Shuffle controls.

instance of the Matrix is created. This means that every note in your pattern is going to be a 16th note in length. You can alter these note lengths by using the Tie button, which you'll use later in this chapter.

▶ **Shuffle**—When activated, this button gives your Matrix sequences a shuffle or swing feeling that's useful with rap and R&B music. The Pattern Shuffle knob in the Transport Panel determines the strength of the shuffle.

DIFFERENT STEPS—DIFFERENT TIME SIGNATURES

Being a musician of many musical influences, I for one enjoy a lot a music that focuses on odd time signatures, such as 3/4, 5/4, 6/8, and my favorite 7/8. I have nothing against good old "four on the floor" time signatures like 4/4 and 2/4, but a little variety never hurts.

If you're like me, you'll be excited to know that the Matrix is fully capable of producing oddly timed sequences. You just have to do a little math to determine the correct number of steps to assign to it.

Here is a list of step numbers to accommodate different time signatures.

▶ **3/4**—12 or 24 steps

▶ **5/4**—20 steps

▶ **6/8**—12 or 24 steps

▶ **7/8**—14 or 28 steps

Matrix Outputs

Press the Tab key to flip the Device Rack and you'll find the CV outputs of the Matrix (see Figure 13.6). Although each of these outputs appears to have a specific destination in mind, you'll find there is more than one possibility for each when you're using them creatively.

▶ **Curve CV**—This CV output is used in combination with the curve pattern data created within the Matrix Pattern window. This output can be routed to just about any type of modulation input on a Reason device. For example, it could be routed to the Modulation inputs of the Subtractor or Malström, or to the Panning controls of reMix.

▶ **Note CV**—This CV output is used in combination with the note pattern data created in the Matrix Pattern window. This output can also be routed to just about any modulation input; however, it is best served by being used with the CV input of a Reason device, like the Subtractor or NN-19.

▶ **Gate CV**—This CV output is used in combination with the note on/off/velocity pattern data created in the Matrix Pattern window. This output is best served by being connected to the Gate input of any Reason device, such as the NN-19 or Malström. Another possible connection is the Level input of reMix.

Figure 13.6
The CV outputs on the back of the Matrix.

Matrix Tutorials

Now that you understand the interface and parameters of the Matrix, it's time to kick things into high gear and learn how to use the Matrix with the Subtractor. Although there are many different Reason devices, the same basic routing and sequencing theory applies to each device, so you can take the information within this tutorial section and apply it to the Malström, NN-19, and the NN-XT. You can also use this information with Dr:rex and Redrum, because they both have CV inputs on their rear panels. After that, the chapter then shows you how to use the Matrix with other Reason devices in ways that you might not have thought possible.

Using the Matrix with the Subtractor

This tutorial shows you how to connect the Matrix to the Subtractor. Once connected, you'll use the combination together to create a melody or lead line. To top it off, you'll see how to use the Matrix creatively with the Subtractor by connecting it in different combinations.

Making the Connection

The first thing you have to do is make a basic connection from the Subtractor to the Matrix. This section shows you how Reason can do this automatically as well as shows you how to manually make a connection between the two devices.

Before getting started, take a minute to start a new Reason song and create a reMix and Subtractor.

1. Click once on the Subtractor to select it. Then choose Matrix Pattern Sequencer from the Create pull-down menu.

2. An instance of the Matrix should now appear under the Subtractor. Press Tab to swing the Device Rack around. The Matrix outputs should already be connected to the Subtractor (see Figure 13.7).

3. Press the Tab key to flip the Device Rack again.

In the next part of the tutorial, you disconnect the Matrix from the Subtractor so that you can get a clear understanding of how to make the connection manually. Before you begin, click once on the Matrix and choose Disconnect Device from the Edit pull-down menu. This will give you a clean slate to start with.

1. Press the Tab key to flip the Device Rack. The Matrix should be disconnected from the Subtractor (see Figure 13.8).

2. Click and drag on the Gate CV output on the Matrix and connect it to the Gate input in the top left of the Subtractor (see Figure 13.9).

3. Now, click and drag on the output of the Note CV output of the Matrix and connect it to the CV input of the Subtractor (see Figure 13.10).

4. Press the Tab key to flip the Device Rack.

Figure 13.7
In the top figure, the
Matrix has been created
and placed just below
the Subtractor. In the
bottom figure, you are
looking at the back of the
Device Rack and you can
see that two of the three
Matrix outputs are
connected to the
Subtractor inputs.

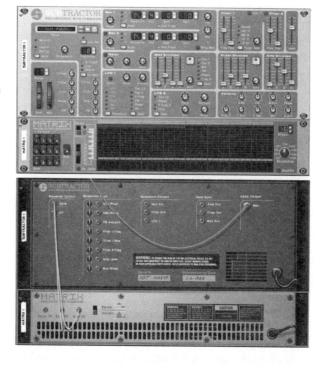

Figure 13.8
The Matrix is not
connected to the
Subtractor.

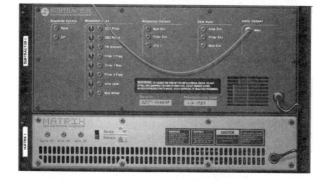

Figure 13.9
First connect the Gate CV
output of the Matrix to
the Gate input of the
Subtractor.

Figure 13.10
Now, the Note CV output is connected to the CV input.

Sequencing the Subtractor with the Matrix

After connecting the Matrix to the Subtractor, you'll probably want to begin sequencing right away. It's extremely easy to do and will only take a minute to learn.

Let's keep it simple and create a 16-step sequence with a resolution of 1/16. This means that there are 16 steps total in this pattern and a single 16th note represents one step.

Before you begin, look at the Pattern window. Notice that there are already notes drawn in along the low C note (see Figure 13.11). This is done by default whenever an instance of the Matrix is created. This means that the Subtractor can already begin to play sequenced notes from the Matrix, but it's missing just one element, which is *Note On/Off and Velocity*. So, what you need to do is assign some velocity to this sequence in order to hear it.

To draw in this pattern, use your mouse to click in the velocity section of the Pattern window, just below the note you want to hear. For example, if you want to hear the first note, click in the Gate section of the first note in order to assign values to it (see Figure 13.12). This will assign a note on/off and velocity value to the note.

Figure 13.11
Looking at the Matrix, you can see that there are notes already drawn in. The only element that is missing is note on/off and velocity.

Figure 13.12
Click in the gate portion of the Pattern window in order to assign a value to its corresponding note.

Click on Play and you should now hear the Subtractor play the C note with whatever value you assigned to it. At this point, you can go ahead and write values for each of the 16 steps in this sequence.

Now, let's write in some proper notes. Once again, the rule of thumb here is to keep it simple, as you'll have plenty of time later to channel some techno heaven out of the Matrix. So, draw in a C Major arpeggio line (the notes are C-E-G) consisting primarily of 16th notes. Use your mouse to select the notes for the sequence. When you're finished, it should look like Figure 13.13.

Click on Play now and you should hear your 16th note arpeggio line play back in all its techno glory. That's pretty much all there is to writing in a Matrix pattern, but let's try a couple of variations.

Listening to just 16th notes in a run can get extremely boring after a while, as it is just begging for some variation. This can be achieved by using the Tie button to tie a couple of 16th notes together to create an 8th note. Here's how to do it.

First, click on the Tie button in the lower-left corner of the Matrix interface. Next, using your mouse, navigate to the gate portion of the Pattern window and click on the first note. Notice that the gate bar, which was once thin, is now much thicker (see Figure 13.14). Click on Play and you should now hear those two 16th notes played together as a single 8th note.

Figure 13.13
A 16th note arpeggio is easy to create with the Pattern window. For some variation in the sound of the sequence, you can use different velocities by clicking on the note on/off/velocity values for each corresponding note.

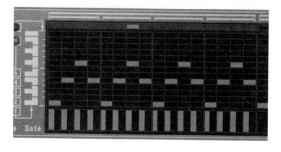

Figure 13.14
Activate the Tie function and click in the gate portion of the Pattern window under the note you want to hear played back as an 8th note.

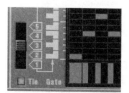

TIE KEYBOARD SHORTCUT
A handy shortcut for accessing the Tie function is to hold down the Shift key while clicking on the velocities of the notes you want to tie together.

SHIFT IT UP, SHIFT IT DOWN, SHIFT THEM NOTES ALL AROUND

As you might recall from Chapter 7, the Redrum is also a pattern-based sequencer. It's therefore safe to assume that these two pattern-based sequencers share a lot of functions that can be used to achieve different effects with the patterns.

Click on the Matrix to select it. Then click on the Edit pull-down menu and you'll see a list of the different options. Because most of these options were mentioned in Chapter 7, I won't go into each one unless there are any differences.

▶ **Cut Pattern**

▶ **Copy Pattern**

▶ **Paste Pattern**

▶ **Clear Pattern**

▶ **Shift Pattern Left**

▶ **Shift Pattern Right**

▶ **Shift Pattern Up**—This option transposes the pattern up one half step.

▶ **Shift Pattern Down**—This option transposes the pattern down one half step.

▶ **Randomize Pattern**—This option randomly generates Note, Gate, and Curve pattern data.

▶ **Alter Pattern**

When you finish writing in your sequence patterns, you can either create another pattern by selecting A2, or you can choose Copy Pattern to Track from the Edit pull-down menu. This will copy the Matrix pattern to its sequencer track between the locator points, which can then be moved to a sequencer track belonging to another Reason device.

MONOPHONIC ONLY

Although you probably have figured this out already, the Matrix cannot be used to sequence chord patterns. Its sole purpose is to create monophonic synth lines and curve patterns to control the parameters of other Reason devices. If you want to create chord progressions for the Subtractor, Malström, and NN-19/XT, you should do so within the Reason sequencer. See Chapter 5, "The Reason Sequencer—Close Up," for more information.

Creative Connections with the Subtractor

Now that you've covered the basics of using the Matrix with the Subtractor, let's look at a few creative connections that you can make between the two devices.

This first example uses the Curve CV to control the pitch of the Subtractor.

1. Click on Play to start the sequencer. Press the Tab key to flip the Device Rack.

2. Disconnect the Note CV output from the CV input of the Subtractor. The Subtractor should now begin playing a 16th-note sequence comprised of single notes.

3. Connect the Curve CV output of the Matrix to the OSC Pitch input on the Subtractor (see Figure 13.15).

4. Press the Tab key.

5. Switch the Edit mode from Key to Curve Edit (see Figure 13.16).

6. Use the Selector tool to draw in a Curve pattern (see Figure 13.17).

7. Click on Play and the Matrix will use the Curve pattern to affect the OSC pitch of the Subtractor. At this point, you can now make additional adjustments to the Curve pattern until you get a sequence of notes that you like. With a little practice, you'll be channeling those old Atari 2600 video game sounds in no time.

You can also route the Note CV output of the Matrix to any additional modulation inputs on the Subtractor. For example, try routing the Note CV output to the FM Amount input on the Subtractor. Additionally, you can increase or decrease the amount of input to this parameter by using the knob to the left of the input. Also note that you must use a Subtractor patch that uses the FM function (see Figure 13.18).

Figure 13.15
Connect the Curve CV output of the Matrix to the OSC Pitch input on the Subtractor.

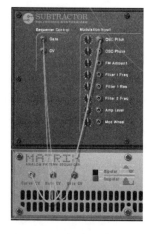

Figure 13.16
Switch the Edit mode from Key to Curve Edit.

Figure 13.17
Draw in a Curve pattern with the Selector tool.

Figure 13.18
Try connecting the Note CV output of the Matrix to any of the modulation inputs on the back of the Subtractor. In this example, I have connected the Note CV output to the FM Amount input.

Creative Connections with the Matrix

If there is one thing that I can say about Reason, it's that it excels at creative solutions. The Matrix is a prime example; it offers a great variety of interesting possibilities and creative connections. In fact, this section shows you some connections that will have you thinking "No Way!"

Using One Matrix with Two Devices

Although I have very few gripes about the Subtractor, I would really love to see some sort of panning control within the interface to automate the panning between the left and right channels. But, with a little research and experimentation, I found that using the Matrix with the Subtractor *and* reMix makes this possible.

Try the following exercise. Get ready by starting a new Reason song and creating an instance of reMix, the Subtractor, and the Matrix.

1. Using your mouse, write a quick sequence into the Matrix in order to trigger the sounds of the Subtractor (see Figure 13.19).
2. Press the Tab key to flip the Device Rack.
3. Switch the Curve mode from unipolar to bipolar.
4. Next, click and drag a virtual cable from the Curve CV output of the Matrix to the Pan CV input of reMix channel 1 (see Figure 13.20).
5. Press the Tab key to flip the Device Rack.
6. Switch the Edit mode on the Matrix from Key to Curve.
7. Draw in a curve pattern using your mouse (see Figure 13.21).

Figure 13.19
Write a quick sequence into the Matrix. Remember to assign gate to your sequence so that you will hear it play back.

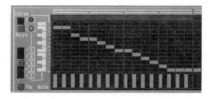

Figure 13.20
Connect a virtual cable from the Curve CV output of the Matrix to the Pan CV input of reMix channel 1. This will make it possible to have the Matrix control the panning assignment of reMix channel 1 by way of the Matrix Curve Edit.

Figure 13.21
Draw in a curve pattern. By switching to the bipolar curve mode, you can draw in curve values that will affect the left and right channels.

8.   Click on Play to start the Matrix Sequencer. You should now hear the sequence panning from left to right.

Using the Matrix with Real-Time Effects

Although the next chapter discusses real-time effects in more detail, I can't resist showing you how to use the Matrix with a few choice effects.

Using the Matrix with Unison

Unison is an effect that is used to reproduce several detuned voices from a single source. It sounds similar to a chorus. In this tutorial, you will connect the Matrix to a Subtractor that is using an instance of Union as an insert effect. Before you begin, start a new Reason song and create instances of the following Reason devices in this order:

1.   reMix.

2.   Subtractor.

3.   Unison. This will make Reason automatically route the output of the Subtractor to the input of the Unison. The Unison's outputs will then automatically be routed to a channel on reMix.

4.   The Matrix. Reason will automatically route its Curve CV output to the Detune input on Unison, and this is fine.

At this point, you should also draw in a quick note sequence for the Matrix, which will be used to trigger the notes of the Subtractor. Note, though, that you won't hear a sound, as you have not connected the Matrix to the Subtractor.

Okay, let's go.

1. Press the Tab key to flip the Device Rack.

2. Click and drag a virtual cable from the Note CV output of the Matrix to the CV input of the Subtractor.

3. Click and drag a virtual cable from the Gate CV output of the Matrix to the Gate CV input of the Subtractor. At this point, you can click on Play to hear your sequence play back. Also, notice that the Curve CV output of the Matrix is connected to the Detune input of Unison (see Figure 13.22).

4. Switch the Curve mode from unipolar to bipolar.

5. Press the Tab key to flip the Device Rack.

6. Switch the Edit mode on the Matrix from Key to Curve mode.

7. Write in a curve pattern that looks like Figure 13.23.

8. Click on Play. You should now hear your Subtractor sequence playing back as well as the Unison detune parameter in action. At this point, you might want to change the number of voices that the Unison creates by clicking on the Voice Count parameter.

Figure 13.22
The Matrix is ready to alter the Detune parameter of Unison.

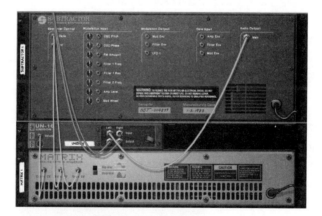

Figure 13.23
Draw in a curve pattern like this.

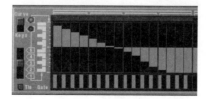

Using the Matrix with the Envelope Controlled Filter

This next tutorial has you double up your pleasure by using two instances of the Matrix along with another really great real-time effect called the ECF-42. For this exercise, you will not have to start over with a new song. You can continue to use the Reason song you created in the last exercise and make a few adjustments to it along the way.

First, get rid of Unison in order to use the ECF-42 instead. Click on Unison once and choose Cut Device from the Edit pull-down menu.

Now, click on the Subtractor once and choose ECF-42 Envelope Controlled Filter from the Create pull-down menu. This will create an instance of the ECF-42 under the Subtractor. If you press the Tab key to flip the Device Rack around, you will also see that the Subtractor's output has been automatically routed to the ECF-42.

Make the following parameter adjustments to the ECF-42 interface.

▶ **Resonance**—Set to 100

▶ **Envelope Amount**—Set between 50-60

▶ **Velocity**—Set to 42

▶ **Filter Mode**—Set to BP12 to use as a band pass filter

▶ **Decay**—Set to 100

▶ **Sustain**—Set to 24

▶ **Release**—Set to 0

Okay, you're ready to begin.

1. Press the Tab key to flip the Device Rack.

2. Connect the Curve CV output of the Matrix to the Frequency CV input on the ECF-42.

3. Click on the Matrix to select it and choose Matrix Pattern Sequencer from the Create pull-down menu to create another instance of it (see Figure 13.24).

4. Click once on the second Matrix to select it and choose Disconnect Device from the Edit pull-down menu. The second Matrix should now be disconnected from the ECF-42.

5. Click and drag a virtual cable from the Curve CV output of the second Matrix to the Envelope Gate input of the ECF-42.

6. Change the Curve mode of the second Matrix from unipolar to bipolar.

7. Press the Tab key to flip the Device Rack.

Figure 13.24
After creating a second instance of the Matrix, notice that the Curve CV and Gate CV outputs have been automatically routed to the Decay CV input and Env Gate CV input, respectively.

The second instance of the Matrix has now been created and you are just about ready to draw in a curve pattern that will affect the Envelope section of the ECF-42. However, you need to make a few adjustments to the second Matrix.

1. Change the number of steps from 16 to 4.
2. Change the resolution from 1/16 to 1/8.

Now, switch the Edit mode on the second Matrix from Key to Curve and draw in a curve pattern similar to Figure 13.25.

Click on Play and now both Matrix sequencers should begin playing in perfect sync. Notice the really cool filter effect that you have just created with the ECF-42.

Figure 13.25
Now that the connections have been made and the parameters have been adjusted, draw in a simple curve pattern that will affect the Envelope section of the ECF-42.

Automating the Matrix

Once you have compiled a set of different pattern sequences for your song, you need to program them into your Reason song. This requires writing automation data into the Pattern section of the Matrix. By doing this, you can program when the Matrix will play different patterns within your song. Writing this automation is simple.

There are two ways to automate the Pattern section of the Matrix:

▶ **Live Automation**—This kind of data is recorded in real time while the song plays back.

▶ **Drawn Automation**—This kind of data is drawn in using the Pencil tool while in the Edit mode with the Pattern Lane.

To see how automation works, you can do a little live automation by trying the following exercise. Before you start, take a minute to start a new Reason song and load it with an instance of the Matrix.

Note that this exercise is meant to teach you about automation, not to actually produce a sound.

1. Make sure that the Matrix is armed for recording by clicking on the In column of the Matrix sequencer track.
2. Click on Record and Play in the Transport panel to have the Reason Sequencer start recording data.

3. As the Matrix track is recording, select different patterns and banks. At the same time, look at the Transport Panel and you will see the bright red Punched In LED in the Automation Override section (lower-right corner; see Figure 13.26).

4. When you're finished recording, click on the Stop button. At this point, a purple framed box should appear around the Pattern section of the Matrix, which indicates that automation data has been recorded here (see Figure 13.27). Also, notice that a tan/brown line with data has been written into the Matrix sequencer track. This also indicates that data has been written in here.

Figure 13.26
As the Matrix sequencer track is recording, change to different banks and patterns. Try something easy, like changing from pattern A1 to A2 and back.

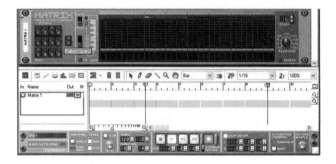

Figure 13.27
There is now automation data recorded on the Pattern section of the Matrix.

AUTOMATION IN DETAIL
You have briefly read about automation in this chapter, but you can learn more about it in Chapter 15, aptly called "Automation."

I have to admit, the first year that I used Reason, the Matrix was not one of my favorite things about the program, because I found it a little awkward and retro. But as I came to desire more pattern-driven elements in my songs, I found the Matrix to be a very welcome device in my Reason studio.

This pretty much finishes up the dinner course of your Reason tour. You should now be ready to move on to the dessert course by getting into the real-time effects.

14

Effects—Close Up

No virtual studio is complete without a horde of virtual effects, and Reason 2.5 is no exception. There are 12 unbelievable real-time virtual effect processors here that are sure to be just what the doctor ordered when a healthy dose of audio spice is needed for your tracks.

This chapter digs into each one of these hotties and shows you how they can be used effectively and creatively.

Effects Common Features

As you begin to look more closely at these real-time effects, you will notice that they all share a few common parameters.

Each real-time effect includes an Input Meter, located on the left side of each graphic interface. This meter shows the level of an incoming audio signal.

Each effect also comes with a Power/Bypass switch that has three modes:

> ▶ **Bypass**—When this mode is selected, the input signal passes through the effect module without being processed. It is a good way to compare "clean vs. processed" audio signals.

> ▶ **On**—When this mode is selected, the input signal passes through the effect and is processed.

> ▶ **Off**—When this mode is selected, the effect is turned off. No audio whatsoever will pass through this effect device.

All of the real-time effects support stereo ins and outs and can be used as either sends or inserts. However, some of these effects were programmed to be used as insert effects only or send effects only. To help you tell the difference, each effect has a signal flow graph that demonstrates how the effect handles mono and stereo signals. To see a device's graph, press the Tab key to flip the Device Rack around.

There are five signal flow charts used to describe the signal flow though the different effects:

 Chart A—This can be used as a mono-in, mono-out device.

 Chart B—This can be used as a mono-in, stereo-out device. This means that the effect will create a stereo effect, or can also be used as a mono effect and panned.

 Chart C—Connecting both inputs and outputs in stereo makes this device a dual mono effect, because both left and right signals will be processed independently.

 Chart D—The left and right signals are summed, or combined before being processed, which does not make it a true stereo signal. However, the effect itself is a stereo effect.

 Chart E—This is a true stereo processor, because the effect uses both left and right signals in order to generate a new signal. This process can be found exclusively in the RV7000 Reverb.

The remainder of this chapter is a guided tour through each of Reason's real-time effects.

RV-7 Digital Reverb

Reverberation is probably one of the most important effects needed to create ambience and space in your Reason songs. The RV-7 Digital Reverb is the first of two real-time reverbs available in Reason 2.5 (see Figure 14.1) and is sure to help you add new life to your pads and snare drums.

The RV-7 offers several presets, including:

▶ **Hall**—Simulates the characteristics of a standard sized hall.

▶ **Large Hall**—Simulates the characteristics of a large hall.

▶ **Hall 2**—Sounds very similar to Hall 1, but with a brighter attack.

▶ **Large Room**—Simulates the characteristics of a large room with hard early reflections.

▶ **Medium Room**—Simulates the characteristics of medium sized room with semi-hard walls.

▶ **Small Room**—Simulates the characteristics of a much smaller room. Suitable for drums.

▶ **Gated**—A reverb that is fed through a gate with a quick release.

▶ **Low Density**—A thin sounding, low-CPU-consumption reverb.

▶ **Stereo Echoes**—An echo reverberation that pans left and right.

▶ **Pan Room**—Similar to the Stereo Echoes, but with softer attacks.

Figure 14.1
The RV-7 Digital Reverb is one of two reverb effects in Reason.

SAVE YOUR CPU—USE LOW DENSITY

Reverbs are without a doubt the most CPU intensive of all real-time effects. With so many variables and algorithms needing to be calculated in real time, using several reverbs like the RV-7 in one Reason song can overload your computer's processor. If you plan to use several instances of the RV-7 within one Reason song, choose the Low Density preset, because it was designed to use less processing power than the others.

Once you have selected the preset you want to work with, you can then begin to edit the preset with these available parameters:

▶ **Size**—This knob adjusts the size of the room. Decreasing this parameter will cause the room size to shrink. Increasing the parameter will have the opposite result. Also note that this knob is used to adjust the delay time when using the Stereo Echoes or Pan Room presets.

▶ **Decay**—This parameter adjusts the length of the reverb's decay. Also note that Decay is not used in the Gated preset.

▶ **Damp**—This parameter is used to adjust the equalization of the reverb effect. Increasing this parameter will cut the high frequencies, making for a warm and smooth effect.

▶ **Dry/Wet**—This parameter determines the balance between a processed or *wet* signal and an unprocessed or *dry* signal. When using the RV-7 as a send or aux effect, this knob should be set to its maximum. When used as an insert effect, it should be set in the middle or 12:00 position so you can hear both wet and dry signals at once.

The Matrix Pattern Sequencer can be used to control the Decay parameter of the RV-7. Just route the Curve CV output of the Matrix to the Decay input on the back of the RV-7. Switch the Matrix from Note to Curve mode, select a note value, and create a curve for your RV-7 Decay.

DDL-1—Digital Delay Line

A *delay* effect is an echo of sorts, but not like that of a reverb. It is used to repeat synths phrases, thicken up pads, syncopate drum sounds, and introduce a funky tempo feeling to your songs. One of the best examples I can think of is the guitar part for "Run Like Hell" by Pink Floyd. The whole rhythm of the song is based solely on a guitar part played through a delay in tempo with the song. Delay is simply one of those effects I can't live without. It's an effect that can be used on any instrument, even the less conventional ones, like bass synths. The DDL-1 (see Figure 14.2) is a delay that does it all and what's more is incredibly easy to understand and use.

Figure 14.2
The DDL-1 Digital Delay is used to repeat synth phrases and syncopate drum sounds.

CHAPTER 14

Take a look at the available parameters:

▶ **Delay Time**—The window to the far left of the DDL-1 displays the currently selected delay time in either note valued steps or in milliseconds. You can have a maximum of 16 steps or 2000 milliseconds (approx two seconds).

▶ **Unit**—This button is used to select either steps or milliseconds for the DDL-1. If you select steps, the delay effect will synchronize with the Reason sequencer. If you select milliseconds, the delay effect will be in *free time,* meaning that it is not tempo related.

▶ **Step Length**—This button is used to select the note value of the DDL-1 when it is set to steps. You can select between 16th notes (1/16) or 8th note triplets (1/8T).

▶ **Feedback**—This knob sets the number of delay repeats.

▶ **Pan**—This knob pans the delay effect within the stereo field.

▶ **Dry/Wet**—This knob determines the balance between a processed or *wet* signal and an unprocessed or *dry* signal. When using the DDL-1 as a send or aux effect, this knob should be set to its maximum. When used as an insert effect, it should be set in the middle or 12:00 position so you can hear both wet and dry signals at once.

The Matrix Pattern Sequencer can be used to control the DDL-1 via CV input. Just connect the Curve CV, Note CV, or Gate CV outputs of the Matrix to one of these two parameters on the back of the DDL-1:

▶ **Pan**—Once connected, the Matrix can pan your delay effect in step mode. Increasing the amount of input on the back panel of the DDL-1 can intensify this effect.

▶ **Feedback**—Once connected, the Matrix can control the amount of feedback in step mode. Increasing the amount of input on the back panel of the DDL-1 can intensify this effect.

D-11 Foldback Distortion

The D-11 is a fantastic-sounding digital distortion (see Figure 14.3). It is a perfect and easy solution for adding a little more growl to your Subtractor bass lines or for going full-on industrial with Redrum. Controlled by just two parameters, the D-11 is a basic real-time effect that can be used as an insert or auxiliary send.

▶ **Amount**—This knob assigns the amount of distortion to be used.

▶ **Foldback**—This knob is used to add character to the shape of the distortion. At its minimum setting, the Foldback knob sounds dark and flat. At its maximum setting, the Foldback becomes the audio equivalent of nuclear meltdown by introducing a sharp and jarring effect into the mix.

Figure 14.3
The D-11 Foldback Distortion is one of two distortion effects available in Reason.

The Matrix can control the Amount parameter of the D-11. Just route the Curve CV output of the Matrix to the Amount input on the back of the D-11 and you're set.

ECF-42 Envelope Controlled Filter

The ECF-42 is a combination filter/envelope generator that can be used to create pattern-controlled filter and envelope effects with any Reason device (see Figure 14.4). This effect should be used as an insert, because it is more of a niche effect used for specific sounds rather than a universal effect such as a reverb or delay.

Let's have a look at the filter parameters of the ECF-42:

▶ **Mode**—This button is used to switch between the different filter modes (BP 12, LP 12, and LP 24). Also note that you can simply click on the name of the filter mode to select it.

▶ **Freq**—This knob controls the Filter Frequency of the ECF-42. When using the ECF-42 in its static or filter-only mode, this knob controls the overall frequency of the audio. When used in combination with the envelope generator, this knob is used as a start and end frequency for the created filter sweep effect.

▶ **Res**—This knob controls the resonance of the filter.

▶ **Env.Amt**—This parameter is used to specify how much the filter frequency will be affected by the triggered envelope.

▶ **Vel**—This parameter is used to specify how much the gate velocity will affect the envelope.

The envelope parameters of the ECF-42 are available only when triggered by another Reason device, such as a Matrix or Dr:rex (read "Triggering the Envelope" for more info). Once the envelope is triggered by another Reason device, you can use any of these standard envelope parameters:

▶ Attack

▶ Decay

▶ Sustain

▶ Release

Figure 14.4
The ECF-42 Envelope Controlled Filter is used to create tempo-based sweeping filter effects.

TRIGGERING THE ENVELOPE

Unlike most of the other real-time effects in Reason, the ECF-42 does not function completely as an independent effect and requires an additional Reason device to trigger the envelope. This is done very easily by routing the gate output of any Reason device that has a gate output on the back, such as Redrum, Dr:rex, and the Matrix.

Here's how to set it up with a Dr:rex:

1. In any Reason song, create a Dr:rex and load it up with any available REX file. Click the To Track button to send it to the sequencer.

2. Click on the Dr:rex to select it, and then select the ECF-42 Envelope Controlled Filter from the Create pull-down menu. Reason will automatically set up the ECF-42 as an insert effect for Dr:rex.

3. Press the Tab key to flip the Device Rack.

4. Route the Slice Gate Output of Dr:rex to the Env Gate input on the back of the ECF-42.

5. Press the Tab key again and click on Play.

You should now see the Gate LED on the ECF-42 light up, because it is receiving gate information from Dr:rex. At this point, you can use the envelope parameters.

The Matrix can control the Frequency, Decay, and Resonance parameters of the ECF-42. Just route any of the CV outputs of the Matrix to any of the three available ECF-42 parameters and you're set.

CF-101 Chorus/Flanger

The CF-101 is a combination chorus/flanger effect device (see Figure 14.5). A chorus/flanger effect is commonly used to add depth and ambience to a sound by introducing a short delay to the fed audio signal. That delayed signal is then mixed with the original dry signal, creating a much larger sound than before. The size and broadness of the delayed signal is determined by the set delay time, feedback, and LFO modulation.

Figure 14.5
The CF-101
Chorus/Flanger is used
to thicken up your pads
and leads.

A CHORUS/FLANGER LINE

To really understand the magic of a chorus or flanger effect, you should hear these beauties in action. Some of the best examples can be found in classic rock tunes of the 70s and 80s. For example, the vocal track from "In The Air Tonight" by Phil Collins is drenched in chorus, whereas "Never Let Me Down Again" by Depeche Mode or "Barracuda" by Heart are examples of flanging at its best.

Sure, they may be "Moldy Golden Oldies" to some, but you can really benefit by exploring the groundbreaking work found in these tunes.

Let's have a look at the CF-101 parameters.

▶ **Delay**—This knob sets the delay time needed to create the chorus/flanger. For best results, use short delay times to create a flanger effect and medium to long delay times for the chorus.

▶ **Feedback**—This knob controls the amount of effect being fed back into the input, which gives character to the effect.

▶ **LFO Rate**—This knob controls the modulation rate of the LFO. Increasing this parameter will speed up the frequency of oscillation.

▶ **LFO Sync**—This button synchronizes the LFO Rate to the tempo of the Reason sequencer. Note that when this button is activated, the LFO Rate knob displays note values rather than the standard numeric value.

▶ **LFO Mod Amount**—This knob is used to assign a depth to the LFO modulation.

▶ **Send Mode**—This button is used to properly integrate the CF-101 with the other Reason devices. When activated, the CF-101 is in Send mode, which means that the device will output only the modulated signal, making it possible to use the Aux send knob to mix in the additional dry signal. When not active, the CF-101 is used as an insert effect, where the device will output a mix of the dry and wet signal.

Aside from parameters on the front of the device, the Matrix Pattern Sequencer can also modify the CF-101. Press the Tab key to flip the Device Rack and you will find two CV inputs, one for the Delay parameter, and one for the LFO Rate parameter.

Just route the Curve, Note, or Gate CV outputs of the Matrix to either of these parameters and experiment.

PH-90 Phaser

The PH-90 is a sweeping effect perfect for use with guitar samples or pads (see Figure 14.6). At times, it can be confused with the likes of a standard chorus/flanger effect, but a phaser is a much different monster once you look under the hood.

A phaser shifts portions of an audio signal out of phase and then sends that effected signal back to the original signal, causing narrow bands (called *notches*) of the frequency spectrum to be filtered out. The aforementioned *sweeping effect* happens when these notches are adjusted.

Figure 14.6
The PH-90 Phaser is a perfect effect for guitar samples.

The PH-90 has four adjustable notches in the frequency spectrum that can be modified by way of seven parameters:

▶ **Freq**—This knob assigns the frequency of the first notch. Once this is set, the remaining three notches will move in parallel within the frequency spectrum.

▶ **Split**—This knob changes the distance between each notch. This alters the character of the overall effect.

▶ **Width**—This knob adjusts the width of the notches. Increasing this parameter creates a very deep effect while also making the overall sound hollow.

▶ **LFO Rate**—This knob controls the modulation rate of the LFO. Increasing this parameter speeds up the frequency of oscillation.

▶ **LFO Sync**—This button synchronizes the LFO Rate to the tempo of the Reason sequencer. Note that when this button is activated, the LFO Rate knob displays note values rather than the standard numeric value.

▶ **LFO F.Mod**—This knob assigns the depth of LFO modulation.

▶ **Feedback**—This knob is used to alter the tone of the phaser, much in the same way as a resonance knob on a filter.

The Matrix Pattern Sequencer can also modify the PH-90. Press the Tab key to flip the Device Rack and you will find two CV inputs, one for the LFO Frequency, and one for the LFO Rate parameter.

Just route the Curve, Note, or Gate CV outputs of the Matrix to either of these parameters and experiment.

Here's an exercise to demonstrate how to use the PH-90 with Dr:rex. Be sure to create a new song, and load it with a reMix and Dr:rex. Also, load a REX file and send it to its sequencer track:

1. Select the Dr:rex by clicking on it once, and then select PH-90 Phaser from the Create pull-down menu. This will automatically connect the PH-90 to the Dr:rex to be used as an insert effect.

2. Click on Play and you will hear the PH-90 in action. By default, it already sounds great, but it would probably sound even better if it was synced up to the tempo of the Reason song.

3. Click on the Sync button to synchronize the PH-90 effect with the song tempo. Then adjust the Rate knob until it reads 4/4, which means that the phasing effect will recycle every bar.

4. Adjust the Split knob to 0 and notice the extra sweep that has been introduced to the low end.

5. Adjust the Width knob to its maximum setting and you will notice that the high and low frequencies are accented, but not the mid frequencies, which makes the overall sound hollow.

6. Finally, adjust the Feedback knob to add a singing tone to the mix.

UN-16 Unison

The UN-16 Unison can be thought of as a simple and straightforward chorus effect (see Figure 14.7). By using the available parameters, it produces a set number of voices that are each slightly delayed and detuned by way of low frequency noise. This produces a very thick stereo-friendly chorus that can be used on vocal samples, guitar/drum loops, and so on.

Figure 14.7
The UN-16 Unison
Module is a basic chorus
effect.

Let's have a look at the UN-16 parameters:

- ▶ **Voice Count**—This assigns the number of voices to be produced. You can select 4, 8, or 16 individual voices.

- ▶ **Detune**—This knob increases/decreases the detuning of the individual voices.

- ▶ **Dry/Wet**—This knob determines the balance between a processed or wet signal and an unprocessed or dry signal. When using the UN-16 as a send or aux effect, this knob should be set to its maximum. When used as an insert effect, it should be set in the middle or 12:00 position so you can hear both wet and dry signals at once.

The Matrix Pattern Sequencer can control the detune parameter of the UN-16. Just connect the Curve CV output of the Matrix to the Detune input on the back of the UN-16.

PEQ-2 Two Band Parametric EQ

The PEQ-2 is a two band parametric EQ that allows very precise control over the equalization curve of any Reason device (see Figure 14.8). Its features and sound quality far surpass those found in the EQ controls of reMix, making it a perfect solution for advanced mixing.

The two bands of equalization, EQ A and EQ B, are controlled independently within the interface of the PEQ-2. EQ A is always active and ready to use when an instance of the PEQ-2 is created within a Reason song. In order to use EQ B, you must first activate it by clicking the B button, found in the lower-center portion of the interface. Once activated, its individual parameters are at your disposal.

The graphical display in the left portion of the PEQ-2 is used to show the frequency response curve as it is being created by the EQ parameters. This is a fantastic visual aid that helps you sculpt your EQ curve.

Figure 14.8
The PEQ-2 two band
parametric EQ is a
fantastic parametric EQ
for adjusting the
frequency bands of any
Reason device.

Let's have a look at the parameters of the PEQ-2:

▶ **Freq**—This knob assigns the center of the EQ curve. When setting this parameter, you should first increase the Gain parameter to hear the effect. The range is 31Hz to 16Hz.

▶ **Q**—This knob determines the frequency width of the EQ curve around the set center frequency.

▶ **Gain**—This knob boosts and cuts the gain of the EQ curve.

The Matrix can control Frequency A and B by connecting the Curve CV, Note CV, or Gate CV outputs of the Matrix to the Frequency 1 or 2 inputs on the back of the PEQ-2.

USING THE PEQ-2 AS AN INSERT/MASTERING EFFECT

The PEQ-2 is best used as an insert or mastering effect. If you recall, an *insert effect* is when the dry signal of a Reason device is completely sent to the effect. The effect then processes this signal and sends it back to an input of reMix.

To review how to create and use an insert effect, try the following exercise:

1. Create a Reason device, such as a Dr:rex or Subtractor. Once created, it will appear on the channel strip of reMix.

2. Click on the interface of the created Reason device to select it.

3. Select the PEQ-2 from the Create pull-down menu. This will create an instance under the selected Reason device.

4. Press the Tab key to flip the Device Rack around. You will see that the outputs of the Reason device have been automatically routed to the inputs of the PEQ-2. Also notice that the PEQ-2's outputs have been routed to the channel strip of reMix.

The concept of using a Mastering effect is very similar to creating and using insert effects. Essentially, the outputs of reMix are routed to the inputs of the real-time effect. The processed signal is then sent off to the outputs of the audio card.

To demonstrate how to use the PEQ-2 as a mastering effect, try the following exercise:

1. Click on the MIDI IN/AUDIO OUT interface to select it.

2. Select the PEQ-2 from the Create pull-down menu. This will place a PEQ-2 effect module in between the MIDI IN/AUDIO OUT and reMix.

3. Press the Tab key to flip the Device Rack around. You will notice that reMix is not routed to the PEQ-2. You will have to do this manually.

4. Click and hold on the Master Out Left of reMix and select Disconnect from the pop-up menu. This will automatically disconnect both channels of reMix from the AUDIO IN device.

5. Click and drag a virtual cable from the Master Out Left to the Input Left of the PEQ-2. Release the mouse and reMix will automatically route both output channels to the PEQ-2.

6. Click and drag a virtual cable from the Output Left of the PEQ-2 to the first input of the AUDIO IN device. Release the mouse and notice that both of the outputs of the PEQ-2 have been routed to Audio In 1 and 2.

7. Press the Tab key again to flip the Device Rack. Click on Play to use the PEQ-2 as a mastering effect.

COMP-01 Auto Make Up Gain Compressor

The COMP-01 is a real-time compressor that is typically used to level out audio signals that are too loud in the mix and are in danger of digitally clipping. The COMP-01 is a great solution to combat this problem and can be used as an insert effect or send effect (see Figure 14.9).

Figure 14.9
The COMP-01 auto make up gain compressor will level out any signal with too much amplitude.

> ▶ **Ratio**—This knob sets the gain reduction of the audio signal according to the set threshold.

> ▶ **Thresh**—This knob sets the level that dictates when the compressor effect will kick in. Any audio signal that meets this set level or goes above it will be compressed, whereas signals that fall below this level will not be affected.

> ▶ **Attack**—This knob adjusts the attack of the compression effect.

> ▶ **Release**—This knob adjusts the length of time needed before the audio signal is unaffected by the COMP-01, once its level has fallen under the threshold. At its lowest setting, a short release will cause a pumping sound, which is good for kick drums. At its mid to high settings, the release will become long and sustained, which is good for pads or pianos.

> ▶ **Gain Meter**—This meter displays the amount of gain reduction and increase in decibels.

In order to use the COMP-01 as an insert or mastering effect, refer back to the tutorial found in the PEQ-2 section of this chapter.

The BV512 Vocoder/Equalizer

One of the best additions to Reason 2.5 is the BV512 vocoder (see Figure 14.10). This effect is commonly used to create robotic voices in dance and performance music. Another popular use of a vocoder is to create a "choir of synthetic voices" as heard in songs by Moby and New Order.

Figure 14.10
The BV512 vocoder/ equalizer is an amazing vocoder that can also be used as an equalizer.

What Is a Vocoder?

A vocoder is an effect that uses two separate sources of input to create a new audio signal by applying the frequency bands of one signal to the other. These two separate audio sources are known as the *carrier* and the *modulator*.

The carrier is ideally an audio source that is constantly generating sound. A good example of this is a string pad playing from the Subtractor in a sequence that is looped continuously.

The modulator is typically an audio source such as a spoken voice or vocal track. Another typically used modulator is a drum loop for creating rhythmically enhanced sounds.

Once you have these two elements, they are then routed to their appropriate vocoder inputs. The modulator is divided into a set number of bands (4, 8, 16, 32, or 512) by using band pass filters. These separate bands are then sent to an envelope follower (a device that continuously monitors and analyzes the signal levels).

Meanwhile, the carrier is processed with the same number of bands as the modulator. The same frequency ranges used in the modulator's band pass filters are also applied to the carrier. By doing this, the carrier will have the same frequency characteristics as the modulator. This means that if the modulator gets louder or more dynamic in shape, the carrier will follow and emulate this as well.

THE VOCODER IN ACTION
If you want to hear good audio examples of vocoding, listen to just about any CD by Laurie Anderson ("O'Superman"), Daft Punk ("Around the World"), Air ("Remember"), or Zapp and Roger ("More Bounce to the Ounce").

Let's have a look at the basic parameters of the BV512.

▶ **Level Meters**—These meters display the signal level of the carrier and the modulator.

▶ **Band Switch**—This switches between the number of filter bands (4, 8, 16, 32, or 512).

▶ **Equalizer/Vocoder Switch**—This switches the BV512 between vocoder mode and equalizer mode. Note that when using the BV512 in equalizer mode, the modulator input is not used.

▶ **Modulation Level Display**—This displays the overall spectrum of the modulation signal.

▶ **Frequency Band Level Adjust**—This display is used to adjust the levels of the individual filter bands. When using this section in vocoder mode, each band adjusts the sound and shape of the vocoder. When using this section in equalizer mode, each band adjusts the amplitude of the individual frequencies in the EQ curve. After making adjustments to the individual bands, you can use the Reset Band Levels option from the Edit pull-down menu.

▶ **Hold Button**—When activated, this button freezes the current filter settings. The modulator signal will no longer affect the carrier in this mode. Clicking it again will release the filter settings.

▶ **Attack**—This parameter affects the overall attack of the frequency bands. Increasing the attack amount can create some very cool pad sounds. Note that when the BV512 is in equalizer mode, this parameter is not available.

▶ **Decay**—This parameter affects the overall decay of the frequency bands. As with the Attack, this parameter is not available when the BV512 is used as an equalizer.

▶ **Shift**—This parameter shifts the carrier signal filters up and down, creating a sweeping effect.

▶ **High Frequency Emphasis**—This knob increases the high frequencies in the carrier signal.

▶ **Dry/Wet**—This knob mixes between the unprocessed (or dry) signal and the processed (or wet) signal.

The BV512 as an Equalizer

The BV512 can also be used as a graphic equalizer. Capable of supporting up to 512 bands of equalization, the BV512 is perfect for enhancing individual devices in a Reason song, or even being used as a mastering equalizer.

Follow these steps to learn how to use the BV512 as a mastering equalizer:

1. Press the Tab key to flip the Device Rack around.
2. Click on the AUDIO IN device to select it.
3. Select the BV512 Vocoder device from the Create pull-down menu. This will place the BV512 between the AUDIO IN and reMix.
4. Route the outputs of reMix into the carrier inputs on the BV512.
5. Route the outputs of the BV512 to inputs 1 and 2 of the AUDIO IN device.
6. Press the Tab key again to flip the Device Rack around.
7. Set the Equalizer/Vocoder switch to Equalizer. Also, set the Band Switch to 512 for the best quality equalization (read "FFT Vocoding and Equalizing" below).

At this point, you can now load some Reason devices, sequence them, and play them through the BV512 as a mastering EQ.

FFT VOCODING AND EQUALIZING

As you know, the BV512 supports up to 512 bands of EQ, but what does this really mean? If you use the band switch to change between 32 bands and 512 bands of EQ, there is no visual difference in the interface of the BV512, but there is a noticeable auditory difference, thanks to FFT.

FFT (*Fast Fourier Transform*) refers to a very detailed and precise form of analysis and processing in which waveforms are represented as a sum of sines and cosines (math geeks rejoice!).

To the rest of us, this means that using the BV512 as a vocoder or as an EQ in 512FFT mode produces very precise and detailed control over the shaping of the effect. One thing to keep in mind is that when you are making adjustments to the BV512 in 512FFT mode, a majority of the available bands in the interface will control the high frequencies, rather than the low frequencies.

Basic Vocoding Tutorial

Let's apply what you have just learned about vocoding by going through a basic vocoding tutorial. In this section, you will open a Reason song that I have prepared that consists of an NN-19 (the modulator) playing a single sample, a Subtractor (the carrier) playing chords, and the BV512 Vocoder. Through a step-by-step method, you will learn how to route the carrier and modulator to the BV512, adjust the frequency band, and create a unique signal that you can edit further by using the synth parameters of the Subtractor.

BEFORE YOU GET STARTED

Before you start this tutorial, take a minute to visit the Muska & Lipman website, where you will find a Reason 2.5 song called Vocoder Tutorial. This song file is a *published* song, which means that all of the elements specifically created for this tutorial are self-contained within the song file.

You'll learn more about published songs in Chapter 18, "Mixing and Publishing Your Reason Songs."

1. Open the Vocoder Tutorial song. You will see reMix, the DDL-1 delay, a Subtractor, the NN-19, and the BV512 at the bottom. The NN-19 has a loaded sample of my voice, and the Subtractor has the Bowy patch loaded. Also notice that there is a sequence written for both the Subtractor and the NN-19, but if you click on Play, you won't hear anything, as the audio has not yet been routed.

2. Press the Tab key to flip the Device Rack and notice that there are no audio signals routed to reMix. This gives you a perfect starting point to begin routing your carrier and modulator.

3. Route the output of the Subtractor to the carrier input left of the BV512 (see Figure 14.11).

4. Route the left output of the NN-19 to the modulator input on the BV512 (see Figure 14.12).

5. Route just the left output of the BV512 to the channel 1 left input of reMix; this is a mono signal.

6. Click on Play on the Transport. You should now hear the BV512 in action. It should be a strong signal that is very bass heavy and slightly distorted. This means

Figure 14.11
First the carrier . . .

that some adjustments will need to be made to the frequency band level section of the BV512.

7. Because this is your first time using the BV512, switch to the 16-band display using the Band switch, and make some adjustments to the lower frequency bands (see Figure 14.13).

This should give you a pretty good idea of how the BV512 works. You can experiment further by changing the band range of the BV512, making further adjustments to the synth parameters of the Subtractor, or replacing the Subtractor with the Malström for a whole new sound.

Figure 14.12
Then the modulator.

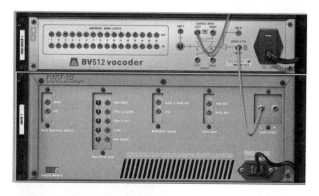

Figure 14.13
Make adjustments to the frequency band level to ensure that you will not digitally distort your signal.

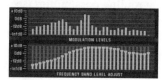

USING DR:REX AS THE MODULATOR

Another interesting application for the BV512 is to use a drum loop as the source of modulation. This creates a very interesting rhythmically driven audio signal. Try the following exercise:

1. Create an instance of Dr:rex and load a 16th note patterned REX file. (For example, something from the Abstract Hip Hop folder in the Reason Factory Sound Bank should work well.)

2. Click on the To Track button on the Dr:rex interface to load the REX file into the Reason sequencer.

3. Press the Tab key to flip the Device Rack. Disconnect the NN-19 from the BV512.

4. Disconnect Dr:rex from channel 2 of reMix. Connect the left output of Dr:rex to the modulator input of the BV512.

Now click on Play and you will hear the rhythmic bliss of vocoding in action. Try to add some delay to the signal or use some of the synth parameters of either Dr:rex or the Subtractor for a whole new sound.

Automation

All of the parameters in the BV512 can be automated in the same way as any Reason device. The only hoop you have to jump through in order to begin automating is to create a sequencer track and route its output to the BV512.

Let's see how this works by working through the following exercise. Before you begin this exercise, start a new Reason song and create an instance of reMix and the BV512.

1. Navigate to the Create pull-down menu and choose Sequencer Track. This will place a new track below the NN-19 track that is called New Track 1. You can rename this track to BV512 if you want.

2. To the right of the Track Name column is the Output pull-down menu, which is used to assign the output of the sequencer track to any created Reason device within a song. Select the Vocoder 1 option.

3. Highlight the BV512 track and click on the Switch to Edit Mode button in the sequencer to show the Controller lane for creating automation.

4. Select any BV512 parameter from the Controller's pull-down menu and write in your automation information.

CV Connections

As if it couldn't get any better, the BV512 offers many individual inputs and outputs on the back of the device that allow for some very interesting routing possibilities (see Figure 14.14).

Figure 14.14
The BV512 offers many routing possibilities by providing a wide assortment of ins and outs.

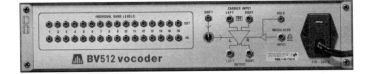

▶ **Frequency Band Outputs**—These CV outputs use the amplitude of an individual frequency band to control the parameter inputs of other Reason devices. For example, you could use the output of band 8 and route it to the FM Amount input of the Subtractor.

▶ **Frequency Band Inputs**—These CV inputs can be controlled by the Matrix to alter the amplitude of each frequency band in the BV512. Note that once you make a connection from the Matrix to a specific frequency band, the Matrix exclusively controls that band's amplitude.

▶ **Shift**—This input controls the Shift parameter on the front of the device and can be used to create fantastic sweeping effects.

▶ **Hold**—This input is to operate the Hold parameter and can be used to create a step-driven vocoder effect. Perfect for creating percussive vocoder stabs on vocals and pads. Note that you must use the Gate CV output of the Matrix to make this input work.

Scream 4 Sound Destruction Unit

Aside from the comical Wes Craven-esque name (programmers always have a good sense of humor), the appropriately titled Scream 4 is the digital distortion that takes distorted vocals, drums, and synth patches to a whole new level (see Figure 14.15). Divided into three sections (Damage, Cut, and Body), Scream 4 can shape, mold, and destroy any audio signal it comes into contact with.

Another welcome addition to the Scream 4 and the upcoming RV7000 (discussed later in this chapter) is the ability to load, edit, and save customized presets. The Scream 4 already comes with a lot of great sounding presets, but it never hurts to make your own.

For those of you who were looking for something better than the D-11, this *is* it!

Figure 14.15
The Scream 4 is the kind of distortion that non-Reason users can only dream of.

The Damage Section

Let's have a look at the various parameters of Scream 4. This section starts by looking at the parameters and presets for the Damage section (see Figure 14.16).

Figure 14.16
The Damage section of Scream 4 is used to select the type of distortion and edit its characteristics.

▶ **Damage Button**—Turns the Damage section on and off.

▶ **Damage Control**—This knob is used to assign an amount of input gain to the Scream 4. The higher the value, the more distortion there is.

▶ **Damage Type**—This knob lets you select the type of distortion.

▶ **P1/P2 Knobs**—These knobs work differently with each damage type. These types are covered next.

There are 10 damage types available with the Scream 4:

▶ **Overdrive**—This is a standard analog-type distortion that responds well to variable dynamics. When selected, the P1 knob is used as a tone control. The P2 knob controls the presence, which increases the mid to high frequencies before it's passed through the distortion effect.

▶ **Distortion**—This is similar to the Overdrive preset, but is capable of creating a much thicker distortion effect. Note that the P1 and P2 knobs work the same here as they did with the Overdrive preset.

▶ **Fuzz**—This preset is a heavy distortion that is strong even at low damage control settings. Note that the P1 and P2 knobs work the same as they did with the Overdrive preset.

▶ **Tube**—This preset simulates a classic tube distortion (a la Led Zeppelin or Jimi Hendrix). When using this preset the P1 knob acts as a contour, or high pass filter. The P2 knob controls the Bias, or balance of the tube distortion. When set to a 12:00 position, the Bias is very balanced in shape. When set to its maximum resolution, the Bias knob will create an uneven balance to the distortion, which sounds very close to a tube-driven amplifier.

▶ **Tape**—This preset is a simulation of tape saturation, which can add compression and punch to the distortion. The P1 knob acts as a tape speed, which helps to preserve the higher frequencies when set to high speeds. The P2 knob controls the compression ratio.

▶ **Feedback**—This preset is a combination of heavy distortion and looped feedback. Feedback is created when a sound source is fed back to itself. A good example is an electric guitar or microphone that is placed too close to its amplifier or speaker. The Damage Control knob assigns the amount of gain to the feedback loop, whereas the P1 and P2 knobs control the size and "howl," or frequency of the feedback respectively.

▶ **Modulate**—This preset creates a distortion that resonates by combining two copies of itself before it is fed through a distortion. The P1 knob controls the resonance ring, whereas the P2 knob controls the filter frequency.

▶ **Warp**—This preset creates a strong, stinging distortion by multiplying its incoming signal with itself. The P1 knob controls the sharpness of the distortion, whereas the P2 knob controls the bias, or balance, of the distortion.

▶ **Digital**—This preset is meant to be used as a low fidelity, gritty distortion. The P1 knob is used to alter the bit depth from the highest resolution possible to a down and dirty single bit of resolution. The P2 knob alters the sampling rate of the distortion and ranges from clean and pristine to crunchy and static.

▶ **Scream**—This preset is similar to the Fuzz preset, but includes a band pass filter including high resonance and gain before distorting. The P1 knob controls the tone of the distortion, whereas the P2 knob controls the filter frequency.

The Cut Section

The Cut section of Scream 4 acts as EQ controls, allowing for many creative possibilities in carving and shaping an interesting EQ curve for your distortion (see Figure 14.17).

Figure 14.17
The Cut section is a simple yet effective three-band EQ.

Click on the Cut button to activate the EQ. At this point, you can then adjust the low, mid, and high bands of equalization to your liking. At any time, you can reset any of the three bands by holding down the Ctrl key on your PC or Apple key on your Mac and clicking on the band slider to reset it to its default position.

The Body Section

The Body section of Scream 4 is used to create different effects such as speaker cabinet simulations and auto-wahs (for us guitarists), by placing the signal in different simulated enclosures (see Figure 14.18). There are five body types that can be selected and then edited by resonance and scale parameters.

Figure 14.18
The Body section places the signal in a resonant body, which makes it possible to simulate speaker cabinets and other effects.

▶ **Body Button**—This button switches the Body section on/off.

▶ **Type**—This knob is used to switch between one of five available body types.

▶ **Reso**—This knob creates a resonance effect for the selected body type.

▶ **Scale**—This knob is used to control the size of the selected body. Please note that this knob is inverted and that turning the knob clockwise creates a smaller size, whereas counter-clockwise increases the size.

▶ **Auto**—This knob is used to control the amount of the Envelope Follower (see the following note box).

THE ENVELOPE FOLLOWER

The Envelope Follower is used to change the body scale according to the incoming dynamic level. The louder the incoming sound, the more the scale parameter is increased. This creates what is commonly known as an "auto-wah" effect, which is set by the Auto knob.

To demonstrate the versatility of this effect, try the following exercise. Before you begin, start a new Reason song and create an instance of reMix.

1. Create a Dr:rex and load a REX file from either the Abstract Hip Hop folder or the Techno folder in the Reason Factory Sound Bank. Click on the To Track button to load the Dr:rex pattern into the Reason sequencer.

2. Create a Scream 4 and route it to be used as an insert effect.

3. Activate the Body section, select Body Type B, and turn the Auto knob clockwise.

4. Click on Play and notice how the Body Scale opens up with the various dynamics of the REX loop.

CHAPTER 14

SCREAMING MIX

Aside from using the Scream 4 as a send or insert for your individual Reason devices, the Scream 4 can also be used as a mastering effect. By using the Tape preset in the Damage section, you can introduce a very warm and welcome tape saturation that will give your mix the kick it needs.

To use the Scream 4 as a mastering effect, try the following exercise. Before you begin, open any Reason demo song, located in the Demo Songs folder in the Reason Program folder.

1.   Press the Tab key to flip the Device Rack.

2.   Click once on the AUDIO IN device and select the Scream 4 from the Create pull-down menu. This will place an instance of the Scream 4 in between the AUDIO IN and reMix devices.

3.   Disconnect the Master outputs of reMix and re-route them to the inputs of Scream 4.

4.   Connect the outputs of Scream 4 to the AUDIO IN device.

5.   Press the Tab key again to flip the Device Rack.

6.   With the EQ and Body sections disabled, set your Damage Control knob to a low setting.

7.   Set your Damage Type to Tape.

8.   Set your P1 and P2 knobs at the 12:00 position.

At this point, you can begin to play back your Reason song and make adjustments to the Damage parameters. Use the P1 knob for brightness and the P2 knob for more compression.

The CV Connections

Using CV outputs can enable the Matrix to control any of four Scream 4 parameters.

▶   **Damage Control**—Changes the amount of distortion.

▶   **P1 Knob**—Increases/decreases the P1 parameter. Note that the Damage Type will determine what this parameter affects.

▶   **P2 Knob**—Increases/decreases the P2 parameter. Note that the Damage Type will determine what this parameter affects.

▶   **Scale**—Increases/decreases the size of the selected body.

Additionally, the Scream 4 includes an Auto CV Output, which can be routed to the CV input of another Reason device. For example, Scream 4 could be routed to a modulation parameter of the Subtractor or Malström.

RV7000 Advanced Reverb

Reason 2.5 was a big breakthrough for users worldwide, because it included a vocoder, an ultra distortion unit, and, above all, a true stereo pro reverb effect called the RV7000 (see Figure 14.19). The RV7000 is the kind of reverb that sounds too good to be true. It has nine reverb and echo

Figure 14.19
The RV7000 advanced reverb is one of the best software-based reverbs you'll ever hear.

algorithms that can be used along with an included EQ and Gate for molding and shaping your reverb in ways that just can't be done by most hardware and software reverbs.

The Main Panel

The RV7000 is a two-part effect unit; much in the same way the NN-XT is a two-part sampler. When you first load the RV7000, the part of the device you will see is the main panel, which controls the global parameters of the device (see Figure 14.20).

Notice that the RV7000 has a Patch Browser in the left corner of the main panel. This makes it possible to load, edit, and save customized patches for the device.

Figure 14.20
The RV7000 main panel.

WHERE ARE THE PRESETS?

All of the presets for the Scream 4 and the RV7000 can be found within the In Full Effect Sound Bank ReFill, which is located in the Reason program folder if you are using the downloaded version of Reason 2.5.

If you installed Reason 2.5 using the original CDs in your box, the presets are in the Reason Factory Sound Bank ReFill.

Take a look at the global parameters:

▶ **EQ Enable**—This button switches the EQ section off and on.

▶ **Gate Enable**—This button switches the Gate section off and on.

▶ **Decay**—This knob controls the rate of decay within a reverb or the amount of feedback within an echo algorithm.

▶ **HF Damp**—This knob assigns an amount of decay time for the high frequencies in the reverb. Increasing this knob makes the reverb sound warm and dull.

▶ **HI EQ**—This knob controls the high shelving EQ. Increase the value of this parameter to boost the high frequencies in the reverb.

▶ **Dry/Wet**—This knob mixes between the unprocessed dry signal and the processed wet signal.

The Remote Programmer

The Remote Programmer is where all of the individual edits of the RV7000 are completed (see Figure 14.21). To activate the Remote Programmer, click on the arrow button next to the virtual cable slot. The RV7000 will then perform a little animation and load up right below the main panel.

Figure 14.21
The RV7000 Remote Programmer.

Once the Remote Programmer is open, you can select between one of nine algorithms. Each of these algorithms emulates a specific type of reverb or echo and offers a number of editable parameters.

> ▶ **Small Space**—Emulates a small room.
> ▶ **Room**—Emulates a standard sized room with adjustable shape and wall composition.
> ▶ **Hall**—Emulates a standard hall.
> ▶ **Arena**—Emulates the characteristics of a large arena.
> ▶ **Plate**—Classic plate reverb.
> ▶ **Spring**—Emulates a spring-driven reverb, which can be found on the back of most old Fender guitar amps.
> ▶ **Echo**—Creates a tempo synced echo.
> ▶ **Multi Tap**—Creates a tempo synced multi-tapped delay.
> ▶ **Reverse**—A well known backwards effect in which the dry signal comes safter the reverb.

As you will notice, each one of these algorithms has its own set of attributes and parameters that can be altered. That said, let's run down the list of each one.

The first algorithm is the Small Space:

> ▶ **Size**—Assigns a size to the space.
> ▶ **Modulated Rate**—Sets the rate of modulation of the space, which helps to even out the character of the reverb. Works alongside the Mod Amount parameter.
> ▶ **Room Shape**—Select one of four room shapes.
> ▶ **Low Frequency Damp**—Controls the rate of decay for the low frequencies.
> ▶ **Wall Irregularities**—Adjusts the positioning of the walls within a small space.
> ▶ **Predelay**—Adjusts the amount of predelay, which is the delay between the source signal and the starting point of the reverb.
> ▶ **Modulation Amount**—Assigns the amount of modulation to the reverb.

The next algorithm is the Room. Note that the Hall algorithm has the same parameters, but much larger size settings.

▶ **Size**—Assigns a size to the space.

▶ **Diffusion**—Clarifies the *bounce*, or reflection, of the reverb.

▶ **Room Shape**—Selects one of four room shapes.

▶ **ER->Late**—This parameter sets the time between the "early reflections" and tail end of the reverb.

▶ **ER Level**—Adjusts the level of the early reflections.

▶ **Predelay**—Adjusts the amount of predelay, which is the delay between the source signal and the starting point of the reverb.

▶ **Modulation Amount**—Assigns the amount of modulation to the reverb.

The Arena algorithm is used to emulate the reverberations of a full-sized area. This particular algorithm is unique in that it controls the left, right, and center reflections that are present in an arena setting.

▶ **Size**—Assigns a size to the space.

▶ **Diffusion**—Clarifies the *bounce*, or reflection, of the reverb.

▶ **Left Delay**—Sets the predelay time for the left side of the reverb.

▶ **Right Delay**—Sets the predelay time for the right side of the reverb.

▶ **Stereo Level**—Adjusts the level for both left and right channels of the reverb.

▶ **Mono Delay**—Sets the predelay time for the center of the reverb.

▶ **Mono Level**—Adjusts the level of the center of the reverb.

There are only two adjustable parameters for the Plate algorithm.

▶ **LF Damp**—Controls the rate of decay for the low frequencies.

▶ **Predelay**—Adjusts the amount of *predelay*, which is the delay between the source signal and the starting point of the reverb.

The Spring reverb algorithm emulates the behaviors of the actual spring found on the back of old guitar amps.

▶ **Length**—Sets the length of the spring.

▶ **Diffusion**—Clarifies the bounce, or reflection, of the reverb.

▶ **Dispersion Freq**—This parameter controls the amount of dispersion of the different frequencies created by the initial reflection. Works in combination with the Dispersion Amount.

▶ **Low Frequency Damp**—Controls the rate of decay for the low frequencies.

▶ **Stereo On/Off**—Determines whether the reverb is mono or stereo.

▶ **Predelay**—Adjusts the amount of predelay, which is the delay between the source signal and the starting point of the reverb.

▶ **Dispersion Amount**—Controls the amount of the dispersion effect.

The Echo algorithm is an echo or delay-like effect, which can be tempo-synced.

▶ **Echo Time**—This parameter adjusts the time between each echo. Note that when Tempo Sync is not active, this parameter has a range of 10-2000 milliseconds (up to two seconds). When Tempo Sync is active, this parameter is set in note values such as 1/8 or 1/16.

▶ **Diffusion**—Clarifies the bounce and number of reflections of the echo. Works in combination with the Spread parameter.

▶ **Tempo Sync**—Turns the tempo sync off and on.

▶ **LF Damp**—Controls the rate of decay for the low frequencies.

▶ **Spread**—Adjusts the space of the additional reflections set by the Diffusion parameter.

▶ **Predelay**—Introduces an additional delay before the first echo.

The Multi Tap algorithm produces four separate delays, each with its own adjustable parameters. The settings of this algorithm differ greatly from the others, as each tap is assigned its own set of parameters.

There are a few common parameters used in taps 1-4, including:

▶ **Tempo Sync**—Turns the tempo sync off and on.

▶ **Diffusion**—Clarifies the bounce and number of reflections of the echoes.

▶ **LF Damp**—Controls the rate of decay for the low frequencies in the echoes.

▶ **Tap Delay**—Adjusts the delay time of each tap. Note that when Tempo Sync is not active, this parameter has a range of 10-2000 milliseconds (about two seconds). When Tempo Sync is active, this parameter is set in note values, such as 1/8 and 1/16.

▶ **Tap Level**—Adjusts the amplitude of each tap.

▶ **Tap Pan**—Adjusts the panning assignment for each tap.

When Repeat Tap is selected, this parameter adjusts the time between each repeat of the entire set of tap delays.

One of my favorite algorithms in the RV7000, the Reverse, mimics the backward effect that you hear so often in ambient electronic music.

▶ **Length**—Adjusts the time between when the source signal is processed and then played back. Note that when Tempo Sync is not active, this parameter has a range of 10-4000 milliseconds (about four seconds). When Tempo Sync is active, this parameter is set in note values, such as 1/8 and 1/16.

▶ **Density**—Used to control the thickness of the reverse effect.

▶ **Rev Dry/Wet**—Mixes between the dry unprocessed signal and the wet processed signal.

▶ **Tempo Sync**—Turns the tempo sync off and on.

The CV Connections

You can connect the Matrix CV outputs to one of three CV inputs on the back of the RV7000 to control the three parameters in step time:

▶ **Decay**—This CV input controls reverb decay or echo/delay feedback.

▶ **HF Damp**—This CV input controls the HF Damp parameter on the RV7000 main display.

▶ **Gate Trig**—This CV input is used to trigger the Gate section of the RV7000.

The Spider Audio Merger & Splitter

New to Reason 2.5, the Spider Merger & Splitter is not an actual real-time effect (see Figure 14.22). However, it is a utility that serves two basic functions:

Figure 14.22
The Spider Merger & Splitter can be used to split a single audio signal to four outputs. It can also be used to merge four audio signals into one.

▶ Merges up to four separate audio inputs into a single output.

▶ Splits one audio input into four separate outputs.

Press the Tab to flip the Device Rack around. You will see that the Spider is split into two sections (see Figure 14.23). On the left is the Merge section, and the Splitter is on the right. In the next two sections, I will show you how to use the merging and splitting capabilities of the Spider.

Figure 14.23
There are two separate sections to the Spider: The Merge section and the Split section.

Using the Spider to Merge Audio

Merging audio with the Spider might not seem like such a hot idea the first time you think about it. But as this tutorial progresses, you might find yourself coming up with some interesting routing ideas that you might not have thought possible.

First, the basic idea: You can route the outputs of any Reason device to any of the four stereo inputs on the Spider. For example, you could route the outputs of the Malström, the stereo outputs of Redrum, the outputs of Dr:rex, and the outputs of two Subtractor synths to the Spider inputs (see Figure 14.24). These signals are then merged internally and routed to the stereo outputs of the Spider, which can be sent off to reMix, a stereo compressor, and so on.

Figure 14.24
The Merge section can accept the outputs of four stereo devices, or up to eight mono devices.

Additionally, the Merge section of the Spider has a couple of rules when it comes to using mono signals from Reason devices such as the Subtractor, or individual outputs from Redrum or the NN-XT.

▶ When you route the mono output of a Reason device to the left mono input of the Spider and don't connect anything to its corresponding right input, the Spider will output the signal to its left and right outputs.

▶ When you route the mono output of a Reason device to the right mono input of the Spider and don't connect anything to its corresponding left input, the Spider will output the signal to its right channel only.

Let's look at an example of how to use the Merge section effectively, by routing Dr:rex and Redrum to the Spider in order to send them all to a single insert effect.

1. Create a new Reason song and load it with reMix, Redrum, and Dr:rex. Additionally, write a pattern for Redrum and load a REX file into Dr:rex. Send it to its sequencer track.

2. Create a Spider Audio Merger & Splitter at the bottom of the Device Rack.

3. Create a COMP-01 Compressor next to the Spider. Notice that the output of the Dr:rex device has automatically routed itself to the COMP-01 in order to use it as an insert effect.

4. Press the Tab key.

5. Disconnect Redrum from reMix and Dr:rex from the COMP-01. At this point, if you click on Play, you won't hear any signal.

6. Route the left output of Redrum to any of the left inputs of the Spider's Merge section. The right output of Redrum should automatically route itself to the Spider's right input as well.

7. Route the left output of Dr:rex to any of the left inputs of the Spider's Merge section. The right output of Redrum should automatically route itself to the Spider's right input as well (see Figure 14.25).

Figure 14.25
The outputs of the Redrum and Dr:rex have now been routed to the inputs of the Spider.

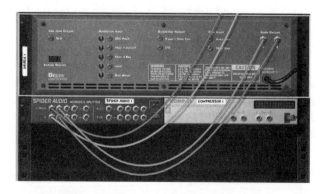

8. Route the left output of the Spider's Merge section to the left input of the COMP-01.

9. Route the left output of the COMP-01 to the channel 1 left input of reMix.

10. Press the Tab key again and then click on Play. You should now see and hear the COMP-01 processing both Redrum and Dr:rex (see Figure 14.26).

Figure 14.26
The audio outputs from both Redrum and Dr:rex are now being processed by COMP-01.

Using the Spider to Split Audio

The Splitter section of the Spider performs the exact opposite function of the Merger section. Simply put, its purpose is to split an audio signal into four separate stereo pairs of outputs. This allows you to then route the audio signal of one Reason device into many other devices, such as real-time effects.

Try an example:

1. Start a new Reason song and load it with a reMix and Dr:rex. Load a REX file and send it to its sequencer track.

2. Press the Tab key.

3. At the bottom of the Device Rack, create a Spider Audio Merger & Splitter.

4. Create a few real-time effects, such as the RV-7, the DDL-1, and the D-11. Notice that Dr:rex has automatically routed itself to the first effect as an insert.

5. Disconnect all of the Reason devices to start off with a clean slate. If you click on Play, you should not hear any audio now.

6. Route the left output of Dr:rex to the left input of the Spider's Splitter section. The right output of Dr:rex should automatically route itself to the Spider's right input accordingly (see Figure 14.27).

7. Route the left output of the first Spider channel to the channel 1 input of reMix. This will give you one dry signal of Dr:rex.

Figure 14.27
After all of the devices have been disconnected, route Dr:rex to the input of the Spider.

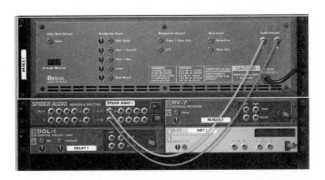

CHAPTER 14

8.   Route the left output of the second Spider channel to the left input of the RV-7 (see Figure 14.28).

Figure 14.28
Route the second output channel of the Spider to the RV-7.

9.   Route the outputs of the RV-7 to channel 2 of reMix.

10. Route the outputs of the third Spider channel to the DDL-1 and route its outputs to channel 3 of reMix.

11. Route the outputs of the fourth Spider channel to the D-11 and route its outputs to channel 4 of reMix.

At this point, you now have four channels of reMix playing the same REX loop with different processors (see Figure 14.29).

Figure 14.29
The same REX loop is now playing back through four inputs on reMix. Channel 1 is dry, channel 2 is a reverb, channel 3 is delay, and channel 4 is a distortion.

The Spider CV Merger & Splitter

Along with the Spider Audio Merger & Splitter, Reason 2.5 has a Spider unit that merges and splits CV signals, called the Spider CV Merger & Splitter (see Figure 14.30).

Figure 14.30
The Spider CV Merger & Splitter is used to split and merge CV signals.

The Spider CV Merger & Splitter serves two purposes:

▶ It merges four separate CV outputs from other Reason devices into one master CV output.

▶ It splits CV or Gate inputs into several outputs.

Next, take a look at a couple of examples for effectively using the merging and splitting functions of this wonder.

First, try the following exercise to learn how to merge:

1. Start a new Reason song and load it with reMix, Redrum, the ECF-42, and a Spider CV Merger & Splitter.

2. Write in a Redrum pattern using four different drum sounds (such as kick, snare, hi-hat, and cymbal).

3. Press the Tab key.

4. Route the audio outputs of Redrum to the ECF-42, and route the outputs of the ECF-42 to reMix.

5. Route the Redrum channel Gate outputs that have pattern data written on them to the inputs on the Merger section of the Spider (see Figure 14.31).

6. Route the merged output to the Envelope Gate input of the ECF-42.

7. Press the Tab key.

8. Select the Low Pass 24dB filter mode and set the ECF-42 parameters to the following values: Frequency 42, Resonance 91, Envelope Amount 22, Velocity 22, Attack 18, Decay 55, Sustain 43, and Release 127.

9. Click on Play. Notice the robotic sounds that Redrum makes now, thanks to a little CV merging.

Figure 14.31
The Gate Outputs of Redrum Channels 1, 2, 6, and 9 have been routed to the Merging inputs of the Spider.

SPLIT OUTPUT 4 IS INVERTED

Look at the Split section of the Spider. Notice that the abbreviation INV is displayed next to output 4 of both Split A and B. This means that these outputs send inverted CV data to any CV input they are routed to. Be sure to pay close attention to this in the upcoming tutorial.

Now, let's take a stab at splitting. Note that the CV Splitter section of the Spider includes two input points, Point A and Point B.

Try the following exercise:

1. Start a new Reason song and load it with a reMix, Dr:rex, and Redrum. Load a REX file and send it to its sequencer track. Write a drum pattern using channel 1 of Redrum, which is a Kick Drum sound.

2. Press the Tab key.

3. Create a Matrix and place it at the bottom of the Device Rack. Make sure that it is not connected to either Dr:rex or Redrum.

4. Create a Spider CV Merger & Splitter below the Matrix. Route the Curve CV output of the Matrix to Split input A (see Figure 14.32).

5. Connect an output of Split A to the Pitch CV input of Redrum's channel 1. Increase the Pitch CV amount of channel 1 to its maximum setting (see Figure 14.33).

6. Route output 4 of Split A to the Filter Cutoff CV input of Dr:rex. You can also increase the amount of its CV pattern.

7. Press the Tab key.

8. Switch the Matrix from Keys to Curve mode and write in a quick curve pattern (see Figure 14.34).

9. Click on Play. You should now hear the kick drum of Redrum pitch shift up or down according to the curve you drew. Also notice that the cutoff filter of Dr:rex is modulating as well, but it's inverse to the effect of Redrum. So, if the pitch of Redrum is bending down, the cutoff filter of Dr:rex should be opening rather than closing.

Figure 14.32
The Curve output of the Matrix has been routed to the CV inputs of the Spider's Splitter section.

Figure 14.33
Routing Curve CV control to Redrum makes it possible to create some twisted pitch bends to the loaded drum sample.

Figure 14.34
Write in a quick Curve pattern to modify the pitch of Redrum and the Filter Cutoff of Dr:rex.

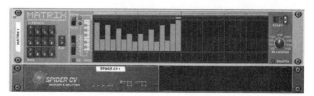

Judging by the length of this chapter, the amount of possibilities with the effects in Reason should keep you happy and occupied for a long, long time to come.

CHAPTER 14

15

Automation

A necessity for any studio, virtual or hardware, is the capability to automate your mix. Automation means the capability to automatically control equipment by recording its movements. A good example of automation is a hardware mixer with motorized faders that are programmed to automatically move with the mix (also known as *flying faders*). Reason's automation can record the movements of any device parameter, and those movements recur as you play back the song.

In this chapter, you learn to automate Reason's parameters. It's easy and fun.

Reason is simply one of the easiest programs to automate. Any parameter in the Device Rack can be automated just by doing the following.

1. Create a sequencer track. Note that this is already done when you create any virtual synth device, such as the Subtractor or NN-19.

2. Route the output of the sequencer track to the device that you want to automate. Once again, this is done for you when you create any virtual synth devices.

3. Arm the sequencer track for recording. Note that this step is not necessary when manually drawing in automation data (more on this later).

Once you have followed these steps, you can then choose one of two ways to create your automation data.

One method of creation is *live automation*. It involves using an external MIDI controller that is capable of sending out controller data that's read by the Reason sequencer and recorded as automation data.

Another method of creation is *drawn automation*. This method involves using the sequencer in Edit mode and drawing in Controller data, which is automation. You might recall that you did this back in Chapter 5, "The Reason Sequencer—Close Up." However, in this chapter, you are going to look at automation with the *Pattern lane*.

Let's look at both of these methods in detail.

Live Automation

Live automation is generally the first choice of most Reason users, because it gives you a real-time, hands-on approach to channeling your creativity. I have to admit; there is nothing quite as cool as using knobs and wheels on MIDI controllers to mix while demonstrating Reason to my students.

There are two ways to automate live in Reason:

▶ Using your mouse

▶ Using an external MIDI controller

Using the Mouse to Automate

If you do not have an external controller, you can use your mouse as a means of automating your Reason parameters. In this tutorial, you will automate a couple of reMix faders and knobs.

Before beginning, start a new song and create an instance of reMix. Ready? Follow these steps:

1. Choose Create > Sequencer Track. Note that the created sequencer track is armed to receive MIDI data (see Figure 15.1).

2. Click on the Output pop-up menu of the new sequencer track. You should have two choices—Disconnect (which is grayed out) and Mixer 1. Choose Mixer 1 so this sequencer track will be able to receive MIDI data (see Figure 15.2).

3. Click on the Record button on the Transport Panel. This will make the sequencer ready to record.

4. Now click on the Play button on the Transport Panel, or just press the spacebar key on your keyboard to start recording.

5. As soon as the sequencer begins to record, select a reMix channel fader to automate and begin to make volume changes to it by clicking and dragging up and down with your mouse (see Figure 15.3). Notice that Automation Override LED lights up to indicate that automation has been recorded.

Figure 15.1
A new sequencer track called New Track 1 has been created. Double-click on the track name to change it to reMix.

Figure 15.2
The output of the reMix track has now been assigned to reMix.

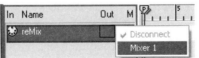

Figure 15.3
Click and drag on any
reMix channel fader to
automate it while the
sequencer is recording.

6. Press the spacebar again to stop recording. Notice the new data that has been
    written into the sequencer track and a neon green framed box has been drawn
    around the reMix channel (see Figure 15.4).

At this point, you can begin to automate any additional reMix parameters.

Figure 15.4
After recording your
automation, it will be
displayed within its
sequencer track.
Additionally, a framed
box has been drawn around
the automated parameter.

CLEARING YOUR AUTOMATION

At some point, you might decide that you want to clear the automation from a
particular parameter and start over. You can do this by right-clicking on any
automated parameter (or Control-clicking on the Mac) and choosing Clear
Automation from the pop-up menu (see Figure 15.5).

Once you select this, the neon green box will disappear, and you can now record
new automation data.

Figure 15.5
Right-click on any
automated parameter (or
Control-click on the Mac)
and choose Clear
Automation to erase its
automation data.

Using an External Controller to Automate

The use of an external controller is a great solution for those of you who find using a mouse to automate Reason parameters a bit cumbersome. An external controller can send MIDI controller data to any of the Reason devices, making it perfect for creating volume changes, synth parameter changes, and transport controls.

This tutorial shows you how to automate reMix by using the M-Audio Ozone, which has eight knobs that send out MIDI controller information (see Figure 15.6). I have set up the Ozone so that Knob 1 controls reMix channel 1.

Make sure that you have started a new Reason song and have created an instance of reMix.

Additionally, make sure that you have set up your external controller as a MIDI input device by choosing it from the MIDI page within the Preferences window (see Figure 15.7).

1. Choose Create > Sequencer Track. Once the track is created, rename it reMix.

2. Set the output of the reMix sequencer track to Mixer from its pull-down menu.

3. Click on the Record button on the Main Transport. This will make the sequencer ready to record.

4. Now click on the Play button on the Main Transport, or just press the spacebar key on your keyboard to start recording.

5. As soon as the sequencer begins to record, begin to make volume changes to channel 1 by turning the external controller's knob clockwise to increase its value and counter-clockwise to decrease (see Figure 15.8).

6. Press the spacebar again to stop recording. The automation data will be written on the reMix sequencer track, and there will be a neon green framed box around the channel 1 fader.

Figure 15.6
The M-Audio Ozone is a keyboard controller, external controller, and audio card, all rolled into one.

Figure 15.7
Ozone has been selected as the MIDI input device.

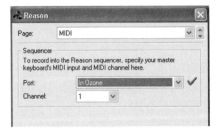

Figure 15.8
In this example, I have set up the first knob on the Ozone to control channel 1 of reMix.

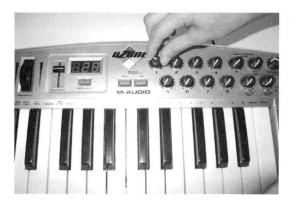 

WHICH CONTROLLER IS RIGHT FOR YOU?

After reading through this tutorial, you might find yourself wanting to get an external controller for your studio. You'll be happy to know that there are many affordable solutions that you'll find at your local music instrument shop.

In order to select the right controller, you should first decide whether you want to purchase a controller with knobs, faders, or both. They can all be used to automate Reason's device parameters, but you might find controlling reMix's faders with controller knobs a little confusing.

My advice is to purchase an external controller that has both knobs and faders. At around $225, the UC-33 controller from Evolution (see Figure 15.9) is a great solution. It is a USB device, so there is no need for additional MIDI inputs to your computer, and it comes complete with templates created especially for Reason.

There are of course many other external controllers to choose from, but it comes down to a question of how much money you are willing to part with. Visit your local music instrument shop for more information, or possibly try some online resources such as Harmony Central (www.harmony-central.com) or KvR Instrument Resources (www.kvr-vst.com).

Figure 15.9
The UC-33 by Evolution is an external controller that has both knobs and faders for use with Reason.

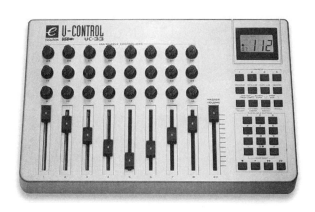

Automation Override

Once you have written in your live automation data, you might want to either add more automation data to the same parameter or redo it entirely. There are two ways to do this. One way is to switch to Edit mode and use the Editing tools of the Sequencer toolbar to redraw and erase automated parameters. This method is covered later in this chapter.

The other way to edit your live automation data is to use the Automation Override function, which is found in the Transport Panel of the sequencer (see Figure 15.10).

The Automation Override function makes it possible to replace an entire automation movement, or simply add to an existing one. Notice in Figure 15.10 the Reset button. This button is used to make the previous automation active again while still keeping the newly recorded automation up to that point.

You can see for yourself how to use the Automation Override by performing the following exercise. Get ready by starting a new Reason song and creating an instance of reMix and an instance of Subtractor.

1. Start by recording a quick automation of the Subtractor's Modulation Wheel with either your mouse or a MIDI controller. Use the previous tutorials as examples if you are unsure how to do this.

2. Once the automation data has been recorded, click on Stop and you should see it in the Subtractor sequencer track (see Figure 15.11). Click on Play to view the automation data playback.

3. Click on Stop twice to go back to the beginning of your sequence. Click on Record and Play to begin recording a new automation.

4. Record a new automation performance of the Modulation Wheel and take note that the Punched In LED is lit up, indicating that a new automation is being recorded.

5. About halfway through the automated sequence, click on the Reset button and notice the previously recorded automation has become active again and is controlling the Modulation Wheel.

6. Click on Stop and you should see your new and old automation data displayed in the sequencer track. Click on Play to verify.

Figure 15.10
The Automation Override is used to overwrite already written automation data.

Figure 15.11
The Modulation Wheel has been automated. Note the neon green frame around the Modulation Wheel.

AUTOMATING WITH OVERDUB

When recording automation, take a minute to verify that your Record mode is set to Overdub and not Replace before you begin. If you record automation while in Replace mode, you will erase any recorded MIDI performance on that sequencer track. Although there are unlimited levels of Undo in Reason, it is very annoying to go back and fix a mistake that could have been avoided.

That pretty much covers live automation. As I stated before, *any* parameter in Reason can be automated live in real time. Next, you'll take a look at drawn automation.

Drawn Automation

Another way of automating Reason's parameters is by manually drawing the automation into the Reason sequencer. This can appear to be a little tedious at first, but it is very helpful for correcting or modifying any previously written automation data.

Drawing Automation in the Controller Lane

In this tutorial, you will automate the individual parameters of the Subtractor by drawing automation in via the Reason sequencer. Before you begin, start a new Reason song; create a reMix and a Subtractor. It's also a good idea to quickly write in a sequence so you can hear the changes as they are being written.

1. Click the Switch to Edit Mode button found in the upper-left corner of the sequencer. Also, set the Snap to 1/64, so the automation data will be smooth.

2. Hide the Key and Velocity lanes by clicking on their corresponding buttons, found in the upper row of the sequencer.

3. Click the Maximize Sequencer Window button.

4. Click on the Show Controller Lane button.

5. To the right of the Controller Lane button is the Controllers button, which will display a pop-up menu of every controller that can be displayed and automated (see Figure 15.12).

6. Choose Master Level and the sequencer will display the Master Level controller (see Figure 15.13).

7. Select the Pencil tool and draw in some automation data (see Figure 15.14).

8. Click on the Restore Sequencer Window button to restore the view of the Device Rack.

9. Click on the Switch to Arrange Mode button.

10. The Subtractor Master Level slider will have a neon green framed box around it. Click on Play on your sequencer and you will see the slider move up and down to match the movements of the automation you drew in.

Figure 15.12
Every parameter of the
Subtractor is available to
automate. If this is your
first time, try an easy
parameter, such as the
Master Level or the
Modulation/Pitch
Wheels.

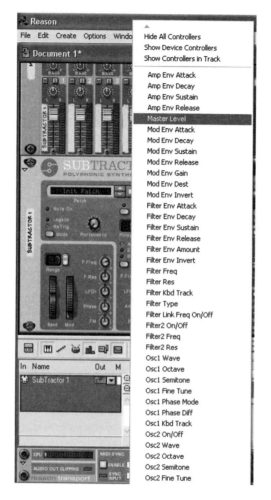

Figure 15.13
This is the Master Level
Controller lane.

Figure 15.14
Draw in some
automation for the
Master Level parameter.

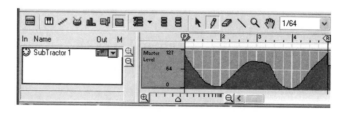

SHORTCUT TO AUTOMATION

Here's a handy shortcut to view the Controller lane of any parameter you want to automate in the Edit mode. Hold down the Alt key on your computer keyboard and click on any Reason device parameter (or use the Alt/Option key and click on your Mac). Let's use the previous tutorial as an example. If you are in the Arrange mode and you want to view the automation data of the Subtractor's Master Level parameter, hold down the Alt key and click on the parameter with your mouse. The Reason sequencer will switch to Edit mode and display both the Velocity lane and the Master Level Controller lane.

Automating the Pattern Lane

The Pattern lane is found in the Edit mode of the Reason sequencer and is used to write in automation data for the Pattern section of the Matrix and Redrum, which are pattern-driven devices (see Figure 15.15).

The next tutorial shows you how to draw in pattern data to automate the Pattern section of the Redrum. Before beginning, take a minute to start a new Reason song, create a reMix and Redrum. Although it's not necessary, you might also want to load up a Redrum kit and create a few patterns (refer back to Chapter 7, "Redrum—Close Up," for details on this).

1. Click on the Switch to Edit mode and you'll see the Drum lane, the Velocity lane, and the Pattern lane.

2. Set the Snap pull-down menu to Bar, because this will allow you to write in automation that is one bar in length at a time.

3. Select the Pencil tool and draw in a pattern change in the Pattern lane at bar one (see Figure 15.16).

4. Click on the pattern pop-up menu located in the lower-left corner of the Pattern lane and choose A2 (see Figure 15.17).

Figure 15.15
The Pattern lane is used to automate the changing of patterns for the Matrix and Redrum.

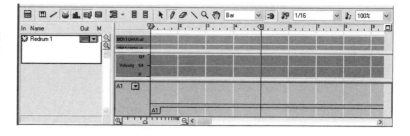

Figure 15.16
Use the Pencil tool to draw in your first pattern change. Note that the pattern data extends much farther than the first bar.

Figure 15.17
The pattern pop-up menu is where the other available patterns are selected.

5. Navigate your mouse to bar two in the Pattern lane and click to write in a bar of pattern A2 (see Figure 15.18).

6. Switch back to Arrange mode and you will see that the pattern data has been written onto the Redrum sequencer track. You'll also see the neon green box around the Pattern section of Redrum, so you know that automation exists on this parameter (see Figure 15.19).

Figure 15.18
Write in a bar of pattern A2. Notice that pattern A1 is used again at bar three.

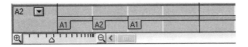

Figure 15.19
The pattern changes have now been written in and can be viewed in the Arrange mode of the sequencer.

AUTOMATING LIVE PATTERN CHANGES

As you know, any parameter in any Reason device can be automated live, and this definitely includes the Pattern section of the Matrix and Redrum. Try the following exercise:

1. Using the previous tutorial, switch to Arrange mode and clear the automation from the Pattern section of Redrum.

2. Select the Selector tool and click on the Record and Play buttons to start recording pattern changes. Pattern A1 should already by playing.

3. While recording, click on Redrum's Pattern A2 button on the downbeat of bar two. As Pattern A2 begins to play at bar two, the sequencer track should now reflect that it has recorded a pattern change (see Figure 15.20).

4. Stop the sequencer. If you switch to the Edit mode, you'll see that Pattern A1 has been automatically drawn in at the bar closest to where the Position Indication was when you stopped recording (see Figure 15.21).

Once the pattern changes have been recorded, you can keep them as is. You can also redo them with the Automation Override or draw them in with the Pattern lane.

Figure 15.20
The sequencer has recorded a pattern change.

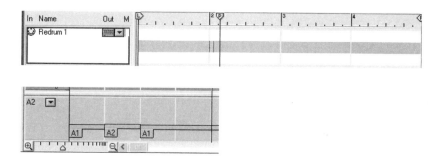

Figure 15.21
The sequencer has automatically inserted a pattern change back to Pattern A1 at bar three, so that Redrum will continuously play audio.

In this chapter, you have learned just about all there is to know about automation within Reason. If you are a seasoned DAW user, I think you'll agree that automating within Reason is much easier than it is with just about any other program out there.

Next, it's on to synchronization!

CHAPTER 15

16

Synchronization

This chapter takes a close up look at the synchronization capabilities of Reason 2.5.

What Is Synchronization?

Synchronization is the capability to make Reason play at the same time and tempo as another device. Additionally, synchronization makes it possible for Reason and another other device to stop, start, and locate different song positions together. This is a great feature if you are a live musician looking to use Reason alongside your rig of drum machines and external hardware sequencers. Although a somewhat simplified definition, it's one that is probably sufficient for most Reason users. Aside from the capabilities offered by ReWire, synchronization is not one of Reason's most versatile features. Reason is meant to be an all-in-one standalone application. But Reason is capable of syncing with other non-ReWire ready programs, as well as external MIDI gear. To find out more, read on.

DIFFERENT SYNCHRONIZATION FORMATS

There are many synchronization formats found in other DAW applications. Although they serve the same basic purpose, each format has been created in order to cater to the needs of a specific audience.

One of the most common sync-related terms you will hear is *SMPTE time code*. SMPTE is a sync format developed and implemented by the Society of Motion Picture and Television Engineers for use in video and film. SMPTE time code has three types or "flavors" that you'll read about in a minute.

Even though you don't learn about most of these formats in this chapter, here is a list of commonly known sync formats that you might hear about from time to time:

▶ **LTC** (Longitudinal Time Code) is a time code format derived from SMPTE that is recorded onto the audio track of a video deck or a multi-track recorder.

▶ **VITC** (Vertical Interval Time Code) is another SMPTE-based format in which the time code is recorded onto a video signal in the first few lines of the picture, which is generally not visible.

▶ **MTC** (MIDI Time Code) is another SMPTE-based format in which the time is transmitted via MIDI outputs found on many moderately priced MIDI interfaces or hardware-based digital multi-track recorders.

▶ **Word Clock** is a digital-based time code used with hardware peripherals that support digital formats, such as AES/EBU, S/DIF, and ADAT lightpipe.

REWIRE—THE SYNCHRONIZATION MASTER

Propellerhead Software has developed a synchronization technology called ReWire. Because many DAW applications support it (Logic, Cubase, and SONAR), ReWire is covered in detail in Chapter 17, "ReWire."

MIDI Clock

The synchronization that Reason supports is called *MIDI Clock*. This form of synchronization functions in much the same way as a metronome—its purpose is to synchronize the two devices by way of sending tempo-controlled information from one device to another. MIDI Clock generates and sends what are called *pulses per quarter note* (PPQN) via a MIDI cable. By default, MIDI Clock generates 24 evenly spaced PPQNs, of which the total number of PPQNs per minute is ultimately decided by the assigned tempo of a song. For example, a song that is playing at 60 BPM (beats per minute) sends approximately 1,440 PPQN per minute (or one pulse every 41.67 milliseconds). If you were to double the tempo to 120 BPM, MIDI Clock would generate 2,880 PPQN per minute (one pulse per every 20.83 milliseconds).

There are two basic devices in a MIDI Clock synchronization setup.

▶ **Master**—This is the device that sends the sync data and acts as the "leader" of the two devices. The master device sends a MIDI Start message to the receiver to initiate sync. It also sends a MIDI End message to stop sync. Additionally, a master device must send a Song Position message to the receiver to have it follow the master from within a specific point in a song.

▶ **Slave**—This is the device that receives and interprets the sync data from the master and follows it.

REASON IS THE SLAVE

When using MIDI Clock sync, Reason is *always* the slave device. You'll find that this is also the case when syncing Reason via ReWire.

Synchronization Tutorials

Now that you have a clear idea of what MIDI Clock is and how it works, it's time to learn how to sync Reason via MIDI Clock.

Syncing Reason to External Devices

This first tutorial involves synchronizing Reason with an external hardware device. This can include any external hardware that has its own internal sequencer and can generate a MIDI Clock signal, such as a drum machine, a sampling workstation like the EMU MP-7, or a standalone multi-track recorder like the Roland VS series.

This tutorial shows you how to synchronize a PC running Reason to a Mac iBook running Cubase SX. Cubase will generate MIDI Clock, send it out through its MIDI interface, to a MIDI interface connected to the PC, and then to Reason (see Figure 16.1).

Follow along with these steps.

1. First, you must assign a MIDI out to the MIDI Clock feature of Cubase (see Figure 16.2). Note that this window looks much different in other DAW applications, such as SONAR or Logic.

2. Activate the Sync feature in the Cubase SX transport bar (see Figure 16.3). This will enable Cubase to generate and send a MIDI Clock from the iBook to the PC. Once again, this will look different in another program.

Figure 16.1
This diagram demonstrates how to sync an iBook to a PC via MIDI Clock.

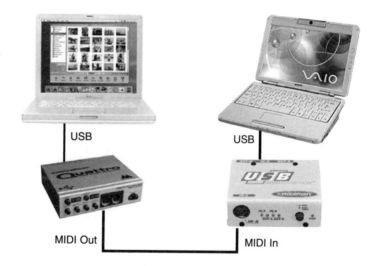

USB   USB

MIDI Out   MIDI In

Figure 16.2
Assign a MIDI output to the MIDI Clock window in Cubase. Because the MIDI interface on the iBook has only one MIDI output, Port 1 is the only available output.

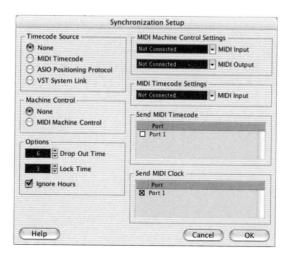

Figure 16.3
Activate the Sync feature
on the Cubase transport
bar.

3.   On the PC, open the Preferences window of Reason from the Edit pull-down
     menu. Switch to the Advanced MIDI page and assign a MIDI input to the MIDI
     Clock Sync pull-down menu (see Figure 16.4).

4.   Close the Preferences window and activate the MIDI sync by selecting it in the
     Transport Panel (see Figure 16.5).

5.   Click on Play in Cubase. Reason will immediately follow along. Try stopping the
     Cubase song a few times and you'll see that the Reason song stops accordingly.

Figure 16.4
Assign a MIDI input to
the MIDI Clock Sync
pull-down menu.

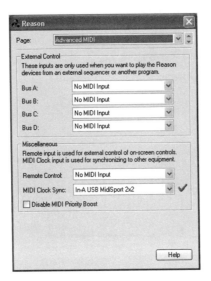

Figure 16.5
Enable MIDI Sync from
the Transport Panel.
Also, make sure that you
turn off the looping
function in the Transport
Panel. Otherwise, the
Reason song will play in a
loop while the Cubase SX
song continues. Notice that
when the MIDI Sync is
enabled, the Reason tempo
indicator reads 0, because
it's waiting to receive tempo
information from the master
device (Cubase).

LATENCY COMPENSATION

As you begin to synchronize your programs, you might hear a timing offset between the two applications during playback. This is most likely due to an excess of latency, or delay. This can be easily remedied by adjusting the Latency Compensation indicator found on the Audio page of the Preferences window (see Figure 16.6). This adjustment needs to be made only once, and it will be stored in the Reason Preferences.

To properly adjust the latency compensation for tighter sync, do the following:

1. Activate the Click option on the master program so it emits a solid timing reference.

2. Activate the Click option for Reason from the Transport Panel.

3. Click on Play on the master program to begin synchronization and make sure you can hear the click sounds of both applications.

4. Open the Audio page of the Preferences window and adjust the Latency Compensation controls until the click sound on both applications occur at exactly the same time. This indicates that the two programs are in sync.

5. Close the Preferences window.

Figure 16.6
Adjust the Latency Compensation to tighten up the synchronization between your applications.

Page:	Audio

Master Tune
440 Hz +0   cent

Audio Card Driver: MME VIA AC'97 Audio (WAVE)

Sample Rate: 44100
Buffer Size:

5632 samples
Output Latency: 127 ms
Latency Compensation: 127 ms
Active Channels: 2 out of 2   Channels...
Clock Source: Built-in

Control Panel...

☑ Play in Background

Syncing Reason with Internal Applications

Reason can also sync internally with another program via MIDI Clock, all within one computer. This is a perfect solution for users of Reason who want to use another program that does not function as a ReWire Master, such as Project5 by Cakewalk.

However, an additional utility called MIDI Yoke must be installed and configured to make this work (see Figure 16.7). MIDI Yoke makes it possible to connect two programs that reside in the same computer via MIDI without any MIDI hardware connections.

Figure 16.7
MIDI Yoke is a free
utility that makes it
possible to internally
connect two MIDI
applications within the
same computer without
using any MIDI
hardware.

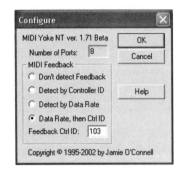

GO GET MIDI YOKE

MIDI Yoke is a free utility that can be downloaded at **www.midiox.com**. This site also contains some handy tutorials to show you how to easily install and configure MIDI Yoke.

MAC OS X USERS READ THIS

Mac OS X users will be happy to know that there is now a Mac solution called iMIDI by Granted Software (see Figure 16.8). It is a free utility program that internally connects two programs within one computer. It also has the capability to link two computers running MIDI applications via Ethernet.

You can download iMIDI free by going to the Granted Software website at **www.grantedsw.com**. You will also find some other utility software that Granted has written especially for Reason, such as ReMIDI (for creating arpeggios) or ReVision (a ReWire-enabled QuickTime movie player).

Figure 16.8
iMIDI is a free Mac OS X
utility that works in
much the same way as
MIDI Yoke.

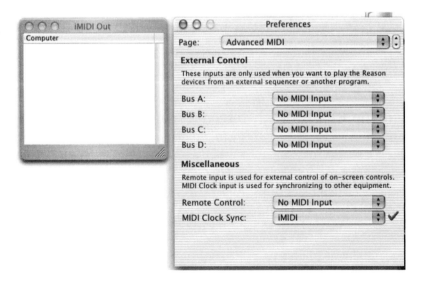

Assuming that you have installed and configured MIDI Yoke, you're ready to sync Project5 to Reason.

1. Start Project5.

2. The first time you start Project5, a pop-up window will appear asking you to assign the available MIDI ports (see Figure 16.9). Assign the MIDI Clock output to MIDI Yoke: NT1 and click OK to close the window.

3. Once the Project5 interface opens, navigate to the upper-right corner of the screen, which displays the Transport Controls, and turn on the MIDI Sync button (see Figure 16.10).

4. Start Reason.

5. Open the Preferences window and select the Advanced MIDI page.

6. Set the MIDI Clock Sync to MIDI Yoke: NT1 and close the window (see Figure 16.11).

Figure 16.9
Project5 will ask you to assign your MIDI ports in a pop-up window. Note: At the bottom of this window is the option to assign a MIDI output for the MIDI Clock signal.

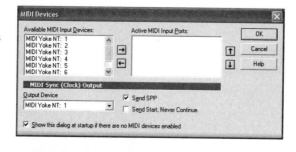

Figure 16.10
Turn on the MIDI Sync button in the Transport Controls of Project5.

Figure 16.11
Set the MIDI Clock Sync to MIDI Yoke: NT1.

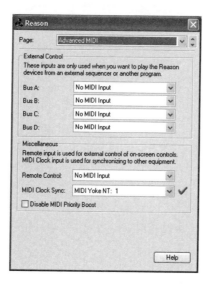

7. Enable the MIDI Sync feature in the Transport Panel. Also notice that the Sync Input LED is glowing bright green, which indicates that it is receiving input.

8. Switch to Project5 and click on Play. Reason should immediately follow in sync. You can verify that the two programs are syncing up by activating the Click track on both programs. Once activated, they should be in perfect sync with each other.

9. If you want to stop the programs, you must do it from Project5, because it is the master application.

SHARING APPLICATIONS—SHARING AUDIO CARDS

As you begin to sync and use Reason with another program like Project5, you might encounter some audio problems with your sound card. This happens because the driver you are using is not capable of sharing audio processing duties for both programs.

If you're using Windows XP, this is typically not a problem, because you can switch between different driver formats very easily. For example, if you are using your audio card's ASIO driver for both applications, try switching to the WDM drivers for both programs. For a review of how to deal with drivers, see Chapter 2, "Installing and Configuring Reason."

If you are using Mac OS X, this is not a problem, as Core Audio is multi-client. This means that two programs can use your audio card simultaneously.

If you are using another application that doesn't support ReWire or isn't a ReWire master program, syncing via MIDI Clock is a good solution, especially if the other program records audio, because this is something that Reason can't do.

Now that you've learned about MIDI Clock synchronization, you're ready to move on to ReWire!

17

ReWire

You can incorporate the creativity and sounds of Reason 2.5 into your own virtual studio environment by using a supplied Propellerhead technology known as *ReWire*. Included with Reason 2.5, ReWire gives you the ability to internally synchronize Reason with any other MIDI sequencing/audio recording software that supports it.

Although this is not a new concept to experienced virtual studio musicians, ReWire offers two key benefits that make it a unique technology. With ReWire, you can:

▶ Synchronize two programs with sample-accurate precision.

▶ Route the virtual outputs of the ReWired program into the virtual mixer of the host application. This makes it possible to then internally mix the two programs together within one mixing environment.

How Does ReWire Work?

ReWire is an internal technology shared between two programs within one computer, and the same rules of synchronization (see Chapter 16, "Synchronization") apply both in the real and virtual world (that is, units of measurement, rate of measurement, and timing reference). However, you will find that using ReWire simplifies synchronization, because there are no specific parameters to adjust when using two programs that support ReWire. You just need a *ReWire master* and a *ReWire slave* to make it work.

The *ReWire master* (a program such as Cubase SX or Logic 6) sends synchronization information, including transport functions and tempo/time signature information, to the slave program. The ReWire slave then reads this information and reacts in the blink of an eye, thanks to the wonders of sample-accurate timing.

To show you how tight sample-accurate sync is, consider this example. As discussed in Chapter 16, SMPTE time code has a standard resolution of 30 frames per second, which mathematically works out to 120th of a second, or 367 samples. The waveform displayed in Figure 17.1 is represented in samples, and reads from left to right. At the right side of the figure, you will see that the selected portion of this waveform is positioned at approximately 367 samples. This is precisely how long it would take before SMPTE time code would lock up and sync.

Sample-accurate timing calls for synchronization to occur within *1-2 samples* after playback of the master device. Look at Figure 17.1 again and you will see that sample-accurate timing is far superior to any other method of synchronization.

Figure 17.1
Sample-accurate
synchronization is as
tight as it gets.

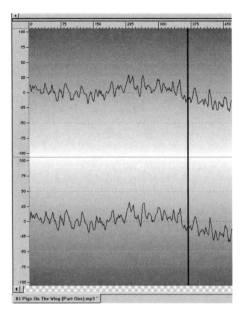

The *ReWire slave* is the program that reads the synchronization information and follows the lead of the ReWire master. A good example of a ReWire slave program is Reason 2.5.

Additionally, the ReWire master receives the virtual audio outputs of the ReWire slave program and routes these signals to its own virtual mixer. In the case of Reason, there are 64 individual outputs that can be routed to its ReWire Master application. This function is referred to as Audio Streaming.

KEEP AN EYE ON YOUR CPU
ReWire is a fantastic technology that will certainly become a permanent fixture in your virtual studio environment for years to come. Keep in mind, though, that running two programs together such as this can lead to CPU overloads and audio dropouts. So, keep an eye on the CPU meter in your ReWire Master program.

ReWire Tutorials

Now it's time to learn how to use ReWire with other DAW programs. Throughout the rest of this chapter, you'll find tutorials for using Reason with most of the popular ReWire host applications via ReWire.

Using ReWire with Cubase SX/SL 1.06

Steinberg's Cubase VST (Mac/PC) was the first program to integrate ReWire into its applications, so it seems only appropriate to begin with Cubase SX/SL (see Figure 17.2).

Figure 17.2
Cubase SX/SL in the
flesh.

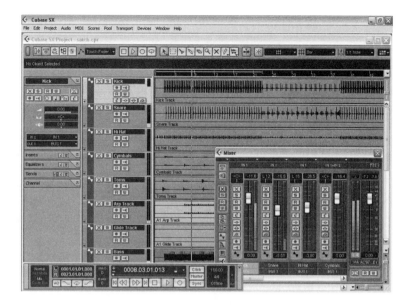

Make sure you are using the built-in song for Reason, so you can follow along.

1. Launch Cubase and create a blank project.

2. Navigate to the Device's pull-down menu. If you have installed Reason, it will appear halfway down the menu list. Select this device. The ReWire window will pop up (see Figure 17.3).

Figure 17.3
The Reason ReWire
window in Cubase
SX/SL.

3. In the ReWire window, you will see that Cubase SX/SL can activate up to 64 individual channels of ReWire. This can lead to some extremely complex routing, with both virtual effects and synths. Assuming this is your first time using ReWire, this example is simple and just uses Reason's main mix. Activate the first pair of ReWire channels (called Mix L and Mix R) by clicking on the dark green bars located in the middle of the window.

4. Close the ReWire window. Open the Cubase mixer by pressing the F3 key on your keyboard. Notice that a new stereo channel has been opened. Also notice that the track classification logo is different from the logo on your mixer's other tracks (see Figure 17.4).

5. Launch Reason. Once it has launched, look at the Audio Out device in the Reason Device Rack. Notice that Reason is now set to ReWire Slave Mode, which means that Reason will follow or chase to Cubase. Also notice that the tempo of Reason's built-in song is set to the same tempo as Cubase.

6. Click on Play in either Reason or Cubase. Switch over to Cubase. On the mixer, you should now see the active ReWire channels lit up with joy. The Reason mix is playing straight through it, as shown in Figure 17.5.

7. Click on Stop.

Figure 17.4
Cubase creates a specific ReWire channel on its virtual mixer.

Figure 17.5
Reason is now following Cubase in sample-accurate sync.

8. Should you want to quit Cubase and Reason, remember to quit Reason first, followed by Cubase. If you try to quit Cubase first, an alert window will pop up to remind you.

Additionally, Cubase can also trigger the individual instruments and real-time effects of Reason via MIDI through ReWire.

Make sure that you are using the built-in song for Reason, so you can follow along.

1. Following the steps in the previous tutorial, activate the ReWire channels in Cubase and launch Reason.

2. In Cubase, create a MIDI track in the Project window. Make sure that the MIDI track is record enabled by clicking on what looks like a Record button on the track (see Figure 17.6).

3. Click on the Out pull-down menu of the MIDI track and you will see a long list of routing possibilities, including all of the active devices in Reason. For this example, choose the Reason Drums option. This will give you access to Redrum (see Figure 17.7).

4. Press the C1 key on your MIDI keyboard. This should trigger the first Redrum channel, which is typically a kick drum.

5. You can now begin to sequence in Cubase using Redrum as your drum machine.

Now that you have seen the granddaddy of ReWire-ready programs, you can also apply this knowledge to Steinberg's post-production wonder called Nuendo, because they are similar in both interface and functionality.

Figure 17.6
Create a MIDI track in Cubase and make sure that it is record enabled.

Figure 17.7
Set the output of the MIDI track in Cubase to Reason Drums in order to trigger Redrum.

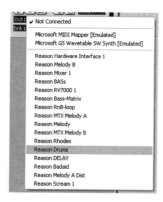

FOR MORE INFO

Many DAW applications are covered throughout this chapter. You will be happy to learn that Muska & Lipman's *Power!* series has books dedicated to most of these programs.

For example, if you want to know more about Cubase SX, you can read *Cubase SX Power!* by Robert Guerin. If you want to know more about SONAR 3, pick up *SONAR 3 Power!* by Scott Garrigus. If you want to know more about Logic 6, read *Logic 6 Power!* by Orren Merton (Muska & Lipman). To see what else is available, visit **www.courseptr.com**.

TWO MONITOR HEADS ARE BETTER THAN ONE

While writing this chapter, I felt compelled to purchase a second monitor so I could view both Reason and the ReWire host application at the same time. If you should feel that same urge, here are some tips.

First, you need a second monitor that supports a pixel rate equal to or better than the pixel rate of your primary monitor. For example, if your primary monitor can display a 1024×768 pixel resolution, make sure your second monitor does the same. It will save you a lot of eyestrain and headaches when switching back and forth. Also make sure that both monitors support the same color depth.

Second, you need a video card that supports dual monitors (or dual heads, as we call them). This is more affordable than it used to be, with dual-monitor cards available for around $110. Make sure to get a good brand name, such as Matrox or MSI.

After you have your dual monitor set up, you'll wonder how you ever lived without it.

Using ReWire with Logic 6.0 (Mac Only)

Emagic's Logic 6.0 (Mac only) is without a doubt the most complex of all the MIDI sequencers/audio recording programs (see Figure 17.8). Purchased by Apple Computer in 2002, Logic is the flagship program for Apple's new standard in digital audio, called *core audio* (see Chapter 2, "Installing and Configuring Reason," for more details). Logic is the choice software for musicians who want to stay true to the Mac platform and be able to incorporate different technologies into one lean, mean, music machine.

1. Launch Logic. The Arrange window will open with the default assortment of audio and MIDI tracks. This is a fine place to start.

2. Launch Reason. At the top of the Audio Device in the Reason Device Rack, you'll see that Reason is automatically set to ReWire Slave Mode. Also take notice that the tempo of the Reason built-in song is now set to Logic.

3. In Logic, navigate to the Audio pull-down menu and select the audio mixer.

4. Scroll to the far left of the audio mixer and select Audio 1 by clicking on it at the bottom of the channel strip (see Figure 17.9).

Figure 17.8

Logic Platinum, by Emagic, is for those who appreciate every nuance MIDI has to offer.

Figure 17.9

Scroll to the far left of the audio mixer in Logic and select Audio 1.

5. Just to the left of the channel strip is the channel properties section of the audio mixer. The mixer displays all of the information about the selected channel. Looking back to Figure 17.9, you can see all of the properties of Audio 1, including its routing information. This is where you make your ReWire settings.

6. Follow the channel properties down until you find the Cha section. It should be set to Track 1. Click and hold this pop-up menu to select a new input source from the supplied pull-down menu. For this tutorial, select ReWire > RW: Mix L (see Figure 17.10). This will route the left Reason channel of the stereo mix into the Logic audio mixer.

7. Now, select Audio 2 and repeat Step 6. Just make sure that you route RW: Mix R into Audio 2, so both Reason channels of the stereo mix will be routed to the Logic audio mixer.

Figure 17.10
Select RW: Mix L to
route the left Reason
channel of the stereo mix
into the audio mixer.

8. Before you click on Play, pan Audio 1 to hard left, and Audio 2 to hard right. This is necessary in order to achieve a true stereo mix.

9. Click on Play in Logic, and Reason should now chase to Logic without a problem.

As is the case with Cubase, Logic can send MIDI data to Reason, making it a perfect solution for using Reason as a virtual synth module from within the Logic environment. However, the process to do this is pretty complicated, so follow along closely.

1. Open the audio mixer in Logic. Select New > ReWire from the Internal submenu. This will create a ReWire object, located at the bottom of the audio mixer (see Figure 17.11).

2. The channel properties portion of the audio mixer lists all of the properties for the ReWire object. In this tutorial, you are going to route this object to Redrum, so rename the object *Drums*.

3. Navigate to the Cha portion of the properties portion of the audio mixer, which should be set to All. Click and hold this pop-up menu to view the list of available Reason devices that can be controlled. Locate the Drums device and select it (see Figure 17.12).

Figure 17.11
Create a ReWire object in
the audio mixer.

Figure 17.12
After re-naming your ReWire object to Drums, select Drums from the Cha pull-down menu. This will route MIDI data from Logic to the Redrum device in Reason.

4. In order to begin sequencing Redrum from Logic, you must now click and drag the Drums object from the audio mixer to the Arrange window (see Figure 17.13). Once this is done, a Drums track is created on the Arrange window. Logic is now ready to send MIDI data to Redrum. Note that the created track is also armed for recording.

Figure 17.13
Click and drag the Drums object onto the Arrange window to prepare it for sequencing.

Suffice it to say, Logic is a bit more complicated than your run-of-the-mill MIDI sequencer, but many professional musicians rely on its solid feature set and musical potential.

Using ReWire with Pro Tools LE 6.1

Just about anybody who has delved into this side of music technology has certainly heard of Pro Tools by Digidesign (Mac/PC). Pro Tools is the first tool of choice for post-production applications, with its basic and straightforward approach to audio recording and editing (see Figure 17.14). Within the last few years, Digidesign has pursued the consumer market by introducing some great hardware audio interfaces at affordable prices that come included with a light version of Pro Tools called *Pro Tools LE*. This version, although a bit stripped down, is a formidable solution for audio and MIDI productions. With the recently released version 6.1, Pro Tools LE is now a ReWire-ready host application.

Figure 17.14
Pro Tools LE by
Digidesign is an
affordable all-in-one
solution for digital audio
and MIDI.

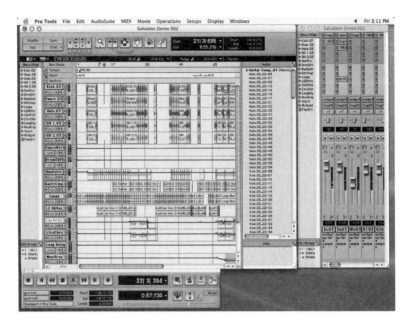

Here's how to set up ReWire with Pro Tools LE.

1. Launch Pro Tools LE and create a new project.

2. Select File > Create Track. When the dialog box appears, have Pro Tools create a stereo audio track. After it is created in the Edit view, double-click on it and name the track ReWirMx, as shown in Figure 17.15.

3. Select Display > Show Mix. This will open up the virtual mixer. You will find the Reason Mix channel strip on the far left.

4. On the insert section of the Reason Mix channel strip, locate the first insert point. Click and hold here to display the available plug-ins for your session. Select the Reason plug-in (see Figure 17.16). Reason will launch automatically.

5. Once Reason is loaded, you will see in the Audio Out device that it is automatically set to ReWire Slave Mode. Click Play and Reason will immediately chase to Pro Tools, but you won't hear any audio. Just open the ReWire plug-in interface (see Figure 17.17) and route its output to Mix L-R.

6. Should you want to quit Pro Tools LE and Reason, remember to quit Reason first, followed by Pro Tools LE. If you try to quit Pro Tools LE first, an alert window will pop up to remind you.

Figure 17.15
Create a stereo audio
track and name it ReWire
Mix. If you are familiar
with Pro Tools, you will
notice that this is indeed
a stereo track, because it
has a pair of meters.

Figure 17.16
Pro Tools integrates
ReWire into its interface
by using Reason, or any
other ReWire-ready
program, as a plug-in.

Figure 17.17
Route the output of the
ReWire plug-in to Mix
L-R.

Once you have successfully synced up Reason and Pro Tools LE, you can send MIDI data to
Reason by way of a Pro Tools MIDI track. Just follow these steps to do so:

1. In Pro Tools LE, select File > Create New Track. Repeat Step 2 from the last
    tutorial, but create a MIDI track rather than an audio track. This will place a MIDI
    track just below the Reason Mix audio track created in the previous tutorial.

2. Select Display > Show Mix to bring up the virtual mixer. As shown in Figure
    17.18, route the output of the MIDI track to Redrum by selecting Drums from the
    pull-down menu.

3. At this point, you can switch back to the Edit view, arm your MIDI track, and
    sequence in some MIDI data that will now be sent to Redrum. With a little
    experimenting, you can easily come up with a sequence such as the one shown in
    Figure 17.19.

Figure 17.18
Pro Tools LE can route
MIDI data to any Reason
device. You simply select
it from the MIDI Out
pull-down menu.

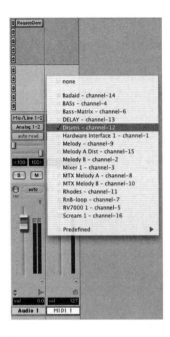

Figure 17.19
Sequencing in Pro Tools
LE is a cinch.

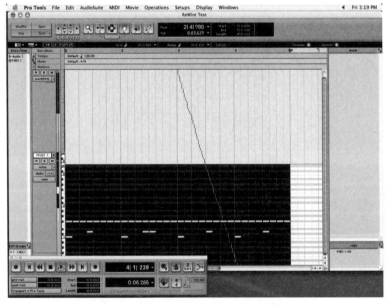

Although Pro Tools LE is not the most complete MIDI sequencer ever made, adding the power of
Reason 2.5 via ReWire is sure to make your tracks sparkle with creativity.

Using ReWire with SONAR 2.2 (Windows Only)

There's no doubt that the last couple of years have been good ones for Cakewalk, because SONAR (Windows only) has accumulated a long list of great reviews from the press and its user base (see Figure 17.20). Now with ReWire, you can integrate the synths and sound modules of Reason with the audio recording and MIDI sequencing capabilities of SONAR 2.2.

Make sure that you are using the built-in song for Reason, so you can follow along.

1. Launch SONAR and start a new blank project.

2. Select View > Synth Rack. You can also click on the DXi button, which is located in the Project window. Once you select it, the blank synth rack will open, as shown in Figure 17.21.

3. In the top-left corner of the Synth Rack window, click on the Insert DXi instrument and Reason devices button. A pull-down menu will then appear with a submenu for DXi synths and one for ReWire devices. Select the Reason option from the ReWire devices submenu.

4. SONAR will then pop up a window asking for synth and ReWire options (see Figure 17.22). If this is your first time performing this task, make sure that you specify SONAR to create a MIDI Source track and a First Synth Output track as well. Click OK.

Figure 17.20
SONAR 2.2 has a killer graphical interface and exceptional audio/MIDI editing features.

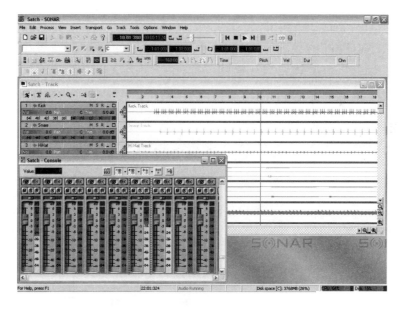

CHAPTER 17

Figure 17.21
The SONAR DXi synth rack is where you begin to load your ReWire programs.

Figure 17.22
The SONAR DXi synth options can be very useful when using virtual synths for the first time, because these options take all of the guesswork out of the picture.

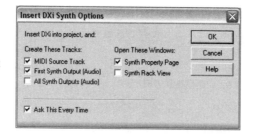

5. SONAR will then automatically launch Reason. SONAR will also create a Reason device in the Synth Rack window.

6. Once Reason has loaded the built-in song, click on Play and look at the Audio Out device in the Reason Device Rack. Notice that Reason is now set to ReWire Slave Mode, which means that Reason will follow or chase to SONAR. Also notice that the tempo of Reason's built-in song is set to the same tempo as SONAR.

7. Select View > Console. This will launch the SONAR virtual mixer. If you are still playing the built-in song, you will see the SONAR meters jumping with delight.

8. Click on Stop.

9. Should you want to quit SONAR and Reason, remember to quit Reason first, followed by SONAR. If you try to quit SONAR first, an alert window will pop up to remind you.

Just as with Cubase, SONAR can trigger the individual Reason devices via MIDI. If you followed the previous tutorial, this can be done in a heartbeat. With ReWire still running in your SONAR project, select the MIDI track that was created when you first launched Reason from the DXi synth rack. Make sure that the output is still set to Reason and then click on the Channel pull-down menu. As shown in Figure 17.23, you can select any of the Reason devices from this menu, and then proceed to trigger and sequence them from within the SONAR interface.

Figure 17.23
Set your MIDI output to Reason and then use the Channel pull-down menu to select the Reason device you want to trigger and sequence.

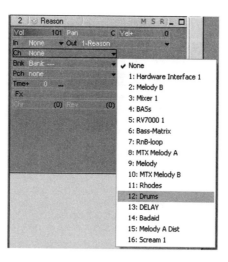

USING REWIRE WITH PROJECT5

Riding high on the success of SONAR, Cakewalk released their answer to Reason, called Project5 (see Figure 17.24). This virtual synth studio functions a lot like Reason in that it has plenty of virtual synths, sound modules, and sequencers. To top it off, Project5 also supports ReWire, which suggests that it could be used with Reason, but there is a catch. Unlike SONAR, Project5 is *not* a ReWire master program. Rather, it is a ReWire slave (like Reason), which can chase to any ReWire master program, such as SONAR.

In all likelihood, Project5 will become a ReWire master program in a future update.

So, in order to use Project5 with Reason, a ReWire master program, such as Cubase SX/SL, Pro Tools LE, SONAR, Orion, or Ableton Live, is required. If you have the money and a fast enough computer to accomplish this feat (remember, you are now running *three* programs at one time, which requires *a lot* of CPU speed), simply use any of the PC-based tutorials in this chapter as a template and you should be able to figure it out with no trouble at all.

Figure 17.24
Cakewalk's Project5 is a virtual synth studio like Reason.

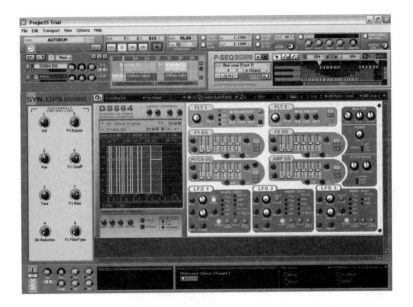

CHAPTER 17

Using ReWire with Orion Platinum 4.0 (Windows Only)

Orion (Windows only) succeeds in filling the void for Reason users who want to use VST and DirectX virtual instruments and effects alongside Reason without the added complications of hard disk recording, as is the case with Cubase and SONAR (see Figure 17.25).

Figure 17.25
Synapse Audio's Orion Platinum has VSTi, DXi, and ReWire support under one roof and sports some very cool synths of its own.

Make sure that you are using the built-in song for Reason, so you can follow along.

1. Launch Orion.

2. Select Insert > ReWire. Orion will then display the different ReWire applications available. As you can see in Figure 17.26, my machine has three ReWire applications available: Reason, ReBirth, and Project5.

3. Select Reason. Orion will then automatically create 16 individual mixer channels for Reason and launch the Reason application.

4. Once Reason is launched and the built-in song is open, click on Play in Orion and you will see Reason sync to Orion.

Figure 17.26
You can access your ReWire devices from the Insert pull-down menu.

5. If you want to send different Reason instruments and devices to their own individual outputs, just press the Tab key on your computer keyboard to swing the Device Rack around. You can then click and drag the outputs of the individual Reason devices to the Audio Out channels (see Figure 17.27). Just keep in mind that stereo Reason synths such as the Malström and NN-19 require two channels in Orion. Additionally, once you have routed them to their ReWire channels, you will need to pan one channel hard left and the other hard right.

6. Should you want to quit Orion and Reason, remember to quit Reason first, followed by Orion. If you try to quit Orion first, an alert window will pop up to remind you.

Figure 17.27
Click and drag the individual outputs of your Reason devices to the audio output device.

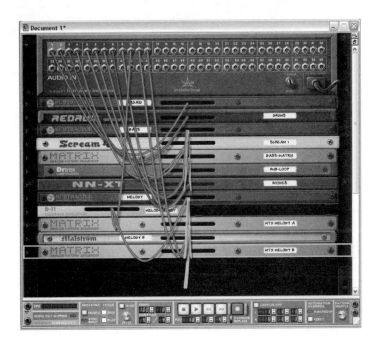

Using ReWire with Ableton Live 2

Ableton Live (Mac/PC) is to remixing digital audio what Reason is to synthesis—ultra freaking cool! Don't let the retro, two-dimensional graphical interface fool you (see Figure 17.28); Live 2 is a perfect solution for audio recording and remixing.

Make sure that you are using the built-in song for Reason, so you can follow along.

1. Launch Ableton Live.

2. Now launch Reason. At the top of the audio device in the Reason Device Rack, you'll see that Reason is automatically set to ReWire Slave Mode. Also take notice that the tempo of the Reason built-in song is now set to the default tempo of Live.

Figure 17.28
Ableton Live 2.03 bends,
twists, and stretches
audio like a rubber band.

3. At this point, you need to activate an audio track in Live and set it to receive the routed audio from Reason. Go to track 1 and locate the Input Type box, which is located just below the send knobs. Click on this box and you will get a pull-down menu listing all of the input options you have. As shown in Figure 17.29, there are two choices: Master Out (for re-sampling) and Reason. Choose Reason.

4. Once Reason is selected, a new dialog box will appear directly below the Input Type. This is the *Input Channel*, which is where you can assign which Reason channels to route to this track in Live. Although you can select up to 64 various outputs, keep it simple and choose 01/02:Mix L, Mix R (see Figure 17.30). This will allow you to listen to the stereo mix of Reason.

5. If you now click on Play in either the Live or Reason transport, you will still not hear any Reason audio. To fix this, activate the Monitor button for track 1 in Live. You will immediately hear Reason in a stereo mix.

Figure 17.29
Located just below the
send knobs on any audio
track in Live, you'll find
the Input Type box.
Although you select
Reason for this example,
any ReWire slave
program that you own and
have installed will appear in
this list.

Figure 17.30
Select the Reason
channel that you want to
route to Live.

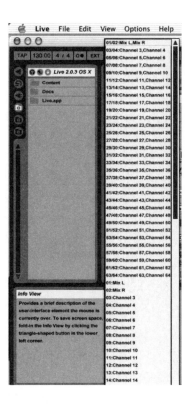

6. Should you want to quit Live and Reason, remember to quit Reason first, followed by Live. If you try to quit Live first, an alert window will pop up to remind you.

DIFFERENT PROGRAMS, DIFFERENT VERSIONS

Although this is a chapter dedicated to the technology of ReWire, it simply can't cover every ReWire-ready program on the market, nor the various versions of each given program. Fortunately, the Propellerhead website is a good place to find most of the answers to your ReWire questions. Have a look at the Reason support section of **www.propellerheads.se** and you'll be sure to find ReWire tutorials that cover software that was not covered in this chapter, such as Digital Performer. You'll also find tutorials covering earlier versions of software, such as Logic 5 or Cubase VST.

ReWire is one of those essential elements that I like to use in new songs that I write. Not only do I get the best of digital audio recording with my ReWire master application, but I also get the best of virtual synths with Reason.

CHAPTER 17

18

Mixing and Publishing Your Reason Songs

When it comes to finalizing and mixing down your song, Reason offers many options. Aside from the typically found Export Audio function that you will see in just about every digital audio program on the market, Propellerhead has included a very interesting Publish feature that saves your song and allows other Reason users to listen to it on their own computers. This introduces a Reason Community concept that encourages users to interact and exchange ideas.

How and What Can Reason Export?

As with many digital audio workstation programs such as Cubase, SONAR, Digital Performer, and Logic, Reason can export many file formats, making it a versatile solution for any digital music junkie (see Figure 18.1).

Reason can export the following file types:

- ▶ Export audio
- ▶ Export MIDI files
- ▶ Publish Reason songs

Figure 18.1
Choose your export option from the File pull-down menu.

The following sections break it down and take an in-depth look at what each export type does.

Export Audio

Exporting audio is synonymous with *audio mixdown,* which is simply the process of combining all of the various signals and real-time effects in your Reason song into a single stereo digital audio file. This file can then be used to make an audio CD that can be played in any CD player.

Reason provides a couple of ways to export audio, each of which serves specific functions. Open your File pull-down menu and follow along.

▶ **Export Song As Audio File**—This option will export your entire Reason song, from start to finish.

▶ **Export Loop As Audio File**—This option will export whatever is contained between the left and right locator points of the Reason sequencer. Although this option might not appear to be immediately useful, the purpose of this function is explained later in this section.

Let's export some audio using both methods.

Export Your Reason Song as an Audio File

In this section, you are going to load a Reason song and learn how to export the entire song as a stereo WAV or AIFF file. Reason offers many choices and options to create the best file possible, so it is important that you understand how the process works.

For this tutorial, I suggest you use the Tutorial Song, so you can follow along seamlessly.

1. First, scroll to the right in the Reason sequencer and locate the end marker (see Figure 18.2). Notice that it is set at measure 101, and that the song itself ends at measure 41. If you were to export the song as an audio file now, Reason would export all of the audio, all the way to measure 101. This would mean that your exported audio would have 60 extra measures of space, which is a lot of blank audio. To avoid this, drag the end marker to the left until you reach measure 45 (see Figure 18.3).

2. Next, look at the sequencer tracks and make sure that all of the tracks you want to include in the mix are not muted (see Figure 18.4). For example, if you want to

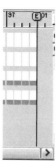

Figure 18.2
Scroll to the right and locate the end marker. In the Tutorial Song, it is located at measure 101.

Figure 18.3
In the Tutorial Song, find the end marker and drag it to the left until it reaches measure 45.

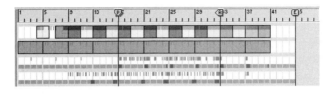

Figure 18.4
Make sure the sequencer tracks you want to export have not been muted.

export a mix without the Redrum module, you can simply mute the Redrum track either on its sequencer track or by clicking on its Mute button in reMix. This way, Reason will not include Redrum in the export of the mix (see Figure 18.5).

3. Choose File > Export Song As Audio File. A new window will pop up and ask you to name your song and select a location for it (see Figure 18.6). For simplicity's sake, save the mix to the desktop and keep its original name (Tutorial Song). At this point, you can also select which audio file format to export your mix as—AIFF or WAV. The golden rule is typically "WAV files for Windows and AIFF for Macs." However, with today's computers, this is generally not much of a concern, because most programs can support and open both WAV and AIFF files, so it is really up to you. Assuming this is your first time out, perhaps AIFF would be just fine. Click the Save button to continue.

Figure 18.5
If you want to exclude Redrum from the audio export, mute it in the Reason sequencer track or click its Mute button in reMix.

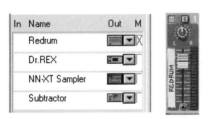

Figure 18.6
Select a place to save your audio file and give it a name.

4. Next you are asked to set your export audio settings (see Figure 18.7). In this case, the sample rate has been set to 44100Hz and has been given a bit depth of 16 bits. These are the standard audio settings found on a commercially available audio CD. If your intention is to burn an audio CD right after exporting your Reason songs, these settings are fine. But just for kicks, click on the pull-down menus in this window to see all of the other possible export audio settings (see Figure 18.8). Reason is capable of creating a 24-bit audio file with a sampling rate of 96kHz. If your intention is to take the digital audio file that Reason creates and import it into a high-end mastering program such as WaveLab or Peak, these settings might be the ticket.

5. After you have made your settings, click OK. Reason will proceed to mix and export your Reason song into a digital audio file. In Figure 18.9, you will see that Reason counts down the remaining bars to be exported.

Figure 18.7
Set your audio preferences to export your Reason song.

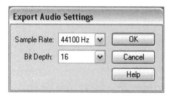

Figure 18.8
Reason can create a 24-bit/96kHz digital audio file, making it the perfect solution to use with a pro-audio application.

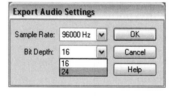

Figure 18.9
Reason counts down the measures as it exports your song.

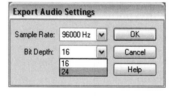

Export Your Reason Loop as an Audio File

Reason can also export just portions (or loops) of your songs as audio files as well. It does this by exporting whatever content is between the left and right locators. This is extremely useful for creating high-quality loops that can be used in pro-audio DAW applications, such as Cubase, SONAR, or Logic.

Why would you want to do this? Although Reason is a great sequencing program, it cannot record audio. There are times when you might find you are working on a piece of music made up of mostly recorded tracks of audio and you need just a little bit of Reason magic here and there. To do this, you have two options:

▶   You can run Reason with your DAW application through ReWire. The problem here is that you'll use a lot of CPU speed that you might need somewhere else.

▶ You can create drum loops and synth loops in Reason, export them as audio files, and import them into your DAW application. This is a much better solution, because it saves your precious CPU speed.

That said, let's get on with it and create a four-bar digital audio loop in Reason. As with the last tutorial, use the Tutorial Song once again so you can keep up with the group.

1. Click and drag the left and right locators to measures 13 and 17, respectively (see Figure 18.10). This will give you a four-bar loop to work with.

2. Make sure your Loop button is set to On in the Reason Transport Panel.

3. Listen to the loop and decide which single instrument you want to export as a digital audio file. This example exports the Redrum track for Figure 18.11, so either click on the Solo button on the Redrum channel in reMix or mute all of the other sequencer tracks except for the Redrum track.

4. Now you are set to export your audio loop. Navigate to the File pull-down menu and select Export Loop As Audio File.

5. As with the last tutorial, you need to name the file and select a location for it. You then need to specify your digital audio settings to export your digital audio loop.

Figure 18.10
Click and drag the left and right locators to measures 13 and 17, respectively.

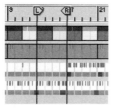

Figure 18.11
To export just one instrument from your mix, either solo its reMix channel, or mute all of the other sequencer tracks except for the Redrum track.

REASON DOES NOT MAKE MP3s

The MP3, or *MPEG Layer 3*, is a digital audio file format that is used primarily to exchange music between friends, family, and, most importantly, fans. It is a popular format because it compresses a high-quality stereo AIFF or WAV file to a much smaller size that can be transferred easily via the web.

Reason 2.5 does not create MP3 files, although this added functionality would seem to be an obvious step for the Internet/digital music junkie.

But cheer up kids; the good news is that there are *many* MP3 encoding programs available at a very small price. For Windows users, a program such as MyMP3 by Steinberg, or Pyro by Cakewalk, can be purchased for under $50. For Mac users, it gets even better, because Apple's iTunes encodes MP3 files like a champ and is a free program that comes with Mac OS X.

CHAPTER 18

Export MIDI

As you read in Chapter 5, "The Reason Sequencer—Close Up," Reason can import any MIDI file to be used within the Reason sequencer. This can lead to some very interesting remixing ideas by routing these various MIDI tracks to some of Reason's virtual synths and sound modules. One of my little musical pastimes involves downloading MIDI files of bands I like from the Internet and remixing them with the Reason synths. I then add new elements to them with REX loops and real-time effects. It's like reinterpreting classic rock tunes and creating a whole new concept around those songs. Believe me, Kate Bush and Depeche Mode never sounded so good!

As luck would have it, Reason 2.5 can also export MIDI files from any opened Reason song. This allows you to import that MIDI file into another program, such as Cubase or SONAR. These MIDI tracks can then be routed to either hardware or software synths for further remixing or so you can record a few tracks of audio.

Let's go over how to export a Reason song as a MIDI file. Open the Tutorial Song, which is located in the Reason folder (see Figure 18.12) and then follow these steps.

1. Find the end marker, which is located to the far right of your Reason song. Click and drag the end marker to the end of your Reason song. By doing this, Reason will export just your song and not a lot of empty measures (see Figure 18.13).

2. Select File > Export MIDI File.

Figure 18.12
Open the Tutorial Song in the Reason program folder.

Figure 18.13
Find the end marker and drag it to the left, so Reason will just export the measures with active MIDI data on them, rather than a bunch of empty measures.

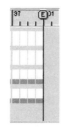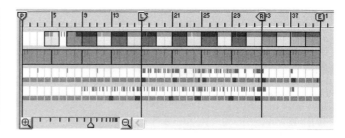

3. Reason will then ask you to name your MIDI file and where you would like to place it. As shown in Figure 18.14, this example keeps the original name and saves the file to the desktop, where it can be located quickly. Click Save. After you quit Reason, you should see the Tutorial Song MIDI file on your desktop (see Figure 18.15).

4. At this point, you can save it onto a floppy drive and pass it to your friend, but let's suppose that you have another audio/MIDI program on your computer, such as Cubase SX. Open that program so you can see what the Reason MIDI file looks like.

5. Import the MIDI file into your audio/MIDI program and you will see all four tracks of the Tutorial Song displayed as MIDI information (see Figure 18.16). Notice that all of the MIDI tracks still have their original names and that each track is set to MIDI channel 1. Because Reason's sequencer is not channel-dependent like a traditional MIDI sequencer, it sets each MIDI track to channel 1. This is easily correctable in any MIDI sequencing software.

Figure 18.14
Select the name and location for your exported MIDI file.

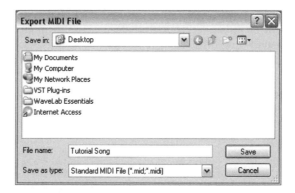

Figure 18.15
The MIDI file is now available on the desktop to import to another MIDI sequencing program.

Figure 18.16

The Tutorial Song imported into Cubase SX. Notice that all of the MIDI tracks still have the same names as they did in Reason. Notice that the first MIDI track is set to MIDI channel 1. All of the other tracks will be set to MIDI channel 1 as well.

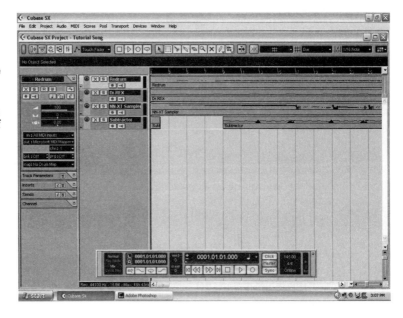

Publishing a Reason Song

Reason's publishing function is a unique idea, because it creates a special Reason song file that can be opened on any computer that has Reason 2.5 installed. Although that might not sound all that exciting at first, the publish song function has a couple of aces up its sleeve.

1. Aside from ReFills (read the "Got ReFill?" note later in this chapter), a published song can be made self-contained. All extra samples and custom presets can be saved within a published song so that they can be opened and heard from any computer with Reason 2.5 installed.

2. Published songs are semi-copyright safe. If a user opens a published song, that song cannot be saved with a different filename, nor can a user make saved changes to a published song. However, a user can export a published song as an audio file.

HOW TO TELL THE DIFFERENCE

Look in your Reason program folder and find the Demo Songs folder. Open this folder and you will see several demo songs that have been prepared by other Reason users.

First, notice that the filename is followed by an .rps extension (Reason Published Song), as opposed to the standard .rns file extension found on new Reason songs that you create and save. This is the first indication that these song files are published songs.

Next, open any of the demo songs and look at the File pull-down menu. As you can see in Figure 18.17, there is no way of saving this published song. That's the second clue that this is a published song.

Figure 18.17
Published Reason songs
cannot be saved, as
indicated by the Save
options being grayed out.

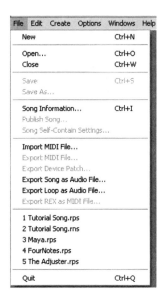

One thing I love about the publish feature 5 is that I can export my song as a self-contained song. This simply means that any extra samples, patches, or REX files will be compressed and saved within the song file. That way, any user who opens my published song will be able to listen to it the way I intended it to be heard.

Let's look at how to make a song self-contained. To follow along with this tutorial, you need one of the REX files I have prepared and made available at the Course Technology site (**www.courseptr.com**). Locate the REX Loops for Chapter 18 folder, download the folder, and place it on your computer's desktop so you will be able to easily locate it.

1. Open the Reason Tutorial Song.

2. Scroll to the bottom of the Device Rack and create a Dr:rex Loop Player (see Figure 18.18).

3. Navigate to the folder icon of Dr:rex to open the browser window.

4. Find your way to the computer desktop. You should see the REX Files folder. Double-click on it to open it, and you'll then be in the REX Loops for Chapter 18 folder (see Figure 18.19).

Figure 18.18
Creating a Dr:rex Loop
Player.

Figure 18.19
Find the demo REX file
folder. Double-click any
of the REX files to load it
into Dr:rex.

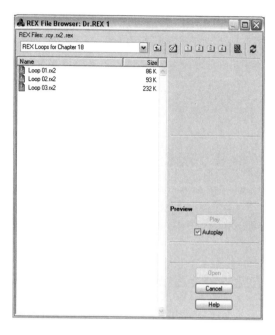

5. Open any REX file to load it into Dr:rex, as shown in Figure 18.20.

6. Click on the To Track button in Dr:rex to place the REX file MIDI notes onto the
    Reason sequencer (see Figure 18.21).

7. Choose File > Song Self-Contain Settings. This will open up the customizable
    settings window so you can specify which files will be included in the published
    Reason song.

8. Look at Figure 18.22 and notice how many files are listed. Included are all of the
    samples that have been loaded into the NN-XT sampler, Redrum, and Dr:rex. Also
    notice that almost all of these samples have lock symbols next to them, signifying
    that they are included from various ReFills. These locked files will not be included
    in your published song. See the note entitled "Got ReFill?" for more information.

Figure 18.20
The REX file is now
loaded into Dr:rex and is
ready to be used in this
tutorial.

Figure 18.21
Click on the To Track
button and the REX MIDI
notes will be placed in
the Reason sequencer.

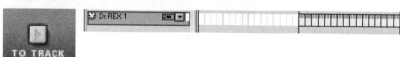

Figure 18.22
The Song Self-Contain Settings window lists all of the samples and REX loops used in a song.

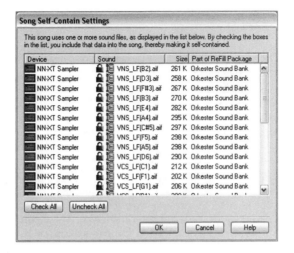

9.   Scroll all the way to the bottom of this list and you will see the only sample that doesn't have a lock symbol next to it is the REX file that you just imported into your Reason song (see Figure 18.23). In place of the lock is a check box. This means that you can include this REX file when publishing your Reason song.

10.   Click on the check box to include the REX file to make your song self-contained. Click OK to continue (see Figure 18.24).

11.   Navigate to the File pull-down menu again and choose Publish Song. You can now rename the song and save it to any location you want. For this tutorial, save the published song to the desktop so it is easy to locate. Click Save and quit Reason.

12.   On your desktop, you should now see the published song file. If you like, you can burn it to a CD and open it on another computer with Reason 2.5 installed. The song should load just fine.

Figure 18.23
The REX file you just imported can be included in the publishing function, because it has a blank check box next to its name.

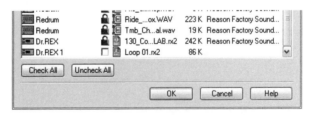

Figure 18.24
Click the check box next to the REX filename and click OK to include it in the publish function.

GOT REFILL?

As previously stated, a published song that is self-contained comes complete with all extra samples and custom presets, making it a great way to pass your composition along to a friend or community.

There is one exception to this rule, and that is when a user creates a song using ReFills. As you have read many times throughout this book, a ReFill is a compilation of sounds and presets created exclusively for use in Reason. When you create and publish your song using the ReFills that come with Reason 2.5, other users will be able to open that published song without a problem, because both you and they own the same ReFill collections.

But what happens when you create a song using a different ReFill collection? Take a trip to the Propellerhead website, and find the link on the front page that's called Reason ReFill. This link will take you to a page that contains all of the known available ReFills, both free and commercial. At last count, there were over 80 available ReFills. That's a lot of sounds and loops, folks!

So, let's say that you have created a song using the "Skip To My Loops" ReFill by AMG and published that song in Reason. Any users who download that published song will also need to have the same ReFill installed on their computers in order to listen to the song as you intended.

To demonstrate my point, I have created a song that uses a ReFill collection called "King Tone Grooves," which can be found at **www.reasonrefills.com**. I then published this song and placed it on a Macintosh computer that has Reason 2.5 installed but does not have the "King Tone Grooves" ReFill available on it. As you can see in Figure 18.25, Reason tries to locate the REX files that I used in my published song, but cannot find them because they are not installed on my Mac.

To conclude, if you are planning to publish your Reason songs to be heard by your soon-to-be adoring fans, just remember that you should try to use samples and REX loops from commonly used ReFill collections, so others can appreciate your eclectic vision.

Figure 18.25
When I try to open the published Reason song on my Mac, I get an error message stating that it cannot find the REX loops used in this song. Reason will then open the song, but the Dr:rex will display that the loop is missing.

GET HEARD NOW!

The Propellerhead website is a fantastic portal to post your published song. Literally hundreds of users a day visit the Propellerhead website to listen to the latest creations and audio innovations of the electronic scene, so why not be a part of the team?

You will need to register your copy of Reason at **www.propellerheads.se** to obtain a username and password. Once you do, you can upload your Reason songs to their server and, with a little luck, you're on your way to creating your own online fan base!

Getting Your Music to CD

At this point, you should now have exported your mix to an audio file, and it is sitting on your computer, waiting for the next step. That step is getting your music onto a CD to play in your car stereo or impress your buddies!

In order to do this, you need the following items:

> ▶ **A CD burner**—If you are using a newer Mac or PC, you should already have one installed and ready to use in your computer. If not, just take a quick trip to your local computer shop and pick one up. With today's prices, you should be able to find a good internal or external CD burner for around $50-150.

> ▶ **Blank CDs**—Six or seven years ago, blank CDs were expensive, usually around $2-3 each. That might not sound like much, but once you start burning 10 to 15 CDs a week, that's a lot of scratch! Thankfully, blank CDs have become very affordable these days. Look in your local newspaper ads for Best Buy or Comp USA and you can be sure to find outrageously priced blank CDs in bulk for $10-20 for a spindle of 50 discs. Oh, how sweet it is!

> ▶ **A CD burning program**—If you already own a computer with a CD burner, you can bet that there is already CD burning software of some kind installed. If not, you might want to have a look at such programs as EZ CD Creator or Nero for the PC, or Roxio Toast for the Mac. If you don't have such a program, and don't want to buy one, have a look at the following tip.

WINDOWS AND MAC CAN BURN CDS!

You might be interested to know that both Windows XP and Mac OS X have the capability to burn CDs without the need for an additional program.

Through the rest of this section, I use screen shots from these burning programs, rather than the optional Roxio or Nero software, so you can become more familiar with these little-known wonders in your operating system.

To be fair to Roxio and Nero, I should point out that these programs come with many extra features, such as back-up programs and the capability to create many different types of discs. So, if you do have the means, pick them up. You won't regret it.

THE FOUR FLAVORS OF BLANK MEDIA

When it comes to selecting blank discs, you should be aware of the four types of discs available. It is important to be able to tell the difference, because you might possibly purchase the wrong kind and cost yourself another trip to Wal-Mart.

▶ **CD-R**—This is the standard blank media used to burn music and data CDs. These blank CDs can be burned one time only. This is also called "disc at once." I recommend using this media.

▶ **CD-RW**—This is the next level up from the CD-R. These discs can be burned and erased several times, making them very useful for backing up files on your computer. However, they are almost useless as music CDs, because most home and car stereo systems will not play them.

▶ **DVD-R**—These blank discs are for use with DVD players and burners. They hold incredibly large amounts of data—up to 4GB, in fact. However, as with CD-RWs, these discs are not compatible with most home and car stereo systems.

▶ **DVD-RW**—These blanks are the same as DVD-Rs, but they can be used over and over again, just as with CD-RWs. But they carry the same restrictions as DVD-Rs.

Make sure you have all the parts so you can start to burn, baby, burn!

Burning CDs with Windows XP

You've got to hand it to Microsoft; they take a lot of the guesswork out of burning CDs with Windows XP. By following a few simple steps, you will be burning your CDs in no time.

1. Start by placing a blank CD in your burner and closing it. Once the blank CD starts to spin, Windows will detect it as a blank and will open a window that has a few options, as shown in Figure 18.26.

Figure 18.26
As soon as Windows detects a blank CD, it will give you a few options. Choose Open Writable CD Folder Using Windows Explorer.

2. Choose the Open Writable CD Folder Using Windows Explorer option by clicking it and clicking OK. Windows will create an open window into which you can simply drag your audio files (see Figure 18.27).

3. At this point, it's a simple task of just dragging and dropping the AIFF and WAV files that you want to burn into the open window (see Figure 18.28). This will then create a temporary file on the CD drive, which means that it is ready to be burned to CD.

Figure 18.27
Windows Explorer will open a blank window for your CD burner.

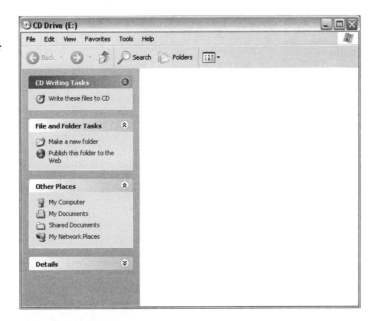

Figure 18.28
Drag and drop any audio files you want to burn to disc into the blank window.

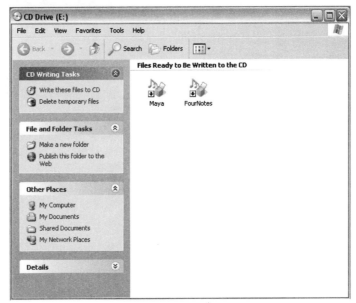

4.   At the left side of the open window is an option called Write These Files to CD (see Figure 18.29). Click on it, and this will start up the CD Writing Wizard.

5.   The CD Writing Wizard (see Figure 18.30) is where you can name your CD, specify whether it is an audio or data CD, and let her rip! Start by typing a name for the CD. Click Next.

6.   Next, specify whether you want to burn an audio CD or a data CD (see Figure 18.31). For this step, choose Make an Audio CD. Click Next.

Figure 18.29
Click on Write These Files to CD to start the burning process.

Figure 18.30
The CD Writing Wizard will guide you through the burning process. Start by typing a name for your CD.

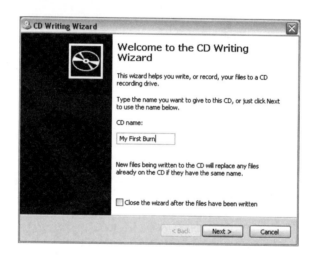

Figure 18.31
Specify whether you want to burn an audio CD or a data CD. For this tutorial, choose Make an Audio CD.

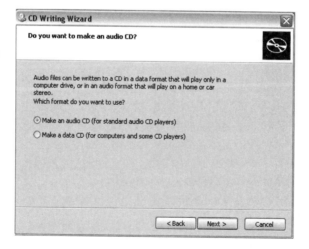

7. Next, the Windows Media Player will launch. Notice in Figure 18.32 that the songs that you want to burn are listed on the left side. This list is known as a *playlist* which is simply a list of songs that can be played or burned in any order you choose. When you have your playlist ready, just click on the Copy Music button located in the upper-right corner.

8. At this point, Windows Media Player will begin to burn your audio CD. This can take anywhere from one minute to 30 minutes, depending on how many songs are being burned (see Figure 18.33).

9. Once this is completed, you can choose to burn another CD by just popping a new blank disc in the CD burner, or just close the Windows Media Player if you are done.

Figure 18.32
The Windows Media Player will now launch. Notice on the left side of the interface that your playlist of audio is ready to be burned. Click the Copy Music button to begin the burning process.

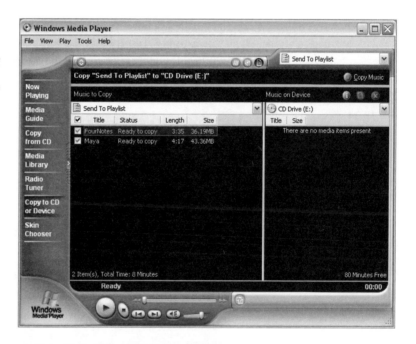

Figure 18.33
The burning process takes a few minutes, depending on how much audio needs to be written.

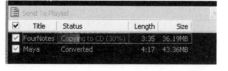

BURNING DATA IN XP

Windows XP can also burn data CDs in a snap. Refer to Figure 18.31 and choose Make a Data CD instead. Click Next. Follow any additional steps. Windows XP will proceed to burn a data CD pronto.

CHAPTER 18

Burning CDs with Mac OS X

With Mac OS X, it simply doesn't get any easier to burn CDs; iTunes is a fantastic program! There are times when I still can't believe it is free.

Follow these steps to burn an audio CD from iTunes:

1. Start by placing a blank CD in your burner and closing it. Once the blank CD starts to spin, OS X will detect it as a blank and will open a window that has a few options that can be selected via pull-down menu, as shown in Figure 18.34. Select Open iTunes and click OK.

2. After clicking OK, iTunes will launch (see Figure 18.35). Once iTunes has launched, it informs you that it has detected a blank CD and gives you a couple of hints on how to burn an audio CD.

3. You will now need to create a playlist. Go to the File pull-down menu and select New Playlist. Once this is done, iTunes will create an untitled playlist on the left side of the iTunes interface. You can click on the playlist and rename at any time (in Figure 18.36, it's been renamed to My First Burn).

Figure 18.34
When you first insert your blank CD, OS X wants to know what kind of CD you are going to create. Select iTunes to create an audio CD.

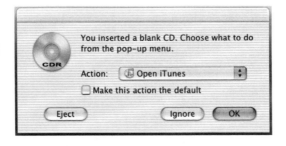

Figure 18.35
The iTunes interface is intuitive and comprehensive.

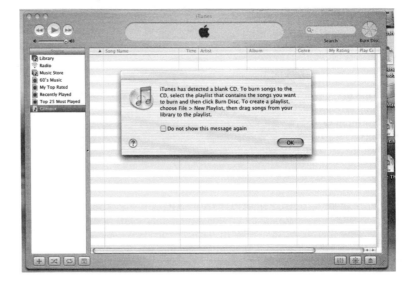

Figure 18.36
Before you can burn a CD, you must create a new playlist.

4.   Now it's time to get iTunes ready to burn a CD. Simply drag and drop the audio files that you want to burn onto your playlist, as shown in Figure 18.37. Once you have done this, you can change the order of songs by dragging the audio files up or down the playlist.

5.   You are now ready to burn your audio CD. Navigate to the top-right corner of the iTunes interface and click on the Burn Disc button (see Figure 18.38). This button will light up and looks a lot like a Caution: Radioactive logo that you see on nuclear reactors.

Figure 18.37
Drag and drop the songs you want to burn to CD.

Figure 18.38
It's time to go radioactive and burn an audio CD in iTunes.

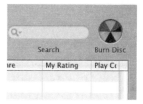

6. Click on the Burn Disc button again, and iTunes will begin to burn a CD. This can take anywhere from 1 to 10 minutes, depending on how much audio is being written.

7. Once the burning process is complete, just quit iTunes and eject the CD.

BURNING DATA IN MAC OS X

OS X can also burn data CDs with ease. Refer back to Figure 18.34. You would select Open Finder from the pull-down menu, and then type a name for the disc. Click on OK and OS X will create a CD-R icon on the desktop. Just drag and drop your files on the CD-R icon and OS X will prep them for burning. Once this is complete, just drag the CD-R icon into the Trash, which will begin the burning process. OS X will ask you at what speed to burn the CD. Select Maximum and let her burn!

BACK IT UP OFTEN

As I have stated many times throughout this book, remember to back up your data. Follow the steps given in these tutorials and make a weekly or bi-weekly habit of backing up important data, such as new Reason songs, ReFills, and other important data.

At this point, you should now have created an audio file from your Reason compositions. From here on, what you do with that capability is up to you. Want to burn a CD for your buddies? Want to make MP3s and upload them to your website? These days, the possibilities for distributing your music are almost endless.

A

The ReBirth of Cool

Believe it or not, Reason is not the first flame of popularity that Propellerhead has lit up in the electronic music community. Long before Reason was even a spark in a haystack, there was ReBirth. ReBirth, on the market in 1997, was, in my opinion, the first *real* virtual synth. Back then, there were numerous attempts to claim that coveted title, such as Reality, Turbosynth, and Generator (later to be Reaktor), but none of them had the versatility, simplicity, and sex appeal of ReBirth (see Figure A.1).

ReBirth is a powerful combination of bass synths and drum machines that look very familiar to connoisseurs of hardware synthesis. They are familiar because the bass synths are physically modeled versions of the very popular Roland TB303 bass synths, and the drum machines are software emulations of the TR808 and TR909 drum machines, all shown in Figure A.2. In the world of electronic music, these three hardware synths were, and still are, among the most sought after, not only due to their classic look, but also because they have a sound that is just *it* for electronic music. Believe me, long before I was a believer in the "virtual studio," I looked high and low for these beauties here in Los Angeles, and if I was ever lucky enough to find one, it would be priced at $1000 or more. So, when I saw ReBirth, I was amazed at how great it sounded at such an affordable price ($199). And this was when it was just version 1.0!

Figure A.1
ReBirth's sleek interface and killer sounds turn any computer into a techno groove box.

Figure A.2
The coveted TB303,
TR808, and TR909 have
their place set in
synthesizer history.

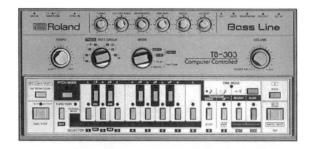

How Does It Work?

ReBirth operates in a fashion similar to the vintage synths that it emulates, as it is not a typical MIDI-triggered synth. ReBirth's sequencer is based entirely on programmed patterns. Each synth module and drum machine in ReBirth contains a pattern sequencer. Each sequencer contains four banks with eight patterns within each bank, giving 32 patterns per synth that can be used in a song. Notice how similar this is to Reason. Although these patterns are programmed in step by step, the process of writing patterns with the bass synths are much different than they are with the drum machines, so let's take a quick look.

Step-Programming the Bass Synths

The bass synths are programmed in a step fashion, which is a little tedious but gives you great control. As shown in Figure A.3, to the far left of the first bass synth, you must first specify the number of 16th note steps within a given pattern. By default, ReBirth assigns 16 steps to all of the machines, which is good for use in four-four time. Although a little tricky, other time signatures can be created by changing the number of steps, but this example sticks with 16 steps for now.

To the right of the bass synth is the step programmer, as shown in Figure A.4. In this section, you must program each step, one at a time, by using either your mouse or your computer keyboard. Some of the available parameters that are at your disposal include step rests, accents, and slides. Slides in particular are one of my favorites to use, because they make it easy to combine two 16th notes in order to create one 8th note.

After programming a single pattern, you can program seven more patterns for just one bank. After that, you have another 24 patterns to create if you want.

Figure A.3
How many 16th notes do you need? ReBirth will provide.

Figure A.4
Step programming in ReBirth is a little tedious at first, but you can learn to use your computer keyboard to quickly program the TB303 synth.

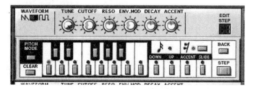

Step-Programming the Drum Machines

The drum machines are a little easier to program. Click on Play and watch either of the drum machines, as the step position runs through its pattern, just like an old control voltage sequencer. Although these two drum machines have the same basic programming principles behind them, there are distinct differences between them.

▶ The 808 drum machine contains 16 step pads, just like the 909. However, the way you choose the sounds played per step is a bit different. With the 809, you must first select the drum sound that you want from the selection wheel, which is found to the far right side of the 808 module (see Figure A.5). Simply use your mouse to click and drag until you find the drum sound you want. If this is your first time, try the bass drum, or "BD." Now, to the left of the sound selection, click with your mouse where you want the bass drum to play within the 16-step pattern. Once you have done this, click on Play and you'll see your rhythm in action. Repeat this with all of the other sounds until you have created a full-on rhythm section.

▶ Selecting different sounds in the 909-drum machine is different, but also very simple. Just locate the sound that you want and click on it to begin programming a pattern for it (see Figure A.6).

Figure A.5
The TR808 drum module is simple to program and sounds just like the real thing.

Figure A.6
The TR909 drum module has a few extra tricks up its sleeve, like the capability to create a rhythmic flam effect.

But Wait . . . There's More!

ReBirth also contains a few extras that will help liven up the mix. Effects from filters to delays will brighten up any techno masterpiece.

▶ The distortion (see Figure A.7) ranges from "subtle" to "down and digitally dirty" in a heartbeat. Included in this effect are an Amount knob and a Shape knob. They change the amount and characteristics of the distortion drastically. Additionally, the distortion can be assigned to more than one synth or drum machine.

▶ The compressor (see Figure A.8) can be used to help the dynamics of an entire mix or just fix a single synth or drum machine. It includes a Ratio knob and a Threshold knob to shape your compression curve.

▶ The delay (see Figure A.9) is a simple yet effective addition to help make your tracks a bit more "ambient." It is automatically synchronized via the ReBirth master tempo and can be used either in straight notes or triplets for that good old swing feel.

▶ The PCF, or pattern controlled filter, was added to version 1.5 in 1998. As shown in Figure A.10, it can be used as a low pass or band pass filter and has 54 possible pattern combinations. As with the delay, the PCF tempo syncs like a champ. The only downside is that only one of ReBirth's synths or drum machines can be assigned to it.

Figure A.7
ReBirth's distortion effect can give you that Nine Inch Nails sound you've been looking for.

Figure A.8

The compressor can be used on just a single instrument, or the entire mix.

Figure A.9

Adding a little delay to your bass and/or drums is the key to ambience.

Figure A.10

The pattern controlled filter, or PCF, can give your drum and bass loops a creative edge.

Getting New Drum Sounds

In 1998, Propellerhead added a new feature to ReBirth called *Mods*, short for modifications. These modifications included alterations to the graphic interface of ReBirth and new drum sounds for the two drum machines. These new features took off like a rocket, and before you knew it, fans and users were creating Mods for ReBirth, such as the "Pitch Black Mod," shown in Figure A.11. Of these different Mods (there are 56 available on the Propellerhead website), ReBirth includes four with the program. The rest can be downloaded free and used at will.

Figure A.11

The Pitch Black Mod comes on the ReBirth 2.0 CD-ROM.

And here's the icing on the cake folks—included on the ReBirth CD is a program called Mod Packer. It allows you to create your own Mods. If you have any old drum machines that you want to breathe new life into, you can sample them and create a whole new Mod on your own. Once you have finished it, you can submit it to Propellerhead Software to see if they will post it on their site for others to enjoy. Isn't that cool?

Hold the Phone! Isn't This Book about Reason?

Indeed, this book is about Reason, but it's also about the technologies that allow Reason to work with other programs and technologies, of which ReBirth is a prime example.

If you recall in Chapter 17, "ReWire," ReBirth was the first program to contain the ReWire technology and it was used very heavily by the Cubase community, because Cubase was the first major host software to support it. Thankfully, Reason was ReWire-ready the moment it was released in 2000. However, ReBirth and Reason work together via ReWire a little differently than the other host applications covered in Chapter 17. That said, I am going to take you through a ReWire tutorial involving ReBirth and Reason. Ready? Set? Let's go!

1. Chapter 17 discussed the difference between a ReWire master and a ReWire slave. In this ReBirth/Reason scenario, Reason is the master and ReBirth is the slave. So, first start Reason with an empty Device Rack and create a reMix device (see Figure A.12).

2. Next, navigate to the Create pull-down menu and select ReBirth Input Machine. The input machine will then appear below reMix, as shown in Figure A.13.

Figure A.12
Start with an empty Device Rack and create a reMix device.

Figure A.13
Create a ReBirth input machine and it will automatically be routed to channel 1 in reMix.

3. Launch ReBirth.

4. Click on Play on either ReBirth or Reason; they should now be in perfect sync. You can switch between programs to see for yourself.

5. On the reMix interface in Figure A.14, you'll see that the signal from ReBirth has been routed into channel 1. Press the Tab key to swing the Device Rack around and you will see the different audio routing possibilities with it. Have a go at routing different ReBirth sounds into different channels.

6. If you are ready to quit Reason and ReBirth, you must first close the slave program—in this case ReBirth. Then close Reason afterward.

Figure A.14
Every sound in ReBirth can be routed to its own reMix channel.

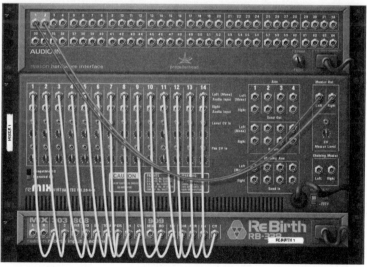

I'm sure once you use it, you'll find that ReBirth has a lot of bells and whistles that will light up any techno tune. For more information on ReBirth, visit your local music store, or just check out the Propellerhead website at **www.propellerheads.se.** From there, you can download a free demo version of the software.

B

ReCycle! 2.0

When it comes to using tempo-based audio loops in music composition, one of the bigger challenges is using the loops in songs of different tempos. Before ReCycle! was available, there were only two ways to do this:

1. Map the loop across a set of keys on a hardware sampler and mathematically determine the tempos.

2. Compress or stretch the audio loops to fit your tempo in a program such as Pro Tools or Cubase Audio.

In either process, you ran the risk of losing audio quality from the loop, and, what's worse, the pitch of the processed audio loop would be higher or lower than the pitch of the original.

Released in 1994, Propellerhead ReCycle! solved this problem by providing an original take on making audio loops fit into different tempos (see Figure B.1).

Figure B.1
The ReCycle! 2.0
graphical interface.

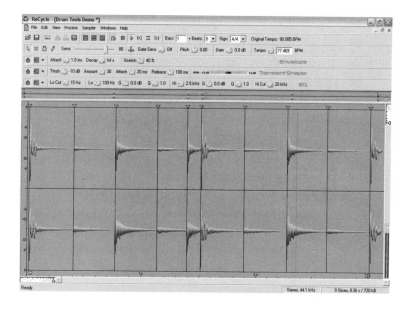

Slice and Dice

ReCycle! uses a unique editing process of virtually "slicing" an audio loop in places it determines by use of a sensitivity slider. Once this process is finished, ReCycle! can finish the job by performing one of two additional tasks:

1. Transmitting the slices to a hardware sampler by way of SCSI or MIDI.

2. Exporting the slices in a different audio format called REX2 (ReCycle! EXclusive).

The REX2 file is a proprietary format created by Propellerhead Software and is supported by many software applications, such as Reason, Cubase SX/SL, and Logic Audio. Essentially, a REX2 file is a series of slices created by ReCycle!. These slices are transmitted as one audio file that is then imported into software that supports the REX2 format. Once the REX2 file has been imported into a program, it can be used at virtually any tempo by simply adjusting the individual slices to conform to the new tempo.

In musical terms, if you have a drum loop set at 110 BPM and you want to use it in a song that is 120 BPM, you can import that loop into ReCycle!, create a REX2 file from it, and import it into your song. Additionally, if you want to change the tempo in your song at a later date, the REX2 file will adjust accordingly to fit that tempo.

Roll Yer Own REX2 Files

Creating your own REX2 files for Reason is less of a challenge than you might think. In this section, I have created a step-by-step tutorial that covers:

▶ Importing an audio loop into ReCycle!

▶ Slicing up the audio loop

▶ Editing the loop with ReCycle! effects

▶ Exporting the loop as a REX2 file

▶ Importing the REX2 file into Reason using Dr:rex

Let's get REXing!

1. Start by clicking on the Folder icon located at the top-left side of the ReCycle! interface, or select File > Open. This will open the Open Sound File dialog (see Figure B.2).

2. Look at the different file types that ReCycle! can open. All of the standard formats are here, such as WAV and AIFF, but there is also the option to open up REX (mono) and REX2 (stereo) files as well. Also notice that there is an Auto Play check box at the bottom-right side of the window so you can automatically listen to your audio files before importing them. Browse to the ReCycle folder and open the file named "Drum Tools Demo."

3. As the selected audio file opens, ReCycle! will ask "Do you want to move the left locator to the first slice point?," as shown in Figure B.3. Click on Yes, and ReCycle! will automatically move the left locator to the first slice point, which is located at the beginning of the loop.

Figure B.2
Use the file browser to locate your audio file for ReCycle!

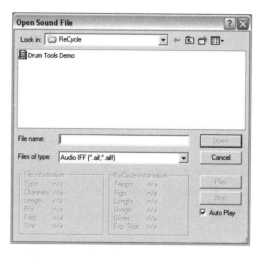

Figure B.3
Click Yes to have ReCycle! automatically move the left locator to the first slice point.

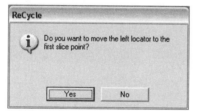

4. ReCycle! will then inform you that you will not be able to hear any effects until you activate the Preview Toggle button (see Figure B.4). As you'll learn about this later, just click OK for now. The audio file will open and is ready to be ReCycled.

5. Press the spacebar to play the loop, and ReCycle! will proceed to play it over and over again. If you are using the "Drum Tools Demo" file, you will certainly hear the extra beat that has been purposely thrown in to show you how to use the ReCycle! looping power. Notice the left and right locators, which are similar to those in Reason's sequencer (see Figure B.5).

6. At the top of the ReCycle! interface is the sensitivity slider, which is used to assign slices to the audio loop (see Figure B.6). With your mouse, click and drag the slider to the right until it reaches 80. Look at your audio loop and you will now see 10 separate audio slices (see Figure B.7). If you want to hear each slice individually, just click on them (see Figure B.8).

Figure B.4
ReCycle! will inform you that you cannot use the effects until the Preview Toggle button is activated. Click OK to continue.

Figure B.5
The ReCycle! graphical interface before slicing.

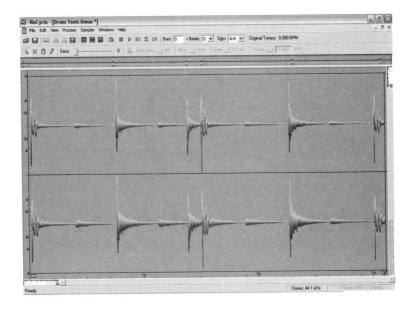

Figure B.6
The sensitivity slider assigns slices to the audio loop.

Figure B.7
ReCycle! has now sliced the audio loop.

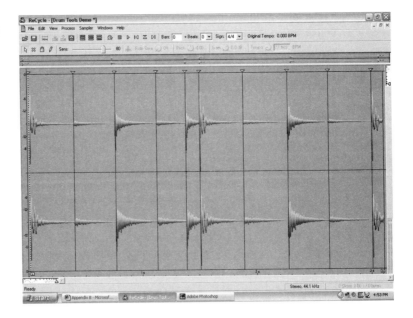

Figure B.8
Click on any slice to
preview it.

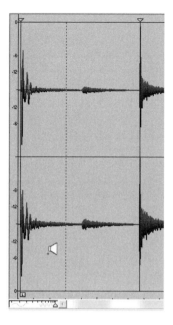

7. If you play the loop again, you will still hear the extra beat, which throws off the entire loop. To correct this, you must click and drag the right locator to the 10th slice, as shown in Figure B.9. Click on Play again and this time the loop should sound just fine.

Figure B.9
Click and drag the right
locator one slice to the
left to correct the timing
problem.

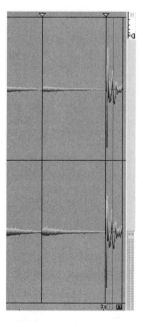

Now that the slices have been created, you are ready to push on and work with the ReCycle! effects. Follow these steps to do so:

1. You must first assign a numeric amount of bars to this loop. Because this tutorial uses the "Drum Tools Demo" file, this is a one-bar loop. Navigate to the upper portion of the ReCycle! interface, where you will find the Bars/Beats/Time Sign toolbar (see Figure B.10). Select the Bars box and enter 1. This will tell ReCycle! that this audio loop is one bar long. Also notice that ReCycle! has automatically assigned a tempo of 80.085 BPM (beats per measure) to this loop.

Figure B.10
The Bars/Beats/Time Sign toolbar is where you assign the number of bars to an audio loop.

2. To the left of the transport controls you will find the Preview Toggle button (see Figure B.11). Click on it once to activate it.

Figure B.11
Click on the Preview Toggle button to allow access to the internal real-time effects or preview your loop at different tempos.

3. After activating the Preview Toggle button, you now have access to the ReCycle! effects, as well as other various parameters to edit your loop. If you want to play back the audio loop at a different tempo, click and drag the Tempo knob (see Figure B.12) up or down.

Figure B.12
Use the Tempo knob to preview the ReCycle loop at a different tempo.

4. To the left of the ReCycle! transport controls is the toolbar containing the real-time effects (see Figure B.13). Click on all three buttons to load the effects into the ReCycle! interface (see Figure B.14).

Figure B.13
Activate the ReCycle! real-time effects to load them into the graphical interface.

Figure B.14
Turn on the real-time
effects by clicking on
their buttons. Now select
a preset from the pull-
down menu.

5. Activate the Envelope effect by clicking on its button, located to the far left of the interface, and then select one of its presets, located just to the right of the button. A good one to try is the "Fake Backwards" preset, which creates a reverse effect on the slices by using a combination of Attack and Decay.

6. If you like, you can edit these parameters more to your liking or just activate the other effects, such as the Transient Shaper (or compression) or the EQ (equalizer).

At this point, you can export your audio loop as a REX2 file and import it into Dr:rex in a couple of clicks.

BEFORE YOU EXPORT

Before you export your audio loop, make sure that you return the tempo to its original setting. In the case of the "Drum Tools Demo" file, the tempo is 80.085 BPM. Otherwise, ReCycle! will export the audio loop as a REX2 file with a default tempo of whatever the Tempo box reads.

1. Select Save As from the File pull-down menu.

2. Select a place to save your REX2 file, and give it a descriptive name (see Figure B.15).

Figure B.15
After you have sliced up
your audio loop, save it
as a REX2 file.

3. Click the Save button. The audio loop will be saved as a REX2 file.

4. Start Reason and load a Dr:rex loop player (see Figure B.16).

5. Click on the Folder icon of Dr:rex to locate a REX2 file to import.

6. Locate your new REX2 file and import it into Dr:rex (see Figure B.17).

Figure B.16
Start Reason and load a
Dr:rex.

Figure B.17
Load your new REX2 file
into Dr:rex.

GET THE DEMO

If you don't own ReCycle!, a demo version is available at the Propellerhead website. Go to **www.propellerheads.se**, find the ReCycle! page, click on Try It!, and you will be taken to a link to download the demo version.

The demo version is fully-functional, so you can save and export your created REX files to Reason. The only limitation in this demo version is that you can work with only one of the four provided audio loops. Nevertheless, it should give you a good idea of the potential of this fantastic program!

Although this appendix is quite brief, I'm sure that you "loop addicts" can see the potential that a program such as ReCycle! can offer. Contact your local music software shop or just visit **www.propellerheads.se** for more information about purchasing ReCycle! or seeing a demo.

APPENDIX B

C

ReFills

There is a well-known saying that "too much is never enough." Although this saying can be applied to many life situations, it fits the modern electronic musician like a glove. In a digital world of samples, loops, and patches, creative electronic musicians are always on the prowl for more goodies to add to their stash. Although many wonderful and creative samples and patches come with Reason, an experienced user will always clamor for more and more content. To meet this demand, I give you *ReFills!*

ReFills are compilations of samples, loops, and patches created specifically for use in Reason. Although files of many formats can be used to create a ReFill, such as WAV, AIFF, REX, and patch files, a ReFill is accessed as one single file of a particular type. This is similar to the idea behind an archived file, such as a ZIP or SIT file. Throughout this book, I have mentioned ReFills many times. This appendix sheds more light on what they are, how they work, and, most importantly, how to make your own ReFills.

FREEBIES

In the ReFill section of the Propellerhead website, you'll find a complete list of available ReFills you can use with Reason. At the time of this writing, I counted well over 80 ReFill titles offering a variety of styles and content. Some titles are dedicated to the NN-XT and NN-19 samplers, whereas others are dedicated to the Subtractor and Malström synths. Sometimes, you can get lucky and find a fully loaded ReFill that has patches and presets for all of the different Reason devices, including Redrum patches and REX files.

The best part of all is that a lot of these ReFills are free downloads from the web. It's great to see enthusiastic users creating products like this free of charge to keep fueling the flames of creativity.

Of course, there are also many commercially available ReFill titles, and these are great too. AMG in particular has a lot of ReFill titles, including loops created by the likes of Norman Cook (a.k.a. Fatboy Slim) and Vince Clarke (Erasure, Yazoo, Depeche Mode). Not to worry, though, because these ReFill titles are competitively priced and won't put a huge dent in your wallet.

ReFill Ingredients

This section analyzes a typical ReFill and explains the different samples and presets included.

▶ REX files

▶ Redrum patches and files

▶ NN-XT and NN-19 patches and files

▶. Malström and Subtractor patches

▶ Real-time effects patches

REX Files

As you read in Appendix B, "ReCycle! 2.0," a REX file is a digital audio file format created by another Propellerhead Software title called ReCycle!. This program imports an AIFF or WAV file, slices it up, and saves the slices in an individual file. Once imported into a program that supports the REX format, that REX file can then be used at different tempos.

On the surface, it might appear that Dr:rex is the only device that supports the REX format, but this is not true. Redrum, NN-19, and NN-XT all support the REX format in their own unique ways. Although they are mentioned throughout this book, let's take a moment to recap and review.

As you may remember from the previous chapters and appendixes, there are several different versions of the REX file (i.e., REX, REX2, RCY), but to keep things simple, I will just use REX for the remainder of this appendix.

Redrum Your REX

The REX file support in Redrum is especially unique and interesting, because it differs greatly from Dr:rex, NN-19, and the NN-XT. Instead of importing an entire REX file as these other devices do, Redrum can import individual REX slices (see Figure C.1). This opens the door to interesting combinations of sounds and styles. On channel 1, you could load up a kick drum REX slice from a techno styled REX file, and then you could import a snare REX slice from an acoustic-styled REX file. The combinations are endless.

NN-19 and NN-XT

Both of these virtual samplers can import entire REX files and map them across their virtual keyboards, as shown in Figure C.2. Although the parameters of the NN-19 might appear to be quite similar to those found on Dr:rex, there are a few tricks and treats that clearly set the two devices apart. For starters, the Spread knob found at the upper-left corner of the NN-19 can create a cool auto pan effect, where the REX slices will randomly pan from left to right in the stereo field. The NN-19 envelope, which sounds great, also contains an additional Invert knob, which is used to invert the effect of the envelope. These are just a couple of differences, but you get the picture.

The NN-XT is the sampler's sampler when it comes to handling REX files. Aside from the individual parameters, the NN-XT can assign REX slices to any of its 16 individual outputs (see Figure C.3). Imagine the routing possibilities.

Figure C.1
Redrum can import
individual REX slices
into each of its 10
channels.

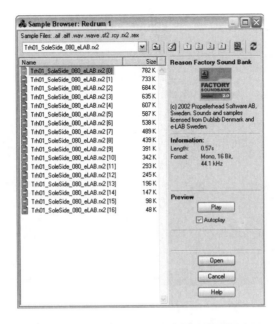

Figure C.2
The NN-19 and NN-XT
can both import REX
files.

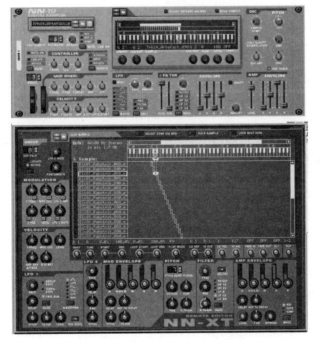

Figure C.3
The NN-XT has 16 individual outputs. By using the NN-XT interface, you can assign each REX slice to its own output.

Redrum Patches

When it comes to drum samples, they are pretty much a dime a dozen in my book. Just type the phrase "Drum Samples" in your local Yahoo search engine and you'll see thousands of web pages that contain freeware and shareware samples to download—not to mention the amount of commercially available drum samples you'll find at your local music shop.

So, once you have all of these drum samples, how are you going to use them? In Reason, Redrum is your best friend for tackling this challenge. Redrum can import many sample file formats, including:

▶ AIFF

▶ WAV

▶ Sound Fonts or SF2

▶ REX files

Once you select and import your various samples, you can then save your patch by clicking on the Save button on the Redrum interface and creating a .DRP file.

NN-19 and NN-XT Patches

Although Reason 2.5 comes complete with a huge sample library, I own other sample libraries that I prefer to use on occasion. Both the NN-19 and NN-XT samplers can import various file formats and then save as individual patches.

RELOAD YOUR SAMPLES

At your local music shop, you can be sure to find a library of samples CDs that will give the Smithsonian a run for its money. Think of any kind of instrument that you want, and you'll be sure to find it on a sample CD. In addition, these sample libraries are formatted for popular hardware samplers, such as Roland, EMU, and the everlasting Akai. The question then becomes how to get these different sample formats into Reason.

Propellerhead wanted to make it possible for Reason users to take advantage of these sample libraries, so they created and released Reload (see Figure C.4). This utility converts Akai formatted samples to the NN-XT format. It will also convert the Akai patch, which contains the sample mapping and individual parameters of the samples, over to the NN-XT patch format. Reload will even go one step further and convert the Akai samples and patches and create a custom ReFill as well.

For more information on Reload, be sure to see Chapter 12, "NN-XT—Close Up."

Figure C.4
Reload expands your sample library by converting Akai formatted samples to the NN-XT format.

Malström and Subtractor Patches

If you are a tweak-head like me, you have probably started to accumulate your collection of patches for Malström and Subtractor. These patches are essential to any good ReFill collection. In the ReFill area of the Propellerhead website (**www.propellerheads.se**), you'll be sure to find ReFill collections that are built primarily for these two synths, such as the "Linkpage" ReFill or the "1001 Subtractor Patches" ReFill.

Real-Time Effect Patches

A ReFill can also include patches for the advanced real-time effects of Reason 2.5. There are already quite a few included in the "In Full Effect" ReFill. These patches are used with the RV7000 Advanced Reverb and the Scream 4 Distortion.

Using ReFills with Reason 2.5

Thankfully, using a ReFill collection within Reason 2.5 is very easy. This section goes through the steps to install a ReFill and shows you how to use it in Reason. Visit the Propellerhead website and download a free ReFill so you can follow along with this tutorial.

Downloading and Installing a ReFill

For the sake of simplicity, download a small ReFill from the Propellerhead website, such as the "Zuwonga Patch Bonanza," which has patches made for the Subtractor and NN-XT or NN-19 samplers. All of the ReFill titles you find on the Propellerhead web page are compressed using the ZIP format. Once you have downloaded the ZIP file, decompress it and place it in the Reason 2.5 program folder. If you're not sure where that is, let's review:

▶ On Windows, you will find it in the Program Files > Propellerhead Software > Reason 2.5 folder.

▶ On the Macintosh, you will find it in the Applications folder.

Once you have placed the downloaded ReFill in the Reason folder, you should now see a total of four ReFills in this folder (see Figure C.5).

▶ Reason Factory Sound Bank.

▶ Orkester Sound Bank.

▶ In Full Effect Sound Bank. (Note that if you installed Reason 2.5 using the original 2.5 CD set, you will only see the Reason Factory Sound Bank and the Orkester Sound Bank. The In Full Effect Sound Bank patches are found in the Reason Factory Sound Bank.)

▶ The new ReFill title you just downloaded, decompressed, and installed. In this example, it is the Zuwonga Patch Bonanza ReFill.

Figure C.5
There are now four ReFills in the Reason program folder.

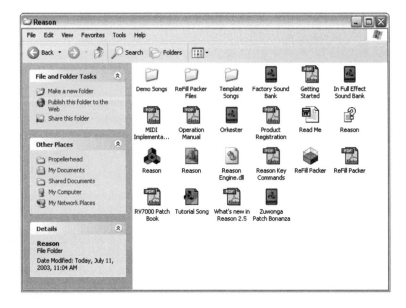

GOT STUFF-IT?

PC users who are running Reason under a pre-Windows XP operating system might encounter some trouble decompressing these ZIP files and installing them into their Reason program folder. The same can be said for Mac owners using OS X. Here's the solution.

OS X Macintosh users will need to use a utility program called Stuff-It Expander. This utility decompresses archived files with the ZIP or SIT extension (for example, refill.ZIP or refill.SIT). Take a quick trip to the Stuff-It website (**www.stuffit.com**), where you can download a trial version for free.

For Windows users, a popular and well-known application called WinZip will be the answer for you. It can be found at **www.winzip.com**.

Of course, should you already be working on Windows XP, you should not need to do this as Windows XP has its own decompression utility built into the OS.

Using the ReFill

Now that you have downloaded and installed your ReFill, it's time to learn how to access it and unleash the patches and loops.

Figure C.6 shows that I have created a new song and loaded a Subtractor, which is set to its default patch. At this point, click on the folder icon. The Patch Browser window will appear (see Figure C.7). Click on the Find All ReFills button at the top-right corner of the Patch Browser window. This will rescan your computer for any installed ReFills within the Reason program folder, or your CD-ROM drive. After you click on the Find All ReFills button, the new ReFill that you installed will be listed, as shown in Figure C.8.

Figure C.6
Create a new Reason song and create a reMix device and Subtractor as well.

Figure C.7
The Reason Patch
Browser is used to locate
and load patches and
audio files to any Reason
device.

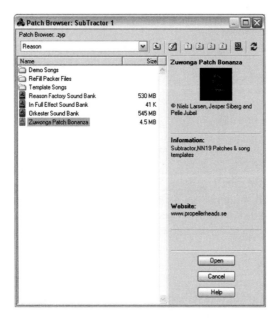

Figure C.8
The new ReFill is now
listed and available to
use.

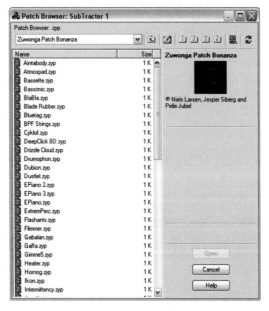

If the new ReFill does not show up, just click on the Re-scan Files button, which is located to the right of the Find All ReFills button (see Figure C.9). This will re-scan your Reason program folder and CD-ROM drive.

At this point, you should now be able to access the new ReFill by double-clicking on it and opening a patch for the Subtractor. Because this ReFill contains samples for the NN-19 and NN-XT, you can access those as well.

Figure C.9
The Re-scan Files button acts as a refresh button.

Sound Locations

At some point, you will probably want to move your soon-to-be-growing sample collection to a bigger hard drive to save space. If this is the case, Reason has a perfect solution called *Sound Locations* (see Figure C.10). These are savable presets that contain references to files that can be used within Reason. Say, for instance, that you have a collection of REX or AIFF/WAV files that you like to use. You can specify where these files are and save their location as a Sound Location. Then, when you use the Patch Browser in the future, you can navigate to these Sound Locations by just clicking on one of the four location buttons at the top. It's an excellent timesaver, which is so important when you are trying to channel creativity!

Figure C.10
Sound Locations give you easy access to your files.

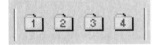

Let's step through an example of working with Sound Locations.

1. Assume that you have a folder of REX files that you would like to set as a Sound Location. Make sure they are all in one folder and place them somewhere on your computer, such as another hard drive, as shown in Figure C.11.

2. Next, navigate to the Edit pull-down menu in Reason and choose Preferences. This will launch the Preferences window (see Figure C.12).

Figure C.11
For this example, I moved a folder of REX files over to my other hard drive.

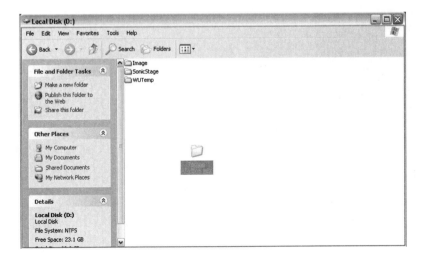

Figure C.12
Choose Edit >
Preferences to open the
Preferences window.

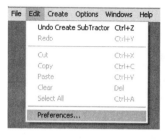

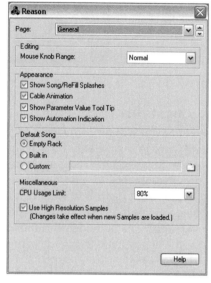

3. Choose Sound Locations from the Page pull-down menu. This is where you set up your Sound Locations (see Figure C.13).

4. Navigate to the right side of this window and click on the first folder to open the location browser (see Figure C.14).

Figure C.13
Choose Sound Locations
from the Page pull-down
menu.

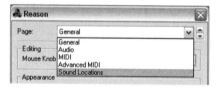

Figure C.14
Click on the first Sound
Location button to
launch its browser.
Locate the folder that
contains your sound files
and click OK.

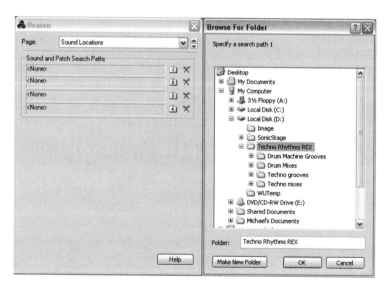

5. Using the browser, locate the folder that contains the files you want to use. Once you locate it, click OK. The first Sound Location should now be listed, as shown in Figure C.15.

6. Close the window and create a new Reason song. Create a Reason device that uses the desired files. For example, create a Dr:rex if you want to use REX files that are in your new Sound Location.

7. Click on the Reason device's Browse Patch button. The Patch Browser window will open. Notice that the first Sound Location button is no longer grayed out as it previously was.

8. Click on the first Sound Location button, and now your REX files should be ready for you to use (see Figure C.16).

Figure C.15
Now the first Sound Location has been specified.

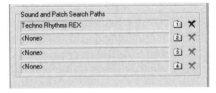

Figure C.16
Make a new Reason song, create a Dr:rex module, and click on the Browse Patch button to launch the Patch Browser window. Click on the first Sound Location folder to see your REX files.

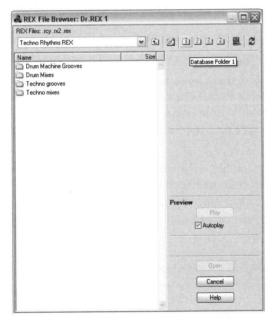

REFILLS CAN BE SAVED AS SOUND LOCATIONS...BUT

Undoubtedly, if you download and install a bunch of ReFills, you might very well want to move these to another hard drive to save space. If you follow the same steps, you can set up Sound Locations for your ReFill collections.

However, once you use these Sound Locations, Reason will automatically recall the location of the included ReFills when you click the Find All ReFills button.

Creating Your Own ReFill

So, now that you have had a crash course in ReFills, you might feel the need to throw caution to the wind and try your luck at creating a custom ReFill. This is much easier than it initially looks, because Propellerhead has created a free utility program that is available at their website called ReFill Packer.

REMEMBER TO REGISTER

In order to obtain access to the ReFills and Propellerhead utility programs mentioned throughout this book, you must register your copy of Reason 2.5 as soon as possible. This is also a very important step to take if you want to receive technical support and updates to Reason.

The ReFill Packer compiles, compresses, and creates ReFills made of your custom patches, samples, and loops made for Reason. After downloading and decompressing the file, you should run the installer and make sure that it installs into the Reason program folder, so it is easily found. After you have installed it, look inside the Reason program folder and you should find these additional files and folders:

▶ The ReFill Packer program

▶ A ReFill Packer manual in Adobe Acrobat Reader format (PDF)

▶ A ReFill Packer Files folder, which contains essential templates and examples

Hopefully, you have found all of these items and are ready to proceed. You can start by having a look at the contents of the ReFill Packer Files folder. As you can see in Figure C.17, this folder contains two subfolders named Sample Folder and Template Folder. Open the Sample Folder and you will find three folders, a text file, and a JPEG graphic file. This is the folder you are going to use for this tutorial.

▶ The JPEG graphic file is the splash-screen graphic that appears when you want to load the ReFill from the Patch Browser window in Reason. It is a very small file.

▶ The text file, called Info, is used to input the credits for your ReFill, include your website address (or URL), and include any additional information.

WRITING THE INFO TEXT

Writing the info text for your ReFill is easy, but you need to make sure that you state everything correctly in order for it to work.

This is how your ReFill info text should be laid out when you create your own. You can change the content to your liking, of course.

NAME="My First ReFill"

COPYRIGHT="© 2003 Mi Musique"

URL="www.yahoo.com"

COMMENTS="This is a ReFill that I made"

Figure C.17
The contents of the ReFill Packer Files folder. Double-click on the Sample Folder to open it.

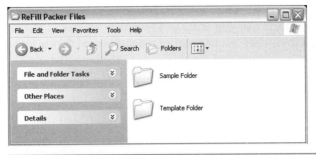

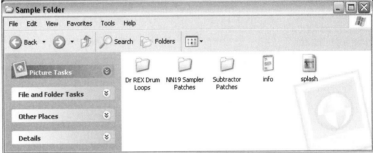

▶ Patch and Sample folders for specific Reason devices are included here. As you can see, there is a folder of REX files for Dr:rex, a folder of patches for the Subtractor, and a folder of samples and patches for the NN-19 sampler.

Compiling Your ReFill Files

At this point, it's important to consider how to organize your patches and samples, so that you will not experience complications when creating your first ReFill. Although it is not that difficult a task to accomplish, it still needs to be spelled out in detail.

In order to make this as clear as possible, the steps are broken down for each Reason device.

▶ **Subtractor and Malström**—These devices are fairly simple, because the patches are stored within their respective folders. For example, all of your Subtractor patches should be stored in the folder entitled Subtractor Patches. The same goes for the Malström. After you have your patches in their correct places, you can then begin to categorize them by creating a subfolder inside the original folder. For example, you could create a Bass or Pad folder inside the Subtractor Patches folder and then place the relevant patches into their correct subfolders.

▶ **Dr:rex**—This Reason device's patches can be organized in the same way as the Subtractor and Malström. First compile your REX files and place them in a Dr REX Drum Loops folder. At this point, you can create subfolders within this main folder and place the relevant REX files into their correct locations.

▶ **Real-time FX**—These patches are very easy to understand, because there are only two Reason devices that can use them—Scream 4 and the RV7000. When creating your ReFill, you can simply create a folder for each device.

▶ **NN-XT, NN-19, and Redrum**—These are a little more complicated. The basic rule of thumb is that you will need two items to make a ReFill for these devices. First, the NN-19, NN-XT, or Redrum patch file, and then a folder containing the samples that are used for that patch. Figure C.18 shows the contents of the NN-19 Sampler Patches folder found within the ReFill Sample folder. Notice both the patch names and the folder that contain the samples.

Figure C.18
The contents of the NN-19 Sampler Patches folder include the patch names and the additional folder that contains the samples.

CREATING THE PATCHES

If you need to review how to create patches for each of the Reason devices, refer to each device's individual chapter.

YOU CAN PACK YOUR REASON SONGS AND MIDI FILES

In addition to Reason patch files and samples, you can also include Reason songs and MIDI files in your ReFills. Why is this useful? If you create a ReFill and you want to demonstrate its potential to another Reason user, creating a few demonstrations with MIDI and Reason song files will do the trick.

USING COPYRIGHTED SAMPLES

As you begin to compile the samples, loops, and patches for your first ReFill, it might be tempting to add in a few samples and loops from your sample CD collection. There is a right way and a wrong way to go about this.

If you plan to use the ReFill just for your own personal use, using copyrighted samples is not a problem. You can create a ReFill containing copyrighted samples and loops and use it within Reason to write and produce songs, just as you can with an audio/MIDI program such as Cubase or Pro Tools.

However, you cannot distribute this ReFill to other Reason users, regardless of whether you charge money for it or not. Doing so results in a violation of copyright law. Musicians, producers, and programmers work tirelessly to create, produce, and distribute these samples. Redistributing these samples in a ReFill is a slap in the face to all of those who worked so hard to create them. It's stealing.

You're almost ready to push forward and run the ReFill Packer and create your first ReFill. But first, you should double-check your organization. Figure C.19 reviews the basic structure of a ReFill. Although you are going to use the pre-made Samples folder for this tutorial, you can always refer to this figure when you create a new ReFill from scratch.

Figure C.19
This is the most commonly found organizational structure in a ReFill.

Using ReFill Packer

In this tutorial, you will launch the ReFill Packer and create your first ReFill by using the Samples folder.

1. Start by launching the ReFill Packer utility. If you are using a Mac, you should find it in your Applications folder. If you are using Windows XP, it will be located in your Reason folder, which is located in the Propellerhead folder in the Program Files folder. Once it's launched, you should see the ReFill Packer program window, which looks just like Figure C.20.

Figure C.20
The ReFill Packer interface.

2. Click on the Input Folder button at the top-right corner of the ReFill Packer interface and select the Sample Folder, which is found within the ReFill Packer Files folder (see Figure C.21). Click OK. All of the relevant information should be listed in the ReFill Packer interface (see Figure C.22).

3. Click on the Output File button, which is located just below the Input Folder button. This is where you can select the destination for your ReFill. Because this is your first time, I suggest saving it to the desktop. Once you have selected the destination, the Output File text box will display the name of the ReFill, as shown in Figure C.23.

Figure C.21
Select the Sample Folder as the input source.

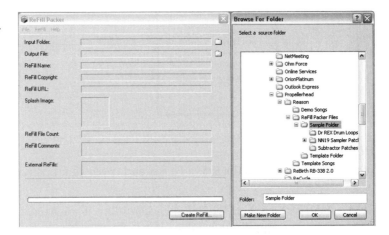

Figure C.22
Now, the Sample Folder is listed as the input source.

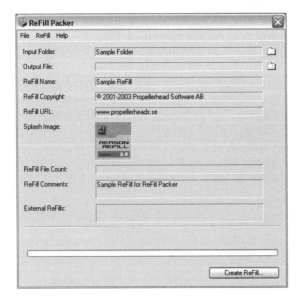

Figure C.23
Once you select the
destination for output,
ReFill Packer will
display the name.

4. Click on the Create ReFill button at the lower-right corner of the ReFill Packer interface. The ReFill Packer should now display a ReFill File Count as it compiles. Once it is completed, ReFill Packer will display a message that the ReFill has now been packed successfully (see Figure C.24).

5. Locate the ReFill called Sample ReFill on your computer's desktop (see Figure C.25).

Figure C.24
The ReFill has been
successfully created.

Figure C.25
Your first ReFill is now
created and located on
the computer desktop.

FOR MORE INFORMATION

This appendix covers a lot of information within its pages. There are a few additional tips and tricks you can learn by taking a peek at the ReFill Packer PDF file, which is located in the Reason program folder.

D

Additional Resources on the Web

Throughout this book, you have explored nearly every aspect of Reason 2.5 and what it can do for your music. You have also learned about many other programs and hardware that might have some of you wanting to know more about refining your approach to making music in the virtual studio. And after all is said and done, you should also learn how to share your Reason songs with other listeners around the world. After all, the whole point of using a program like this is to make music for your friends, family, and fans around the world.

This appendix points out some websites that will help you learn more about additional software and hardware, and some web resources for posting your music.

Propellerhead Software (www.propellerheads.se)

Because this book is about Reason, it seems only right that Propellerhead Software is mentioned first in this appendix (see Figure D.1). This web page is an active hub where Reason users the world over come to download updates for Reason, as well as to share ideas and publish Reason songs.

Figure D.1
The Propellerhead website is a good place to start.

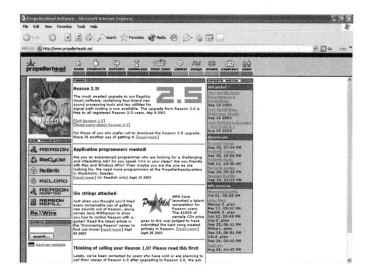

Apple Computer (www.apple.com)

If you are an avid Mac user, you probably already know about this site. However, for all of you new "web jockeys," **apple.com** is the home page of everything that is made, created, and supported by Apple (see Figure D.2). This website has one of the best technical support databases around to answer just about every Apple-related question there is. There is also a comprehensive web store to configure and build a new Mac with those hip new G5 processors.

Figure D.2
The Apple website has, among other things, a great technical support database.

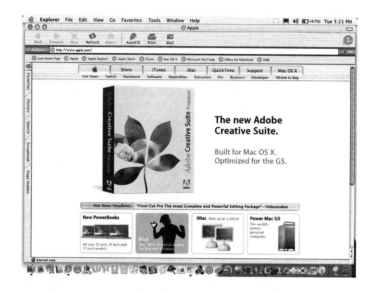

Microsoft Corporation (www.microsoft.com)

For those of you on the other side of the great computer pendulum, **microsoft.com** is the home page for all of the programs and operating systems conceived and created by Microsoft (see Figure D.3). I use this page frequently to download new updates for Windows XP. I cannot stress enough how important it is to check frequently for security updates for your operating system, as there are so many computer viruses out there these days.

Harmony Central (www.harmony-central.com)

Harmony Central is the ultimate musician resource on the web, period (see Figure D.4). On this page, you'll find many informative tutorials and essays to help you better understand the technology behind this program and others like it. It's also the first website I visit when I want to know what's new in music products. Above all, Harmony Central sports one of the most active user forums on the planet. Chances are, if you can't find the answer to your question here, there might not be an answer.

Figure D.3
The Microsoft website is a good source for new software updates and patches.

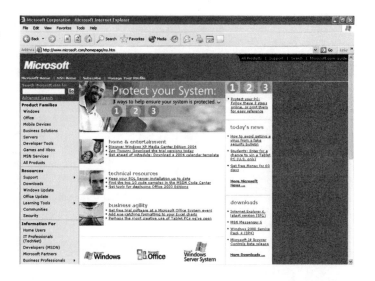

Figure D.4
The Harmony Central website has a very active user forum.

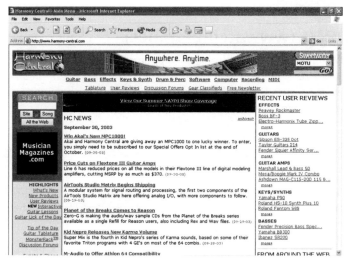

The following websites are those of the companies who create ReWire-ready software products (see Chapter 17, "ReWire").

MP3.com (www.mp3.com)

After mixing your music down, you will need a way to deliver it to the masses. **MP3.com** is a perfect solution, because this website allows you to upload your music in the popular MP3 file format (see Figure D.5).

Figure D.5
The MP3.com website.

Steinberg (www.steinberg.net)

If you know the history of Propellerhead Software going all the way back to the dusty old days of ReCycle version 1.0, you know that Steinberg played a big part in making the Prop Heads as big as they are now (see Figure D.6). Cubase was the first DAW application to support ReWire, and it is one of the best programs to use with Reason.

Figure D.6
The Steinberg website provides updates to their products and offers helpful user forums.

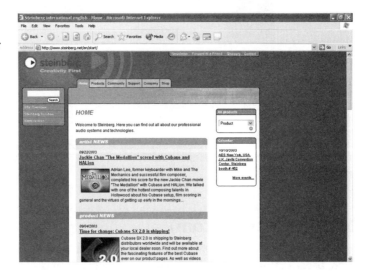

Emagic (www.emagic.de)

Emagic Software is another one of the DAW biggies that has the Mac market cornered with Logic 6 (see Figure D.7). This program, although a little on the complicated side, is one of the most comprehensive music-making applications on the scene. Emagic is owned by Apple Computer, making it a powerful combination of technology and music, to which Reason is a wonderful addition.

Figure D.7
The Emagic website provides updates to their product line and in-depth tutorials.

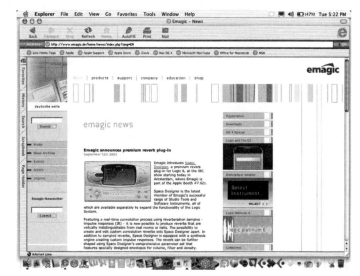

Digidesign (www.digidesign.com)

Digidesign helped define the virtual studio by introducing their DAW application Pro Tools many years ago (see Figure D.8). To this day, Pro Tools is still used throughout the industry for post-production and song creation. Digi is also the manufacturer of some of the best sounding hardware audio interfaces on the planet. They make hardware to match any budget and studio configuration.

Figure D.8
The Digidesign website provides news, updates, and support for the various versions of Pro Tools and Digidesign Hardware.

Cakewalk (www.cakewalk.com)

Cakewalk's SONAR is another DAW software that has taken the virtual studio world by storm (see Figure D.9). Made exclusively for the PC platform, SONAR is the program with several features and impressive graphical interface that meet the needs of both novice and professional musicians alike. Cakewalk also makes the Project5 program, which will soon be a ReWire Master application.

Figure D.9
The Cakewalk website is a well laid out website that provides news and updates for SONAR and Project5.

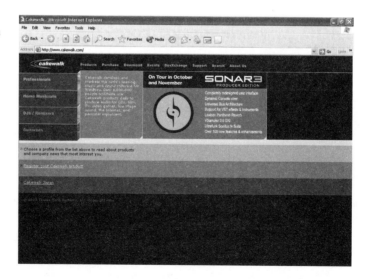

Synapse Audio (www.synapse-audio.com)

Synapse Audio is the company behind the Orion Platinum software (see Figure D.10). Another PC-exclusive program, it is a virtual studio along the lines of Reason and Project5. It is also a ReWire master and slave application. It's a program with great sounds and synths that can complement any PC running Reason.

Ableton (www.ableton.com)

Ableton Live is a program that really is on a level of its own. Released in late 2001, Live has changed the way most of us look at manipulating digital audio (see Figure D.11). It is a PC and Mac application as well as a ReWire master or slave for those who want to record, rewire, and remix!

Figure D.10
The Synapse Audio website is used to provide updates to the various versions of Orion.

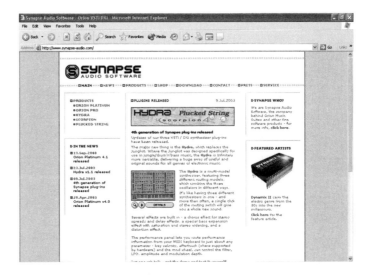

Figure D.11
Use the Ableton website to get the latest information and downloads for the impressive Live application.

Index

Q

INDEX

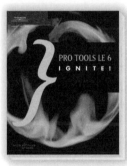

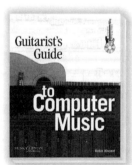